Engagement with the Past

ENGAGEMENT
WITH THE PAST

*The Lives and Works of the
World War II Generation of Historians*

WILLIAM PALMER

THE UNIVERSITY PRESS OF KENTUCKY

Publication of this volume was made possible in part by a grant
from the National Endowment for the Humanities.

Editorial and Sales Offices: The University Press of Kentucky
663 South Limestone Street, Lexington, Kentucky 40508–4008

01 02 03 04 05   5 4 3 2 1

Library of Congress Cataloging-in-Publication Data

Palmer, William, 1951-
Engagement with the past : the lives and works of the World War II
generation of historians / William Palmer.
p. cm.
ISBN 0-8131-2206-6 (alk. paper)
1. Historians—United States—Biography. 2. United States—Social
conditions—1945- 3. History—Study and teaching—United States. 4.
United States—Historiography. I. Title.
E175.45 .P35 2001
973'.07'2022—dc21   2001002579

This book is printed on acid-free recycled paper meeting
the requirements of the American National Standard
for Permanence in Paper for Printed Library Materials.

Manufactured in the United States of America.

If I watch them long enough I see them come together, I see them *placed*, I see them engaged in this or that act and in this or that difficulty. How they look and move and speak and behave, always in the setting I have found for them, is my account of them.

Turgenev

Let the word go forth from this time and place, to friend and foe alike, that the torch has been passed to a new generation of Americans, born in this century, tempered by war, disciplined by a hard and bitter peace.

John F. Kennedy

CONTENTS

INTRODUCTION:
WRITING HISTORIANS' LIVES

This is a book about a generation of historians, and many roads converged in its writing. As the author of two specialized monographs that I virtually had to subpoena people to read, much less buy, I wanted to write a book that would have a broader appeal. I had written several articles on historiographical matters, but it was not immediately clear to me how I could turn that interest into a book for the general reader. But in the mid-1990s several books on historians suggested an answer. In England to do research in the summer of 1995 on other matters, I discovered Adam Sisman's biography of A.J.P. Taylor in a London bookstore. Marveling at Sisman's ability to make Taylor come alive as a person, I devoured the book greedily on the flight home. In Sisman's hands the biography of a historian seemed like promising project.

Now I had to find a subject. Hugh Trevor-Roper, Taylor's occasional antagonist and friend at one time, was my first choice. He was almost as controversial as Taylor. Spotting a book review Trevor-Roper had written in the *English Historical Review*, I wrote to him to ask if he was interested in having someone write his biography. When I did not hear from him after a two-month interval, I pursued some other possibilities, most of which reflected my interest in early modern England. These other possibilities included Christopher Hill, Lawrence Stone, and Geoffrey Elton. All of them, it seemed to me, had students and friends better placed than I to do the job. Besides, doing a biography of any Englishman, especially if I wanted to do as good a job as Adam Sisman had done with Taylor, would require a great deal of hustling in British archives, which I could not afford to do. Thus, if biography was my goal, an American topic appeared to be more practical. Richard Hofstadter, who died in 1970, was the American historian who interested me the most. If one of his students was going to write a biography of him, there had been plenty of time for them to do it. So I briefly explored the possibility of doing Hofstadter until I came upon a solid study of his early life by Susan Stout Baker, which covered what was to me the most interesting part of his career.

At this point I heard at last from Hugh Trevor-Roper. In a charming four-page letter, ranging widely over a number of topics, he apologized for the delay in responding; his entire correspondence, he said, had been suspended while he cared for his disabled wife. He wrote that while he preferred that his biography not be written, he would not stand in the way. And, it turned out that Adam Sisman had already approached him with the same result.

It was at this point that I had an epiphany. The delay in hearing from Trevor-Roper was actually a blessing, because in exploring other possibilities, I discovered what might have been obvious to everyone else, that there was a heavy concentration of renowned English historians born between 1910 and 1921. This group included J.H. Plumb (b. 1911), Christopher Hill (b. 1912), Sir Richard Southern (b. 1912), Hugh Trevor-Roper (b. 1914), Richard Cobb (b. 1917), Eric Hobsbawm (b. 1917), and Geoffrey Elton, (b. 1921). Almost all of them had developed intellectually in the 1930s, did military service during World War II, and exercised an extended period of dominance in their fields after the war. The writings of Christopher Hill, Hugh Trevor-Roper, and Lawrence Stone dominated the study of seventeenth-century England for almost a quarter century. By writing *The Tudor Revolution in Government*, Geoffrey Elton almost singlehandedly made the early sixteenth century again a field of interest. Nearly forty years after its publication, it stands alone among studies of Tudor politics. The same thing might be said for Sir Richard Southern's famous *The Making of the Middle Ages*, which made him the most revered medievalist of his time and has survived intense scrutiny with only cosmetic modification.

It got better. American history was one of my doctoral fields as a graduate student, and for years I have taught an American survey class during summer school at Marshall, so I am fairly knowledgeable about American historians. I quickly found that, like Richard Hofstadter, a number of the most remarkable and productive American historians had also been born approximately between 1910 and 1920. These included David Potter (b. 1910), Kenneth Stampp (b. 1912), Daniel Boorstin (b. 1914), John Hope Franklin (b. 1915), Oscar Handlin (b. 1915), Edmund Morgan (b. 1916), Arthur Schlesinger Jr. (b. 1917), and Anne Firor Scott (b. 1921). If generational boundaries were extended but slightly, C. Vann Woodward (b. 1908) could be included. Like the English cohort, they had been formed to a certain extent by the intellectual and economic convulsion of the Great Depression, they performed some kind of military service in during World War II, and they, too, came to exercise a disproportionately lengthy period of dominance over their fields.

Again, their influence was astonishing. Edmund Morgan looms like a colossus over American colonial history. Arthur M. Schlesinger Jr., was for many years the leading authority on early national America, which he later extended to the New Deal era. Kenneth Stampp's *The Peculiar Institution*, published in 1956, completely redirected the study of American slavery. While today its findings have been revised by other scholars, it remains in many ways the single most important work written on slavery. David Potter was for many years the leading authority on the American Civil War, while Oscar Handlin pioneered the study of immigrant groups in the United States. In fact the dominant figure in American history in the 1950s and 1960s was Richard Hofstadter, whose assessment of the Progressive movement won early notice, but whose work ultimately ranged widely over the entire compass of American history. His tragic, early death in 1970 at fifty-four deprived the profession of one of its most subtle and original minds.

It did not stop there. There was also a surprising number of Americans of the same age group who achieved real distinction in European history. These included J.H. Hexter (b. 1910), Barbara Tuchman (b. 1912), Gordon Craig (b. 1913), Carl Schorske (b. 1915), William McNeill (b. 1917), and Gertrude Himmelfarb (b. 1922).

Was this generation unique? It is doubtful that any other generation has exercised such a pervasive effect on its discipline. So much happened during their lifetimes. Not only did they experience the Great Depression, the Second World War, and the threat to faith in religion and progress posed by these upheavals, but they were also the first generation to confront the prospect of nuclear holocaust and threatening specter posed by Communism and the arms race. Electricity, the automobile, indoor plumbing, the telephone all became commonplace in American and English life during their lifetimes.

Many members of this generation of historians overcame remarkable hardships. Richard Southern wrote *The Making of the Middle Ages* while recovering from tuberculosis, often fatal in those days. Richard Hofstadter's first wife died tragically, shortly after the birth of their first child in 1945. David Potter's second wife committed suicide, and Vann Woodward lost his wife and only child to cancer. Geoffrey Elton arrived in Britain in the 1930s barely knowing a word of English, and rather like Joseph Conrad, eventually became a master of English prose. Beginning in middle age J.H. Hexter suffered for a quarter century with a series of heart problems, which included two strokes, two coronary occlusions, two major hemorrhages, and three bouts of pneumonia. Most of these historians had their careers interrupted by military service. And they entered academic life at a time when academic careers cannot have looked very promising and many members of their generation were actively discouraged from pursuing them. Years later, Carl Schorske remembered with some bitterness an incident at Columbia where the literary critic Lionel Trilling scoffed at the folly of Schorske's teaching aspirations, given the poor state of the job market at the time and Schorske's Jewish heritage.

Most, however, advanced to positions of power and prestige, which placed them in the forefront of English and American academic life. Barbara Tuchman, Oscar Handlin, Richard Hofstadter, Vann Woodward, Carl Schorske, and Daniel Boorstin won Pulitzer Prizes. Arthur Schlesinger Jr., won two. Hugh Trevor-Roper became Regius Professor of History at Oxford; Geoffrey Elton received a similar accolade at Cambridge. Richard Southern was appointed Chichele Professor of Medieval History at Oxford and later become President of St. John's College. His Oxford colleague Christopher Hill became Master of Balliol College. Lawrence Stone, Kenneth Stampp, Carl Schorske, and Edmund Morgan have received the American Historical Association's award for scholarly distinction. Gertrude Himmelfarb, John Hope Franklin, and Vann Woodward have delivered the National Endowment for the Humanities Jefferson Lecture. Lawrence Stone, Carl Schorske, and John Hope Franklin have all given the American Council of Learned Societies' Life in Learning Lecture. Woodward, Franklin, David Potter, Gordon Craig, and William McNeill were elected presidents of the American Historical Association.

Living in the age of the Internet was also fortuitous for my research. With my interest in historiography, I was already aware of a number of memoirs and autobiographical materials concerning these scholars. But a quick check of the Harvard Union Catalogue revealed that there were a number of other resources available. Volume seventeen of the *Dictionary of Literary Biography*, edited by Clyde Wilson, included valuable biographical and critical sketches of Boorstin, Handlin, Hofstadter, Morgan, Potter, Schlesinger, and Woodward.

By this time I had identified about fifteen subjects. I composed a lengthy letter first to those residing in the United States, explaining the nature of my project and asking for their help. I enclosed a separate sheet in which they could disclaim interest in the project or state their preference for responding through writing, being interviewed over the phone, or being interviewed personally.

I then waited with no idea what to expect. In particular I feared that these were people who remained busy and whose advice was still often sought on many matters and who might be annoyed by another intrusion into their lives. I was therefore pleasantly surprised that within a week I had positive responses from Vann Woodward and Edmund Morgan, followed the next day by a similarly encouraging response from Lawrence Stone. All three stated their willingness to be interviewed and appeared to find the project interesting. Within two weeks I had heard from all but two of my initial targets. The two who replied later were out of the country at the time. Oscar Handlin, for example, at age eighty, was in the middle of an extended tour through Southeast Asia. All but two expressed an interest and pledged some level of help.

That help came in many ways. Several referred me to material already in print of which I was unaware. Kenneth Stampp sent me a copy of his biographical sketch from the *Dictionary of Literary Biography* and a copy of his 1981 Wilson lecture at the University of Utah in which he outlined his overall view of history. Others commented directly on the project and suggested to me other promising lines of inquiry. I had originally believed that the Depression was the single most powerful influence on this generation, but in their replies to my initial inquiry, both Lawrence Stone and William McNeill cited the importance of their military experience on their historical work, a point echoed later without my prompting by Hugh Trevor-Roper and Gordon Craig. William McNeill also suggested to me the importance of relatively cheap travel and availability of grants in the 1950s as other reasons for this generation's success, though this was a point disputed by several others. Travel was cheap in those days, Kenneth Stampp pointed out, "but salaries were low." Nevertheless, many of this group did benefit from frequent and generous grants to help them with their research and writing.

Under these circumstances I waited eagerly for each day's mail. The positive initial response convinced me I was onto something of importance. I renewed my correspondence with Hugh Trevor-Roper and wrote to the remaining people on my list, which comprised primarily the historians living in England, asking them if they would be willing to be interviewed if I came over.

There were a few thorns. Two historians in the United States flatly refused to be interviewed, one politely, the other with an intemperate note, implying my insensitivity and incompetence, but also revealing she or he had completely misunderstood what I was trying to do. Two others supplied me with references to material in print, but declined to answer further questions. One of these who would not talk to me, interestingly enough, gave a lengthy interview for a national magazine while the book was in progress. The other pleaded too much work, though, to my knowledge, none of it has appeared in the approximately five years since my query. The material in print, while helpful and illuminating on many matters, often did not answer all my questions, especially on certain subjects. My inability to persuade certain subjects to address specific questions leads to some odd gaps in the narrative. Furthermore, the untimely deaths of Geoffrey Elton before I began the project and Richard Cobb while it was in progress also deprived me of the chance to talk with two subjects who would have been most entertaining.

I was then ready to interview some of my American subjects over the telephone. As exciting as the mail was, the interviews were even better, although I admit that I gained an unexpected admiration for television and radio interviewers. Colleagues in other disciplines whose research depends highly on interviews tell me that a cold, telephone interview, where the subject has never seen and knows little about his interrogator, is the most difficult kind of interview to conduct. This is doubtless true, and I compounded the problem by being a poor interviewer anyway, especially in the first few interviews I did. I made several elementary errors. First, I felt a need to show my subjects that I was bright and worthy of telling their story, so I asked a number of convoluted, highly theoretical questions, designed not to elicit information, but to display my erudition. In fact, at these times I probably sounded more like a babbling idiot than an erudite interviewer. On more than one occasion one of my subjects responded to one of my tortured questions with a confused, "Now, what is the question?" And, eager to confirm my own hypotheses, I asked too many leading questions, designed to direct my subjects to the answers I wanted. That was surely foolish. These were of course not people likely to be led easily into someone else's conclusions.

There were other moments of consternation. When I asked one eminent scholar about his intellectual relationship with another famous historian, who had been dead for a long time, I was surprised when he replied, "It was difficult, and I won't say anymore." A little while later the same scholar related to me a very touching inscription from a friend in his copy of one of the friend's books. When I repeated the quotation back to him to make sure I had gotten it right, he said with irritation, "Why, you can't use that; it's personal." Again I was surprised: the quotation had no malicious content, and, again, the person in question had been dead for decades. I cannot fathom the reasons behind his irritation at my wanting to use the quotation, but to him these were clearly private matters.

When I learned that the stories of these historians were better than anything I could contrive and that I should shut up and let them talk, the interviews went better. There have been few professional pleasures for me greater than the lengthy interviews with Edmund Morgan (nearly two hours over two days) and J.H. Hexter (one hour and forty-five minutes straight). Both were fascinating, and they had me laughing so often and so hard that I had to struggle to maintain my train of thought. I also ached along with Hexter as he recounted his humiliating ordeal of trying to find a job as a Jew in the 1930s. I am not Jewish, but it resembled all too closely my own experience as a new Ph.D. trying to find a job in the early 1980s.

I was often astonished by the sharpness of my subjects' memories. I had noted in Kenneth Stampp's biographical sketch that he had finished his dissertation in 1941, so without checking more carefully, I asked him if he had received his Ph.D. in 1941. "Oh, no," he replied, "I finished my dissertation in December 1941; I did not receive my degree until March 1942." At eighty-seven Vann Woodward remembered every job he had in the 1930s and when and how he got them. Only two years younger, J.H. Hexter recalled many of the slights he had received as a graduate student at Harvard.

I saw occasional moments of self-absorption in certain of my subjects. One of them, after we had finished the interview, said, "Now, let's see, you're writing a biography of me, right?" I also had expected most of them to have a wealth of insights about other historians, but some talked primarily about themselves, offering little about others. Lawrence Stone was an exception to this. He quickly saw the project as a whole, and his expressed regret at some of his tilts with Geoffrey Elton was quite touching. Only a few were curious at all about me. It was a pleasant surprise when J.H. Hexter said at one point during our lengthy interview, "Am I boring you?" Of course he was not. It was also a little hard to get Carl Schorske to talk about himself. He, like Lawrence Stone and several others, had quite a bit of curiosity about the project as a whole. I actually had to convince Schorske that the topic had substance, and he responded by offering a number of helpful insights. Gordon Craig was also a remarkable mixture of a steel-trap memory regarding his own life combined with thoughtful reflections on his generation and others in it as a whole. I enjoyed my interview with him immensely. When I finished, I felt a bit sad, and I tried desperately to come up with some additional questions to prolong the interview. I was disappointed when I couldn't. I perhaps flatter myself, but I had the feeling that he, too, did not want the interview to conclude.

The face-to-face interviews in England had their own delights. Hugh Trevor-Roper exceeded his reputation for charm and witty conversation. Sir Richard Southern shared with me several of the most powerful moments of his spiritual life. J.H. Plumb was also engaging, but about halfway through the interview I had the sense that he had become bored and decided to say some mildly outrageous things just to make it interesting. When I asked him how he developed his prose style, he denied that there was anything to develop, insisting that you either have it or you don't. When I realized that he wanted me to banter back, the interview went better.

With a few exceptions, almost all of the Americans and most of the rest brightened on the subject of teaching. Despite the common complaint that in the modern university teaching has been sacrificed to the almighty god of research, one can find only scant indication of it in the World War II generation. Along with their remarkable productivity as scholars, most of them were dedicated teachers full of ideas about teaching and justifiably proud of their accomplishments in the classroom.

Readers of this book should bear in mind several considerations. First, this is not an exhaustive history of the historians of the World War II generation. It is a selection, decidedly imperfect and perhaps even whimsical in some ways, of several historians of that generation. There are so many historians worthy of inclusion that at several points I felt, rather like a lion tamer, that my project threatened to consume me. But if I was to reach a popular audience, having too many subjects would lose the average reader. I therefore had to be ruthless in my selections, including the excision of several historians I very much wished to include. I focused primarily on those born between 1910 and 1920. I made four exceptions to this rule, Vann Woodward (b. 1908), Geoffrey Elton (b. 1921), Anne Scott (b. 1921), and Gertrude Himmelfarb (b. 1922) because I considered them too important not to include. Among the Americans I tried to limit myself to one person per field.

I regret that scholars of such distinction and estimable achievement as Rodney Hilton (b. 1916), H. Stuart Hughes (b. 1916), James MacGregor Burns (b. 1918), George Taylor (b. 1919), Raymond Carr (b. 1919), Wallace MacCaffrey (b. 1920), Arthur S. Link (b. 1920), David Donald (b. 1920), John Morton Blum (b. 1921), Carl N. Degler (b. 1921), Bernard Bailyn (b. 1922), William Leuchtenburg (b. 1922), and E.P. Thompson (b. 1924) could not be included. I am certain that there are still others worthy of inclusion that have not occurred to me. The reason they have not been included has nothing to do with their achievement; it has everything to do with my desire to keep the project to a manageable number of people.

This book consists of two parts. The first part presents biographical information about these scholars. Some of it will be known, but much will not be widely known. I managed to elicit information from Kenneth Stampp and Hugh Trevor-Roper that was unknown to two of their favorite and most able pupils, John Sproat and Blair Worden. Most biographers find it difficult to generalize about their subjects; it is even harder to generalize about the lives of twenty subjects. All were different, but the information gathered here is valuable both for its personal interest and the fact that in a few years we may not have access to any of it.

The second part of the book deals with the intellectual achievement of the World War II generation. Like the first, this section also presents some expository problems. The achievement of the World War II generation is too immense for me to cover it all, even if I had the erudition necessary to undertake it. I have therefore tried to examine particular aspects of their achievement, usually selecting one or two books along with a few articles, to get at the essence of their work, or least something about it not widely known.

Neither the biographical nor the critical section of the book, therefore, is exhaustive. I should also confess that occasionally during the course of my research, I found things that didn't quite jibe, some areas into which people were reluctant to venture. No doubt some of this is attributable to the failure of memories over time. My colleague at Marshall, Donna Spindel, has recently published an interesting, if disturbing, article on how little attention historians pay to work from other disciplines on how feeble memory really is. If we did take into account this literature, the historical profession might be shattered fore and aft.

Apart from memory, members of this generation of historians probably have some skeletons in more than a few closets. In most cases I chose not to pursue them. In part this was because I wanted to write a book that will be of interest to a more general public, which is probably more interested in the personal lives and achievement of the World War II generation than in their arcane politics. In part this also reflects the dilemma of the contemporary historian. When you write books about dead subjects, you have only reviewers and colleagues to worry about. When you work in part with live ones, the amount of material you can draw out of them depends in large part on your ability to establish a working rapport and understanding with them. Had I probed too deeply into sensitive matters, such as controversial tenure decisions, failed marriages, estranged children, or backroom academic politics, I might have failed to gather much of the information in this book. I recognize this as a flaw, but only to people who are expecting a comprehensive study intended to lay bare tangled webs of deceit and apologia. In the end I decided that it was more important to get the information in print. Future scholars may explore in more depth than I could the issues lurking beneath the surface.

Part I: Lives

Chapter 1

BEGINNINGS

They were born early in the century during which the modern Western world pivoted, which meant something different to those in England and those in America. For the English, the historians of the World War II generation were born at a time when serious and visible signs of decay, such as strikes, feverish foreign competition, and the erosion of confidence, were appearing in the Victorian industrial juggernaut. More seriously, while the members of the World War II generation were learning to walk, Britain was, like Agamemnon, struck deep from a mortal blow from which it has never entirely recovered. During World War I the core of a generation of British youth perished in the fields of Flanders and France, including thousands who might have been expected to be the leaders of the future in politics, science, technology, and the arts, even history. Across the Atlantic, by contrast, the American members of the World War II generation were born into the beginning of what was to become the American century, during which the United States would seize the lead in industry and production, would experience unprecedented economic expansion, and assume leadership of the world at large.

No two childhoods are alike, but several groupings of consequence can be distinguished among this group of historians. Among the English historians, most received their formative educational experiences while attending the English public schools, either as boarders or day students. Among Americans, there are several distinct categories into which the World War II generation of historians can be placed. There is, for example, a group of urban Jews who grew up in the northeast United States, a group of faculty brats, a group with Middle Western roots, and a small cohort with a Southern heritage. Several others, such as Daniel Boorstin, John Hope Franklin, and Gordon Craig, defy easy categorization.

Among the historians raised in England, the English public school education is, with two exceptions, the common denominator. Lawrence Stone has provided a memorable portrait of his own youth and his experience in school. His parents had married immediately after World War I, and his father was a commercial artist whose business prospered in the 1920s. As a child, Stone was an inveterate collector of disparate items, including postage stamps, butterflies, fossils, and cigarette cards. He displayed an early interest in history, reading history books and novels by the time he was ten. At eight he was sent to Charterhouse, the famous London boarding school, to receive what was then termed a "liberal education." It was for Stone utter misery, a dreary and stifling regimen of repeated memorization of the vocabulary and grammar of Greek and Latin. From age eight to sixteen, Stone spent his time translating English prose into Latin prose, Latin prose into Latin verse, Latin verse into Greek verse, and Greek prose back into English, along with every other possible variation. This unsparing program of classical training may have contributed to Stone's forceful and often admired prose style, but he chafed at the regimen. "I was not very good at it," he wrote years later, "partly from natural ineptitude, partly from lack of will. I could not for the life of me see the point of it at all, and I still don't." The rigid approach to learning was applied by his schoolmasters in other areas. At twelve Stone was thought by some to be a promising batsman in cricket, but perhaps typically, his style did not conform to accepted practice. Charterhouse hired an elderly, former professional cricket player to instruct him in the proper technique, insisting that Stone hold his bat straight up in the conventional manner. Stone tried to adopt to his teacher's strictures, but never played a successful game again, a personal disappointment, since he dreamed about playing for England.[1]

Stone was also exposed to several of the other charming traditions of English public school life: segregation from the opposite sex, regular beatings, rituals designed to humiliate, complex hierarchical pecking orders, execrable food, and sexual initiations by the older males. Fortunately, Stone was rescued from this adolescent hell by the intervention of a new headmaster at Charterhouse, Sir Robert Birley, who singlehandedly changed Stone's life. Birley was an intriguing figure, at once a devoted member of the landed elite and devout upholder of the Church of England, who assumed a role as a crusading radical with reformist sympathies. He was sometimes derided by his disapproving aristocratic brethren as "Red Robert" and was one of the few among the English elite to express sympathy with the General Strike of 1926. Birley quickly recognized Stone as a pupil of exceptional promise and in a year and a half of intensive instruction prepared Stone to obtain an open scholarship in history at Oxford. After Stone secured his scholarship, Birley sent him to Paris for six months exposure to another culture. Here Stone encountered indirectly the Paris mandarin intelligentsia, as well as the great

Annales School of historians, then represented by Marc Bloch and Lucien Febvre, which were so important to his later work.[2]

Christopher Hill's early years offer an interesting contrast. Where Stone found the regimens of the English preparatory school repressive, Hill thrived in them, although his highest ambition was to play cricket for Yorkshire. From 1923 to 1931 he attended St. Peter's School, York, first as a day boy and later as a boarder, where he found classical study quite congenial, winning a Headmaster's Prize for Latin Prose in 1930 and prizes in history as well. Unlike most English schoolboys, Hill appears to have been more influenced by domestic circumstances, especially by the striking personality of his father, Edward Harold Hill, a solicitor of the Lodge, Huntington, York. From his parents, Hill acquired a nonconformist background and his famous egalitarian spirit. "My parents had a strong sense of fairness," he recalled in the 1950s. "To them the idea of one race being superior to another was repugnant. . . . I heard my first anti-semitic joke when I was twelve or thirteen, and I didn't get the point." Hill also remembers learning to question authority at an early age. At six, a school mistress insisted that he eat something that he protested would make him sick. The school mistress would not relent; Hill ate the food in question and became violently ill, leaving him with a profound suspicion of authority.[3]

But it was his father who loomed the largest in his universe. Visitors to Hill's house in the 1930s noticed a sharp contrast in Hill's parents. Mrs. Hill was lively and vivacious, while Mr. Hill, quiet and controlled, was the real power in the family. Tall, sandy-haired, and handsome, the elder Hill was a twentieth-century incarnation of the early modern Puritan, genial, but strict and uncompromising. Smoking and drinking were forbidden in the Hill household, so that when the younger Hill and his friends sneaked out to a pub, they took care, upon their return to the house, to disguise the alcohol on their breath.[4]

Hill was from the north of England, a region that has produced many outstanding English historians. G.M. Trevelyan was from Northumberland, while F.M. Powicke and A.J.P. Taylor were Lancashire men. Other northerners of distinction in history include Mandell Creighton, Dame Veronica Wedgwood, and Sir Steven Runciman. Northerners are often as foreign to those in southern England as Scotsmen or Irishmen, and northern historians were often regarded as outsiders in the south, especially at Oxford. Neither Taylor nor Powicke, for example, despite their enormous scholarly achievements, was ever entirely accepted at Oxford.

The tradition of excellence in history among northern men was continued by the World War II generation. Oddly, the two most famous northern men of the World War II generation, Hugh Trevor-Roper and Richard Southern, both became quintessential Oxonians, who prospered in the hierarchical, sometimes snobbish, social climate of Oxford. Trevor-Roper himself has commented on the importance of northern ancestry in his historical development. Raised in rural, north Northumberland, Trevor-Roper was surrounded by a multitude of visible symbols and relics of the north's violent and eruptive past. Hadrian's Wall from Roman times and the castles, fortified garrisons, and peel towers of the Cheviot Hills that cast a wary eye on the Scots, as well as the watch towers of the rugged east coast of Northumberland, suggested the inescapability of the northern past.[5]

Trevor-Roper's father was a country doctor. The family was rather isolated and addicted to the sporting life and avocations of the northern gentry, horse racing (known locally as "the turf") and hunting. There was hardly a book in the household. An able governess provided Trevor-Roper with an opening to the life of the mind, to which Trevor-Roper, a rather solitary child, responded with alacrity. He read widely, but indiscriminately on a variety of subjects. The border novels of Sir Walter Scott were a particular favorite.[6] Trevor-Roper was educated in local public schools and later at Charterhouse. He wanted to study mathematics there, but was informed that pupils of exceptional promise, like himself, studied classics.

Richard Southern is also a child of the English north, born in the industrial city of Newcastle in 1912, the middle of three brothers. Even in later years, a return to Newcastle for him could evoke powerful emotions. His father was a timber merchant, and Southern's brothers eventually entered the family business. Southern, who admired his father very much, planned to enter it as well. But he was also his father's favorite, and his father, sensing that there was something special about Southern, wanted something better for his middle son. Southern attended the elementary and grammar schools in the area, quickly proving to be a superior student. In 1929, he won a scholarship to Balliol College, at the time perhaps the most academically prestigious and rigorous of Oxford colleges.[7]

Neither Trevor-Roper nor Southern has left much in print about their childhoods and upbringing. But Richard Cobb has explored his own childhood in southeast England in the quaint village of Tunbridge Wells in a series of autobiographical sketches. In his *Still Life: Sketches from a Tunbridge Wells Childhood*, published in 1983, Cobb describes his village in a series of frozen images: R. Septimus Gardiner, taxidermist with a shop full of stuffed animals and birds, including hummingbirds and badgers; Dr. Footner, who made his house calls in a carriage and the curious Limbury-Buses: the mother was rarely home, the son never spoke, and the whole family never altered its daily routine. For his part, Cobb recalls his own anxieties about the flats his family lived in, his fears that in some of the places in which his family lived there was no way out, no backdoor "in case of disturbance or revolution." In *Something to Hold Onto*, Cobb remembered his own bizarre family: Daisy, who collected thousands of copies of the *Daily Mail*; Uncle Primus whose daily rituals included winding the clocks, banging the gongs for meals, and taking two walks each day.[8]

The ordinary and settled nature of Cobb's childhood was shattered during his teens by tragedy. One of his closest friends, Edward Ball, had a stormy and distressing relationship with his irrational and vicious mother. Ball regularly poured out his heart to Cobb, as he struggled to come to grips with his mother's behavior. When he could not bear any further abuse, Ball seized an axe and bludgeoned her to death. But the story in Cobb's rendering is yet more subtle. Mrs. Ball often accused Cobb of turning her son against her, and the police suspected Cobb as well of having a hand in the tragedy. In his account Cobb did not deny it.[9]

J.H. Plumb was raised in the midland city of Leicester in a Tory, nonconformist household. His father ran a boot and shoe factory, unusual for its paternalism. Profits were normally returned to workers, then to consumers in the form of reduced prices, and only then to the shareholders, none of whom could hold more than one hundred shares. Plumb's mother believed in one child at a time. Thus, Plumb had two brothers, one thirteen, the other six, at the time of his birth. Too young to be of use to either, he had a rather solitary childhood. His father, however, had a small library, and Plumb soon discovered that he loved to read. At nine a history of Portugal fascinated him for a week. By eleven he devoured the novels of Sir Walter Scott and read the Bible in its entirety.

Plumb's experience in his boarding school was perhaps the most extraordinary of all. Even then, Plumb was iconoclastic and combative, his iconoclasm revealed in the canary yellow sweaters and purple trousers he sometimes wore, his combativeness revealed through his relationship with his schoolmaster H.E. Howard. Howard was known for his unconventional style of teaching, which involved, according to one observer, a "cut and thrust of the claymore variety and the blows, one feels, were sometimes intended to be lethal." While Plumb was never formally taught by Howard, the two did discover a common love of disputation. One legendary argument between Plumb and Howard, over whether emotions can be false, raged all over Leicester, concluding at three o'clock in the morning outside the city gates when the Howard informed Plumb, "You've misunderstood your facts, you've misread your psychology, you've got a third-rate mind, and you're probably impotent. Good night!"[10] A second schoolteacher, Joels, was instrumental in encouraging Plumb to take a shot at getting into Oxford or Cambridge and not be seduced into his father's business.

The early lives of Eric Hobsbawm and Geoffrey Elton are unique among the English historians of the World War II generation. Both were raised abroad and only partially educated in English schools. Eric Hobsbawm was born in Alexandria, Egypt, in the revolutionary year of 1917. His origins reflect partly the history of imperialism. His father was English; his mother was Austrian. Both England and the Habsburg Empire had interests in Egypt, and his parents met and married there. After the war, they went to Vienna, where Hobsbawm was brought up. His parents died in 1931, and he moved to Berlin to stay with relatives.

As far as Hobsbawm was concerned, his life began in Berlin. "Everything I learned began in Berlin. . . . Marx for one thing," he once remarked. In class he had been "shooting his mouth off" when an irritated teacher informed him that he clearly had no idea what he was talking about and that he should go to the library and start reading. Unlike many students taxed with this injunction, Hobsbawm did as he was instructed.[11]

Gottfried Ehrenberg (later Geoffrey Elton) was born in Tübingen, Germany, on August 18, 1921. In 1929 the family moved to Prague where his father, a classical scholar, had taken a university chair. His father, a powerful intellectual force in the household, gave young Elton his first book when he was one week old and lovingly recorded in a sketch book each step of his son's development during his first year. Under his father's influence, history pervaded through the household. "I became a historian through prenatal influence," he once remarked. Before he was a teenager, Elton was writing historical plays. At about age thirteen, he wrote his first book, which he typed himself, at his father's insistence, with both left and right-hand justification. At his father's insistence he also learned the craft of bookbinding so he could bind the book himself.

By the late 1930s Prague was no longer safe for Jews. Elton's mother was the first to realize the enormity of their plight and made arrangements through a woman named Esther Simpson, the secretary of the Society for the Protection of Science and Learning, to bring the family to England. Some of their friends protested that the Ehrenbergs should not remove the manifestly able Geoffrey from school at so critical a point in his education. Nonetheless, the Ehrenbergs fled from Prague in February 1939, a month before the Nazis occupied the city. They tried vainly to persuade Elton's aunt to go with them, but she refused and was killed two years later. The family arrived in England on St. Valentine's Day 1939. More than sixty years later Elton wrote, "Within a few months it dawned upon me that I had arrived in the country in which I ought to have been born." Mrs. Ehrenberg's best friend had married a Methodist minister, who now served as the Rector of Colwyn Bay and chaplain to the Rydal School in Colwyn Bay. The minister and his wife arranged for Elton and his younger brother Ludwig (later Lewis) to attend Rydal. Elton managed the astonishing feat of acquiring a school certificate in four months, though the work had to be done in English, and he had virtually none at the time of his arrival in England. His father had advised him to concentrate on Latin at school, "since you can pick up English at any time in the future."

By any standard, Elton's academic achievement at Rydal was remarkable. Socially, however, he and Lewis struggled to learn the traditions and customs of their new country, and as Lewis remarked later, "we had only been a week in England before we were exposed to the strange and mysterious entity of the English public school. Was it really true that new boys had to have either all three buttons of their jackets done up or none at all, but under no circumstance only one?" Things were perhaps more difficult for Lewis, who was accused during World War II by a member of the domestic staff of leaving lights on to assist German bombers. There is a certain tinge of pain to a remark Geoffrey made in middle age: "I really like marmalade now, and I might even take to porridge, but I am going to wait until I get home to try, as I would like it to be of good quality."[12]

In the United States several of the great historians of the World War II generation reflect the impact of Jewish immigration. Barbara Tuchman is a good example. She was born in New York City in 1912 into comfortable circumstances. Her father, Maurice Wertheim, was a successful banker, patron of the arts, and at one time, the owner of the political magazine *The Nation*. Her mother, Alma Morgenthau, was the daughter of Henry Morgenthau, a prominent diplomat, at one time America's ambassador to Constantinople. Tuchman's interest in history was aroused at age six through her reading of a succession of books called the Twins Series by Lucy Fitch Perkins. The Twins Series was intended to illuminate history for young readers by describing the adventures of twin girls caught up in historical events. Through the series, Tuchman became enchanted by the fortunes of the Dutch twins, the twins of the American Revolution, and the Belgian twins, who suffered at the hands of the German invasion of Belgium in 1914. Tuchman soon advanced to historical novels, especially those of Dumas, through which she acquired an intimacy with French history so acute that when the family vacationed in France she could describe which duke of Guise had been murdered in which castle. Conan Doyle's *White Company* and, above all, Jane Porter's *The Scottish Chiefs* aroused an interest in Scottish history and especially in the Scottish hero William Wallace. When Tuchman attended her first masquerade party at age twelve, most of her friends went as Florence Nightingale or Juliet. Tuchman went as Wallace, in "tartan and velvet tam."[13]

Oscar Handlin's parents were Russian Jews who settled in New York City. One of the several occupations pursued by Handlin's father was that of grocer, and the young Handlin often delivered groceries to his father's customers. Like many of the scholars here, Handlin was a precocious child. He could often be seen reading in the back of the wagon the family used for deliveries, and before he reached the age of eight, he had decided he could write better history books than those he read. A brilliant, but occasionally exasperating pupil, he was expelled from several public schools, but was admitted on the basis of competitive examination to Brooklyn College at fifteen.[14]

Carl Schorske also grew up in greater New York City. His most vivid youthful recollection came following his entry into kindergarten in Scarsdale, New York. His kindergarten teacher Miss Howe asked pupils to volunteer to sing songs. Schorske gladly offered a German song about a soldier contemplating death in battle. It was 1919 and anti-German sentiments from World War I were still rampant. Miss Howe was outraged and dispatched the young Schorske to the principal's office. Here, fortunately, he found a more sympathetic audience. The principal immediately promoted him to first grade with Mrs. Beyer, an excellent teacher who expected him "to work but not to sing."

As a youth, Schorske grew up immersed in radical politics. His father, a banker, was politically active and after World War I, became a socialist. His father was also intensely German, bitterly opposed to American intervention in World War I, and Schorske inherited a subtle German sensibility. When his mother, who unlike his father was Jewish, encountered anti-Semitism, Schorske acquired a second marginal identity.[15]

But no one had a more profoundly Jewish immigrant identity and upbringing than Gertrude Himmelfarb. "The main fact about growing up for me was that mine was an immigrant family. I think that was absolutely crucial," she remarked later. Her parents and grandparents came to the United States from Russia just before the beginning of the First World War. In Russia her maternal grandfather was the village Hebrew teacher who had acquired a great deal of learning on his own. Himmelfarb's grandmother and mother operated a small store and ran the family household while her grandfather devoted himself to reading and religion. Himmelfarb had enormous respect for her grandfather, who was gentle and kindly, as well as learned.

Once in the United States, her father began a small glass-manufacturing business in Brooklyn. The family was decidedly lower middle class and owned only a few books, many of them in Yiddish. Most of the English books Himmelfarb read were either from the library or her public school. The books in the Himmelfarb household were the Bible, various prayer and devotional books, and Yiddish classics. In her family, as well as in other Jewish families of the time and place, if a religious book fell onto the floor, the person who picked it up kissed it before replacing it. Her parents and her older brother regarded Yiddish as their first language. While they did speak English when necessary, they spoke Yiddish as the usual language of the household. Himmelfarb attended Brooklyn public schools and also Hebrew school every afternoon for two hours.[16]

The early life of Richard Hofstadter also reflects the impact of immigration and the sometimes precarious nature of life in early-twentieth-century America. Hofstadter was born in 1916 in Buffalo, New York, to a Polish Jewish father and a Lutheran mother. Though raised as an Episcopalian, Hofstadter came to identify at least in part with his Jewish heritage, though his father, Emil A. Hofstadter, ardently pursued the acceptance and middle-class respectability that so many Jewish immigrants sought. The young Hofstadter sang in the Episcopal church choir; the family took a summer cottage on Grand Island, an area close to Buffalo.[17]

But in 1926 Hofstadter suffered a cruel twist of fate from which he never entirely recovered. His mother died after a lengthy struggle with intestinal cancer. The family was broken up. Hofstadter's sister Betty went to live with his aunt Gertrude, so he lost a sister as well as a mother. Years later, Hofstadter wrote that after his mother's death "his childhood became so difficult . . . [he] no longer remember[ed] or care[d] to remember much before his high school years."[18]

Despite the tragedy, Hofstadter, pushed hard by his father, emerged as a student of exceptional promise. In 1929 he entered Fosdick Masten High School in Buffalo, where he excelled in a variety of activities. He played golf and tennis, was a cheerleader, and eventually joined a fraternity, despite the fact most fraternities did not admit Jews. He was also the star of the debate team and was extremely popular with the opposite sex. In his senior year he was elected class president. Excelling academically as well, he was class valedictorian and won a scholarship to the University of Buffalo. Another award demonstrated the sometimes tense and ambiguous relationship between Hofstadter and his father. While Emil Hofstadter continually had pushed Hofstadter to excel, he remained skeptical about his son's abilities and doubted that Hofstadter could win the prestigious Dartmouth award for outstanding scholarship. When Hofstadter did win it, tears welled in the elder Hofstadter's eyes. Thus, when Hofstadter entered the University of Buffalo in the fall of 1933, he appeared to be destined for academic stardom.[19]

J.H. Hexter was also an urban Jew, but from the American Middle West, and like Hofstadter, he suffered an early family tragedy. His mother committed suicide soon after he was born. His father, crushed by the experience, turned out to be ineffectual, and Hexter was raised primarily by his grandmother and great-grandmother. The circumstances of his birth led to an amusing but annoying confusion about his name. He was born in Memphis, Tennessee, in 1910, named Milton J. Hexter, after his father, Milton K. Hexter. He disliked the name Milton, and his twin cousins, who lived across the street from him in Memphis, called him Jack, which everyone in his family soon began to call him.

Hexter's name was not a problem until a few years later, after the family had moved to Cincinnati and his grandmother enrolled him in kindergarten as Milton K. Hexter. The results were disconcerting. To his family and friends, he was Jack. To every one of his teachers he was Milton; to most of his schoolmates, he was Milton, Milt, or, worse, Miltie. Release did not come for several years until he entered another school. This time he did the registering and enrolled himself as Jack Hexter. This allowed him a period of generalized peace regarding his name for the next thirteen years.[20]

His grandmother's influence was profound. She was often tough on him. When he came home beaten up after a schoolyard brawl, she offered little sympathy. Instead, she sent him back out to learn to take care of himself.[21]

Also urban, but not Jewish, Kenneth Stampp grew up in Milwaukee, the child of German immigrants. His father was a chiropractor, who was also a stern figure who dominated his household and who was strongly influenced by the socialist and pacifist traditions of the German-American community in Milwaukee. Stampp did not always get along well with his father, but he would himself be profoundly affected by his father's socialism and pacifism and consideration of the place of these traditions in a democratic society. Stampp's interest in history can be traced back to elementary school. When he was in the fifth grade, he announced to his class and teacher that he intended one day to be a history teacher. His early academic record was undistinguished in part because he was busy with other things, such as delivering newspapers and working in a pharmacy. [22]

Gordon Craig was also an immigrant. His father was a printer who followed the trade in search of work. Born in Scotland in 1913, Craig moved with his family to Canada at the age of six months. His early education occurred in the Toronto public schools. When he was twelve, his family moved to Jersey City. Like most of the others, Craig excelled in school right from the beginning and was usually the best student in his class. He took no history at all before college, concentrating instead on literature and achieving a particular excellence in Latin. [23]

Of all the historians considered in this book, William McNeill was perhaps the most influenced by his family background. McNeill was born in 1917 in Vancouver, British Columbia, and his family moved to Chicago in 1927, while continuing to spend its summers on Prince Edward Island. McNeill's father had a kind of dual identity, as a college professor and an ordained Presbyterian minister. John T. McNeill's approach to history was fairly ecumenical, and he was increasingly distressed by the divisions that had erupted among Christians.

McNeill's childhood was idyllic in comparison with that of some of his contemporaries. In Chicago his family lived in a Hyde Park neighborhood where he knew his neighbors for ten to twenty houses each way, and many of them were connected to the University of Chicago. He spent his summers on his grandfather's farm on Prince Edward Island in the Gulf of St. Lawrence. The island population consisted largely of Scottish farmers and French fisherman, who nourished thinly veiled and sometimes open hostility toward each other. The young McNeill also worked on his grandfather's farm where farming was still practiced in the traditional way. Like the French historian Marc Bloch, McNeill was able to see one of the most basic human activities, food production, the way it had been done for centuries. He later recalled that this made his "vision of the past more down to earth. Sweating in the field while pitching hay, even the smell of urine—I am very grateful for that slight introduction to what life was like for most people, most of the time in the deeper past." The coming of the Great Depression had little effect on

McNeill. His father kept his university job without even a salary cut. At the same time, the deflationary effect of the Depression meant that a college education actually cost less for him and his brothers and sisters.[24]

Edmund Morgan also came from an academic family. He was born in Minneapolis in 1916, where his father, Edmund Morris Morgan, taught at the University of Minnesota Law School. The elder Morgan was descended from Welsh coal mining stock; his mother, Elsie Smith Morgan, descended from Vermont Congregationalists. In 1925 the elder Morgan accepted a post at the Harvard Law School, and he published prolifically on the rules of evidence, in one instance, as applied to the Sacco and Vanzetti case.

The younger Morgan grew up around Harvard and the Cambridge area, though he never acquired much taste for the law. His early education was as a day student at the Belmont Hill School, which he attended for six years, studying Latin, French, geometry, algebra, physics, and English composition. While he took some history courses, Morgan benefited the most from Latin. Like Lawrence Stone, Morgan was not enthralled by the rigors of Latin composition, but unlike Stone, he believes the focus on grammar and sentence structure, which is the core of Latin instruction, helped him acquire his own elegant and felicitous style.[25]

Arthur Schlesinger Jr. also came from a prestigious academic family. Schlesinger's father, Arthur Meier Schlesinger, was a member of the history faculty at Harvard and in 1942 served as president of the American Historical Association. The younger Schlesinger was often referred to as "young Arthur." As a teenager, Schlesinger admired his father enough to have his name changed from Arthur Bancroft Schlesinger to Arthur Meier Schlesinger Jr. because, as he recalled later, at that time, "I very much wanted to be Arthur Meier Schlesinger, Jr." His mother, Elizabeth Schlesinger, was remotely descended from the famous early American historian George Bancroft and was herself a pioneer in the study of women's history. As important as his father was to him, Schlesinger's mother also played a key role in his development. "One of the great pleasures recalled from my childhood," Schlesinger said in 1979, "was my mother reading to me. She was a splendid reader-aloud, spirited and expressive." Schlesinger was also astute enough to notice that like many parents, his mother skipped what she regarded as dull or lengthy in such Schlesinger favorites as *Ivanhoe* or Francis Parkman's *History of the Conspiracy of Pontiac*. Schlesinger, not fooled, demanded the full and unexpurgated text. He also read voraciously on his own. Victorian literature, the works of Alexandre Dumas, and the historical novels of Arthur Conan Doyle were particular favorites.

Temperamentally, Schlesinger had more in common with his outspoken, activist mother. In 1968 he reflected, "I was always less detached and judicious than my father, more eager for commitment and combat. I think this from time to time disconcerted him, but . . . he always backed me in everything, no matter how misguided he may privately have thought my activities to be." In other ways Schlesinger followed the lead of his father. The elder Schlesinger was a firm liberal Democrat with a distaste for extremist views, especially Marxism. The younger Schlesinger not only became a lifelong liberal Democrat, but easily repelled the Marxism that attracted so many of his generation.

Arthur Schlesinger Sr. joined the Harvard faculty in 1924, and as committed egalitarians, he and his wife at first sent Arthur and his brother Tom to Cambridge public schools, contrary to the practices of most Harvard faculty members. Arthur proved to be a prodigy who was allowed to skip the second and fourth grades. But his parents soon received a sobering awakening on the quality of education in the Cambridge public schools. Among other appalling revelations, Arthur's public school history teacher told the class that the inhabitants of Albania were called Albinos because they had white hair and pink eyes. The Schlesingers promptly pulled the boys from the Cambridge public school system and enrolled them in private school. Arthur graduated from the famous eastern private school Phillips Exeter Academy in 1933, just before his sixteenth birthday. Shortly thereafter, his father was awarded a sabbatical leave from Harvard, which he and his wife used to take Arthur and Tom on a year-long, world tour.[26]

C. Vann Woodward's childhood and environment were unique among this group and a bit Faulkneresque. Woodward was born in 1908 in the small village of Vanndale, Arkansas, deeply embedded in several Southern traditions. His ancestors had owned slaves, and he was part of a large, extended family network of uncles, aunts, and cousins. A grandfather, John Vann, had served four years in the Confederate army. Woodward's father, Hugh Allison Woodward, was a public school administrator and a pillar of the local Methodist church.

The Arkansas of Woodward's youth was rural and a breeding ground for Ku Klux Klan activity. Once in Morilton, Arkansas, Woodward saw the leader of a group of clansmen enter a local church, fully attired in Klan regalia in the middle of a service to make a donation, which the minister accepted. Later he saw a lynch mob being organized on the streets of Morilton. "I saw the mob, I knew what they were going to do. . . . I did not see the man they lynched," he later recalled.[27]

Woodward's father was an educated man with a variety of friends, and many interesting people passed through the Woodward household. Woodward himself was particularly influenced by the powerful personality and ideas of his uncle Comer M. Woodward, a Methodist minister, who in the early 1920s taught sociology at Southern Methodist University. In embattled style C.M. Woodward preached a doctrine of tolerance and good works, rejecting the Klan, racial violence, and segregation, helping to instill a passion for social justice in his young nephew. At about the same time, the family entertained Charles H. Brough, a two-term governor of Arkansas from 1916 to 1920. Brough also had liberal ideas. As governor, he built schools and roads, fought for women's suffrage, and campaigned against racial violence, at one point personally intervening to stop an antiblack race riot in Philips County.

In 1928 the family left Arkansas when Hugh Woodward accepted a position as dean of Emory University's community college in Oxford, Georgia. In Oxford Woodward became acquainted with Howard W. Odum, a sociologist who founded regional studies at the University of North Carolina, who often came to Oxford to visit his parents. Odum's attitudes resembled those of Comer H. Woodward. By 1928, as the young Woodward prepared to enter Emory University, he was already a unique son of the South, a young man increasingly uncomfortable with the strictures of his Methodist upbringing and who both revered and rejected elements of his region.[28]

There is a great deal of information about Woodward's youth, but much less about his fellow Southerner David Potter. Potter's early death in 1971 precluded the writing of a memoir, and he rarely wrote or spoke about his early life. In a rare moment of reflection, he once remarked on the eerie sense of history that often haunts Southerners: "Though I was born in Georgia in 1910, I have always had the feeling that in an indirect, nonsensory way I could remember what was still called 'The War'—as if there had been no other. If I did not see the men in gray march off to battle, I saw a great number of them march in parades on a Memorial Day which did not fall on the same day that was observed in the North. If I did not experience the rigors of life 'behind the lines in the Southern Confederacy,' I lived in the long backwash of the war in a land that remembered the past very vividly and somewhat inaccurately, because the present had nothing exciting to offer, and accuracy about either the past or the present was psychologically not very rewarding. . . . But on balance I have lived longer outside of the South than in it and hopefully have learned to view it with detachment, though not without fondness. Certainly no longer a Southerner, I am not yet completely denatured."[29]

The experiences and remembrances of Woodward and Potter sometimes summon an image of Faulkner and Quentin Compson describing for his roommate in a Harvard dormitory room his ambiguous, love-hate relationship with his native land. But the experience of three other Southerners, Anne Scott, Daniel Boorstin, and John Hope Franklin, was quite different.

Anne Firor was born in Georgia in 1921, a date that has considerable significance to her. She was born nine months after the suffrage amendment was added to the Constitution, in the same year the number of women in state universities first equaled the number of men, and the year that marked the first time women in other occupations outnumbered domestic servants among female wage earners. It was also, she recalled, a year of sudden economic collapse. Her parents lost their savings in a bank failure and encountered some difficulty paying the doctor who delivered her.

Firor's father was an older, but devoted parent. He particularly enjoyed reading to Firor, the oldest child in the family, and her three younger brothers, but scorned conventional children's books, which bored him. Instead, he read his own favorites and regaled the children with long historical tales, dealing with the Indian tribes, which he claimed had lived on the hill by the Oconee River in Athens where the Georgia State College of Agriculture now stood.

There were no intellectual distinctions on the basis of sex in the Firor household. If anything, more was expected of Anne, as the eldest child. These expectations did include that she would be raised in accordance with the traditional standards of behavior for the proper Southern lady. In any case, it never crossed her mind until she was twenty-one, when she heard a rude comment from a favorite philosophy professor, that being a woman in any way limited what she might do.[30]

Daniel Boorstin, born in Atlanta on October 1, 1914, was a fellow Georgian by nativity, but also a Jew. In 1916 his father, Samuel Aaron Boorstin, a lawyer, moved the family to Tulsa, Oklahoma. The elder Boorstin, the child of Russian Jews who had been an immigrant himself, had worked his way through the University of Georgia and practiced law in Atlanta. The move to Tulsa was a calculated risk. Atlanta had many established lawyers, but Tulsa in the early twentieth century was a frontier town ready to expand, and the elder Boorstin prospered as Tulsa developed. Like so many others of his generation of historians, the young Dan Boorstin was a prodigy, graduating first in his class from Tulsa Central High School in 1930 and entering Harvard University the next fall.[31]

Boorstin's father was an extraordinary man, a lawyer with a general practice who preferred helping people to getting rich. He was excessively proud of his gifted son, buttonholing his fellow Tulsans on the street to show them clippings of Dan's latest triumph. Yet he never praised his son to his face. The father's love for his son, however, manifested itself in other ways. The elder Boorstin fervently hoped that Dan would attend the University of Oklahoma and eventually join the law practice. Dan went to Harvard only at the insistence of his mother. When Dan later won a Rhodes Scholarship to go from Harvard to Oxford, his father made no comment, except to note that a neighbor boy had won a scholarship to the University of Oklahoma, surely realizing that Oxford would only take his son farther away from him.[32]

As an African-American, John Hope Franklin provides an exception in almost every aspect of the historical experience of the World War II generation of historians, although he, too, was a student of exceptional promise. Franklin was born in the all-black town of Rentiesville, Oklahoma, in 1915. His parents had settled in Rentiesville after his father, who was a lawyer, had been expelled from court by a judge who refused to allow blacks to represent anyone in his court. His father therefore decided to abandon the white world and make a life among his own people, but the quality of life in Rentiesville was shockingly poor. Fewer than two hundred people lived there, and there was no electricity, running water, or inside plumbing. Still worse, there was no meaningful entertainment or means of diversion, no parks, playgrounds, or newspapers. Most of Franklin's days in Rentiesville were lonely and empty. Franklin's mother was a school teacher who often took him to work with her, so he learned to read at an early age. There was little else for him to do, although he did win the local spelling bee in the county seat of Eufala three years in a row. Reading by dim kerosene light also weakened his eyes, and he had to start wearing glasses at age five.[33]

Franklin encountered racism early in his life. A rare family pleasure was a trip to Checotah, six miles away by train, to go shopping. During one excursion, he, his mother, and his sister were removed from the train because his mother would not move from the whites-only coach, which she had taken because it was the only one available. Her argument failed to convince the conductor, who threw them off, and they had to walk back to Rentiesville through the woods. The grinding poverty of Rentiesville persuaded his parents that they needed to live elsewhere, and they resolved to move to Tulsa. The plan was for his father to move there first and establish his law practice, and the family would follow. After his father's departure, the family received the news of a race riot in Tulsa. Observing his mother's reaction, Franklin deduced that his father was in danger. Happily, the danger passed and the family moved on to Tulsa just before Franklin reached his eleventh birthday.

Tulsa was larger and much more prosperous than Rentiesville and completely segregated. Central High School in Tulsa, where Dan Boorstin had excelled, was a massive building, all white, with every conceivable advantage and contrivance for its students. Franklin's all-black school paled by comparison. By this time Franklin's mother no longer worked and began to introduce the family to certain cultural amenities, like black literature and classical music. Franklin, already playing first trumpet in the high school orchestra, learned to love music. He also spent time in his father's law office. After the onset of the Depression, his father had few clients and had more time to spend with his children. The elder Franklin delighted in the classics, especially in Plato and Socrates. He and Franklin often walked home together, and after dinner, the father went to his books, the son to his. In what might be a good lesson to parents, Franklin grew up thinking that reading and writing were what one did in the evening. Franklin dreamed of getting his law degree and becoming his father's partner.

While Franklin's parents did not consciously oppose or decry the segregation under which they lived, they sought their own ways of protest and maintaining self-respect. They refused, for example, to attend the concerts and recitals held at the Central High School auditorium, even though they were open to blacks and whites. Franklin loved music and with the money he earned from delivering papers was able to buy tickets. He got the chance to hear Paul Whiteman's orchestra perform "Rhapsody in Blue" in 1927 and to hear the annual performances of the Chicago Civic Opera Company. In later life Franklin often reproached himself for having capitulated to this aspect of segregation, recognizing in retrospect that his parents knew best.

It is hard to generalize about the early lives of these historians. There is considerable variation even among seemingly homogenous groups, such as those who attended the English public schools or those who were raised in the American South. One thing, however, does seem fairly clear. With only a couple of exceptions, most of these historians gave evidence of extraordinary ability at a very early age. They loved history books, read voraciously at an early age, and won awards and recognition quickly. Several, such as Geoffrey Elton, overcome severe obstacles to win their recognition. Others had the advantage of being raised in affluence or in an academic family. While several benefited from the guidance of a cherished teacher or parent, others made their way largely by their own resourcefulness.

Chapter 2

HARVARD, THE 1930S, AND THE MAKING OF A HISTORICAL GENERATION

꧁

They were in their teens or early twenties, in college or just ready to enter college, when it happened. The stock market crashed in the fall of 1929. The American economy collapsed like a rickety barn in the face of a prairie tornado. Fortunes vanished. Businesses were destroyed. Five thousand banks failed between 1929 and 1932, bankrupting millions of Americans. By 1933 national incomes had declined by more than half, and industrial production had fallen to roughly half of 1929 levels. Unemployment became a grim reality. During the three years after the market crash, an average of 100,000 American workers lost their jobs each week. By 1932 perhaps a third of the country's 120 million people were either unemployed or belonged to a family of unemployed workers. The psychological and emotional shocks were almost as powerful as the economic ones. He who was in affluence and comfort one day woke up in poverty and ignominy the next. "The stock market crash," wrote the literary critic Edmund Wilson, "was to count for us almost like rending of the earth in preparation for the Day of Judgment." The government appeared helpless in the face of such colossal failure, and millions of Americans who trusted the traditional sources of authority in early-twentieth-century America, such as the government, the business community, the church, and political parties, became profoundly alienated from them.

Americans entering college and graduate school in the 1930s faced a world suddenly full of uncertainty and were also compelled to confront a series of disturbing specters in other areas. First, the cost of a college education was beyond the reach of many Americans following the stock market crash, and even when colleges reduced tuition, students and parents faced the chilling prospect that there would be no material reward at the end of it. Second, the course of history in the first thirty years of the twentieth century was discouraging if not terrifying. The First World War shattered nineteenth-century notions of progress. The world of reason and progress had been replaced by a world of irrationality and mass slaughter. The Bolshevik Revolution posed the possibility of the spread of Communism. For many young Americans, Communism seemed to have better answers for the economic collapse of the 1930s than the hollow assurances of capitalism. Just as ominously, the rise of fascism suggested among other things that authoritarian government might be the world's future and that the Western democratic tradition might prove ephemeral. The World War II generation of historians born in America entered the university, in the phrase of Saul Bellow (b. 1915), as "dangling men and women." Few of them were thwarted by the cost of higher education but many of them were dismayed at their prospects and almost all of them confronted the promises of Marxist ideology.

Harvard University has a special claim to attention here. Many of the stalwarts of the World War II generation of historians received their training or a significant part of it there. Obviously, Harvard was not the only university that produced great historians in the 1930s, but no institution produced as many. While Harvard is likely to produce outstanding historians during almost any time period, its students in the thirties were exceptional by any standard. Barbara Tuchman (b. 1912), Daniel Boorstin (b. 1914), Edmund Morgan (b. 1916), and Arthur Schlesinger (b. 1917) were Harvard undergraduates during the 1930s. Morgan and Schlesinger stayed at Harvard for further study. J.H. Hexter (b. 1910), John Hope Franklin (b. 1915), Oscar Handlin (b. 1915), and Carl Schorske (b. 1915) were graduate students at Harvard in the 1930s.[1] Most benefited immensely from the resources of the university, the erudition of the faculty, and stimulation of other superior students. But roses do have thorns, and the Harvard of the 1930s had its flaws. Several of the World War II generation were scarred by the anti-Semitism, snobbery, and occasional pomposity among the faculty that prevailed at Harvard during that time. "Faculty members at Harvard," J.H. Hexter once recalled, "were not much addicted to speaking to graduate students in the good old days."[2] H. Stuart Hughes found advanced historical study at Harvard "dispiriting" and thought that the Harvard lecture style "exuded staleness and desiccation." Retrospectively, he took some solace from the revelation that it is not unusual for historians to regard the "years of graduate study as the least rewarding of one's life."[3] But for most of them, especially the undergraduates, their experience at Harvard was positive; for all of them it was memorable.

Harvard University in the 1930s had not yet achieved the global renown that it would claim later. Edwin O. Reischauer, who arrived in Cambridge for graduate study in 1932, remembered that Harvard was "still an aristocratic, parochially New England institution . . . heavily centered on the undergraduate college, which was populated largely by preppies . . . a few bright New York Jews and Middle Westerners were tolerated, but not really welcomed."[4] But while bound to its proud traditions, Harvard was slowly evolving from its traditional role of educating Boston's elite. By the 1930s it was attracting a broader base of students, both geographically and religiously.[5] And it had already assembled a formidable array of historians. Medieval studies with such luminaries as Charles Homer Haskins, E.K. Rand, and George Sarton was particularly strong, but Harvard also claimed such eminent Americanists as Samuel Eliot Morison, Frederick Merk, and Arthur Schlesinger Sr., and such distinguished Europeanists as William Langer, Crane Brinton, and R.B. Merriman. In all there were seven past or future presidents of the American Historical Association among the history faculty in the 1930s. In the late 1930s the great Asianists John King Fairbank and Edwin Reischauer would begin their Harvard careers.[6] Department cohesion was sustained through regular Thursday lunches, where Sam Morison often appeared in riding breeches. Members and colleagues in related disciplines also competed in hotly contested late afternoon games of fistball, a variant of volleyball, played in the dingy women's gymnasium.[7] Despite the variety of approaches to history among department members, a general climate of harmony prevailed. William Langer, one of the department's most distinguished members, could not recall "any fundamental difference of opinion or effort at factional conflict."[8]

Closely connected to history, History and Literature also emerged in the 1930s as a stimulating major, largely due to the influence of Kenneth B. Murdock and the arrival of Perry Miller and F.O. Matthiessen.[9] Other figures of distinction in American Studies included Howard Mumford Jones and Bernard DeVoto of the English department, and Ralph Barton Perry in philosophy.

The history students at Harvard in the 1930s who confronted the questions posed by the Depression and the collapse of capitalism most directly were, with one exception, urban Jews. Most of these scholars, such as Carl Schorske, Oscar Handlin, J.H. Hexter, and, an African American, John Hope Franklin, entered Harvard as graduate students. Carl Schorske's father had become a socialist, despite his profession as a banker. Schorske's college career began in 1932 at Columbia College, then awash in radical politics, including rallies for Norman Thomas, the socialist candidate. Schorske eschewed a history major, concentrating on a self-designed humanities curriculum, centering on great-book seminars and taught by such exceptional faculty members as Moses Hadas, Theodore Westbrook, Lionel Trilling, and Jacques Barzun. As he completed his humanities curriculum, history was the discipline that interested him the most. However, having done virtually nothing in the way of writing papers or historical research at Columbia, Schorske was dubious about his ability to succeed in graduate study in the discipline. Despite his reservations, he finally settled on history, even in the face of two experiences that might have daunted a lesser spirit. At the 1935 American Historical Association meeting in New York City he managed an audience with Charles Beard, a leading American historian and former president of the American Historical Association. Pontificating from his bed in a steamy room at the Hotel Pennsylvania as though his words should be handed out on tablets, Beard dismissed the profession in which he achieved such distinction as trivial. "Choose a commodity," he told Schorske, "like tin, in some African colony. Write your first seminar paper on it. Write your thesis on it. Broaden it to another country or two and write a book on it. As you sink your mental life into it, your livelihood and place in the esteemed halls of learning will be assured." Schorske also approached his Columbia teacher and literary critic Lionel Trilling for advice. He was wounded when Trilling laughed at him for his folly in dreaming, as a half-Jew, of trying for an academic career in the middle of the Depression.[10]

Undaunted, Schorske entered the Harvard graduate school in the fall of 1936, convinced of his own capacity to do historical research, but without a strong vocation. Harvard might as well have been another planet compared to Columbia. Where Columbia is part of New York City and reflects its ethnic makeup and restless energy, Harvard is aloof, above the madding crowd, a citadel of learning for young gentlemen. But if patrician Harvard required a period of adjustment for an urban Jew, it had its own charms. Where Columbia had developed Schorske's capacity for independent thought and reading texts, Harvard developed his professional vocation. Harvard's leading Europeanist, William Langer, urged Schorske to take as many seminars as possible, to gain as wide a historical understanding as possible. Whatever misgivings Schorske had about his calling quickly evaporated as he took Langer's advice to heart. Though he lacked sufficient command of Greek, Schorske took an in-depth tutorial on the ancient Greek world with William Scott Ferguson. Meeting weekly for two hours at Ferguson's house, Schorske explored a wide range of Greek authors and approaches to Greek history. For his general examination Schorske prepared a special subject on Aristophanes. Under Ferguson's guidance Schorske began to see the possibilities of integrated cultural analysis and the impact a dedicated and learned teacher can have on a student.[11]

By 1938 Harvard was roused from its political slumbers as the international scene became increasingly threatening. As emotions became passionate, Schorske found himself caught in a vise of tension between his political and pedagogical duties. As a graduate teaching assistant, Schorske watched Roger Merriman actively and dramatically campaign for American intervention in Europe. Merriman, according to Schorske, was a "colorful, salty instructor of the old school," passionately devoted to aristocratic Britain, and disturbed by the threat German invasion posed to the sceptered isle. Schorske, dismayed to find the classroom a tool of political indoctrination, organized a conspiracy with his fellow graduate students Barnaby C. Keeney and Robert Lee Wolff to resist Merriman's propaganda.[12]

Politics also filtered into the activities of the Harvard history club, in which student members often prepared papers on topics not covered in regular seminars. German history naturally emerged as a subject of deep interest during this time, and Schorske examined German historians under the Weimar Republic and Third Reich to understand the political pressures upon them and the ways the different cultural traditions in historiography, clashing with a changing present, led to new visions of the past. Schorske was shocked to find out that the most nationalistic historians often justified their nationalism with explicit philosophic relativism. The exercise reminded Schorske and his graduate student colleagues that the present can both impede and enhance the understanding of the past. Moreover, previous generations, even those with aspirations to objectivity, could not free themselves from the distortions that resulted from their participation in the present.[13]

If Carl Schorske entered graduate school with some trepidation, Oscar Handlin, another urban Jew, roared into fair Harvard like a nor'easter coming up the New England coast. At Brooklyn College during his freshman year, he turned in a paper that was so good his instructor believed it had been plagiarized. She summoned Handlin for a conference and quickly recognized her error. Handlin was indeed capable of writing such a paper. Handlin, a Brooklyn Jew of working-class background, seemed to be the type likely to be attracted to Marxist doctrine during the Depression. But with typical independence, he eschewed the many heated discussions of Marx and capitalist collapse that swirled around the campus, remaining suspicious of ideologies that promised easy answers.[14]

In fact the first attraction that Harvard held for Handlin was its glittering array of medievalists. Undeterred by a remark from a Brooklyn College dean that no one in Cambridge had ever heard of Brooklyn College, Handlin decided to visit Cambridge for himself. In 1934 $3.50 bought him a round-trip New York to Boston ticket. Handlin arrived in Cambridge unannounced, but with a letter of introduction to Michael Karpovich, then an assistant professor of Russian history. At 8:30 A.M. Handlin rang the doorbell at Karpovich's house on Trowbridge Street and offered his letter, which seemed at first to create some level of confusion on the part of Karpovich, who was still in his pajamas and robe. Karpovich, however, quickly recovered and guided Handlin on a tour of Harvard, including the river houses, the fabled Yard, and into the Widener Library, where Handlin gazed in awe at the breathtaking resources and the marvel of open stacks. They spent the entire morning talking about Harvard and history. Karpovich was, however, somewhat uncertain about the mechanics of admission into graduate school, and Crane Brinton, who knew them thoroughly, would be out of town until the next day.[15]

Handlin therefore decided to stay another day. Brinton proved to be as engaging and friendly as Karpovich. He and Handlin talked easily about history, and Brinton took him to see the dean of the graduate school, who chatted with Handlin for a while and then admitted him, without application, undergraduate transcripts, or Graduate Record Examination scores.

When Handlin entered Harvard in the fall, he was dismayed to find a different place from the one he encountered in the spring. The plan to study medieval history crumbled quickly. Haskins was seriously ill, Rand did only classics, and Sarton was buried in his own work. Even Brinton was a bit distant, suggesting that his Enlightenment course was for undergraduates and too superficial for Handlin. Handlin was left to his own devices. With no regulation to limit the number of courses he could take and no additional tuition involved, Handlin signed up for as many courses as he dared handle. In his first semester he completed the Latin, French, and German requirements and enrolled in five other courses. Having overextended himself, he received mostly mediocre grades.[16]

Despite this inauspicious beginning, he quickly became a Harvard legend, disdaining to take notes at lectures and constantly hectoring even Harvard's most distinguished history faculty. To William Langer he "seemed to seize upon every occasion to differ."[17] Graduate students normally challenge faculty at their own peril, and for Handlin, a Brooklyn Jew at patrician Harvard, the risks of defiance were even greater. Anti-Semitism was a basic fact of American academic life in the 1930s. At Columbia the careers of Lionel Trilling and Moses Finley were both hampered by prejudice. At Harvard the prejudice existed, but Handlin escaped it, largely, he believes, because he made no attempt to conceal his identity. Occasionally he heard jokes from peers and professors with references to Brooklyn and the Dodgers given in "Toid Avenue" accents. If there was an anti-Semitic meaning to them, Handlin chose to ignore it. In any event the faculty with the most impeccable pedigrees, such as Morison, Murdock, and Elliot Perkins, went out of their way to be helpful.[18] His dazzling performance on his comprehensive examinations established him as a student of unquestioned brilliance, destined, according to Ray Alan Billington, "to rank among the great historians of his day."[19] Handlin chose Arthur Schlesinger Sr., whom he admired greatly, to supervise his dissertation. Schlesinger suggested that Handlin study Boston immigrants in the late eighteenth and early nineteenth centuries, a subject abandoned by another student.[20] Handlin's doctoral thesis, supported by a Sheldon Fellowship that enabled him to pursue his research in Dublin and London, allowed him to receive his Ph.D. in 1940 and was published in 1941 as *Boston's Immigrants*. From 1938 to 1939 he returned to Brooklyn College as an instructor before going back to Harvard in 1939 as an instructor.

The career of J.H. Hexter resembled Handlin's in some ways. Both were urban Jews who began their college careers at city colleges and came to

Harvard to pursue their doctorates. Raised in Cincinnati, Hexter entered the University of Cincinnati in the spring of 1929 and enrolled in an introductory course in Western Civilization. The course began in 1517 and proceeded to modern times, using Ferdinand Schevill's basic text. But Hexter's real education began in his sophomore year. By a dependence on H.L. Mencken and Mencken's generally cynical approach to life, Hexter generally avoided reading, especially great books, until one day he accidentally walked into a graduate class in philosophy where the teacher, Benjamin Fuller, held Hexter's "head down in Spinoza's *Ethics* for seven weeks."[21] In this class, Hexter recalled, "you had to wade into Spinoza," line by line, and he wrote ten or twelve papers during the course. An English major, Hexter was a superior student at Cincinnati, graduating in 1931, with practically straight A's.[22]

He entered the Harvard Graduate School in 1932, but his experience there was distinctly unsatisfying. Deciding that an English major was too easy, he elected to concentrate on history, a field in which he had little preparation. He also felt shunned by his mentors, as a Jew, and the fact that, as a Midwesterner and something of a plodder, he may have been regarded as a bumpkin by the faculty. "I was brighter than I looked," he recalled. His first year's record was poor. But he soon began to show signs of genuine promise, publishing an article in the *Journal of Modern History*, already a highly respected journal, and winning several Harvard history prize competitions, including the Toppin and Bowdoin Prizes. Most of the Harvard faculty, he believed, "never noticed."[23]

Hexter largely stood above the great political debates of the 1930s. His family environment was not impassioned politically, and as far as the great intellectual figures of the age, Marx and Freud, were concerned, Hexter recalled that while people at the time were immersed in their writings, he was not: "I never believed either of them; it was just too silly." He rejected the ideas of Marx almost instinctively and congratulated himself on the time saved by not reading them.[24]

Some of the perplexities about his name were resolved at Harvard. At a meeting of the Graduate History Club he was approached by his advisor Wilbur Abbott with a suggestion that he change his name. It soon became clear that Abbott thought that Hexter might someday be a good historian, and in that case he would have to have a more distinguished name than Jack. Hexter persisted in wanting to be called Jack, but after some high-level deliberation, the two agreed that professionally he could go by initials. That Hexter should use "J" for his first initial was obvious, but since he didn't have a middle name, there was no clear middle initial. Abbott told Hexter that he had a spare one, an "H" he didn't use, which Hexter could use. So Hexter became J.H. Hexter.

The encounter with Abbott was curious in two ways. First, Hexter's record at Harvard up to that point had not been promising, and Abbott was the first Harvard faculty member who ever expressed the slightest hint that Hexter had any kind of future as a historian. Second, a year or so later, after Hexter related the story to two fellow graduate students, one of them speculated that since Abbott's full name was W.H.C. Abbott and that the W.H. stood for Wilbur Hernando, it was exceedingly likely that the C. stood for Cortez. This meant that Hexter's new name must be Jack Hernando Hexter. However, in a subsequent conversation with Abbott's secretary Hexter discovered that the "H" stood for something other than Hernando.

But there was no way to escape the harsh economic realities of the 1930s. In 1936 Hexter was a Jew with a Harvard Ph.D. trying to find a job at the height of the Depression. For two terrible years, with little help from the faculty, he tried to find a job. His advisor, Abbott, was a Boston Brahmin, largely cut off from the profession. In those days senior professors usually tried to procure the few available jobs for their students, but Abbott, according to Hexter, "couldn't have gotten Leopold von Ranke a job." Crane Brinton made a valiant effort on Hexter's behalf, but the situation was so bleak Brinton feared that Hexter might be unemployable."[25]

One thing of value did come out of this trying period. Hexter had written a promising dissertation called "The Rise of the Independent Party during the English Civil War," but had based it solely on printed sources available in the Widener Library. Harvard's treatment of his dissertation was breathtakingly cavalier. At one point, Elliot Perkins carried the only copy, written out by Hexter in longhand, around Europe for a month. Hexter soon realized that the dissertation could be turned into a book, which might improve his job prospects, if his research from printed sources could be supplemented by archival materials. It was the height of the Depression and Harvard would not be of any help. For years, his mother and grandmother had made him squirrel away the money he usually received at holidays and birthdays, so he had a small amount saved up. He used the money to travel to England, visit the British Museum (now the British Library) to examine the pertinent manuscript collections, and expand his dissertation into a book based now on manuscript materials and get it published as *The Reign of King Pym.*[26]

In 1938 he finally cracked the job market. After spending two years in Cincinnati, supported by his grandmother and great-grandmother and a brief stint of teaching at Cincinnati, he returned to Cambridge to make one last effort to get a job. At one point Carl Bridenbaugh, then teaching at the Massachusetts Institute of Technology, got a job at Brown. Hexter and Bridenbaugh ate at the same delicatessen off Harvard Square, and Bridenbaugh helped him get the job at MIT, although the job was not exactly a plum. Hexter began his teaching career by teaching English to engineers, their first assignment being to write patent specifications.[27]

John Hope Franklin also ended up in the Harvard Graduate School in the 1930s, though his career path followed a rather different trajectory from the others. He entered Fisk University in 1931 in the midst of the Depression on a tuition scholarship, also working at several other jobs to make ends meet. At the end of his freshmen year he was stunned to discover that his father's law practice had declined markedly. His parents lost their home and were compelled to move to a four-family apartment building. Franklin, like many of his generation facing similar circumstances, felt deeply his parents' loss and the feeling of humiliation that accompanied it.[28]

Despite these dispiriting experiences, Franklin returned to Fisk, determined to make the most of it. The Fisk faculty, half white and half black, was excellent, taking pride in both teaching and research. Franklin's decision to major in history at Fisk was almost accidental. He had been excited by the lectures of the chair of the history department, Theodore S. Currier, who was white. Franklin decided to take more courses with Currier, which deepened his interest in historical problems and processes, and the two became fast friends. Under Currier's influence, Franklin scrapped his plan to study law, replacing it with a new desire to undertake further study in history. With the encouragement of Currier, a Harvard Ph.D., Franklin applied to Harvard.[29]

Unlike Handlin, whose admission was secured by a meeting with a dean, Franklin had to take an aptitude test comparable to the modern Graduate Record Examination. The test was administered at nearby Vanderbilt University, and there Franklin received a blunt reminder of who he was. When he arrived at the appointed place to take the exam, the person in charge *threw* (Franklin's italics) his examination at him, leaving Franklin a bit shaken. After he finished the examination and left the room, an African American custodian walked up to him and told him that Franklin was the first black person he had ever seen sitting in a room with white people. Franklin feared that he had done wretchedly, but Harvard admitted him unconditionally although it did not award him a scholarship. Fisk had just received accreditation from the Association of American Universities, and Franklin may have been the first student from an historically black institution to pursue graduate work at Harvard without having done some undergraduate work there.[30]

It remained for Franklin to find the money to go to Harvard. Despite their financial troubles, his parents scraped together a small sum to assist him, but here Franklin was again fortunate in his friendship with Theodore Currier. Currier informed Franklin that he would not allow money to stand in the way of Franklin's going to Harvard, went immediately to a Nashville bank, borrowed $500, and gave it to Franklin.[31]

Franklin arrived in Cambridge in September 1935 and took jobs washing dishes and typing dissertations. He was academically confident. At Fisk he had taken two modern foreign languages, had learned how to use the library, and had written research papers in Currier's seminars. He was not in the least intimidated during his first meeting with his dissertation advisor, the distinguished Arthur Schlesinger Sr. He completed his M.A. degree in nine months and soon won a fellowship. Other parts of his experience at Harvard were also fortuitous. Franklin took a room with an African American family that had been taking in black students for years. He had extensive contact with white students, "who," he recalled, "never showed the slightest condescension toward me."[32]

But Harvard proved to be prickly in other ways. If Franklin did not personally encounter racism at Harvard, he did encounter anti-Semitism. He was active in the Henry Adams Club, composed of graduate students in American history, and he served on the committee to nominate officers for the club, which of course might have been a devious way to make sure he never became one. When he nominated the most active, brightest graduate student for president, he was shocked when he was informed that while this particular student did not have some of the more reprehensible Jewish traits, "he was still a Jew." Franklin had never heard people speak of others in such terms, and he lost respect not only for the person who made the remarks, but for the entire group for tolerating such views.[33]

Another disturbing experience occurred at the beginning of his second year at Harvard. He watched one of the department's outstanding faculty members verbally abuse a student visiting from another institution because the student had asked an awkwardly phrased question. Another professor told Franklin that a doctoral committee failed a student because the student did not *look* (Franklin's italics) like a Harvard Ph.D. When the committee told him that he would have to study four more years before he could be reconsidered, the student dutifully appeared at the library the next morning, clearly failing to grasp the unspoken message the committee was sending him. At that point the chair of the committee went to inform the student that his graduate career at Harvard was over. While Franklin felt well treated at Harvard, when he left in the spring of 1939, he knew that he did not wish to spend another day there.[34]

In the 1930s undergraduate education remained the heart and soul of Harvard, and the experience of the group of historians who were undergraduates there during this time was much better than that of those who were graduate students. During the 1930s Harvard produced an array of stellar undergraduates in history, including Barbara Tuchman, Daniel Boorstin, Edmund Morgan, and Arthur Schlesinger. Most of them found their greatest intellectual stimulation from the History and Literature program. After attending the Walden School in New York City, Barbara (Wertheim) Tuchman entered Radcliffe College in 1929. Tuchman, like several of Harvard's finest students in the 1930s, was Jewish, but she was from a more privileged background. Her father was a prominent banker in New York City. Tuchman elected History and Literature as her concentration. Three courses impressed her the most. The first was Irving Babbitt's Comp

Lit 11, and the second was John Livingston Lowes's English 72. Babbitt and Lowes stood in sharp contrast to each other. Babbitt, a classicist, despised zeal and enthusiasm in teaching, depending on his massive erudition to stimulate student interest. Lowes, by contrast, rode a tidal wave of enthusiasm, especially for the poetry of Samuel Taylor Coleridge. Lowes, Tuchman recalled in 1963, "waved at Wordsworth, bowed briefly to Keats and Shelley, and really let himself go through twelve weeks of lectures on Coleridge's 'The Rime of the Ancient Mariner' and 'Kubla Khan.'" Lowes' enthusiasm for it kept Tuchman poised on the edge of her seat all semester.[35]

Enthusiasm was also the basis for Tuchman's enchantment with C.H. McIlwain's course in the constitutional history of England up to the signing of the Magna Carta. It did not matter to McIlwain, a formidable scholar of the English constitution, that only four students had signed up for the course. He was, in Tuchman's words, "conducting a passionate love affair with the laws of the Angles and the articles of the charter, especially Article 39. Like any person in love, he wanted to let everyone know how beautiful was the object of his affections." Tuchman could recall little of Article 39, but the blaze in McIlwain's blue eyes as he discussed it remained etched in her memory. She sat entranced and yearned to show her appreciation by writing a brilliant final examination to dazzle McIlwain with her wealth of knowledge. When the examination came, Tuchman was dismayed to find that half of the questions were in Anglo-Saxon, a curiosity that McIlwain had neglected to mention to them. In any case, it did not matter. He gave them all A's anyway.[36]

For Tuchman, however, Harvard's most marvelous resource was the Widener Library. By the time she was ready to write her undergraduate honors thesis, she was allowed to have her own small private carrel, deep among the 942s (library catalogue numbers for British history). There, she recalled, "I could roam at liberty through the rich stacks, taking whatever I wanted. The experience was marvelous, a word I use in its exact sense meaning full of marvels. The happiest days of my intellectual life, until I began writing history again some fifteen years later, were spent in the stacks at Widener."[37]

One afternoon, lost in her research, she emerged from Widener into a darkened Harvard Yard to discover that she had stayed out past the dinner hour at her dormitory and that she had only a nickel in her purse. The weather was freezing, and having missed dinner, she was extremely hungry. She had to decide whether to spend the nickel on a chocolate bar and walk home in the cold or spend the nickel on a trolley and go home warm, but hungry. Thirty years later, Tuchman could recall the difficulty in reaching the decision, but not the decision she made.[38]

The honors thesis on which she worked in the library was titled "The Moral Justification of the British Empire." For Tuchman, the experience of working on it was both wonderful and terrible. On one hand it filled her with the excitement of discovery in historical research. On the other hand she could not get the thesis to come out the way she wanted. The characters, so vivid in her mind, were lifeless on paper. Her faculty mentors agreed. "Style undistinguished," was their solemn verdict. Reading it again, years later, Tuchman could only concur.[39]

In 1933 she graduated from Radcliffe and left immediately with no desire to pursue an advanced degree. "I was dying to get out of the cloister," she said years later. "I didn't even stay for my graduation. You see, it was 1933—the year both Hitler and Roosevelt came to power. The world was in such turmoil, the natural thing to do was to go out and be in it."[40]

The colonial historian Edmund Morgan entered Harvard as an undergraduate in 1933, and his first history examination was a shock. He took the survey of European history with "Frisky" Merriman, as Merriman was sometimes known, but made one of the lowest grades. Morgan persisted, majoring in history and literature. He intended to concentrate on English history and literature, until he took a course in American literature in which Perry Miller was one of the lecturers.[41]

Morgan was captivated by Miller, one of the most exciting lecturers he had ever heard, and soon shifted his emphasis to American history so he could have Miller as his tutor. In the mid-1930s Miller was already well on his way to becoming a Harvard legend. An outspoken, Hemingwayesque character, given to telling tall tales about himself, he was a dynamic lecturer and charismatic teacher.[42] As a tutor, he helped students find and develop their own ideas. His enthusiasm was infectious. He was also at the beginning of his ground-breaking studies of American Puritan thought, having just published *Orthodoxy in Massachusetts*, so an air of excitement swirled around him.[43]

Morgan was also influenced by Miller's colleague and occasional rival, F.O. Matthiessen. Matthiessen was also at the beginning of his career, almost as dynamic as Miller and even more competitive. A defeat at fistball could devastate him.[44] While Matthiessen was too serious to joke with, he made himself available to students, and he and Morgan had numerous long conversations in languid Cambridge afternoons. Morgan was struck by the seriousness with which Matthiessen took ideas.[45]

During Morgan's junior year at Harvard, Felix Frankfurter, a family friend (Morgan's father was a law school professor), took an interest in Morgan's work. When Morgan completed his degree in 1937, Frankfurter persuaded him to attend the London School of Economics and study with Harold Laski. So Morgan went to England and spent a year at LSE, though it was not Laski who impressed him the most. Laski was personable and generous, but Morgan found his lectures abstract and uninspiring. By contrast he found the lectures of R.H. Tawney to be specific "with a marvelous sort of humanistic resonance."[46] Tawney, a Christian socialist, combined scholarship with political commitment. His considerable reputation rested upon books depicting the plight of tenants in sixteenth-century England and the economic bases of English Puritanism.[47]

Lured by the offer of a fellowship in American history, Morgan returned to Harvard in 1938. In that year someone gave Harvard money to assist undergraduates who wanted to study American history as an extracurricular activity, and two counselors were appointed for every Harvard house and two for the freshman class, which didn't live in the houses. Morgan received an extremely lucrative stipend to serve as a counselor in Lowell House, where he had lived as an undergraduate. With the number of people seeking his wisdom on American history rather low, he had plenty of time to pursue his doctoral program, working with Perry Miller. Harvard gave him credit for his courses at LSE and after a year of course work at Harvard, Morgan passed his preliminary exams, covering six fields.[48]

He then elected to write a dissertation on Puritan political thought, reading intensively on Luther and Calvin. Over the next summer he completed a 250–page draft and turned it in to Miller. Here he received the first real blow of his career. Miller, his mentor and inspiration, was disappointed and told Morgan to "try again, for God's sake. What do you think this is, an enlarged senior essay?" After he recovered from Miller's harsh reaction, Morgan decided to expand the chapter of his draft on the family into a dissertation topic, which he did after two more years of reading, which included anthropology and Freud. The additional work resulted in *The Puritan Family*, which became Morgan's first book, published in 1945.[49]

Morgan was also caught up in politics. Though he had leftist leanings and many friends in the Communist Party or who were "fellow travelers," Morgan did not join them. The Soviet trials of the 1930s were too disillusioning, and Morgan was repelled by the sweeping generalizations made by many Marxists about history without sufficient grasp of the facts.[50]

Morgan's political commitment was to pacifism. Like many of his generation, he interpreted World War I as the classic case of a war that should never have been fought and should have been adamantly opposed. If war broke out again, Morgan intended to be a conscientious objector, but several factors caused him to change his mind. He had been in Germany briefly just before Munich and watched the Hitler phenomenon unfold, but he did not withdraw his conscientious objector status until the beginning of the war. That decision was not difficult. He decided first of all the Nazis were worth fighting against. Second, conscientious objection would be more difficult than it would have been earlier, since he was recently married with a child on the way. Finally, because of the war, Harvard would not be renewing his position as a tutor.[51]

Two other members of the World War II generation of historians who were Harvard undergraduates in the 1930s were captivated by Perry Miller and F.O. Matthiessen. Arthur Schlesinger Jr., whose father was the Harvard historian Arthur M. Schlesinger Sr., entered Harvard in the fall of 1934 in the History and Literature program. Matthiessen was his tutor for one year, and Perry Miller for two. To Schlesinger both were superb, but with vastly different styles. Miller, while charismatic, was demanding and occasionally intemperate, teaching by the power of his personality. One entered a tutorial with Miller like the Light Brigade entering the valley of death. Matthiessen in Schlesinger's eyes was softer, more forgiving, but just as inspiring. Like Miller, he was poised on the brink of academic prominence, having just published *The Achievement of T. S. Eliot* and in the midst of work on his masterpiece, *American Renaissance*. Under Matthiessen's guidance, Schlesinger learned to appreciate the profundity of Eliot's *The Waste Land*, which had previously seemed inaccessible, and to acquire a taste for contemporary poetry.[52]

Even more vivid, though for different reasons, than Miller or Matthiessen was a lecturer in the English department, Bernard DeVoto. In today's university DeVoto might not survive. He was opinionated and testy, full of defects, and even more combative than Miller. A savage critic, he would engulf a student essay with insulting and abusive comments. His demeanor was too overwhelming for most students, but Schlesinger was secure enough to see that DeVoto's criticism, however unsparing, did improve his writing.[53]

Quite apart from his tutors, Schlesinger was an instant star at Harvard. As a freshman he was one of 613 people who submitted a historical essay for the LeBaron Russell Briggs Prize. Schlesinger's essay won. He was elected to Phi Beta Kappa during his junior year. At his father's suggestion, he chose Orestes A. Brownson, a neglected New England literary figure of the Jacksonian era, as the subject for his senior honors thesis. Brownson enjoyed a varied career in Jacksonian politics, as a Transcendentalist, and as the leading Catholic intellectual in America at the time. Schlesinger graduated summa cum laude from Harvard in 1938, and with the encouragement of his father, decided to revise his honors thesis for publication. During the summer of 1938 he traveled to Indiana to examine the Brownson Papers at the Notre Dame University Library. With this additional work, he quickly revised his manuscript and submitted it to Little, Brown, who agreed to publish it.[54]

In the fall of 1938, despite a threatening international situation, he arrived at Cambridge University to spend a year as a Henry Fellow. Political tensions resounded everywhere in Britain. Schlesinger was in London the night that Neville Chamberlain returned from the Munich Conference, proclaiming that he had wrung "peace in our time" from Hitler. Schlesinger was also in Yugoslavia during the dangerous summer of 1939.

At Cambridge he met a number of remarkable people, including a Communist history student named Eric Hobsbawm. The two worked on the Cambridge undergraduate literary journal *Granta* and began a friendship that has lasted until this day, a surprising union of a firm anti-Marxist and one of the foremost Marxist historians of our time. Schlesinger studied medieval economic history with the economic historians Michael Postan and Eileen Power. He found a much higher level of methodological sophistication at Cambridge than at Harvard. Schlesinger returned to Harvard in the summer of 1939 as an isolationist, though this conviction did not last.[55]

By the time of his return, his *Orestes A. Brownson: A Pilgrim's Progress* had appeared to favorable reviews. Schlesinger then accepted a three-year appointment to Harvard's Society of Fellows, which had been founded a few years before by Harvard president A. Laurence Lowell to allow students of the highest promise and distinction to avoid the occasionally dreary regimen of Ph.D. programs. Under the generosity of the Society of Fellows, Schlesinger pursued his research on the Jacksonian era much further and began to work out the details of a new interpretation of the period, which formed the basis of his first great book, *The Age of Jackson.*[56]

The Harvard career of Daniel Boorstin was just as dazzling as Schlesinger's. Boorstin entered Harvard at sixteen, like Schlesinger, majoring in history and literature. Boorstin served as an editor of the student newspaper the *Harvard Crimson*, and his senior honors essay on Edward Gibbon's *History of the Decline and Fall of the Roman Empire* won the Bowdoin Prize. In 1934 Boorstin graduated summa cum laude from Harvard and won a Rhodes Scholarship to study law at Balliol College, Oxford. During the next three and a half years, he read law at the Inner Temple in London and pulled off the astonishing triumph of winning a double first at Oxford in jurisprudence and civil law.

While in England Boorstin sampled the aristocratic life of Oxford and the bohemian lifestyle of the Continental left banks. He briefly considered settling in England, but returned to the United States in 1937. Here Boorstin pursued a variety of interests. Like many in the 1930s, he saw the power of Marxist analyses and in 1938–39 was a member of the Communist Party. World War II and the events leading up to it led him to reassess his position and to look more favorably on the unique virtues of American democracy. In 1937–38 he was a Sterling Fellow at the Yale Law School and after that, spent four years teaching a series of courses in legal history and history at Harvard and Radcliffe. In 1940 he received a doctor of Judicial Science degree from Yale, and in 1941 the Harvard University Press published his first book, *The Mysterious Science of the Law*, a detailed analysis of Sir William Blackstone's famous *Commentaries on the Laws of England.*[57]

While Harvard historians form a cornerstone of the World War II generation of historians, it is hard to generalize about them and their Harvard experiences. Clearly these were all people of exceptional gifts and energy who would have succeeded anywhere, and they came from different cultural, religious, and socioeconomic backgrounds. Several had immensely beneficial experiences elsewhere, such as Carl Schorske's experience in the Columbia humanities seminars or John Hope Franklin's friendship at Fisk with

Theodore Currier. Historians of comparable greatness were produced at other institutions.

Yet Harvard produced the core of the World War II generation of historians, and a Harvard influence on these scholars seems unmistakable. Harvard's greatest gift to students is to place its estimable resources at their disposal, while leaving it to the students to select which ones they will utilize. As Oscar Handlin once remarked, "Harvard doesn't educate you. It lets you use Widener."[58] For Barbara Tuchman, the main resource was indeed the Widener Library. But the main resource at Harvard in the 1930s for most of these scholars was the extraordinary faculty. The quality of the teaching they received reverberates through their Harvard careers. Oscar Handlin and John Hope Franklin found Arthur Schlesinger Sr. Carl Schorske found William Scott Ferguson. Edmund Morgan, Daniel Boorstin, and Arthur Schlesinger Jr. found electrifying teaching in the History and Literature program and in Perry Miller and F.O. Matthiessen in particular. Handlin and Morgan found the main subject to which they would devote the bulk of their scholarly careers. Schorske found the seeds of the interdisciplinary methodologies he would later perfect in his own work. While anti-Semitism and pomposity persisted among certain members of the Harvard faculty in the 1930s, most of the scholars considered here managed to find quality faculty who were learned, humane, and without prejudice.

Harvard seems to have had more impact than the times. While these historians were forced to confront in some way the political realities of the 1930s, few can be described as being influenced by the tempests of their time. Political talk was certainly extensive at Harvard in the thirties. Roosevelt, the New Deal, appeasement, and the Spanish Civil War all aroused discussion. Most Harvard undergraduates hated Roosevelt and the New Deal; the Republican Alfred Landon claimed a majority of their votes in the 1936 election.[59] Carl Schorske, Barbara Tuchman, Arthur Schlesinger Jr., and Edmund Morgan were perhaps the most affected by contemporary politics. J.H. Hexter and John Hope Franklin felt most acutely the economic circumstances of the Great Depression. Several of them certainly had leftist sympathies. But there was no great attraction to Marxism or other leftist doctrines among the scholars examined here, no dramatic sacrifices made to advance political causes or to save the world. There is a striking contrast between Harvard historians and historians at a comparable stage in their training in Great Britain, where a great many outstanding young scholars, including Christopher Hill, Eric Hobsbawm, Victor Kiernan, Rodney Hilton, and others became Marxists in the 1930s. Even Hugh Trevor-Roper, by the 1950s almost reactionary in his politics, had a lengthy flirtation with Marxism.[60] At Harvard, by contrast, with the exception of Daniel Boorstin, they all rejected it. For most of these historians, Marxism was a body of doctrine that did not add up, and they tended to dismiss it almost instinctively rather than as the result of intense study and reflection. Perhaps it is not odd that Marxism failed to seduce a group of aspiring historians, however disparate, at Harvard in the 1930s. Apart from the role played by the scholars' own critical acuity, Harvard and its patrician traditions, at least as they stood in the 1930s, may have exercised their influence in other, unseen ways.

Chapter 3

OTHER AMERICAN COLLEGES AND UNIVERSITIES

♏

While Harvard served as the promised land for many young American historians in the 1930s, it was not the only university to produce gifted historians. The Depression and the rise of fascism in a sense increased interest in history because they raised many questions that historians were uniquely situated to answer. Many talented young people pursued history degrees even though the job prospects for historians were not encouraging.

In 1932 Gordon Craig entered Princeton as a day student, intending to study law. By his second year he won a scholarship and had become interested in history in part because he supported the New Deal passionately and wanted to work for Roosevelt. Adolf Hitler came to power at the same time, and Craig's interest shifted to Germany, an interest especially nourished by the guidance of his favorite professor, Raymond Sontag.

Political discussion at Princeton was intense in the 1930s. The banks were closed when Craig entered college, and there were vicious discussions at Princeton about the economic hard times of the thirties. Craig, as president of the Princeton Philosophical Society, was in the middle of it, although there were few Marxists at Princeton during his time.

Oxford, however, was another story. In 1936 Craig won a Rhodes Scholarship to Balliol College, Oxford. Political debate was just as fierce at Oxford, though now centering on the Spanish Civil War and appeasement. There were also more Marxists, including at Balliol, Dennis Healey, later minister of the Exchequer, but in the 1930s a member of the Communist Party. Craig himself joined the Labour Club, a socialist group with a Communist wing.

Craig profited immensely from his time at Oxford, spending his first year in a "haze of energy and enthusiasm." He discovered outstanding tutors, including Humphrey Sumner and Llewellyn Woodward, made friends that he kept for the rest of his life, and met Phyllis Halcomb, the woman who became his wife. At the end of his Rhodes tenure, unable to find a job, he went back to Princeton on a scholarship. The inability to find a job meant that he and Phyllis Halcomb could not be married right away. Marriage was postponed until June 1939, and Craig soon got a job at Yale, where he began teaching and finished his dissertation.[1]

Entering the University of Chicago in 1934 William McNeill encountered an exciting and intense atmosphere. While the Chicago curriculum paid practically no attention to Marx, McNeill later recalled, "you couldn't grow up without Marxism and in 1934 the Depression was at its bottom." Fierce debate erupted over the Stalinist treason trials. McNeill listened a great deal to the debates, saw the power of the arguments in the *Communist Manifesto*, but remained skeptical. Deeply cynical about Chicago politicians, he nevertheless retained a faith, as did many Chicago undergraduates, in national politicians.

The temper of the debate changed with the Munich Conference. Few were deceived by the promises of appeasement, and most could see that it meant war was imminent. McNeill remembers one of his professors telling the class, "most of you young men will be killed in the next war."[2]

Undergraduate education at Chicago in the 1930s held many delights. The atmosphere was extremely intense. McNeill followed what was called the New Plan, which meant four required survey courses in physical science, biological science, social science, and the humanities. Each was for McNeill "an enormous revelation, helping [him] to put the world together in a fashion that would not have occurred otherwise." Even today McNeill can claim some security in the sciences and continues to read and take an interest in fresh developments. The humanities course, as created by Ferdinand Schevill some years before, was the best for him, combining art, history, and literature within the framework of the Western world from the Greeks to the twentieth century. It was, he said later, "the central intellectual experience of my late adolescence—I was 16 years of age when I took that course."[3]

Another powerful influence was serendipitous. Quite accidentally, McNeill enrolled in a summer course, called "The Folk Society," taught by the famous Chicago anthropologist Robert Redfield, who was at that time trying to construct a general typology for human societies. Uninterested in historical development, Redfield sought to match certain types of cultures and develop a series of antinomies between civilized societies and remote villages. Another one of his goals was to devise a means of defining and distinguishing between civilized and primitive societies. McNeill retained his interest in the historical underpinning, but came to believe that his principal intellectual stimulus came "not from historians but from anthropologists."[4]

Upon reflection, McNeill came to recognize an obvious flaw in his Chicago education, one that he spent much of his professional life attempting to correct. He noted how completely his studies at Chicago "excluded the vast majority of humankind, even though Japan had begun to challenge the Eurocentric vision of the globe, and European domination over Asia and Africa was already wearing thin." The Chicago curriculum was constructed on the assumption that the study of the European cultural roots was all that mattered.

McNeill also was active in extracurricular activities. He wrote for the Chicago student newspaper the *Maroon* and served as editor during his senior year. He also played tennis, a sport at which Chicago excelled, but did not make the team. After graduation, he stayed at Chicago to take a master's degree, writing a thesis on Herodotus and Thucydides as part of the history of culture program. His approach sparked some controversy. The Chicago professor of ancient history believed that the classics should be studied phrase by phrase line by line. McNeill preferred studying Herodotus and Thucydides to compare how they explained historical processes. But taking on two of the great texts of classical antiquity at once was not the way classics was to be done. Richard McKeon, a professor of philosophy, felt that such a broad approach as McNeill proposed was a little like "Jonah swallowing the whale."[5]

Unlike most graduate students, McNeill conceived a broad plan by which he would study in sequence ancient, medieval, and modern history. Such a program was common in his father's student days, but was increasingly rare by the 1930s, as history was already becoming specialized. The M.A. thesis on Herodotus and Thucydides was the first step. By the time he received his Ph.D. he was indeed prepared to offer these three fields.[6]

In 1939 McNeill went to Cornell to study with Carl Becker, then one of the giants of the profession. Cornell was much more informal and its intellectual climate less intense than that of Chicago. There were no graduate courses, although graduate students were encouraged to sit in on undergraduate lecture courses. Graduate seminars did meet, but of the three McNeill attended, only one required a paper and that was a perfunctory exercise. Cornell's principal gift to graduate students was to give them time. "Let them read," Carl Becker said regarding graduate education, "they'll never have the time again."[7]

Becker himself turned out to be a disappointment. He was a terribly shy man, who lectured with his face buried in his notes, disdained classroom interaction, and was already seriously ill with the stomach problems that would later kill him. He was also past his prime and reportedly spent much of his time shooting pool in the Cornell student center. In any case McNeill had heard almost everything Becker had to say as an undergraduate from the lectures of Becker's pupil Louis Gottschalk at Chicago.

Becker nevertheless exerted some indirect influence on McNeill. Becker was an eighteenth-century specialist, but with a broad range of interests within that specialty, including American colonial politics, the Enlightenment, Thomas Jefferson, the French Revolution, and historiography generally. He liked to explore big themes, with the intent to discover and provoke; he denied history could ever be "proven," and was an important figure in the school of historical relativism, the argument that there is no truth in history because each generation rewrites history in terms of its own experience. He was not, as R.R. Palmer, another Becker student at Cornell, noted, "an archival scholar, nor primarily a research scholar, nor in the most technical sense, a scholar at all. He laughed at the idea of exhausting the sources, and preferred published to unpublished materials."[8] In his approach to history he developed a line of thought and then looked things up to support it. When he found enough supporting material, he wrote. Here Becker was at his best. He was an engaging stylist, capable of conveying complex ideas and historical patterns to a general audience. He wrote most mornings at his home in Ithaca, and his best books, *The Heavenly City of the Eighteenth Century Philosophers* and *The Declaration of Independence: A Study in the History of Ideas*, and his presidential address to the American Historical Association, are models of subtle thought, urbane wit, and gracious learning.

Another epiphanous moment at Cornell occurred when McNeill encountered Arnold Toynbee's massive, multivolume *A Study of History* in the Cornell library. The name of Toynbee was unfamiliar, but the title *A Study of History*, with its promise of grand sweep and big theory, matched McNeill's interests precisely. He had read Oswald Spengler's similar volume, *Decline of the West*, in 1936 while still at Chicago and had even given considerable thought to writing his own one-volume history of civilization. Discovering *A Study of History*, McNeill immediately planted himself in a comfortable chair in the central bay of the White Library and for the next two or three days greedily devoured the first three volumes. (He did not read volumes four, five, and six until after World War II.) McNeill immediately and completely identified with Toynbee: "His thoughts were my thoughts, or so it seemed when I first read him in my early twenties."[9]

At Cornell McNeill was also introduced to the French *Annales* School of historians by Cornell's medievalist, Carl Stephenson, then in the middle of writing his book on feudalism. Stephenson had been a pupil of Henri Pirenne, the eminent Belgian medievalist, and he introduced McNeill to the works of French *Annales* School of historians, such as Marc Bloch and Lucien Febvre. Bloch was particularly important, as much for approach as content. "Bloch," according to McNeill, "got right down to earth, describing how real people made a living from the land: his rural France smelt of the barnyard, not of dusty archives."[10] McNeill wrote his dissertation on the potato in Irish history. However, at Cornell he also recognized an elementary, but crucial distinction, that Eastern Europe differs markedly from Western Europe, an idea that informed his later work, *Europe's Steppe Frontier, 1500–1800*. He was at work on his dissertation when he was drafted into the army in 1941.

Vann Woodward's college career began at Henderson-Brown, a small Methodist college in Arkansas. Between his freshman and sophomore years, he decided to go to Europe. With twenty dollars in his pocket, and hitching rides on freight trains and highways, he left for New York. By the time of his arrival, he had spent most of his money and failed to find a job on a transatlantic freighter. Instead, he managed to find work on a coastal freighter headed for Norfolk, Virginia, where he was hired on another freighter, this time one bound for Europe. Years later, he marveled at his parents' tolerance of his independence.[11]

After two years at Henderson-Brown, Woodward transferred to Emory University in Atlanta, after his father took a job as a school administrator in Oxford, Georgia. He found himself in an undergraduate American history course seated next to David Potter, a future friend. Ironically, Woodward found his first college course in American history too dull to encourage further interest.[12] He did, however, graduate from Emory in 1930 with a degree in philosophy. The following year he managed to get a job teaching freshman English at the Georgia Institute of Technology and then attended Columbia University in New York City. Woodward went to Columbia solely for the purpose of seeing the big city, although he was also interested in studying sociology. This interest evaporated after two classes, given by the same man. In the first class, the man read Rudyard Kipling's poem "If" to the class; in another class, a seminar later the same day, he read "If" again. Woodward switched to political science, and in 1932 he earned a master's degree from Columbia in that discipline.[13]

That summer he went to Europe. Only marginally affected in material terms by the Depression, he was nevertheless powerfully affected intellectually by it. Woodward had listened to considerable talk to the effect that the Great Depression represented the collapse of capitalism, and he had many Communist friends who were convinced that Communism provided the answer to capitalism's failure. Woodward decided to see for himself and borrowed money to spend a month in Russia, as well as a month in Paris and Berlin. The trip brought many revelations. He was in Germany on the eve of Hitler's assumption of power, and he left Russia skeptical about Communism. In fact the trip on the whole caused him to "abandon easy optimism about any solution, which included capitalism, as well as Communism and Nazism."[14]

In 1932 he returned to Atlanta for a second stint of teaching English at Georgia Tech where he immediately found himself in the center of controversy. A young black Communist named Angelo Herndon was arrested and charged with the capital crime of inciting insurrection. Woodward became part of a informal committee of concerned citizens organized to defend Herndon. In Georgia in the 1930s there were few causes riskier than defending a black Communist agitator. The experience, not surprisingly, was not positive. The committee's work was hampered by internal bickering and the efforts of some members to exploit the case for political purposes.

Woodward soon found himself out of a job. He was fired, along with about twenty others, by Georgia Tech in 1932. Budgetary cutbacks were the official explanation. This was probably correct, since about twenty others were also fired, but Woodward's support of an unpopular cause cannot have endeared him to the administration. Not only was this his first brush with unemployment, but the college owed Woodward and the other fired members three months' back pay. Woodward saw his enforced sabbatical as an opportunity to write a book. He stayed in Georgia for several months and worked briefly on a farm survey for the WPA. He then began to conceive writing a book about seven Southern radicals, including Ben Tillman and Tom Watson, eventually deciding to focus on Watson, a complex and contradictory figure. Watson, vilified by liberals as a racist, had also been a populist agitator, advancing social and economic reforms to benefit poor farmers, black and white, and had occasionally risked his political future by supporting black leaders.[15]

The discovery of Watson and the possible significance of his life was a pivotal moment in Woodward's career. Watson's career, riddled with ambiguity and irony, contradicted the easy assumption that all Southerners were narrow-minded bigots and segregationists. Watson had challenged prevailing opinion and devoted much of his life to tearing down racial barriers. Woodward paid scant attention to Watson's early career as a vitriolic racist; instead he studied Watson's later career where he attempted to build bridges over troubled racial waters. Woodward had already cast an interested eye on the meaning of Watson's career for the existing problem of race relations in the South. "If there had indeed been no exceptions, no breaks, and things had always been the same," as the standard historical interpretation of the postbellum South maintained, Woodward declared, "there was little hope of change." Watson's career held out the promise of change and hope for change in the South, and Woodward became an apostle of hope for the South.[16]

Woodward went to the University of North Carolina at Chapel Hill in 1934 to began doctoral studies in history simply because the Watson papers were there and history was the most obvious discipline in which to pursue his Watson project. He found Chapel Hill an enchanting place. Even though money for higher education in North Carolina was tight in the 1930s, Chapel Hill still enjoyed a reputation as an oasis in the middle of a vast Southern wasteland. The shadow of the novelist Thomas Wolfe, hung like fading sunlight on the campus. The Chapel Hill sociologist and family friend Howard Odum helped to arrange a fellowship for Woodward, although Odum knew that Woodward had no intention of becoming a sociologist.[17] But there were occasionally some problems. Three weeks after Woodward's arrival, he was summoned to Odum's office and asked how he could have so quickly fallen in with the wrong crowd, those intellectuals whose hangout was Abernethy's Bookstore just across Franklin Street from the main campus.[18]

Woodward did manage to right himself. Under the direction and encouragement of his mentor Howard K. Beale, Woodward studied Watson. He also continued to seek sociological insight from Odum and Rupert Vance, another Chapel Hill sociologist. He met such diverse figures as Gertrude Stein and Carolina's personable president Frank Graham, behind whose house Woodward had rented a room. Woodward also encountered the group known as the Southern Agrarians, defenders of traditional Southern culture and society. In 1936 he joined William T. Couch, director of the University of North Carolina Press and a Southern liberal, on a trip to Nashville to debate the Agrarians. Couch singlehandedly stated the case for the liberals, and the exchange became quite heated. At the height of the debate, the Agrarians, led by Allen Tate, stormed disgustedly out of the meeting, with Tate shouting additional insults on the way out. At a bar later Woodward fell into a conversation with a man who turned out to be one of the Agrarians and who invited him to an informal gathering where the discussion could be continued. After some initial awkwardness, Woodward was able to make some friendships, several of which turned out to be of lasting importance.[19] Back at Chapel Hill, Woodward also met a young woman named Glenn Boyd MacLeod, whom he married in 1937. She had actually been a student in one of the large lecture classes Woodward had taken at Columbia, but they did not meet until both were at Chapel Hill.[20]

Woodward entertained some doubts about history as a vocation. His first assignment was to master the volumes in the old *American Nation* series. This turned out to be a brain-deadening experience. The volumes were already out of date, and plodding through them, Woodward found the prose pedestrian, the chapters lacking in ideas, and whole volumes wrongheaded. Was this mass of boredom and platitude something to which he wanted to devote his life? He spent a great deal of his first year in Chapel Hill pounding the pavement of Franklin Street late at night, wondering if his life might be better spent as a fish peddler or hack writer.[21] Woodward was held in history by two things. First, a seminar in ancient history introduced him to the delights of Edward Gibbon, the great historian of the fall of the Roman Empire, and an absorbing study of second-century Rome. Second, his encounter with the documents involving Tom Watson's career, "stirred the sporting blood and the spirit of the hunt. Research evidently could be fun."[22] Choosing between the delights of ancient history and the blood stirred by Southern history was an easy call. The majesty of Gibbon clearly paled before the possibilities and prospects of Southern history. "A Southern historian I must be," Woodward concluded. He was not, however, a stellar student, and he admitted that, since the book on Watson was his central concern, he cut as many classes as he could and failed to distinguish himself at all in graduate study.[23]

Finishing his degree in 1937, he found the job market extremely tight, but eventually obtained a position teaching social science at the University of Florida in Gainesville, though the teaching load was heavy and he was not able to teach Southern history. The following year, when he was twenty-nine, his dissertation on Watson was published as *Tom Watson, Agrarian Rebel,* and the book received a laudatory, front-page review in the *New York Times Book Review* from the University of Chicago historian Allan Nevins. Woodward vaulted immediately into the forefront of Southern history.[24]

Little is known about the career of Woodward's fellow Southerner and friend David Potter. After attending public schools in Augusta, Georgia, Potter graduated Phi Beta Kappa from Emory University in 1932. From there, Potter went to Yale University to pursue graduate study with U.B. Phillips, at the time the leading authority on Southern history. Potter quickly received an M.A. degree from Yale in 1933 and spent three more years in graduate study there, and then began his teaching career in 1936 at the University of Mississippi. In 1938 he left Mississippi for a teaching post at Rice Institute, which he held until 1942. In 1940 he finished his dissertation, an account of politics between the time of Lincoln's election as president in November 1860 and the attack on Fort Sumter in April 1861.[25]

Another Southerner, Anne Firor, was one of several of the World War II generation of historians who emerged from college without a clear interest in history. She entered the University of Georgia in 1937. A stimulating freshman course on the English constitution encouraged her to take other history courses. Without planning it, Scott discovered one day that she had a history major, even though she found other disciplines such as literature and chemistry equally compelling. She nursed other dreams, such as becoming a medical doctor or having a large family. She expected one day to have a career and family, but had no clear-cut ideas or sense of direction about how that would come about. As she wrote later, "if my journal is to be believed, I went out into the world in 1940 in search of fame, fortune, and a husband, in no particular order. As to how that search would be conducted, the journal is significantly silent."[26]

After graduation she drifted into several career paths. But a job at IBM and a brief stint in a graduate program in personnel management did not prove sufficiently fulfilling, though her boss at IBM promised advancement if she would be patient. She finally accepted an internship with a young California congressman, Jerry Voorhees, a Yale man who had once run an orphanage and was an ardent supporter of the New Deal. Scott later recalled that Senator Paul Douglas of Illinois once said that he had known three saints in politics, and Voorhees was one. Writing speeches for him and listening to his grasp of ideas made Scott recognize some inadequacies in her own training. She went back to school to get an M.A. in political science, but had still not found a calling that truly inspired her.[27]

Kenneth Stampp also entered college during the throes of the Depression. His parents felt the bite of the economic collapse, and the Stampp family finances were tight in the 1930s. Stampp felt "lucky to go to college at all."[28] A bout with pneumonia delayed his entry into college until February 1931, at which time he entered Milwaukee State Teachers' College. He remained an indifferent student, and his experience at Milwaukee State was not happy. Intending to become a high school history teacher, Stampp emphasized secondary education. In February 1933 the dean of his college and two professors summoned him to the dean's office and forbade him to continue in secondary education. "I will never recommend you for a teaching job in secondary education," an English professor told him. "You won't have to," an angered Stampp replied, "I quit." Stampp was furious; his parents were devastated.

The University of Wisconsin at Madison was the only place he could go, and his parents did not have enough money to send him. Fortunately, his father's sister, who had never married, helped him get through. He was assisted by the relatively cheap cost of living in Madison in the 1930s. His room in a rooming house cost $2.50 a week and could he eat on 60 cents a day, which came to a total of $6.70 a week for living expenses. Tuition at Madison in the mid-1930s was $32 a semester.

His estrangement from Milwaukee State Teachers' College proved to be an intellectual blessing as well. Stampp took the courses in the Old South, Civil War, and Reconstruction given by William Best Hesseltine and was enthralled. Stampp was not a really serious student until he went to Madison, and at Madison he became a superior student, graduating as a Phi Beta Kappa in 1935. After graduation, he taught high school for a brief period, and given the nature of the job market for historians in the 1930s, he gave serious thought to law school.

The quality of the Wisconsin history department rekindled his interest in history. The university itself was a wondrous place. Situated on an isthmus, the University of Wisconsin combines a campus of spectacular beauty with winters whose numbing cold defies description. The history department at Wisconsin in the 1930s rivaled Harvard's in quality. In particular it cherished a great tradition, dating back to Frederick Jackson Turner, himself from rural Wisconsin, and had become a center for the study of social and economic history. Turner had become famous largely on the basis of a single paper, "The Influence of the Frontier on American History," which suggested that the distinctive character of America came not from America's European heritage but from the experience of the westward movement. As Americans interacted with the frontier, a distinctively American character emerged, pragmatic, individualist, and anti-intellectual. Observers often referred to a "Turnerverein," consisting of those both in and out of Madison who had been influenced by Turner.

The influence of Charles Beard also pervaded in Madison, and the members of the history faculty were legendary for their reverence to him. Through his stress on the importance of economic motivation in understanding historical events and the relative nature of historical truth, Beard struck resonant chords with many young historians. His *The Rise of American Civilization* reached a wide audience. Beard's work became perhaps the single most powerful influence on Stampp, who adopted Beard's relativist position on historical truth, which he never abandoned, and wrote his doctoral dissertation, a study of Indiana politics during the American Civil War, from the perspective of economic determinism.

Stampp also studied colonial history with Curtis Nettels, who stressed the importance of economic factors. He studied labor economics with Selig Perlman, who displayed a rare sensitivity to the hardships of working people. The most powerful influence among the faculty Stampp encountered at Wisconsin was that of Hesseltine. Hesseltine was a brilliant scholar, specializing in Southern history and the Civil War, and author of the famous one-liner that studying intellectual history was "like trying to nail jelly to a wall." Hesseltine stimulated Stampp's interest in Southern history and provided him with an example of dynamic teaching to emulate. But like many brilliant people, Hesseltine could be abrasive and arrogant, and he reveled in his ability to say outrageous things and scoff at conventional wisdom. While admiring Hesseltine greatly, Stampp occasionally chafed under his tutelage and with enormous ability himself, often could not overcome the urge to respond in kind. The two developed a close, but tense relationship. Part of their problem stemmed from a misunderstanding early in Stampp's graduate career. At Wisconsin graduate students attached themselves to a particular professor and attended that professor's courses and seminars. After a year of taking all of Hesseltine's offerings, Stampp felt he had learned all he could from Hesseltine. He and another student asked Hesseltine if they could be excused from further attendance in the spring of 1938 while they studied for their qualifying examinations. They thought Hesseltine agreed. Later, Hesseltine exploded at them in his office, asking "who do you guys think you are, not coming to my seminar?" and he did not support Stampp for the extension of his assistantship, although Stampp kept it when he received the support of Curtis Nettels. The relationship between Stampp and Hesseltine continued to be stormy and heated, but they did manage to cooperate well enough for Stampp to complete his dissertation under Hesseltine's direction in December 1941 and receive his doctorate in March 1942.[29]

Another historian influenced by Beard in the 1930s was Richard Hofstadter, who was also perhaps the most radical and politically active in the 1930s. Hofstadter was introduced to activist, left-wing politics during his undergraduate years at the University of Buffalo, where, like Stampp, he majored in history and philosophy. At Buffalo, a "street car" college serving primarily students from the area, Hofstadter came under a variety of contradictory, but important influences. The first was the philosophy professor Marvin Faber, who, in almost Beardian terms, emphasized the materialist underpinnings of political and social phenomena, and the historically determined nature of all philosophies. Faber led his classes through intense, wide-ranging, and exciting discussions, described by one participant as "some of the most illuminating I have engaged in."[30]

Faber's materialist influence was tempered by Hofstadter's association with Julius Pratt, Buffalo's most distinguished historian. Pratt's historical reputation had been made by challenging the Progressive viewpoint, especially the Progressive arguments regarding the economic bases of American foreign policy. The dynamic tension between Hofstadter's progressivist sympathies and the anti-Progressive spirit of Pratt, emerged in Hofstadter's senior thesis, "The Tariff and Homestead Issues in the Republican Campaign of 1860," a portion of which Hofstadter published as a note in the *American Historical Review* in 1938. In the thesis Hofstadter took vigorous exception to the Beardian notion that the American Civil War was not, as most observers thought, a clash of North and South over slavery or secession. Rather, according to Beard, it resulted from the desire of Northern capitalists to control the federal government. Exploring the tariff and homestead issues, Hofstadter discovered that most capitalists opposed the Republicans in 1860, a seeming refutation of Beard. But he did not follow it all the way. The basis of capitalist opposition to the Republicans was, nevertheless, economic, resulting from their calculation that they would benefit more from Democratic economic policies. Hence Hofstadter did not entirely divorce himself from Beard and the Progressives.[31]

Perhaps the key element in his development at Buffalo was his relationship with Felice Swados, with whom he began a romantic relationship in 1934 and married in 1936. Felice was a dominating personality and a left-wing Jewish activist. Her father was not pleased by her involvement with a half-Gentile, and once slapped her across the face when Hofstadter brought her home a half hour late.[32] The father's opposition, however, may have intensified her involvement with Hofstadter, and the two quickly became inseparable. Felice was two years older than Hofstadter, much more sophisticated at this stage politically, and deeply enmeshed in Buffalo's Jewish community. She was also a striking individual. A 1932 yearbook picture reveals a large, tall woman, with her hair pulled severely back into a bun. Energetic, extroverted, she liked being at the vortex of events, although some thought she took up too much space for her level of intellect. Undaunted, she was not afraid to be the lone woman at meetings or to speak out. In part because of her influence Hofstadter recognized and nourished a strong sense of personal identity as a marginal Jew, political leftist, and committed intellectual.[33]

Graduating from Buffalo in 1937, Hofstadter with Felice Swados, now his wife, moved to New York City. He arrived, as Alfred Kazin later wrote, "as the All-American collegian just in from Buffalo with that unmistakable flat accent."[34] On his father's insistence, he entered the Columbia University Law School, but quickly switched to the Columbia graduate program in history, where he received a master's degree in 1938 and a doctorate in 1942.

Once again at Columbia he became deeply engaged in radical politics. He and Felice attended Communist Party meetings and they also became involved with the Communist-sympathizing National Maritime Union in Brooklyn. The Hofstadter household soon became a center for activism, as sailors, workers, and intellectuals gathered there for political talk and free meals. In 1938 he also joined the Columbia unit of the Communist Party, although he mustered little enthusiasm for his choice. "I join without enthusiasm but with a sense of obligation," he explained to his brother-in-law, Harvey Swados. "My fundamental reason for joining it is that I don't like capitalism and want to get rid of it. . . . The party is making a profound contribution to the American people. . . . I prefer to go along with it now."[35]

Lacking the zeal of the true party convert, Hofstadter came to identify more closely with Alfred Kazin and the network of young intellectuals associated with the Trotskyite *Partisan Review*. Members of this group had broken with the Communist Party and Stalinism by 1937 and were committed to finding a way to make Communism work without the excesses of Stalin.[36] The writers associated with the *Partisan Review* also helped Hofstadter develop his ideas about intellectuals and their role in society. The *Partisan* circle regarded small-town America, especially that west of the Hudson River, in the manner of Mencken and Sinclair Lewis, as poisoned by ignorance, prejudice, and anti-intellectualism. The *Partisan* circle deplored the intellect and spirit of the common man, choosing instead to place their faith in a Plato-like group of philosopher-kings: the educated, Eastern elite, to which the writers of the *Partisan Review* were certain they belonged. Exposure to Mencken while at Buffalo had already convinced Hofstadter to be repelled by rural buffoons. "I soaked up everything of Mencken's when I was an undergraduate at the University of Buffalo," Hofstadter remarked in 1960.[37] Under the group's influence, Hofstadter found Mencken's analysis of small-town buffoonery and ignorance amply confirmed and began to perceive deeper and most sinister implications for the power of anti-intellectual forces in American life, ideas that would inform much of his best work.[38]

By the late 1930s Hofstadter also began to throw off his remaining Communist shackles. Where he had once seen the world of the early 1930s as holding the promise of rejecting a reactionary and decadent past in favor of a radical future, events began to drive him in another direction. He had already concluded that the Moscow purge trials were "phony," and he found the party meetings at Columbia dull and excessively regimented. By February 1939 he had quietly abandoned the party.[39] The German-Soviet Pact of

August 1939 shattered Hofstadter's remaining confidence in the promise of radical change.[40] In the next few years, he became increasingly disillusioned with the bureaucracy and totalitarianism of the party and finally with Marxism itself. Yet he continued to consider himself a radical. "I hate capitalism and everything that goes with it," he told Harvey Swados shortly after leaving the party. Part of his dissatisfaction came also from the conviction that intellectuals, which he also now considered himself, would have no place in the regimented, totalitarian socialist state: "We are not the beneficiaries of capitalism, but we will not be the beneficiaries of the socialism of the twentieth century. We are the people with no place to go."[41]

At Columbia Hofstadter found ways to combine his radicalism with history. His master's thesis, written in 1938, considered the plight of Southern sharecroppers. Hofstadter exposed the total inefficiency and hypocrisy of New Deal agricultural policies, where the money ostensibly appropriated to relieve the suffering of poor sharecroppers went preponderantly to large landowners while sharecroppers' plight worsened. The thesis was a bitter condemnation of the Roosevelt administration's policies. At the same time, the influence of Charles Beard was manifest in Hofstadter's work. "Beard was the really exciting influence on me," Hofstadter later remarked. Here again Beard's emphasis on the economic superstructure of political ideas and programs was readily apparent.[42]

But Hofstadter was already beginning to distance himself from Beard. Beard paid minimal attention to ideas, regarding them as mere ideological cover for economic motivation. Hofstadter by contrast found an increasing attraction to American social thought and to ideas as forces in their own right. This interest was encouraged through Hofstadter's association at Columbia with Merle Curti, a leading figure in American intellectual history. By 1939, according to Felice Swados, Hofstadter and Curti had formed a "mutual admiration society."[43]

Despite the heady air of intellectual excitement that surrounded him at Columbia, Hofstadter encountered difficulty there. For three consecutive years, despite his immense intellectual promise and the early publication of an article in the *American Historical Review*, he was denied financial aid. He nursed a continuing sense of resentment over this slight, remarking acidly that "the guys who got the fellowships are little shits who never accomplished or published anything."[44] The reason for Hofstadter's troubles with the history department is not clear, but anti-Semitism was rampant at Columbia in the 1930s. The literary critic Lionel Trilling was one of its victims, and Hofstadter may have been, too. To survive, Hofstadter was forced to seek a teaching job. In the spring of 1940 he began teaching evening classes at Brooklyn College. A year later, he found a full-time position at a downtown branch of City College. Ironically, the position was available because of the forced resignation of Jack Foner, a professor accused of membership in the Communist party. Hofstadter's classes were initially boycotted by students in a show of support for the professor in question, though they eventually returned. Ironically, many years later, Hofstadter's position as DeWitt Clinton Professor of History at Columbia would be occupied by Jack D. Foner's son, Eric Foner.[45]

While beginning his teaching career in the early 1940s, Hofstadter also finished the doctoral dissertation that became his first book, *Social Darwinism in American Thought, 1860–1915*. The dissertation was completed in 1942 when Hofstadter was a mere twenty-six and published by the University of Pennsylvania Press in 1944. In many ways the book represents Hofstadter's first skirmish with his avowed enemy, modern conservative ideology and its intellectual origins. *Social Darwinism in American Thought, 1860–1915* explores the American impact of the ideas of Charles Darwin and such Darwinian notions as "survival of the fittest" and "natural selection," which were often used to justify the rapacious behavior of Gilded Age entrepreneurs and in particular by William Graham Sumner. Hofstadter began with an examination of the idea of Social Darwinism as conceived by Herbert Spencer, followed by a study of Spencer's American acolytes and concluding with a consideration of the rise of what Hofstadter called a "new collectivism" expressed by such thinkers as Thorstein Veblen and John Dewey. Hofstadter's preference clearly lay with the new collectivists with their hopes of improving the world with education and intellectual ideals inspired by a social conscience. Hofstadter, however, remained deeply pessimistic that these ideas could ever be realized.

Gertrude Himmelfarb was another historian who went to college in the New York City of the late 1930s and who experienced the intense political discussions in which the intellectuals and college students of the time often engaged. Himmelfarb entered Brooklyn College and also attended the meetings of the Trotskyist organization, the Young People's Socialist League, sometimes known as the Fourth International. One night at a YSPL meeting in Brooklyn, Irving Kristol, another member of the organization, asked her if she would like to go to a movie. Kristol, later a leading figure in the neoconservative movement, was at that time a leftist who had once jumped on the back of a policeman at a 1939 demonstration at City College in New York City. He was bright and charming, at the same time sharing her lower-class, Jewish origins. One movie date led to another. Kristol worked in the Brooklyn Navy Yard as a machinist, which paid him enough to marry Himmelfarb, while she worked for her degree at Brooklyn.[46]

Himmelfarb decided to go on to graduate school in history, though she harbored few illusions about her prospects. She might engage in research and write books, but being a professor was out of the question. She was a Jew and woman, and Jewish women were not likely to become professors in American universities of the 1940s. Undeterred, she applied anyway to the doctoral program in history at the University of Chicago, where she was interviewed by Louis Gottschalk, later to be her mentor at Chicago. The interview went well. Gottschalk praised her record and offered her a scholarship, saying that Chicago would be delighted to have her in their program. But he admonished her not to expect to find a teaching job. "I want to disabuse you of that. That's not going to happen," he said. He noted that she had three strikes against her. As a woman and Jew, she was acutely aware of two. But the third? The third, according to Gottschalk was that she was a New Yorker, and most Midwestern colleges had a strong bias against Easterners.[47]

Himmelfarb thus entered Chicago almost purely for the love of learning. Professional prospects and financial remuneration appeared to be virtually inconceivable. She and Kristol lived in the same Hyde Park boarding house where Saul Bellow had written "Dangling Man," about a young man waiting to be called up for military service. In 1944 her husband was drafted and saw action in France. At Chicago, fascinated by the French Revolution, she wrote a master's thesis on Robespierre to consider how high-minded ideals degenerated into the Terror. The master's thesis led her to the study of Lord Acton, an English historian who had written a provocative book on the French Revolution exploring that very theme. Acton also had devoted much of his life to a history of liberty, regarded by some as the "greatest book never written."

After the war Himmelfarb won a fellowship to study Acton, and she and her husband went to Cambridge University to examine Acton's manuscripts. She quickly encountered Acton's great dilemma: the French Revolution was a key element of the spread of liberty, but it also collapsed into mass murder and military rule. How could the historian justify the French Revolution and its nobler achievements without endorsing its reprehensible acts?[48]

It is hard to generalize about the experiences of historians who attended other colleges besides Harvard in the 1930s. Several, Craig, McNeill, Hofstadter, and probably Potter, were clearly golden boys, with records that promised lofty achievements in the profession. Stampp and Woodward took somewhat longer to find themselves as students. While Anne Scott found it hard to decide what she wanted to do, Gertrude Himmelfarb had no doubt that history was her calling even if the deck was stacked against her. The job market was tight, and she was a Jew and a woman.

Teaching was important to the intellectual development of this group. Gordon Craig had the inspiration of Raymond Sontag. McNeill had the experience of the New Plan at Chicago, which remained the central intellectual experience of his life. Hofstadter encountered Marvin Faber and Julius Pratt at Buffalo. But for this group the impact of teaching was sometimes ambiguous. McNeill found Carl Becker a disappointment. Stampp found William B. Hesseltine at once enthralling and infuriating. Even such an obvious star on the rise as Hofstadter was denied financial aid at Columbia.

Like their contemporaries at Harvard, they engaged in intense political discussion, and they were tempted by radical philosophies and politics.
Radical thought gained more ground among the members of this group than
those at Harvard. Stampp was probably the most left-wing of any of the
generational cohort. Hofstadter was a member of the Communist Party.
Woodward was a civil rights activist, interested enough in Communism to
visit the Soviet Union to see how it worked.

Chapter 4

THE ENGLISH UNIVERSITY EXPERIENCE IN THE 1930s

ℳ

With its antiquity, dreaming spires, and the haze from the Thames and Cherwell clinging to its majestic buildings, Oxford often appears to be a magical kingdom. The oldest colleges, Merton, University, and Balliol, date back to the 1200s. One measure of Oxford's antiquity is that New College, Oxford, was founded in 1379. Most of the oldest buildings and traditions were established in the Middle Ages, including the traditionally deplorable food. To Americans, used to seeing old buildings on their campuses torn down and replaced by soulless, vertical ice cube trays, Oxford appears to stand in welcome and direct contradiction to the encroachments of modernity.

Oxford bears little resemblance to American universities. There is the apocryphal but understandable story of the American tourist walking along the High Street through central Oxford, inquiring about where the campus is. There is no campus of Oxford University in the American sense. Oxford consists of thirty-seven independent colleges, each with its own grounds, faculties, rules, and traditions. Even Oxford's legendarily primitive living conditions contribute to its myth. Frigid rooms, little hot or running water, are all part of the Oxford experience. L.P. Curtis, an American research student at Christ Church in the 1950s, had done his basic military training in subzero temperatures in the Colorado mountains, but recalled that nothing had prepared him for the relentless chill of his Oxford sitting rooms.[1]

Undergraduate education and the tutorial system are the heart of Oxford. Unlike American students who take classes in a variety of disciplines and eventually select an area in which to major, Oxford pupils are admitted to pursue a particular subject with a series of tutors, called dons. The academic year is divided into three eight-week terms. Once a week, either individually or in small groups, pupils meet with their tutors. One of the pupils has usually been assigned to write an essay on a specified topic, which is read aloud and then discussed and critiqued by the other pupils and the tutor. Oxford students do not have regular examinations as American university students do. Nor are they graded by their tutors. Instead, they are subjected to an annual ordeal, usually called collections, where their tutors comment publicly on their progress. At the end of their three years at Oxford they face the still greater ordeal of the examination schools, at which they are examined on a wide range of questions in their discipline. Their examinations are evaluated by independent examiners who do not know the identities of the pupils whose papers they are evaluating. The examiners confer marks ranging from a "first" to a "fourth," and it is possible to fail altogether. A first-class degree is highly sought and usually guarantees a successful entry into English life and is a virtual *sine qua non* to teach at Oxford. "Schools" are the subject of fierce competition among Oxford colleges, and colleges take pride in the number of their pupils who receive first-class degrees. Schools are also meant to be intensely rigorous, though they are not always an infallible indicator of intellectual power. Many who have later claimed great distinction in English life were humbled by them. A.E. Housman, the author of *A Shropshire Lad*, failed entirely. W.H. Auden, later Professor of Poetry at Oxford, received a third-class degree. The novelist Evelyn Waugh never entirely recovered from the third he received in 1924.[2]

At its best Oxford provides a magnificent undergraduate education. Instead of the impersonal lecturing to thousands of students common in the American university, Oxford pupils receive highly individualized instruction, often from some of the best scholars in their fields. The writing of the weekly essay and its scrutiny by the tutor helps produce a graduate with estimable writing skills, and is often said to account for the superior prose of historians trained under it. Oxford graduates are often intensely loyal to their individual colleges and look back upon the Oxford experience as one of the most memorable of their lives.

The reality, of course, is occasionally different. Class pervades England, and Oxford students can be snobbish, drunken, and more devoted to rowing than to study. Tutors can be indifferent and graduate education is relegated to secondary status behind undergraduate education. The library system can only be described as bizarre. The Bodleian Library has incomparable holdings, but books cannot be taken out, and it is sometimes impossible to locate the books that are there. Legend has it that even Charles I was denied the right to check out a book from the Bodleian Library, a precedent cited when Oliver Cromwell wanted the same privilege. Individual colleges have their own libraries. But in 1995 Hugh Trevor-Roper had not been able to get from any of his college libraries a copy of Caroline Hibbard's important study *Charles I and the Popish Plot*, first published in 1983.

In the 1930s the Oxford History School produced a cluster of exceptional historians, including Sir Richard Southern (b. 1912), Christopher Hill (b. 1912), Hugh Trevor-Roper (b. 1914), Richard Cobb (b. 1917), and Lawrence Stone (b. 1919), who combined to alter completely the landscape of their fields of study. Sir Richard Southern's *The Making of the Middle Ages*, published in 1952, changed medieval studies forever. Christopher Hill's Marxist interpretation of seventeenth-century England dominated the field for most of the 1950s and 1960s. Hugh Trevor-Roper emerged as one of the earliest and one of the most penetrating critics of the Marxist interpretation and offered a reinterpretation of the English Civil War by which the war appeared to be made not by rising gentry in the Marxist sense, but by declining gentry, desperate to save their waning power at court. Lawrence Stone, a pupil of Trevor-Roper's at Christ Church, first endured a scalding riposte from his former tutor for writing an article that offered support for the rising gentry theory, but later produced a stunning work on the English aristocracy and a steady stream of groundbreaking studies in other areas, such as the nature of the civil war itself, the role of the family in English history, and a comprehensive study of divorce and marriage. Richard Cobb did more than any other historian, with the possible exceptions of George Rude and Albert Soboul, to study the role of the masses in French history.

Under normal circumstances Oxford naturally will contribute many of the scholars who do the most to enhance historical understanding, especially in fields concerning English history. But there is something especially remarkable about the scholars who emerged from Oxford in the 1930s. They did not simply contribute to their fields; they dominated them. Few books have had a greater or more lasting impact on their fields that Richard Southern's *The Making of the Middle Ages* or Lawrence Stone's *The Crisis of the Aristocracy*.

In the 1930s Oxford was in the midst of a lengthy and sometimes painful transition, dating back to the 1870s. It would perhaps be unjust to describe Oxford before 1850 in Gibbon's words, as mere "port and prejudice." But it would also not be far from the truth. In the nineteenth century most Oxford colleges were in the hands of clerics, marriage was forbidden, the dons were required to live in college, and they were often men more devoted to port and high-table conversation than to students and learning. In midcentury Oxford underwent a series of reforms in which dons were allowed to marry, which in turn allowed for teaching to be professionalized. In the 1870s Benjamin Jowett of Balliol College took the lead in implementing further reform. Under his leadership, Balliol stressed dedicated tutorial teaching, abolished the celibacy requirement, and began hiring tutors for their intellectual powers. Jowett also began admitting students on the basis of their intellectual ability and performance instead of on their family and institutional ties. In the early 1900s Balliol was already producing first-rate historians such as R.H. Tawney, Keith Feiling, and Lewis Namier. But most colleges retained an amateur quality. When the Regius Professors, such as Sir Charles Firth or F.M. Powicke, attempted to promote research and place more emphasis on graduate instruction, they were often greeted with derision. The typical don often remained an amateur, more interested in the college performance in "eights," than in firsts and intellectual distinction. The subordination of research to teaching was usually defended on the grounds that the mission of the university was to educate a political elite not to train historians. There were of course exceptions. Hastings Rashdall, a dedicated tutor at New College, was also a distinguished historian of the medieval university.[3]

Some indications of change, however, can be seen in the best Oxford colleges. In the 1920s Oxford history schools produced three men of genuine distinction, A.L. Rowse at Christ Church, Bruce McFarlane at Exeter, and A.J.P. Taylor at Oriel, though Taylor has disclaimed any Oxford influence upon his development. By the 1930s Christ Church and Balliol took the lead in the development of historians. Christ Church produced, among others, Hugh Trevor-Roper and Lawrence Stone, while Balliol produced Richard Southern and Christopher Hill.

At Christ Church the reasons for this success are elusive. Christ Church possesses some of Oxford's most spectacular architecture and is perhaps the most conservative and traditional of Oxford colleges, where pedigree and pretense prevail. L.P. Curtis remarked that it would be impossible for one, looking out on Christ Church's magnificent Tom Tower and Quad, to write working-class history. J.C. Masterman, a Christ Church history don, has written that before World War I the Christ Church history faculty claimed no special distinction, but emerged dramatically in the 1920s, despite some internal differences of opinion about philosophy. The senior tutor, Arthur Hassell, took some of the pupils all to himself, leaving Masterman and Keith Feiling to share the rest. Hassell also believed that Feiling was too kind to pupils. Feiling for his part believed that he prepared students both for examinations and to think for themselves and expressed concern that "we did not just blither over a pipe or allow that someone was a self-teaching genius."[4] Hassell retired in 1924, and the Christ Church history school eventually expanded to include scholars such as the medievalist Ernest Jacob. In the early days, according to Masterman, most of the first-class degrees went to Balliol or New College, but by the end of the First World War, Christ Church had forged ahead, and since 1919 had secured more firsts in the History Schools than any other college. In this regard Masterman believed that Christ Church had "outJowetted Jowett."[5]

Ironically, little of Christ Church's progressivity reached Hugh Trevor-Roper or Lawrence Stone, its two great products of the 1930s. Trevor-Roper came up to Christ Church in 1932. By the thirties Christ Church was a blend of the frivolous world of the twenties and *Brideshead Revisited* and the grim, new world of the thirties and economic deprivation. As a student, Trevor-Roper was a blend of this frivolity and seriousness.

On one hand, he pursued an admittedly epicurean life, not entirely different from that of the northern gentry from whence he came and in harmony with the traditions of the gentleman's college of which he was a member. He kept a horse outside of town, devoted a great deal of his time to hunting, and entered unreservedly into the seemingly endless succession of Oxford parties. On the other hand he was a celebrated student, winning all of Oxford's fiercely sought classics prizes. But he gradually became disenchanted with classics as a discipline. At Oxford study of the classics entailed extensive reading in the literature of antiquity, with little concern for the study of the thought contained in the literature or of the context from which the thought emerged. A particularly mind-calcifying encounter with the "inexpressibly tedious" Greek epic poem of Nonnus convinced Trevor-Roper that he had hit the bottom of the barrel when it came to classical literature. Without a great deal of reflection, he decided that he now had sufficient command of Greek and Latin to read the literature, which was what he was the most interested in, and that he preferred to read modern history rather than ancient history or philosophy.[6]

None of his Christ Church classics tutors tried to dissuade him from changing his field to history, which is surprising, since Trevor-Roper was an obvious star on the rise in that discipline. His new history tutors were an odd mix. On one hand there was J.C. Masterman, who was not really a scholar, but a high-class schoolmaster. Trevor-Roper would read his essay for Masterman, who would stroke his nose and talk about cricket. When Masterman took a sabbatical leave, Trevor-Roper recalled, "there was no nonsense about research. He went to India and played cricket with Maharajahs." Masterman was, however, a great mover and fixer in the corridors of power, good at preparing his pupils for careers and with the necessary connections to help them find jobs. Masterman was, as Trevor-Roper became later, the ultimate Oxford insider. Trevor-Roper's other tutor, Keith Feiling, was a serious historian, the author of a book on the history of the Tory Party, and much more rigorous.[7]

After seven terms instead of the usual nine of reading history, Trevor-Roper took schools in June 1936 and received a first-class degree. After schools, he did some teaching at Christ Church and in 1937 was elected to a research fellowship at Merton College. In those days, promising Oxford undergraduates rarely pursued doctorates; it was not required to get a teaching position at Oxford, and it was not the gentlemanly thing to do. Instead, they were awarded research fellowships, which allowed them to take an extended period of self-directed study and reflection, while remaining in the queue for teaching positions. During this time Trevor-Roper continued to enjoy his epicurean life, but also decided to pursue a doctorate by writing a book on Archbishop Laud. Unfortunately the supervisor to which he was assigned was useless even to the point of supervising another student on the same subject. Trevor-Roper tried vainly to wrangle a transfer and eventually wrote his book on Laud without supervision.[8]

Until 1936 Trevor-Roper generally eschewed politics. Indeed, raised in the rural isolation of Northumberland and educated in the enclosed enclave of Charterhouse, he was not even aware of the Depression when he arrived at Christ Church. He did not attend the meetings of the Communist October Club, but by 1936 the Spanish Civil War had roused him from his dogmatic slumbers. He had gone to Germany in 1935 and been horrified by the Nazis. As debates about the meaning of the Civil War raged over Christ Church and Oxford, Trevor-Roper steadfastly defended the Republican cause.

In his valedictory address delivered as he retired from Oxford as Regius Professor of History, Trevor-Roper described an encounter with a young Christ Church history don during his first term of reading history. The don had invited Trevor-Roper and his contemporaries to his rooms for a discussion of the Marxist interpretation of history. The Marxist interpretation, the don informed the assembled group, had predicted the course of events since Marx's time with remarkable accuracy; it could now be regarded as scientifically valid. "The vast pageant of history," Trevor-Roper wrote later, "hitherto so indeterminate, so formless, so mysterious, now had, as it seemed, a beautiful, mechanical regularity, and modern science had supplied a master key which, with a satisfying click, would turn in every lock, open all its darkened chambers, and reveal all its secret workings."[9]

When, however, Trevor-Roper tried to turn the magical key, he encountered difficulty. What, he asked, was the great problem of 1930s? For Trevor-Roper, "it was of course the sudden and apparently irresistible rise of aggressive dictatorships in a world which, we had always been told, had been made safe for democracy by the victory of 1918." Had Marx, or any other Marxist "tipster," predicted the rise of fascism? The answer for Trevor-Roper was a resounding no.

The Munich conference of 1938 also contributed to his political development, giving him a growing sense of the inevitability of war in Europe. He did not for a minute believe that Hitler had made his last territorial demand in Europe. Moreover, shortly after the conference he read an article by R.C.K. Ensor in which Ensor had predicted that there would be an international crisis leading to Western capitulation to Hitler or war in 1939. Ensor argued that Hitler was a man of his word in the sense that the expansionist theories adumbrated in *Mein Kampf* were to be taken seriously.

Trevor-Roper, too, read *Mein Kampf*, the "whole bloody thing," he recalled later, and instead of appeasement, he argued at the time that Britain should have resisted Hitler at once. Retrospectively, he conceded that resistance at that time would have been a mistake. He failed to recognize how weak Britain was. Had there been war in 1938, Britain would probably have lost it.

When Hitler invaded Poland in September 1939, Trevor-Roper was in Northumberland. Hearing the news, he and Gilbert Ryle, a Christ Church philosophy don, returned immediately to Oxford that night. With war imminent, a blackout was in force, and they drove the entire way in the dark, without lights, inching blindly but cautiously, like the world in 1939, down barely visible roads in an eerie darkness. The journey took all night. They knew that not only was their comfortable, indulgent life at Oxford about to change, but that of the world as well.[10]

In retrospect, Trevor-Roper felt a bit failed by Oxford. His history tutors were uninspiring, and his graduate supervision virtually nonexistent. He never submitted a thesis and therefore never received a doctoral degree, and he doubts that with the qualifications he had in the 1930s he could have been elected to a fellowship in the Oxford of the 1990s. His work on Archbishop Laud, published in 1940, he believes, would have been much better had it been supervised by a competent historian. It was not until World War II that he began to think seriously history, and whatever he learned about it, he said years later, "I learned as I went along."

Lawrence Stone's experience at Oxford was only slightly better. The Depression had rendered his family's existence somewhat precarious, so the continuance of his educational career depended upon scholarships. With the help of his Charterhouse mentor, Sir Robert Birley, Stone won a scholarship to Christ Church in 1938. He had hoped for Balliol, which was Birley's college, but when Christ Church's offer came before he heard from Balliol, he could not risk turning it down.

Stone's first sight of Christ Church was memorable. He came up to take scholarship examinations in December 1937 in the middle of a howling blizzard. With snow swirling about the Cathedral and Tom Tower, the college appeared to be suspended in a dreamy, magical haze. Stone experienced a rare moment of awe. A more sobering moment came later that fall. Stone came up in the fall 1938, just after the conclusion of the Munich Conference. Few were fooled by Chamberlain's promise of peace in our time, and Stone arrived at Christ Church with a sense of impending doom, brought chillingly home by the memorial to the Christ Church undergraduates killed in World War I, a tribute to a devastated generation. In the fall of 1938 Stone felt similarly doomed, fearing that his name and those of many of his contemporaries would soon be engraved on a second memorial.[11]

Stone had many of the same tutors that Trevor-Roper had, including Masterman and Feiling, and his impressions of them were similar to Trevor-Roper's. He found Masterman engaging but superficial. They drank sherry in late afternoon tutorials and gossiped. Stone learned nothing. Feiling was competent and professional, without being very stimulating. The Oxford tutor with the greatest impact on Stone was not at Christ Church, but at Queen's College. Stone heard John Prestwich, a Queen's don, lecture and decided that he wanted to work with him. Oxford colleges often farm out their best students to tutors in other colleges who can better address the interests of the students.

Prestwich was typical of a certain kind of Oxford history don in the 1930s, especially prevalent among medievalists. Like Bruce McFarlane at Magdalen, Prestwich was incomparably learned, but with a phobia about publishing. His work was extensive, but in his exacting judgment, never quite ready. Stone studied the Third Crusade with Prestwich, found him erudite and delightful, and acquired from him a sense of what history could be. There was also an element of hand-to-hand combat in Prestwich's teaching method. Stone studied the Third Crusade with Prestwich as a special subject. Having found his earliest essays on the subject systematically demolished by Prestwich, Stone sought out original documents, including little-known accounts by Moslem chroniclers. Armed with obscure and recondite facts drawn from these arcane sources, Stone recovered his confidence and succeeded in momentarily rattling Prestwich. It was a hard-fought, but fleeting victory, as Prestwich recovered to deliver counterblows.[12]

The Spanish Civil War loomed large in Stone's political consciousness. The politics of the 1930s, he recalled, "entirely centered on the Spanish Civil War, which drove many, though not me, to join the Communist Party." Like Trevor-Roper, Stone opposed fascism and staunchly upheld the Republican cause. And, like Trevor-Roper, he was not deceived by Munich and continued to expect war at any minute. If there was a solution to the political and economic crises of the 1930s, he and many of his contemporaries thought, it was most likely to be found in the French socialist government under Leon Blum. By contrast, Stone recalls, the British government was regarded with scorn by many students for its failure to provide jobs at home or to deter the imperialism of Germany and Italy. Few students believed that the Munich Conference brought, as Neville Chamberlain claimed, "peace in our time."[13]

Many students were tempted by Marxism. Stone was not. He was interested, even sympathetic, and tried to read Marx. But he never came close to accepting it. He himself suggests that this has a great deal to do with the year he came up. "Had you come up to the college in 1936, you would have been more likely to end up a Marxist. If you had came up in 1938, when I did, the good guys and the bad guys in the Spanish Civil War were more complicated. The bloom was off. In my year I don't think any of us went off to fight in Spain. In 1936 I think that some of them did."[14]

Stone's education was interrupted by the outbreak of war, but with the exception of his experience with Prestwich, he had benefited little from his experience at Oxford and Christ Church. Like Trevor-Roper, he found the tutoring generally uninspiring. His historical inspiration, outside of Prestwich, would come later from a variety of mentors and stimuli, most of them outside Oxford.

The situation was better at Balliol, where building on the tradition of Jowett, the history faculty prided itself on academic rigor and devotion to teaching. When Christopher Hill came up to Balliol as Brackenbury scholar in Michaelmas term 1931, he was already a renowned student. In 1930 at St. Peter's School, York, he won a County Major Scholarship and the Headmaster's Prizes for history and for Latin Prose. His Balliol interview was already the stuff of legend. Shy and stammering, Hill felt completely intimidated when he was interviewed by V.H. Galbraith and Kenneth Bell, two Balliol history dons, and was barely able to muster the courage to speak. He returned in disgust to the chilly room at Balliol to which he had been assigned, when Galbraith and Bell abruptly burst in and began a furious argument about religion, so intense that it was impossible for Hill to get a word in. When, at one point, Galbraith demanded to know one good thing the Church of England had ever produced, Hill suddenly blurted out, "Swift." The astonished dons thought this was a superb answer and the conversation quickly turned into a high-level discourse, becoming the interview Hill had almost missed. He was offered a scholarship, which they persuaded him to accept, although he had already accepted one from Cambridge.[15]

Hill proved to be an outstanding and versatile student. Despite his small frame, he was regarded as a useful rugby player, "tackling large, bony opponents without flinching." He was also known for his gentle, but sardonic sense of humor. When the first three volumes of Toynbee's *Study of History* appeared Hill delivered a typically Oxfordian judgment to V.H. Galbraith, "P-p-platitude, supported by great learning." Among the Balliol history tutors, Galbraith was his favorite.[16]

At Balliol Hill succeeded through a powerful work ethic. Samuel Beer recalled that, "in spite of his gaiety, there was no frivolity in Hill. He spent his time not in politics or womanizing or chit-chat, but working." During the spectacular summer of 1934 in which many Oxfordians reveled in long periods of glorious, warm, sunny weather, so unusual for Oxford, Hill rarely joined them. Visiting the Hill family home in Yorkshire, Beer recalled a moment of self-revelation when Hill pointed to a window seat and remarked with emotion, "that is where I spent all those hours reading." His hard work paid off. In 1932 he was awarded the Lothian Prize for his essay on Jansenism, and in 1934, he won the prestigious fellowship to All Souls' College at Oxford. At All Souls he continued to work prodigiously. In 1935 Beer wrote to his wife that "poor Christopher Hill fainted the other day after one glass of sherry—fell into a dead clammy sweat from overwork."[17]

Hill's undergraduate years were also characterized by an abiding love of poetry. *The Excursion* was a particular favorite. When a new book of poetry appeared, such as one by Auden or Eliot, Hill bought it. Peter Brown, a distant admirer of Hill's at Oxford in the 1950s, remembers Hill's telling him of the excitement he and his friends experienced when Sir Lewis Namier's *The Structure of Politics* and a book of T.S. Eliot's poems appeared at about the same time. Hill was especially drawn to the Metaphysical poets, and when Eliot's famous essay on them appeared, describing the "dissociation of sensibility," Hill realized he needed to understand the history of the seventeenth century in order to understand the meaning of the poetry. At the same time, he began to see the seventeenth century as the key to understanding Britain's modern development. "I wanted to show that England's peaceful gradualist evolution after the seventeenth century was the consequence of what happened then," he recalled in the early 1980s.[18]

Hill's radicalism began to develop shortly after his arrival at Balliol, as he stared into the abyss of the economic collapse of the early 1930s. "The bottom fell out of our universe in 1931, the year I went up to Balliol," Hill later recalled. Slump, dreadful unemployment, the danger of World War II, the apparent success of the USSR, Hill thought, were especially distressing to middle-class English children, brought up to believe that even if England was no longer the top nation, it was immune from economic collapse and accompanying anxieties.[19]

Hill also recalled that a great deal of Marxist discussion went on at Oxford in the early thirties, and he was greatly influenced by his undergraduate friends. One of these friends, another Balliol undergraduate, Norman O. Brown, one year ahead of Hill, was especially persuasive in furthering Hill's leftward drift, telling Hill that it was his moral duty to join the Communist Party, although Brown did not do so himself. Hill was active in several Oxford radical groups including the October Club and the peace movement, where he first encountered his future Balliol colleague Richard Southern, who had come up two years earlier. Southern recalls that the night before his final examinations in 1932 George Bernard Shaw came to speak to the October Club. Southern decided to study, but Hill went to hear Shaw, and came away wanting to write a book on Bunyan.[20]

Hill was not completely converted to Marxism until he left Balliol. He had received his first in schools in 1934, and then applied for a fellowship at All Souls, the unique Oxford college that has only fellows and accepts no pupils. While the All Souls fellowship was perhaps the most prestigious in Oxford (other holders have included A.L. Rowse, Stuart Hampshire, Peter Brown, J.P. Cooper, and Keith Thomas), it was not something that Hill sought eagerly. He wanted a teaching job, but was turned down at Eton, one of the few openings available. He also wanted to save humanity, but there were few openings there either. So he was fortunate to have the fellowship to fall back on. All Souls, however, seemed to confirm much of the Marxist critique of aristocratic society. "The college had a lot money that the Fellows just spent on living the good life," he said later. "A lot of junior fellows felt, as I did, that the college was just a place of privilege." But the time he spent at All Souls had undeniable benefits for him. A librarian at Worcester College tipped him off that Russian historians were producing cutting-edge work on seventeenth-century England. He learned Russian with the help of gramophone records in order to get in touch with that research, specifically that by Arkhangelsky on Cromwell. The Warden of All Souls, W.G.S. Adams, while sympathetic to the idea that Hill should study abroad, was disappointed at Hill's choice of Russia. The visit was difficult but intellectually rewarding. During it, Hill suffered an infection that required a mastoid operation, but his conversion to Marxism was completed and he gained further ideas on how Marxist doctrines could be applied to the English Revolution.[21]

These insights were expounded in an early article, "Soviet Interpretations of the English Interregnum," which summarized the ideas of Soviet historians and suggested an agenda for future work. Equally important, Hill's arrival in the Soviet Union coincided with an apparent industrial miracle. Where the Western economy lay paralyzed by the collapse predicted by Marx, the Soviet economy thrived. The other alternative, fascism, depended upon the fearful specter of jackbooted storm troopers and the acquiescence of terrified industrial elites. Hill soon saw the Soviet Union as the answer to the crisis of the thirties.[22]

But the Soviet Union had its own demons in the thirties. Hill was there in 1936 while the purges were in progress. For many tempted by the intellectual force of Marxist ideology, the purges were a pivotal point. One who wished to continue to defend the Soviet Union as the answer to the crisis of the thirties had to find a way to justify the purges. Hill found several means by which they could be justified. He had taken lodgings with a woman whose husband had been sent to Siberia for speculation. By taking him in she, too, was engaging in illegal behavior. When the husband returned, he was a picture of health, and Hill concluded that the gulags were not as bad as people thought. An English engineer, unsympathetic to Communism, suggested that many of the victims were guilty, and Hill became convinced in any event that he could not trust any of the accounts in the English press. When the Soviets signed the 1939 nonaggression pact with the Germans, clearing the way for Hitler to invade Poland, Hill blamed Chamberlain for it, since he had for several years advocated that Chamberlain circumvent the Nazis by making his own pact with the Soviets against Hitler. Even after World War II, Hill continued to hope for a British alliance with the Soviets.[23]

Hill's Marxism was further nurtured by the work of the committed Christian socialist, R.H. Tawney, with whom Hill did not have an academic connection, but whom he saw frequently at college functions. Tawney was a luminous Balliol undergraduate, who sacrificed more comfortable and prestigious positions to teach adult, working-class students as part of the Worker's

Educational Association. After years of adult education, he accepted a professorship at the London School of Economics. His research was diffuse and broadly conceived. His *The Agrarian Problem of the Sixteenth Century* described the exploitation of the rural peasantry by ruthless landlords. His *Religion and the Rise of Capitalism* tried to connect Puritanism with capitalism. His famous articles on the rise of the gentry between 1540 and 1640 developed the idea that the English Revolution of 1640 was the product of a long-term struggle for power between a rising class of gentry and a declining aristocratic class.

Tawney's personality was as compelling as his historical vision. The American colonial historian Edmund Morgan, who attended LSE briefly in the 1930s as a graduate student intending to study with Harold Laski, turned to Tawney instead.[24] Tawney lived his life in accordance with his Christian socialist vision. He despised money and once tried to refuse his salary at LSE. Gentle and saintly, his humility knew no bounds. When an undergraduate asked him a question about enclosure, a subject to which he devoted much of his scholarly life, Tawney demurred. "I'm sure you know the field better than I do," he replied. Tawney was famous for saying that instead of more documents, historians needed stronger boots, meaning that they needed the courage to offer bolder generalizations.

Hill found much about Tawney congenial, both intellectually and temperamentally. Like Tawney, Hill believed that historical understanding advanced through bold generalizations and was willing to offer them. And he preferred analytical to narrative history, placing class struggle at center stage. Like Tawney, Hill yearned to combine scholarship with his personal beliefs. And like Tawney, he was overwhelmingly humble.[25]

In one sense Hill's attraction to Marxism was understandable. Not only was Hill pushed toward it by mentors and friends, but during the 1930s it had a powerful appeal. World War I shattered liberal illusions about progress, and the economic collapse of the early 1930s seemed to affirm Marx's contention that capitalism was poised on the edge of collapse. From another angle Hill in some ways resembles the affluent American radicals of the 1960s. Friends going to his family home in Yorkshire for a visit were stunned when they pulled up at the correct address in front of a magnificent mansion on the outskirts of the city, replete with a tennis court and a high wall around the grounds. A servant served lunch at a table on the lawn. The visitors had been apprehensive about their visit. In virtually all matters Hill seemed quite classless. In fact his visitors feared his family might be slightly impoverished and their visit a strain on the family's resources. They need not have worried. Unknown to them, Hill's father was prosperous solicitor who was also a fervent Methodist. In middle age the senior Hill, having made plenty of money, retired from the practice of law to concentrate on promoting the Methodist cause.[26]

Sir Richard Southern's experience at Balliol was also quite positive. "I owe a very great deal to my tutors at Balliol from 1929–1932 and to F.M. Powicke," Southern wrote decades later. One of the first was the famous "Sligger" Urquhart, one of Oxford's legendary characters, known for his devotion to pupils. Southern did not find Urquhart to be particularly stimulating as a tutor, but Urquhart was willing to lend his books. For Southern's first summer vacation, Urquhart lent him his copy of J.A. Round's *Feudal England* and John Henry Newman's *The Idea of a University*, the books that first kindled Southern's interest in history and a life in learning.[27]

Two other tutors, Kenneth Bell and Humphrey Sumner, were competent, but it was V.H. Galbraith who influenced Southern the most. In particular Southern was attracted to the air of excitement that sometimes swirled around Galbraith, then relatively anonymous, but later Regius Professor of History at Oxford and the author of important work on the Domesday Book. Galbraith put everything into his teaching, pouring himself out in talk, whether in tutorials or in casual conversation, arousing in his listeners a high pitch of excitement. Southern later recalled his first experience with this approach to teaching. After hearing Galbraith expound with a vivid and seemingly profound historical discourse, Southern raced back to his rooms in Balliol to write down everything he could remember about it. Upon the cold light of reflection, Southern was surprised to discover how much of it had been plainly wrong. Though initially disappointed by this discovery, Southern then realized that he had just witnessed the greatest gift a teacher can make to his pupils, a willingness by the teacher to lay "himself open to criticism and dissent." Galbraith, he wrote, "kept nothing back, was never pompous, never self-important, and—unless some irritable nerve was touched—he was generous to excess and deeply perceptive of every quality in others except those of formality and prudent reserve." [28]

Despite Galbraith's electrifying presence, the path to a career in medieval history was not straight. In the mid-thirties, England, like most of the Western world, was being crushed by the Depression. What future would there be in medieval history in such desultory times? Southern tried to get away from medieval history by studying economics. But economics, however contemporary, had its own disappointments. At one point Southern told his economics tutor that he wanted to write an essay on how to cure unemployment. The tutor replied that there was no cure for unemployment, except a drastic reduction in population.

Sufficiently discouraged about economics, Southern went back to history, received his first-class degree and won the Alexander Prize of the Royal Historical Society for an essay on Ranulf Flambard. He soon attracted the attention of Sir F.M. Powicke, the Regius Professor of History at Oxford, theoretically the head of the History School and the most prestigious historical position at Oxford. For many Powicke was a difficult man, short and imperious with a Napoleonic complex. Powicke thought that medieval history was the only history of any value, that anyone who wrote about things that occurred after 1500 was merely writing journalism. He was also bitterly critical of the amateurism of most Oxford dons and repeatedly advocated the advancement of research and graduate education to the irritation of many at Oxford. But Powicke was also a dynamic teacher and scholar, eager to advance the careers of those he favored. Southern found Powicke enchanting, and Powicke responded by making Southern his prime protégé, helping him win a research fellowship at Exeter College in 1932, and it was Powicke who also suggested the subject that would become central to much of Southern's work, St. Anselm. Southern spent the next five years in a period of idiosyncratic study, largely on Anselm, including a year in Paris and a few months in Germany.

The intellectual union between Southern and Powicke was unusual. Southern was handsome, graceful, with a sensitive, gentle manner, who had gotten the best Oxford had to offer. By contrast, Powicke, who had failed as a pupil at Oxford, and had to work his way back, was fiery and driven, bitter that Oxford failed to crown him as the new messiah of professionalism, and he approached life with the intensity of an embattled Norse warrior. But there was a common ground. Like many medievalists, Southern seemed to resemble in manner and temperament the saints he would come so often to write about. Despite his combative nature, Powicke also had a saintly side. Peter Brown, an Oxford undergraduate in the 1950s, remembers seeing Powicke lost in serene contemplation in the Merton College chapel. Both men were interested in the spiritual side of religion and its effect on people's lives. In 1937 with Powicke's help Southern returned to Balliol as a fellow and tutor, a position he held, with an interruption for World War II, until 1961, when he received a university chair.[29]

The Oxford of the 1930s was of course swept up in politics. With his working-class origins, Southern was perhaps more sensitive to left-wing ideas than many at Oxford. He was also influenced by his friendship with F.S. Mayer, an American undergraduate at Balliol. Mayer was the founder of the October Club, one of the main Marxist groups at Oxford. Southern attended almost all of its meetings, but neither joined the club nor became a member of the party. Upon reflection, he decided that the Marxists would ultimately comprise a new and more frightening aristocracy than the one they wished to replace. At the meetings Southern did meet another celebrated Balliol undergraduate reading history named Christopher Hill, who would join him as a fellow at Balliol in 1938.

The specter of fascism hung over the decade as well. Recalling the day in 1932 on which he took his final examinations, Southern remembers falling into conversation with another student, Adam Cantroff. Cantroff had been unable to sleep that night, after hearing Hitler speak over the radio. Cantroff was distressed by the fury of the speech and its enthusiastic reception. Southern remembers being moved by Cantroff's vivid description, but thought he was exaggerating.

The Spanish Civil War brought many smoldering issues to the surface. Southern was once asked by a coal miner in 1938 what he thought about the Spanish War. Southern knew the correct, but to him unsatisfying, answer was that the Republicans should win. To Southern one side seemed as bad as the other.[30]

For Trevor-Roper, Stone, Hill, and Southern, the salient experiences of the 1930s were, if not always satisfying, nevertheless at Oxford. For Richard Cobb, an undergraduate at Merton College, the most meaningful experience of the thirties was in a curious odyssey that extended several years. In December 1934 Cobb was a pupil at the Shrewsbury School when he was awarded a Postmastership in History at Balliol. His headmaster and housemaster both wrote to his mother to suggest that "Shrewsbury having done all it could for Richard, it would be better for Shrewsbury if Richard were not to return in January." The reasons were a little vague, but the meaning of the letter was clear. Cobb was no longer welcome at Shrewsbury. His superiors went on to suggest a year abroad before going up to Balliol, and Cobb suddenly found himself in the midst of an enforced hiatus in his education.[31]

Cobb had little notion of what to do or where to go. France was not a promising option. Cobb's knowledge of French was thin and he disliked the language. His own historical interests were English. And the "English public schools in the 1930s took every possible precaution to prevent any of their pupils from becoming Francophiles." France become his choice almost by accident. Germany was quickly ruled out. German barons were bad company for blond English adolescents. Cobb first selected Austria and spent six weeks in Vienna, where he was arrested, beaten up in a series of police stations, and imprisoned for ten days as a Czech student, among other indignities, which was enough to make the idea of a further stay in Austria overwhelmingly repellent.

France became his choice almost by default. When his mother, playing her thrice-weekly bridge game, listened to a friend tell of her daughter who had spent a wonderful year with a family in Paris, the site of his stay was determined. In January 1935 Cobb went to Paris. The family with which he stayed had a flat in a district that placed Cobb in the center of Parisian life. The metro rumbled by at regular intervals. The streets were filled with peddlers, street bands, flame swallowers, and prostitutes. Theaters and restaurants abounded.

Paris was sometimes a shock for a boy raised in the confines of Tunbridge Wells. Three days after his arrival, Cobb was taken to a party by friends where "a naked girl, an admiral's daughter, was being cleaned up. The fact that an admiral's daughter could end up naked at a party shocked him, and for a few days he wanted to return to Tunbridge Wells."[32]

When he went up to Merton, he was fortunate to have J.M. Thompson as one of his tutors. Thompson was a former cleric, who as an intellectual exercise, attempted to demonstrate the validity of the evidence for the miracles supposedly performed by Jesus of Nazareth. This, he thought, would clinch the veracity of Christian teaching. When Thompson instead discovered the evidence insufficient, he immediately renounced Christianity and turned to the study of the French Revolution. Cobb responded to the teaching and interests of Thompson, but he was not an outstanding student at Oxford, going down in June 1938 with a second-class degree.[33]

In 1937 Cobb visited Georges Lefebvre, the Marxist doyen of historians of the French Revolution, and attended his lectures on the Revolution along with an exuberant and cheering audience at the Sorbonne. A fierce, ramrod man of the French north, Lefebvre, thought Cobb, could almost have been a character in the Revolution, so effective was he in his depiction of Marat or Saint-Just.

In the summer of 1938 Cobb returned to France and began a lifelong communion with the Archives Nationales, in which he found shelter from the impending European storm. Violence and revolution, he thought, should "never lap into that elegant, semi-oblong courtyard." Remarkably, the Archives Nationales stayed open from 1939 to 1944. Lefebvre had suggested that Cobb study the Hébertiste leader François-Nicholas Vincent, one of the most violent and hysterical figures of the French Revolution.

Returning to England just before the outbreak of the war, Cobb wrote up the results of his research. The product was a historical disaster, as Cobb was snared by all the traps that lay in waiting for the unwary biographer. Cobb made extravagant claims for Vincent, often based on the thinnest evidence, reinterpreted the entire Revolution on the basis of his understanding of Vincent, who was at best a secondary figure, and essentially flung the kitchen sink at his examiners by his desperate attempt to include all of his discoveries, whether germane or not.

People sometimes think of Cambridge and Oxford as identical, and there are indeed similarities. Like Oxford, Cambridge consists of individual colleges loosely governed by the university, but which operate according to their own statutes and which choose their own fellows and admit their own undergraduates. Each college has a master or mistress as the superior administrator, although the terminology may differ from college to college. The teaching staff of the college, called fellows or dons, are elected at least in theory on the basis of their academic ability and publications. From the fellows of their college, each undergraduate is assigned a tutor and a director of studies. The tutor looks after the student's social welfare and development. The director of studies supervises the undergraduate's academic progress, assigning students to supervisors who offer instruction either individually or in small groups. During their undergraduate years, the Cambridge undergraduates will study under several supervisors, who may be fellows in other colleges if their skills and expertise compliment the students' needs. Supervisions usually consist of hour-long meetings between the supervisor and one pupil or a small group of pupils where the pupils prepare weekly essays and discuss them with their supervisors and the other students. At the end of each term the supervisors report upon their pupil's progress to their tutor. Most undergraduates take examinations at the end of each year. At Cambridge each course in a discipline is called a tripos. It usually lasts a year and concludes with an examination. The results of tripos examinations are posted outside the Senate House where they are keenly awaited by anxious pupils. At the end of three years, the best examinations are given first-class degrees, with a starred first used to identify those examinations of uncommon merit. There are also upper and lower seconds awarded and third-class degrees as well as "special degrees" conferred for those who fail altogether.

Like Oxford, Cambridge also boasts an extensive social life as well as academic rigor. Many undergraduates become consumed by sports, especially rowing. "May races" along the Cam (actually held in June) rouse large and enthusiastic crowds, and May balls last all night, with the survivors "punting" along the Cam to Granchester for a sunrise breakfast. Debating clubs, choral societies, and theatrical productions are also popular undergraduate diversions.

Between Oxford and Cambridge there exists a historic rivalry, which extends to academics as well as sports. Oxford was perhaps the first to implement the reforms that moved the English university away from being the terrain of clerics to that of professionals. But during the recent academic competitions between the two schools, out of five possible points, Oxford received a four, Cambridge a five.

In the 1930s Cambridge produced two historians who went on to remarkable careers, J.H. Plumb and Eric Hobsbawm. In Plumb's case the route to Cambridge was not direct. In 1929 he took examinations for a scholarship at St. John's College, Cambridge, and failed to obtain one, largely, it is said, because he advanced Freudian interpretations. He did make the Exhibitioner List, by which he could have attended St. John's on his own, without financial aid. Making the Exhibitioner List was by itself an impressive achievement for a grammar school lad. But, unable to afford St. John's, he went to the hometown University of Leicester. At Leicester he was taught first by G.E. Fasnacht, a desperately dull man, who appeared in the lecture room in gown and mortarboard and spoke in a "low, sepulchral voice." Fasnacht was so boring that with only three pupils in the class, they took turns cutting it so Fasnacht would not be embarrassed when no one showed up. Plumb was rescued from Fasnacht by the arrival at Leicester of a new Ph.D. from Oxford, Rosalind Hill, who taught medieval history and brought with her, energy, exciting lectures, and the latest historical fashions from Oxford.[34]

Leicester did not examine for degrees, so Plumb had to take his examinations in London. In the summer of 1933 London was intolerably hot and humid as Plumb waited to take his exams, and to make matters worse, C.P. Snow, a friend from Leicester, kept him up all night before the examination, drinking and talking about sadomasochism. Despite the lack of sleep and the presence of such formidable examiners as R.H. Tawney and Eileen Power, Plumb received the first first-class degree ever achieved by a pupil from Leicester.

He then won a research studentship, which he could hold anywhere. At C.P. Snow's urging he decided to take it at Cambridge, but before going he managed to meet two important historians. Through Fasnacht, he met Sir George Clark in Clark's study at All Souls in 1933. Clark was friendly and encouraging about Plumb and his proposed research topic on elections to the House of Commons during the reign of William III. Some time later, Plumb arranged a meeting with the vaunted Lewis Namier on the steps of the British Museum. When Plumb described his project on elections and told Namier that he intended to employ Namier's methods, Namier replied, "How else could you do it?" and returned abruptly to the museum.

At Cambridge Plumb feared that as a student with a degree from a lightly regarded provincial university, he would be consigned to the margins. If he could be accepted as a pupil of the Regius Professor of History at Cambridge, George Macaulay Trevelyan, he might be taken more seriously. Plumb received two notes from Trevelyan, both terse. The first informed him that in order to become Trevelyan's pupil, Plumb would have to be accepted by the Board of Graduate Studies to which Plumb then applied; two weeks later a second note appeared with the information that, having been accepted by the Board of Graduate Studies, Plumb could now be accepted as Trevelyan's student. The note further summoned Plumb to Trevelyan's forbidding house on West Road in Cambridge. Despite family wealth, Trevelyan lived austerely. The house was cold, the furniture ugly and uncomfortable. Trevelyan was also austere in his personal demeanor and for what seemed an eternity remained silent. Finally he asked what Plumb wished to work on. Plumb prattled on for at least ten minutes. When he stopped talking, the silence returned. Finally, in a harsh, grating voice, Trevelyan said, "Good, quite good." Then he rose from his chair, escorted Plumb to the door and said, "Come and see me at the end of the term. If you have any problems let me know." As he opened the door, he asked whether Plumb was living in college or not and then showed him out. Plumb received two supervisions from Trevelyan per term, though Trevelyan remained aloof and forbidding. But he wrote like an angel and was good at teaching his pupils to write, although his method was to seize upon, dissect, and rewrite but one paragraph, slowly reworking the words and rhythms.

Taking his Ph.D. in 1936 and unable to find a job, Plumb had to live by his wits for two years with a little help from his family. He directed studies at

Girton and taught at Newnham. In 1938 the Ehrman Fellowship at King's College in history and geography came open, Plumb applied for it, was examined by John Maynard Keynes, and won the fellowship. After getting the news, he and C.P. Snow got drunk on whiskey. When they finished, they threw their glasses into the fireplace, assuring themselves that "fellows of King's never starve."

By this time politics caught up with Plumb. His family escaped the Depression, but the Spanish Civil War, like chemistry, separated young people in the 1930s into their component parts. There were riots in Cambridge between opponents and supporters of Franco. Many undergraduates went to Spain to fight. Plumb was passionately pro-Republican and responsible for starting a hostel for orphan children from Bilbao. He and some friends found an old rectory, repaired it, and created some shelter and solace for fifteen to twenty orphans.

He was never in such despair as when he heard the news about Chamberlain's capitulation at Munich. There was in his judgment no politician in England to whom he could turn. Plumb was taking his bath at King's when the Dean of the college, Milner-White, came rushing into the room, shouting, "Let's celebrate, we're at war," after hearing that Britain had declared war on Germany. Plumb shared his enthusiasm. It was time to stand up to Hitler. Czechoslovakia was already lost.

Educated on the continent, Eric Hobsbawm experienced a cultural shock when he arrived in England in 1934. In his judgment English grammar schools were roughly five years behind the comparable German schools he attended. At Cambridge he managed to find people interested in some of the same questions he was, though most were ignorant of what was going on in Germany. Unlike his contemporaries at Oxford whose tutors left indelible impressions for good and ill, Hobsbawm got little from his Cambridge supervisors. "Most of us," he said later, "educated ourselves. With the exception of one or two, there wasn't anybody [at Cambridge] we took very seriously. It was unbelievable how provincial English academic life is."

At Cambridge in the thirties, unlike Harvard, Hobsbawm recalls that the brightest people were on the Left. The Spanish Civil War radicalized people and the lectures of Michael Postan on the economic and demographic forces in medieval history attracted large numbers of listeners. "All Marxists," recalls Hobsbawm, "went to Postan's lectures."[35]

Among the English historians, Geoffrey Elton's university experience was the most unconventional. After earning his school certificate at Rydal and still struggling with English, he tried for a scholarship at New College, Oxford, where he was interviewed by the distinguished diplomatic historian, H.A.L. Fisher. But he was rejected, and his Rydal headmaster advised him to stay on at Rydal and teach German while reading for an external degree at the University of London. In 1943 he completed the degree, took his examinations, won a first-class degree in history and a Derby Studentship, which would allow him to pursue postgraduate work at London. Because he had taken his degree externally, Elton knew none of the London faculty, except for a professor of ancient history who was a friend of his father's. The professor recommended that Elton study with the eminent Elizabethan historian Sir John Neale, who by coincidence, had left blitz-ravaged London and taken refuge at Colwyn Bay, not far from the Eltons. Elton paid a visit to Neale, who told him that if he survived the war, a prospect that Neale seemed to suggest by his tone of voice he deemed unlikely, Elton should come to London and become one of Neale's research students.[36]

The experiences of these historians as university students in the 1930s vary considerably. Despite pockets of inspired teaching, such as that received by Hill and Southern at Balliol or Stone from John Prestwich, the English did not receive the high quality of teaching that, say, the Harvard historians received. In several cases, the worst features of teaching of history at Oxford, Cambridge, and elsewhere in 1930s prevailed: amateurism, indifference, and pomposity. The brilliance of Stone and Trevor-Roper, for example, appears to have emerged in spite of Oxford instead of being nourished by it. Even more remarkable is the case of Geoffrey Elton. Rejected by Oxford, he took an external degree and won first-class honors virtually on his own.

Chapter 5

V Was for Victory

꧀

On December 7, 1941, Jack Hexter, then teaching at Queen's College in New York, was living at 334 W. 12th St. in Greenwich Village in an apartment with seven or eight other men. Already a skilled chef, he was preparing an large Sunday lunch for his roommates and for his girlfriend Ruth Mullin, a Queen's graduate who had been in one of his classes. As he prepared the lunch, the news came over the radio that Japan had attacked the American naval base at Pearl Harbor and that President Roosevelt had asked Congress to declare war on Japan. As they discussed what war would mean for their lives, Hexter and Ruth Mullin made one firm decision. They decided they had better get married as quickly as possible because Hexter would be called up for military service soon. He was indeed drafted shortly after Pearl Harbor, which meant, among other things, that he had to sacrifice part of his year as a Guggenheim Fellow. He spent three and half years as a stateside soldier. It may have been fortunate that he was not sent to a combat zone. He never learned to march in step, and while he was attempting to negotiate an obstacle course, he blew out a knee.[1]

Every generation has defining moments, and for this generation, the Depression and World War II were two of their most powerful. For them, it would always be "the War," and most of them would remember where they were or what they were doing when they heard the news of its beginning. To a generation that had been forced to cope with the grim realities of the Great Depression, the beginning of the Second World War must have seemed like another one of Job's travails that they were born to suffer. Most of them had completed their education and had either started or were about to start their careers and families. Once again buffeted by events out of their control, most of them interrupted their studies or careers (one was even fired) and left their wives and small children behind.

The members of the World War II generation served their countries in a variety of ways. Only a few fired a shot in anger or were exposed to danger, but they participated in the war effort in a variety of other ways. Some taught; some were active on the home front. But the primary means by which historians contributed to the war effort was through intelligence work. Most historians, especially the Europeanists, had language skills and expertise essential to intelligence gathering and analysis. In the spring of 1941 Colonel (later General) William "Wild Bill" Donovan convinced Roosevelt of the need for an organ of government with intelligence gathering capability. Donovan then assembled a staff of experts, many of them historians, including William Langer of Harvard to analyze policy.[2] Langer himself, given the liberty to hire extensively, was eager to recruit more historians, especially those with Harvard and Ivy League backgrounds.

Great Britain had already been at war with Germany since 1939, and historians in Britain assumed roles similar to those in the United States. Lawrence Stone was one of the few who saw combat. He decided to enlist in the Royal Navy, believing that naval warfare was the most civilized form of combat, and during the war he spent five years at sea.[3] Writing about the experience, he recalls, that "as anyone who experienced it knows, war is 99.9 per cent boredom and discomfort, and 0.1 per cent sheer terror." In his case the discomfort and boredom were to a certain extent alleviated by the bountiful rations of food and alcohol aboard ship.

During the war, while in London on leave, Stone met R.H. Tawney, already a figure of legend for early modern historians. Stone was a callow Oxford undergraduate and a sailor, but Tawney always had time for him. He and Stone took numerous long walks and discussed both the state of the world and the state of seventeenth-century historiography. From Tawney, Stone learned that the documents of seventeenth-century history had survived in much greater profusion than those of the Middle Ages, which, along with Tawney's influence, converted Stone from a medievalist to an early modernist.

Tawney was also a great character. By then he had fled from his bomb-devastated house and was living in utter squalor in a tiny flat in Bloomsbury, cluttered with books, papers, cats, and plates of uneaten food. In his presence, Stone recalled, one also had to be on guard against possibility that he would set himself on fire, as bits of burning tobacco fell out of his pipe and would land on the sleeves of his tweed jackets, sometimes igniting them.

In a sense Stone began his life of learning as the navigator of a destroyer patrolling the south Atlantic. He was perhaps not the most able navigator; he has admitted to running his destroyer aground twice. In 1942 he wrote his first article on board ship, discussing the shameful treatment by the government of the English sailors who had fought in the Armada campaign in 1588. Stone was supplied with the necessary research materials by the London Library, which, even at the height of the war, dispatched books to remote corners of the earth, even when it sometimes took months for them to reach their destination.

While the ships on which he served regularly encountered combat, Stone's most harrowing experience came at the war's end. By that time, he was attached to the American Seventh Fleet off Japan. Eager to go home, he elbowed his way onto a flight in September 1945, only to discover that his plane was piloted by a man who had flown fifty missions over Germany and was a psychological and physical wreck. Each landing was an adventure. Landing in Malta, they nearly crashed. Stone returned to Oxford in November 1945, just in time to enroll for the year.[4]

Geoffrey Elton was another combat veteran. In 1943 he was summoned for military service, and the British army required him to change his name from Gottfried Ehrenberg to Geoffrey Elton. He joined the infantry, seeing combat in Italy and later serving as a guard for German and Italian prisoners of war. His service as a guard was an oddly formative experience. In his speech and manners, and in the eyes of most of his English friends, Elton was still a German. But to the prisoners of war he guarded, he was indelibly a British soldier and they treated him like one. While he had felt an instant kinship with Britain upon his family's arrival in 1939, he had yet to be regarded by anyone as an Englishman, and he very much wanted to be.[5]

When the war began, Richard Southern, who had been a fellow and tutor at Balliol College since 1937, quickly enlisted. A rather scrawny youth, Southern was asked by one recruiter if he really wanted to be a soldier. Southern replied that he certainly did, and he served in the British army for five years. He was denied the chance for combat by an odd twist of fate. His university education allowed him to become an officer. Officers were subject to a wartime regulation, usually ignored, requiring them to do physical training. Southern was perhaps the only officer in the British army who adhered to the regulation. He had just finished his physical training one morning when he was summoned by his commanding officer, who was considering which officers to recommend for combat service. Southern walked into the office soaked in sweat and dressed in shorts. Perhaps for that reason, he was not taken. He ended up spending eighteen months attached to a less glamorous but safer force, an experimental unit trying to develop a new means of assault called infantry tanks, a tactic by which soldiers would advance across battlefields inside tanks instead of being exposed to fire.

The infantry tank idea was eventually scuttled, and Southern was transferred to London to work in intelligence in the foreign office for the last two years of the war. At the end of the war he spent four months in Germany assessing conditions there. During his time in intelligence, he met his wife, a widow whose first husband was an RAF hero.[6]

J.H. Plumb and Christopher Hill also served in intelligence. Plumb was connected to the famous Bletchley Park intelligence unit under Sir Harry

Hindsley that cracked the German code fairly early in the war. While Plumb did not help crack the code, he was sent to India while the Japanese were still threatening to overrun southern Asia and spent a year there.[7] After the war began Christopher Hill tried hard to get a job in which he could use his ability to speak Russian, but was always told, "we aren't fighting Russia yet." He ended up in the Intelligence Corps arranging education courses for officers and was ultimately attached to the Northern Department of the Foreign Office. After the war knowledge of Russian became vastly more important, and Hill was the only member of the Northern Department who had it or had firsthand acquaintance with the USSR, so he was in high demand educating other officers about Soviet affairs.[8]

The experiences of Eric Hobsbawm and Richard Cobb are harder to classify. Hobsbawm served in the Army Pioneer Corps and the Army Education Corps, teaching European history to army officers. Cobb's military experience was the most varied among the English. He had witnessed the sense of impending war and panic that gripped Paris in the weeks before the Munich Conference and the tumultuous welcome Daladier received upon his return from Munich and the hope it held out for peace. In May 1940 he tried to join the Free French Army, but ended up in the British army, to be trained as a storeman. At one point he endured a long stretch in "sanitary," where his job was emptying latrines in the neighboring countryside. From this experience Cobb learned a valuable lesson in military survival: work too hard, empty too many latrines too quickly, and you will be asked to do more. Cobb soon learned how to make the emptying of a few buckets last all day.[9]

However distasteful "sanitary" duty was, Cobb was nevertheless lucky; he would be spared combat. Like several of his generational cohort, he was also an educated person thrown into the milieu of less well educated, coarser persons with whom he had had little previous contact. Many of his colleagues, who were generally tradesmen and lorry drivers, boasted of their prison experiences. Here the army performed the valuable service of divesting him of his sense of class. His time in France had helped him learn to adjust to alien cultures, and he was soon accepted by his comrades. He was also exposed to other parts of the British Isles, since he was stationed at various times in the north of England, Scotland, and south Wales, which also required some cultural adjustments.

Cobb served as a liaison to the Polish army and was transferred later to the Czechoslovak Independent Brigade Group. Though he did not know either language, Cobb was able to enhance his awareness of Europe and of national minorities. He did undertake a serious attempt to learn Polish and for a while considered studying Polish history. In the spring of 1944 he was transferred to the 21st Army Group, which eventually took him to several parts of France, but kept him generally on only the edge of combat. During the day ambulances rolled by in endless caravans past his post. At night he could see flashes of light from bombardments, though the countryside remained eerily silent. In the winter of 1944 the German offensive in the Ardennes Forest threatened to engage the 21st Army Group. They were each issued a weapon, which Cobb repeatedly misplaced, but did not have to use when the threat receded.

As the war drew to a close, Cobb asked several French girls to marry him. All refused, although they did let him down gently. On VE-Day he joined a wild celebration, a whirling circle of dancers on the Grand'Place in Roubaix, in a spontaneous release of collective joy.

The most famous military experience of the World War II generation of historians was probably that of Hugh Trevor-Roper.[10] Before the outbreak of the war, he was a member of the unmechanized Life Guards, for whom his duties consisted of riding a "steaming black charger" up and down the sandy knolls of Surrey. When the war broke out, he returned to Oxford to await orders. E.W.B. Gill, an intelligence veteran of World War I and in 1939 Bursar of Merton College, where Trevor-Roper was a Junior Research Fellow, asked Trevor-Roper to join an intelligence unit he was in the process of forming. Trevor-Roper's astonishing mastery of languages, including French, Spanish, German, Greek, Dutch, and Latin, suited him perfectly for intelligence work.

Gill had created a niche for himself in a small unit called Radio Security Service (RSS). The purpose of RSS was to seek out unidentified radio signals that might emanate from German spies planted in Britain who might be helping the Luftwaffe to locate targets. If spies were identified, the RSS tried to locate the hidden transmitters and arrest the perpetrators, who were dealt with by the internal security service, MI 5, which at the time was housed in Wormwood Scrubs Prison. Gill and Trevor-Roper thus began their work in a tiny prison cell.

Gill and Trevor-Roper dutifully performed their work, gathering evidence of their own and from a network of enthusiastic amateurs throughout the country. They dispatched their findings to the Government Code and Cypher School (GCCS), at Bletchley Park, so the messages could be decoded. Their labor, however, turned out to be superfluous. There was only one German spy active in Britain when the war broke out, and he was being fed misinformation by MI 5.

The higher officials were therefore not terribly interested in decoding and assessing the material assembled by the RSS unit. Gill and Trevor-Roper, who shared a flat in Ealing, decided to work on it themselves in the evening after their normal work day. Gill knew cryptography and Trevor-Roper knew German. After a few weeks they succeeded in breaking the cipher and realized that they had stumbled upon a finding of some consequence, the radio transmissions of the German Secret Service, or *Abwehr*. With some excitement they reported their finding to Colonel Worlledge, their commanding officer, an honorable but not terribly astute signals officer from World War I. Worlledge was impressed enough to ask Trevor-Roper to write a summary of their findings. Trevor-Roper responded with a report that Worlledge circulated among his colleagues, no doubt expecting that it would demonstrate that the RSS, though it had no nest of German spies to monitor, was nonetheless earning its keep.

The circulation of the report, however, resulted in a bloody bureaucratic battle. When the document reached MI 6, Major Cowgill, the chief of its counterespionage section, was furious that his turf had been encroached upon and declared on more than one occasion that "Lieutenant Trevor-Roper ought to be court-martialed." In the end Gill and Trevor-Roper were reprimanded for having deciphered the documents and forbidden to do so again, since this work was the province of the GCCS.

In true bureaucratic fashion, after the storm had blown over, relations between the units were patched up, and business continued as usual, but with a twist. Raw materials continued to be sent to GCCS, and deciphered materials were simply sent to a new source at Bletchley Park, Oliver Strachey, elder brother of Lytton Strachey, who was interested in their work and uninterested in turf protection. Later Oliver Strachey was succeeded by Trevor-Roper's former classical tutor at Oxford, Denys Page, which made things easier.

Trevor-Roper continued to specialize in German intelligence, but by the early summer of 1944 the goals of MI 5 began to change. By this point the war was essentially won; it was just a question of how long and how many men it would take. In the eyes of the intelligence community, it was also time to prepare for the rebuilding of Germany and for the postwar world. In September 1945 Trevor-Roper went to Germany to assess conditions there. The war in Europe had been over since May, and Trevor-Roper believed that this would be his last military assignment. His prewar position as a research fellow at Merton College allowed him to apply for an early release from the service, which he did in the autumn of 1945. However, his immediate superior, Dick White, later head of MI 5 and MI 6, was growing impatient with the Russians. Even by the fall of 1945 there was still no conclusive evidence about what had happened to Hitler. The Russians, who had reached Berlin first, claimed that Hitler was alive. Dick White wanted to find out, and having read several of Trevor-Roper's intelligence reports on earlier matters, asked him to do it. Trevor-Roper was given complete access to all materials and facilities in the British zone, and American authorities in Frankfurt quickly offered the same privileges to him in the American zone.

Commencing his investigation, Trevor-Roper soon discovered that most of the existing information was false, usually based on ignorance, willful distortion, or self-aggrandizement. The most promising lead came from Field Marshall Zhukov, the Russian commanding general. Zhukov announced that before his death or disappearance, Hitler, according to diaries discovered in the bunker, had married Eva Braun. The diaries referred to by Zhukov suddenly loomed large as a source of information. Trevor-Roper decided to collect as much evidence as possible from sources in the British and American zones and use it to negotiate with the Russians for the diaries and any other information they might have.

Luckily, a few facts could be established with some level of certainty. Already in Allied hands were a core of men who had spent considerable time with Hitler, particularly high-ranking military officers, such as Doenitz, Keitel, and Jodl, as well as high-ranking civilians, such as Speer. While Hitler had dismissed these men along with many others from his bunker on April 22, 1945, they were able to testify to Hitler's state of mind in the last days of the war and to identify those who remained behind.

From this information Trevor-Roper was able to find and interrogate seven people who had remained in the bunker with Hitler and who were in the best position to know what happened to him. Trevor-Roper also chose this time to ask the Russians for access to the diaries mentioned by Marshall Zhukov, but while the Russians acknowledged these requests, they never filled them. As it turned out, Trevor-Roper was not able to examine the diaries until after he had submitted his report to MI 5. But, from those who had remained in the Bunker with Hitler, Trevor-Roper was able to ascertain that Hitler had first married his longtime mistress, Eva Braun; the two of them had then committed suicide, and their bodies had been soaked with gasoline and burned, the explanation now almost universally accepted about Hitler's demise.

At the time, however, it was not widely accepted. Trevor-Roper turned his findings in to MI 5 in a fairly terse report on November 1, 1945. Dick White was entirely satisfied, but it raised some protest and acrimony in other circles of MI 5, and the Russians said it was "very interesting." Trevor-Roper, a little bruised by its reception, also had acquired from his earlier work in intelligence a certain level of understanding and a wealth of materials on the Nazis in general. Dick White suggested that he write a longer book, which would take his findings about Hitler's death to the public, and also interpret some broader themes about the collapse of the Nazis. Trevor-Roper returned to Oxford in 1946, first to his research fellowship at Merton and later to a position as a fellow and tutor (known as "student") at Christ Church, his own undergraduate college. During the summer of 1946 he wrote the manuscript that became *The Last Days of Hitler*. Published in 1947, the book became a best-seller and vaulted Trevor-Roper into academic prominence. The journalist Malcolm Muggerridge remembers having Trevor-Roper to dinner shortly after the book had been published. Muggerridge described his guest as a "youthful don, intelligent, rather full of himself as a result of the great success of his book."[11] Recently into its fifth edition, *The Last Days of*

Hitler remains as fresh and readable as it was when it was first published, fifty years ago. At several points in his later career, Trevor-Roper returned to the Nazis and to the cloak and dagger world of spies and espionage, clearly interests nurtured during his military service.

The involvement of American historians in World War II generally parallels that of British historians, although there are some striking differences. Almost all the English served in the military in some capacity. Among the Americans, some taught, some worked on the home front, still others opposed at least intellectually the war, and some did little for the war effort. But there are some clear similarities. Few Americans were in much danger, most of the Americans who did military service served in intelligence, and several, like Trevor-Roper, managed to write books.

William McNeill was in the midst of graduate school at Cornell when he was drafted in the summer of 1941, even before Pearl Harbor. He entered the peacetime army and received a cultural shock. The peacetime army was a motley group, containing people from the lowest, most uneducated and unrefined elements of American society, similar to the dregs described in James Jones's *From Here to Eternity*. As a faculty brat who had spent all his life in the genteel cloister of academic life, McNeill received a jolting introduction to the behaviors and attitudes of people with whom he was completely unfamiliar. McNeill did basic training in Texas and joined the regular army as a private in Hawaii in 1942. After nearly a year in that rank, he was summoned to Officer Candidate School and then rose to command a battery of Puerto Rican troops in the Caribbean. Then, discovering McNeill's expertise in languages, the army personnel system caught up to him, and he spent almost two years as an intelligence officer in Greece, where the U.S. Army worked uneasily with the British. He wrote a book about Greece in World War II, *The Greek Dilemma: War and Aftermath*. In 1947 he returned to Cornell to complete his graduate work.[12]

In December 1941 Gordon Craig was teaching at Yale when the news of the attack on Pearl Harbor came over the radio. He had been married since 1939, and he and his wife had already had a small child. When the war came, Yale got nervous about the possibility of declining enrollment and fired all of its faculty who did not have a Yale connection. The faculty who were terminated included Douglas Adair, Theodore Mommsen, and Craig. "It was a stupid thing for Yale to do," Craig recalled later with some bitterness; "I would have stayed at Yale, but money talks."[13]

Despite his disappointment, Craig rushed to Washington to see about a job in the Office of Strategic Services (OSS) and found himself surrounded by historians already assembled by William Langer, including Carl Schorske and Stuart Hughes.[14] In the OSS, Craig worked in the African section where he became an expert in the topography of Africa, and he later worked in the State Department. From 1944 to 1946 he was a captain in the United States

Marine Corps and a member of the Strategic Bombing Survey. Part of his Marine service included duty in the Pacific in the Marshall Islands and Rabaul immediately after the war.[15]

In many ways the war experience was valuable for him. In Washington he learned the machinery of diplomacy and made many new friends with similar interests and backgrounds. The most difficult part of the experience concerned his family. During the war his wife and their young children were essentially marooned in Arlington, Virginia, while Craig worked in Washington. The State Department was a demanding taskmaster. Craig's hours were often long and unpredictable. He saw his family when the demands of the job permitted, which placed an enormous burden on his wife and was very disruptive to his family.

Carl Schorske also served in the OSS, which he had joined a few months before Pearl Harbor. The Research and Analysis Branch of the OSS to which Schorske was attached has sometimes been called a second graduate school, and it certainly served this function for Schorske. He was exposed to a wide range of colleagues, fellow Ph.D.'s and graduate students in European history, German émigrés, and a stellar group of economists. One of the Ph.D's was another Harvard student, Stuart Hughes. The two developed a jovial friendship. On pleasant evenings Hughes would say to Schorske, "Lieber Carl, jetzt sollen wir singen," and Schorske would sing in German in his fine baritone, with others joining in whether or not they knew the language or the words to the song.[16] As much as he benefited from exposure to a diverse group of intellectuals, however, Schorske discovered intelligence gathering and policy formulation were not what he wanted to do.[17]

Intelligence work was not limited to those who specialized in European history. Vann Woodward and Arthur Schlesinger Jr. both Americanists, also worked in this area. After temporary teaching posts at the University of Florida and at the University of Virginia, in 1940 Woodward secured his first permanent post in history at Scripps College in California. Woodward's early years in teaching were fairly lean. His salary at Florida was $1800 a year; at Virginia it was around $2000. But Woodward's years at Scripps were happy. California weather was great, and his only child, a son named Peter, was born in 1943.[18]

When the war came, the faculty at Scripps were divided along pro-French and pro-German lines. Woodward had a German colleague, whom Woodward defended when he was imprisoned and accused of being a spy. Woodward was summoned to the office of the college's president, who attempted to intimidate him into remaining silent. It did not work. Woodward organized other colleagues concerned about academic freedom and succeeded in getting rid of the president, aided by the fact that the faculty member in question had married the daughter of the chairman of the Scripps Board of Regents.[19]

In 1943 Woodward entered the Navy as a lieutenant in the Office of Naval Intelligence and in the Naval Office of Public Information. One of his assignments was to analyze operations in the Pacific theater of the war. His analysis of the operations in the Philippines resulted in his second book, *The Battle for Leyte Gulf*, published in 1947 and the only one of his books that is entirely outside the area of Southern history. Woodward described the engagement as "greatest naval battle of the Second World War and the largest engagement ever fought on the high seas." Outside his usual area of research, *The Battle of Leyte Gulf* demonstrated Woodward's ability to master rapidly a range of new sources and construct a readable and authoritative narrative account from them.[20]

Arthur Schlesinger also managed to write a book while in the service of his country, though in his case it was a book based upon his own research, not that undertaken for intelligence. Before the war, during his tenure as a member of Harvard's Society of Fellows, Schlesinger had begun to work on a new interpretation of the Jacksonian era. In the fall of 1941 he delivered a series of lectures to Boston's Lowell Institute that were the basis for his new interpretation. On December 7, 1941, he and his first wife, Marian Canon, were having a Sunday dinner with his parents in Cambridge when Bernard DeVoto, his formidable undergraduate tutor from the history and literature program at Harvard, called with the news.[21]

Schlesinger, already the father of two little boys, quickly moved to Washington, D.C., to serve first with the Office of War Information and later with the OSS. But he was also close to finishing his projected work on the age of Jackson. While in Washington he worked during the day at his intelligence duties. At night and on weekends he labored on the Jackson book. In June 1944 as he awaited a transfer to a new OSS assignment in Europe, he signed a contract for *The Age of Jackson* with Little, Brown. Here he was fortunate to have an educated wife and a historian for a father. Serving in Europe, he was unavailable for any of the odious tasks that comprise the final stages of book production. *The Age of Jackson* was guided through the final stages of publication by his wife and father.[22]

Other historians served on the home front. Edmund Morgan's situation was perhaps the most unusual. Like Gordon Craig at Yale, he was an early academic casualty of the war. Recently married, with a child on the way, Morgan was informed by Harvard after Pearl Harbor, that his tutoring position would not be renewed. In 1940 he had also withdrawn his application for conscientious objector status as a pacifist, and he had not yet finished his dissertation. He decided not to join most of his Harvard cohorts by going to Washington and joining the OSS. Instead, he took evening classes at a local high school to become a machinist. The class was supposed to last three months. But after six weeks Morgan decided he knew as much as they could teach him, and he took a position as a machinist in a radiation laboratory at MIT, immediately making more money there than he had as a Harvard tutor. Always good at working with his hands, Morgan advanced quickly at the laboratory, finding the work generally challenging. After several years of eleven-hour days during the week and six-hour days on Saturday, however, it ceased to be challenging. By the war's end Morgan was glad to be out of the machinist's business and back to academic life.[23]

Although he worked grueling hours at the laboratory Morgan did manage to do research and finish his dissertation. With his continuing interest in the Puritan family, he had come across the diary of Michael Wigglesworth, on which he spent what little free time he had deciphering and transcribing. While working in the rare book room of the Boston Public Library, he met the library's rare book specialist, Zoltan Haraszti. Haraszti took an interest in Morgan's work, asked to see his dissertation, and eventually brought it out as a book called *The Puritan Family* under the library's imprint in 1944. In the book Morgan argued, among other things, that the Puritans were not always the austere, humorless, witch-hunting bigots they were often portrayed as being.

Barbara Tuchman's wartime experience was also unique. She had left Radcliffe College in 1933, eager to escape the shelter of academe for a more active life. She first went to work at the Institute of Pacific Relations, initially in New York City and later in Tokyo. In 1936 she returned from Asia and began working for *The Nation*, which her father had bought to keep it from going bankrupt. Her first job was clipping newspaper articles, but soon she was writing feature articles and covering important stories, including Roosevelt's 1936 presidential campaign and the initial stages of the Spanish Civil War, which she covered from Valencia and Madrid. She also managed to find the time to write a short book on British policy toward Spain and the western Mediterranean, *The Lost British Policy: Britain and Spain since 1700*, published in Britain in 1938. In later life Tuchman made only modest claims for the book and sometimes omitted it from her list of publications. Like many others, she also became energized by the Spanish Civil War and devoted some time to raising money in America on behalf of the Republican cause and also contributing articles to London's *New Statesman* about American attitudes to events in Europe.[24]

In 1940 she married Lester R. Tuchman, a New York internist. At an early stage in the marriage Tuchman exhibited her steely will. Before their marriage her husband told her that in a world gripped by depression and threatened by war, it was a mistake to have children. Tuchman, who wanted children badly, replied that if they had to wait for the world to improve, they might wait forever. Their first child, a daughter, was born almost exactly nine months after their wedding. After Pearl Harbor, Dr. Tuchman was sent to a military hospital overseas, and Tuchman found time to care for her baby and to assist the war effort by working in New York for the Office of War

Information, preparing material on the Far East for use in broadcasts to Nazi-occupied areas.

Anne Firor spent the early 1940s working for a California congress-man and acquiring a master's degree in political science. The war served in many ways to provide new avenues for women to advance in government. In 1944 the president of the National League of Women Voters, watching her staff depart for better opportunities in government, offered Firor a position on her staff. While the league still concentrated on getting women to vote, Scott found herself dealing with a multitude of issues, including public policy, economics, and international problems, and she learned a great deal about the mechanics of a women's voluntary organization.[25]

Most of the other American men taught during the war. In 1936 David Potter began his teaching career as an instructor at the University of Missis-sippi, and in 1938 he moved to what was then Rice Institute. While teaching at Mississippi and Rice, he worked on his dissertation, which concerned the policies of Lincoln and the Republican Party during the secession crisis of 1860–61 and for which Potter received his doctorate from Yale in 1940. In 1942 he returned to Yale as an assistant professor.

He quickly submitted his dissertation to the Yale University Press, which published it in 1942 as *Lincoln and His Party in the Secession Crisis*. In this book Potter argued that historians had been misled by hindsight and the feeling that the outbreak of Civil War in the United States in 1861 was inevitable. Potter discovered that by 1860 Lincoln and the Republicans tended to dis-miss Southern threats of secession since Southerners had threatened this course of action so many times before that they now lacked credibility. Lin-coln conceived a strategy of ignoring the secession of the Deep Southern states in the hope that the more moderate states would remain in the Union and eventually convince the others to remain as well. Moreover, Lincoln tried to ignore the slavery issue, but his hands were tied. The Republicans were a minority; concessions to the South on slavery would be political sui-cide. So Lincoln pursued a policy of calculated indecision, saying nothing inflammatory about either secession or slavery and hoping the crisis would eventually subside. The strategy failed when Lincoln decided that he had an obligation to resupply Fort Sumter.

John Hope Franklin, Daniel Boorstin, and Oscar Handlin also taught during the war. By the time the United States entered the war, Franklin had already accumulated considerable teaching experience. A year at his under-graduate alma mater, Fisk College, while still pursuing his degree, proved a trial by fire. With five preparations in disparate fields and over two hundred students, he learned more history in his first year of teaching than in all of his graduate work. In 1939 he began teaching at St. Augustine's College. When the United States entered the war, Franklin was prepared to serve, but sev-eral blatant examples of prejudice shook his faith in his country and its leaders. He was aware that white historians who did not hold advanced degrees were serving in the War Department. Franklin made application, but was denied. Later the Navy sent out an urgent plea for men of education to do office work who would be given the rank of petty officer. Franklin again made application, but was denied. When his draft board ordered him to report for a physical, he was not allowed inside the doctor's office and was told to wait on a bench in the hall. When he insisted that the doctor see him immediately, a clerk interceded on his behalf, but Franklin had concluded that the United States "did not deserve me." He spent the remainder of the war outwitting his draft board, in part by taking a position at North Carolina College for Negroes, whose president was on the draft appeal board. The passage of time has not diminished Franklin's anger at his treatment by his country nor of its treatment of a million black men and women who did serve but under conditions of segregation and discrimination.[26]

Since 1938 Daniel Boorstin had been teaching a course in legal history at Harvard and courses in American history and literature at Radcliffe and Harvard. At the same time his seemingly magical glide to the top of the academic ladder continued. In 1940 he received a Doctor of Judicial Science degree from Yale, and in 1941, when he was twenty-seven, the Harvard University press published his first book, *The Mysterious Science of the Law*. In 1942 he was admitted to the Massachusetts bar. After the outbreak of war, Boorstin worked briefly for the lend-lease administration and then taught at Swarthmore College. In 1944 Robert Maynard Hutchens, president of the University of Chicago, hired him to teach in a new interdisciplinary social science program at Chicago, where Boorstin remained for the next twenty-five years.[27]

Like Boorstin, Oscar Handlin already had published a book, *Boston's Immigrants*, before the outbreak of war and had also begun his teaching career at Harvard. During the war he taught in the V-12 program, which was designed to teach history to naval officers.[28] Handlin and his wife, Mary Pflug Handlin, also found time to work on another book, *Commonwealth: A Study of the Role of Government in the American Economy: Massachusetts, 1774–1861*, eventually published in 1947.

Most of the World War II generation, especially the English, served their countries willingly, clearly regarding the war as morally just as war would ever be. There were several scholars, however, who remained ambivalent, and almost all of them were Americans. Pacifism had been a natural reaction of many of this generation to World War I, where it seemed that millions had died due to the incompetence, arrogance, and blundering of diplomats. This disgust with war spilled over into historiography where some historians argued that even the American Civil War was by no means inevitable and could have been prevented but for the blundering of those in power. It also spilled over into the attitudes of several young historians in their attitudes toward World War II, and a small cluster of them taught together at the University of Maryland in the early 1940s. Isolationism in the aftermath of Pearl Harbor was politically very risky. Preparing for his Ph.D. oral at Wisconsin in 1941, Frank Freidel feared that Curtis Nettels, an ardent interventionist, would be on his committee and outraged by Freidel's isolationism, would sabotage his examinations.[29]

The principles of another Wisconsin leftist, Kenneth Stampp, were also tested by the coming of the war. When the news of Pearl Harbor came, Stampp was teaching at the University of Arkansas and preparing for his oral examination on his dissertation, which he passed later in December 1941. Nearly thirty years old, married, and a father, he was never called by his draft board, but he had clear pacifist tendencies anyway. His year at Arkansas was generally pleasant. It was his first real university teaching job; he finished his dissertation, and his son, Ken Jr., was born in Fayetteville. Arkansas was poor, and Stampp was surprised to find himself in the upper income bracket with his university salary. There was a tense moment when Stampp discovered that he would be required to teach a course on the importance of national defense, which he feared he might not be able to teach without compromising his isolationist principles. Writing to Hesseltine, his mentor at Wisconsin, he wondered if he could teach the course "without getting myself run out of town as a Fifth Columnist," but added, "I'll be darned if I'll turn the course into anything but a propaganda machine for the isolationists."[30]

In 1942 Stampp moved to the University of Maryland, which proved more intellectually stimulating. Among Stampp's colleagues at Maryland were Richard Hofstadter and Frank Freidel in history and C. Wright Mills in sociology. Stampp did not see much of Mills, but Hofstadter and Freidel became valued friends, and they met regularly for lunch and family gatherings. Politically very compatible, they shared with Mills a disdain of Roosevelt, a commitment to radical politics, suspicion of draft boards, and distrust of the Maryland administration. They talked and argued history by the hour. Most of the ideas in Hofstadter's first great book, *The American Political Tradition and the Men Who Made It*, had been thoroughly tested on Stampp and Freidel. Stampp also profited by his proximity to the Library of Congress, which had extensive holdings in mid-nineteenth-century newspapers and manuscripts, essential to a book he planned to write on the secession crisis.[31]

Stampp and Freidel were also activists in the American Historical Association. In 1944 Carlton J.H. Hayes of Columbia, a right-wing extremist who believed that liberalism was responsible for the chaotic state of the world and who harbored sympathies for the Franco regime in Spain, had been nominated for the presidency of the association. Stampp and Freidel were part of a group of young radicals determined to prevent Hayes's election, and they started a petitioning campaign on behalf of another candidate, Sidney B. Fay. In the end Hayes, the establishment candidate, prevailed, but not before the insurgents had managed to embarrass him by siphoning off sixty-five votes. It was a mild disappointment to Stampp and Freidel that while Hofstadter signed the petition against Hayes, he shrank from wholehearted support of it and from activism in general.[32]

For Richard Hofstadter the war years brought triumph marred by deep personal tragedy. After his initial struggles at Columbia, Hofstadter concluded his graduate career in a surge of glory, garnering accolades like a victorious Roman general. He had published articles in such important journals as the *American Historical Review*, the *New England Quarterly*, and the *Journal of the History of Ideas*.[33] His dissertation, supervised by Merle Curti, was approved in 1942 and was awarded the Albert J. Beveridge Fund Memorial Award. His oral examination over the dissertation was reportedly judged by the faculty the best at Columbia in twenty-five years. A revised form of the dissertation was shortly accepted for publication by the University of Pennsylvania Press. In the same year, Hofstadter left his teaching post at City College to become an assistant professor of history at the University of Maryland. He and Felice found an apartment in Washington, from which he had to make a long and malodorous bus trip from the central city to suburban College Park. He found Maryland students pleasant and quickly established an intimate friendship with C. Wright Mills, also a member of the Maryland faculty, who was at the time a rising star in sociology. Hofstadter, Mills, and their wives soon became close friends.[34]

But the war threatened to engulf everyone, and Hofstadter was torn by the prospect of military service. Part of him yearned to serve his country, but he was also disgusted by the regimentation of the military and the effect that service would have on his life. Moreover, his radical distrust of politicians made him skeptical of the war aims. He hoped that he would be exempt from the draft because he was teaching courses to fresh army enlistees. He was briefly classified 1A, which he successfully appealed, on the grounds of his status as an "essential civilian." He was later reclassified as 4F because of stomach and allergy problems.

At Maryland he soon befriended Stampp and Freidel, and they located a common enemy in the university's president, "Curly" Byrd, a former football coach who ran the university as though it was a banana republic and he was its dictator. With the American entry into the war, the university was suddenly swamped with students, in part because Byrd had secretly contracted with the army to teach introductory classes to new recruits. To accommodate the mass of new students, Byrd simply changed the existing two-semester system to a three-semester system and proposed to increase the standard teaching load from twelve to eighteen hours, without offering any increase in pay to the faculty.

When Byrd appeared at a meeting organized by Hofstadter and his allies, he was bombarded by angry questions. In response, according to Hofstadter,

Byrd "wrapped himself in the flag," demanding to know why the teaching staff was complaining about working eighteen hours a week when others were out risking their lives in combat, and stormed out of the meeting. Hofstadter and his friends managed to push through a resolution proposing a faculty investigation of how the university had obtained its military contracts.[35] In the end the insurgents triumphed; they did not have to February 14, 2001teach eighteen hours.

Already haunted by the pain of his mother's early death, Hofstadter was again visited by tragedy when his wife, Felice, became ill after giving birth to their son Daniel in December 1943. The delivery was difficult, and Felice remained in the hospital after Daniel's birth to receive treatment for an abscess along the spine as well as for additional exploratory surgery, which revealed a long, embryonic cyst running up her back. A few months later in the early summer of 1944 Felice asked Kay Stampp to feel a thick lump near her waist about which she had become alarmed. The lump turned out to be cancerous. Hofstadter took a leave of absence from Maryland, and the family returned to Buffalo to spare Felice the agony of spending a sweltering summer in Washington and to be where her parents could help Hofstadter care for her and the baby. The Hofstadters were forced to leave most of their books and possessions behind in the hands of the Stampps. In pain and unable to keep food down, Felice suffered mightily over the next year. She died in July 1945, leaving Hofstadter to raise Daniel, who was eventually left in the hands of Felice's grandparents when Hofstadter returned to Maryland.[36]

Even during this terrible time, Hofstadter's career prospered. In 1944 his *Social Darwinism in American Thought* was published by the University of Pennsylvania Press to excellent reviews. Hofstadter also began another work. According to Alfred Kazin, who had known the Hofstadters since the mid-1930s, Hofstadter began to write *The American Political Tradition and the Men Who Made It* on a note pad in Felice's hospital room.[37] The book's melancholy and alienated overtones may emanate from the sad circumstances of its composition. In 1945, still grieving over Felice's death and its grim reminder of the precariousness of life and happiness, Hofstadter found at least some small consolation when he received a fellowship from the publisher Alfred A. Knopf to finish *The American Political Tradition*. In 1946, delighted to leave Maryland, he accepted a new position at Columbia University.

While this group of historians did not include an Audie Murphy or an RAF hero, they did, with a few exceptions, serve their countries admirably and without hesitation. Generally convinced of the rectitude of their cause, they regarded the war as a crusade. While survival was always a major consideration, they fought, they analyzed, they taught, they wrote, and they volunteered on behalf of the crusade against fascism. Some of them were even able to keep up their scholarship while in the service. More subtly, many of them also developed further insights about their discipline from the crucible of military service. Several echoed Gibbon, who believed that he learned more about the fall of the Roman Empire from his two years in the Hampshire militia than from the standard works on the subject. Hugh Trevor-Roper recalled that even though he had written a biography of Archbishop Laud before the war, he did not begin to think seriously about history until his experience in it. He had also considered a career in politics, but he was not impressed by the politicians he encountered during the war, making the choice of history as a career easier.[38] Lawrence Stone remarked that his military service was an important part of his intellectual development, strengthening an existing tendency toward cynicism about human nature.[39] William McNeill and Richard Cobb found that their military experience broadened their understanding of various socioeconomic groups with which they were previously unfamiliar, something doubtless experienced by others as well.[40]

Chapter 6

BUILDING CAREERS IN THE POSTWAR WORLD

With the thousand year Reich and its evil variants vanquished, the heroes dispersed, returning to their homes and loved ones, with a new generation of Homers to sing their songs and tell their tales. But if fascism lay in ruins, other new threats loomed ominously on distant horizons.

In the summer of 1945 Anne Firor shared a house with three other women. On a sweltering August night, she and her housemates heard the news that a hydrogen bomb had been dropped on the Japanese city of Hiroshima, and gathering on an upstairs porch, they could hear the sounds of celebration resound in the streets around them. But with the day of triumph at hand, they were oddly subdued, filled with a sense of dread. If nuclear power could destroy Hiroshima, it could destroy them as well. Firor and her housemates decided to form a club, which they called the "Ten Years to Live Club," in the belief that it would take that long for nuclear war to destroy the entire world.[1]

The prospect of annihilation, however, was not the only ominous cloud on the horizon. If fascism lay in shambles, a new malevolence was rising, one that had already required Americans to reverse their fields on more than one occasion. In the 1930s, especially after the 1939 Russo-German pact, most Americans regarded the Soviet Union as just another totalitarian enemy of freedom. But after the German invasion of the Soviet Union in the summer of 1941, the Soviets were recast as allies with whom we maintained an uneasy but necessary alliance. By the end of the war serious differences between the United States and the Soviet Union had been exposed that raised disturbing issues regarding the nature of the postwar world. Both sides believed that they were primarily responsible for winning the war, the Soviets by tying down millions of German soldiers on the Eastern front, the United States by mounting the assault on Western Europe and winning the war against Japan, against whom the Soviets did not even declare war until August 1945. As the war wound down, the victorious powers began jockeying for the dominant position in the postwar world. In the immediate aftermath of the war the Soviets took steps to assert their control over the buffer state territories, such as Poland, Czechoslovakia, and Hungary, between their borders and those of Germany. The United States seized several Pacific Islands to serve as strategic bases and took steps to assert its control over defeated Japan. Assessing the postwar ambitious of both powers with Richard Kern, a friend teaching at Mills College, Kenneth Stampp echoed Mercutio in wishing to visit a plague on both houses.[2]

Historians had clear roles to play in these disputes. The "Free" world needed to be defended against its totalitarian adversaries, whether Nazi or Communist. Delivering his presidential address to the American Historical Association in 1949, Conyers Read declared, "Total war, whether it be hot or cold, enlists everyone and calls upon everyone to assume his part. The historian is no freer from this obligation than the physicist." Many historians also felt the need to rethink the prevailing doctrine of historical relativism. Relativism suggested that there were no right or wrong answers, just answers that were tailored to particular times. Rejection of relativism and the need to defend the West were certainly linked. In this case defense of the West required that Western institutions and values be shown to be not only superior, but timeless and perdurable.[3]

The pressure to defend Western values mounted as the Soviets began to increase their military might. By 1949 the Soviets possessed nuclear weapons themselves, constructing an A-bomb in 1949 and a hydrogen bomb by 1953. In 1950 the United States Army had one tank division; the Soviet army had thirty. And by the early 1950s the Soviet army had four times as many soldiers as the United States Army. The United States had been gripped by a "Red Scare" before, but the prospect of nuclear annihilation was now part of the stakes, a horror that was compounded when it became apparent that scientists working on nuclear projects had passed information to the Soviets. An obscure senator from Wisconsin named Joseph McCarthy vigorously promoted the idea that there was a widespread Communist conspiracy in progress in the United States and that an extensive network of spies working for the Soviets had penetrated the deepest recesses of American government. For nearly five years McCarthy raged against the Communist menace, holding American politics prisoner to his messianic vision. As remorseless as a medieval inquisitor, McCarthy repeatedly deplored the pervasive influence of Communism in American life. So potent was his message that he ruined dozens of lives without having to produce the evidence behind his charges. Those who opposed him or demanded to see the evidence supporting the charges were denounced as obvious dupes of the conspiracy. People in academic life, at the mercy of easily intimidated trustees and state legislatures, were particularly vulnerable to charges that there were Communists teaching at their institutions.[4]

For the World War II generation of historians the end of the war was both euphoric and sobering. On one hand they survived the war and could now resume their lives. On the other hand there was now the very real possibility they would all be blown up, and there were new subtle and insidious threats emerging. Again various patterns to their behavior in the postwar era emerge. Some continued with the teaching careers they had already begun. Others returned to the university to finish their education. Still others took up their first appointments.

Barbara Tuchman defies these categorizations. First of all, unlike the others, she always remained outside academic life. Moreover, as the wife of a physician, raising three small children in the 1940s, she had little time for scholarship. For a while she chafed at her position as a "Park Avenue matron with no status." As the children grew older, it became a bit easier. In 1948 she began work on the history of the Palestinian Question. With the help of a nanny to care for the children, she began research, although she could never work more than half-days on it. After nearly seven years of interrupted, sporadic effort, she finished the book. It took somewhat longer to find a publisher, and the book was not published until 1956. In the meantime she began to work on World War I, and in particular on the Zimmerman telegram, which heightened tensions between the United States and Germany before the American entry into the war. *The Zimmerman Telegram* was published in 1958 and helped provide some of the background for her greatest book, *the Guns of August*, also about World War I, which was published in 1962, winning the first of her Pulitzer Prizes.[5]

For those who were teaching or ready to begin their teaching careers immediately after the war, the opportunities were enormous. The American university in the late 1940s was still a largely sleepy, not entirely formed institution, leagues from the megaversity of the 1990s. Department heads and deans were often petty despots, but all in all a mantle of gentility swathed academic life. After the war this changed. The G.I. Bill paid for the college education of veterans, and returning veterans stampeded into unprepared universities. Eager to make up for lost time and driven to succeed as quickly as possible, the students of the immediate postwar generation comprised possibly the best generation of students American universities have ever had. "My God, you people were the best," Gordon Craig said at the end of his career to some of his former students at Princeton from those days. He remembers them, taking notes furiously, discussing issues passionately, often with their pregnant wives sitting next to them in the lecture hall, knitting baby clothes. Edmund Morgan remembers his University of Chicago pupils as a strange amalgam of "baby fat and bomber jackets." At Harvard Arthur Schlesinger found the G.I. Bill students to be a vast improvement over the mandarins of the 1930s. At Queens College J.H. Hexter thought the post-war students were wonderful because "there was no goddamn nonsense about them." At least part of the bond between the students and faculty in the immediate postwar period concerned their closeness in their age and experience. Craig felt particularly close to his fellow veterans and faintly suspicious of those, student and faculty, who were not.[6]

For some, there was little change. David Potter, Oscar Handlin, John Hope Franklin, and Daniel Boorstin had taught during the war and continued teaching at the same institutions. At Yale David Potter began to gather accolades for his work on the beginning of the Civil War. In 1947–48 he served as the Harmsworth Professor of American History at Oxford University. In 1950 he was appointed William Robertson Coe Professor of American History at Yale. In the same year he delivered the Walgreen Lectures at the University of Chicago, which served as the basis for his greatest book, *People of Plenty*, published in 1954. He also found the time to edit the *Yale Review* from 1949 to 1951.[7]

Oscar Handlin had been teaching at Harvard since 1940, and after the war he continued his prodigious rate of publication in collaboration with Mary Flug Handlin. In 1951 he published his greatest book, *The Uprooted*, a modern epic, biblical in its scope and dimension, about the exodus of some thirty million immigrants who left Europe for the United States after 1820. By the late 1950s Handlin was publishing almost a book a year. In several of them he expanded his research about immigrants and ethnicity, but in others he explored new frontiers, such as a study of New York's governor in the 1920s, Al Smith, the philosopher John Dewey, and race relations. He also served as the chief editor for *The Harvard Guide to American History*.[8]

In the early 1950s Handlin received a generous offer from the University of Chicago, which amounted to roughly four times his Harvard salary. He took the offer to McGeorge Bundy, then the Dean of the Harvard Faculty of Arts and Sciences. Bundy offered little comfort and pleaded with Handlin to stay on the basis of loyalty to the department and university. The ranks of the History Department, Bundy asserted, were about to be depleted. Samuel Eliot Morison, Frederick Merk, and Arthur M. Schlesinger Sr. were ready to retire. Handlin's departure would essentially destroy the Americanist section of the department. Bundy urged Handlin to stay at Harvard, even though he made no effort to match the Chicago offer. Handlin found Bundy's appeal to his institutional loyalty compelling, and he stayed at Harvard out of a sense of duty, never asking, even at the height of his success, for additional compensation.[9]

John Hope Franklin was teaching at North Carolina College at Durham when the war was over. In 1947 he moved on to Howard University in Washington, D.C., where he stayed until 1956. Less than ten years into his career, while writing his second book, Franklin was approached by the president of a respected, historically black liberal arts college about becoming the dean of that college. The president flew to Howard the next day to persuade Franklin to accept. But Franklin was adamant, as he would be for the rest of his career, in his determination to remain as a teacher and a writer of history.[10]

The 1950s saw the rapid growth of the civil rights movement, and Franklin, having regularly felt the sting of racism and segregation throughout his life, became deeply involved. In the early 1950s the National Association for the Advancement of Colored People asked him to serve as an expert witness in the case of Lyman Johnson, who sought admission to the all-white graduate program at the University of Kentucky. This was an issue close to Franklin's heart. He had been barred from entering graduate school at the University of Oklahoma in the thirties. He was able to demonstrate that Johnson could not get the same training at Kentucky State College for Negroes that he could at the University of Kentucky. The case was clinched when the university put one of its history professors on the stand and asked him about teaching Negroes. He replied that he did not teach Negroes; he taught history.

Soon after that, Thurgood Marshall asked Franklin to serve on his non-legal research staff when the NAACP Legal Defense Fund sought to challenge segregation in public schools. Throughout the late summer and fall of 1953, Franklin left Washington every Thursday afternoon for New York, where he worked for the NAACP until Sunday afternoon. He wrote historical essays, coordinated the work of other researchers, and provided the necessary historical context for the lawyers preparing the case.

In 1956 Franklin accepted a position as head of the History Department at Brooklyn College. A great deal of fanfare and celebration accompanied the appointment, which was an astonishing breakthrough. Brooklyn was an important college, and Franklin would chair a department of fifty-two historians. It was quite unusual for anyone in the 1950s to have appointed an African American, even one as distinguished as Franklin, to such a position. But even in a moment of triumph, Franklin was not spared the indignities that accompanied his race. When it came time to buy a house, the new chair of the Brooklyn College history department could not find any of the thirty-odd realtors who offered homes in the Brooklyn College area to show him any of their listings. Consequently, he had to hunt for a house privately. When he found one he liked, he discovered that his insurance company, which promoted the fact that it had fifty million dollars to lend potential home buyers, would not lend him its money because the home he wanted was several blocks beyond where blacks should live. Franklin canceled the insurance policy and was turned down for a loan by every bank in New York, except one in Brooklyn where his lawyer had connections. All in all it took him over a year to find a house, secure the loan, and move in.

Daniel Boorstin's immediate postwar career was the most controversial. Teaching at Chicago since 1944, he continued his career as a productive scholar. In 1948 he published *The Lost World of Thomas Jefferson*. Even in 1948 so much had been written about Jefferson that it was hard for a scholar to say something original about him. But Boorstin managed. Jefferson has sometimes been viewed as an Enlightenment ideologue, deriving his ideas and values from the European Enlightenment. According to Boorstin, no understanding of Jefferson is possible unless one understands the juxtaposition of the intellectual and the frontier in his life. Jefferson was an intellectual, but one must also grasp the fact that he was at the same time a frontier farmer, who had to be pragmatic and practical. Jefferson, like most other early Americans, arrived at a flexible philosophy. Abstract thought was important, but limited. No ideas were valid unless they were tested in the beaker of real-life experience.

Boorstin applied the ideas of practicality and pragmatism to the broader sweep of American history in 1953 when he published *The Genius of American Politics*. In the book Boorstin argued that America has succeeded by approaching problems pragmatically, without ideas based on preconceived ideologies. *The Genius of American Politics* served as a trial run for Boorstin's great trilogy on the "American Experience," which began with *The Americans: The Colonial Experience*, published in 1958. In this book Boorstin employed a bold and inventive narrative style. Instead of constructing, as most historians do, a narrative based on a chronological structure, he told his story through anecdotes, aphorisms, and the masterly marshaling of crucial details.

The Americans: The Colonial Experience repeated several of Boorstin's themes from earlier books. Over and over again, he demonstrated the futility of preconceived plans for the American colonies. Once again, he stressed the pragmatic, practical ways by which the colonists transformed the colonial wilderness into a civilization. *The Americans: The Colonial Experience* was awarded Columbia University's Bancroft Prize for books in American history, diplomacy, and international relations in 1959.[11]

The Americans: The Colonial Experience aroused a lively intellectual debate, but Boorstin was also at the epicenter of another distressing academic debate in the 1950s. With the rising Communist menace and the need to defend Western values manifest, the question arose about whether membership in the Communist Party disqualified one to hold an academic position. A number of alleged former Communists were summoned before congressional committees to answer questions about their own activities and to implicate others. Several distinguished historians and intellectuals, including Samuel Flagg Bemis, Richard Hofstadter, and Sidney Hook, argued that it was the duty of Americans to implicate those suspected if Communist leanings. Others, such as Arthur Schlesinger Jr., argued that it was not. In this debate Boorstin occupied a frontline position. In 1938–39 he had been a member of the Communist Party, but he had resigned from it. In his own public work he had clearly renounced his former positions and advanced new arguments that served to strengthen the idea of the superiority of the West.

In 1953 Boorstin was called to testify before the House Committee on Un-American Activities. He cooperated fully with the committee. He not only reported on his own activities in 1938–39, but also gave information about his associates and concurred with his questioners that no Communist should be allowed to teach at an American university and that the committee had not in any way impinged upon his academic freedom. He concluded by describing the ways he had personally opposed Communism. First, in the belief that religion was a bulwark against Communism, he explained that he was active in the Hillel Foundation at Chicago and had opposed Communism in his own work by discovering and endeavoring to explain to students the unique virtues of American democracy.[12]

Several of this group of historians returned to school. Anne Firor's world changed rapidly after she and her friends had formed the "Ten Years to Live Club." Within a few months, two of her housemates had married, and a third enrolled at Columbia's Russian Institute. Firor was left to find new housemates and continue work with the League of Women Voters, which put her to work writing pamphlets about the control of atomic energy. An even bigger change occurred when a brash young man named Andrew Scott asked her to marry him and go to Harvard with him, "an offer [she] couldn't refuse."[13]

At Harvard Scott was intrigued by the program in American civilization, but needed financial help. When she asked Bernice Cronkhite, then the Dean of the Graduate School, for a fellowship, Cronkhite fixed a steely glare upon her and said, "do you expect to complete the Ph.D.?" Scott had given no previous thought to the matter, but needed the fellowship badly, so she said yes. At Harvard Scott worked hard, learned how to challenge authority, and found inspiring teachers, such as Benjamin Wright, Kenneth Murdoch, and F.O. Matthiessen.

Her most inspiring teacher was Oscar Handlin. She had originally thought of herself as a political scientist, but when her political science advisor became a college president, she turned to Handlin, her most challenging professor. Together they decided that Scott would investigate the Southern Progressives, a group sometimes thought to be a contradiction in terms. So Scott found herself, almost accidentally, studying for a Ph.D. history.

Scott's path to the doctorate was destined to be circuitous. When her husband received his Harvard degree, they moved to Washington, D.C., where he planned to work in international affairs. The sum of their planning focused upon his career, which Scott did not at the time find odd. She used her time to work on the Southern Progressives at the Manuscript Room of the Library of Congress. The atmosphere of the Manuscript Room was congenial, and she found reading the manuscripts fascinating. She was occasionally disconcerted by the sight of renowned scholars who would appear briefly in the Manuscript Room go precisely to the required collection, find exactly what they wanted, and depart. She envied them. For her, archival research would be a longer haul.

The delights of archival discovery came to an abrupt halt with the birth of her first child in 1950. Children, and especially a first child, seem to require all a parent's time and devotion. For a while Scott looked into her future and "saw nothing but diapers and baby food for years to come." The baby, however, turned out to be charming and agreeable, not always a little demon devouring Scott's time and sanity. Soon she could be left with a nursemaid. Scott eventually took a part-time job the League of Women Voters, this time as the editor of the league's magazine the *National Voter.*

Child rearing and editorial duties pushed her work on the Southern Progressives aside. But in the mid-fifties, Andrew Scott returned to academic life, first at Dartmouth College and later at Haverford College. In "the snow-enclosed and male-dominated environment of Dartmouth College" she managed to finish several chapters of her dissertation. But by then the next baby had arrived, and by the time they moved to Haverford, there was a third child. The burgeoning family appeared to be quite sufficient to discourage scholarly ambitions. At this point, Scott was rescued from complete domestic drudgery by the American Association of University Women, which provided funds to pay for a nursemaid while Scott worked, which was perhaps the first time that funds were appropriated by the AAUW for that particular purpose. Seven years after she passed her Ph.D. examinations, Scott had reached a summit: the dissertation was now completed. Part of the drive to complete it had been supplied by the constant hectoring of Oscar Handlin. When her children were born, Scott would write Handlin with the news. Handlin would respond with congratulations, and a question, "are you back at work?" When she successfully defended her dissertation, Scott sought out Bernice Cronkhite, the dean who had asked if Scott intended to complete her degree, to thank her for her help. "I always knew you would finish," Cronkhite replied, indicating a prescient confidence Scott had rarely felt.

Before the degree had quite been completed, Scott, emerging one spring afternoon from the Haverford Library, encountered one of Haverford's historians who was about to take a sabbatical leave. He asked if Scott knew a young man in the profession who would be interested in a one-year appointment at Haverford. Scott agreed to think about it, but as she walked across the campus, it occurred to her that this was a job that she would like. She wheeled around, raced back across campus, and intercepted the friend. "Tom, why not me?" she asked. He looked perplexed, but open to the idea, and agreed to present the matter to the acting president of the college, who was, she noted later, fortuitously a sailing companion of her husband's, and she got the job.

The career of Gertrude Himmelfarb and that of Anne Scott have some interesting parallels. After the war Himmelfarb won a fellowship to study at Cambridge University to which her husband, Irving Kristol, followed her while he worked on an abortive novel that aimed to understand the mind of the anti-Semite. With her fellowship Himmelfarb was the family breadwinner, and she decided to keep her maiden name, though this was mostly accidental; she preferred not to bother with hassle of the paperwork. At Cambridge Himmelfarb worked on the papers of Lord Acton, the great nineteenth-century historian and the subject of her dissertation.

In 1947 they returned to the United States. Kristol took an editing job with *Commentary*, then a fledgling magazine of the American Jewish community, while Himmelfarb finished her dissertation, which was completed in 1950. In the early 1950s Kristol resigned from *Commentary* and moved back to Britain to assume the editorship of another fledgling journal, *Encounter*, secretly funded by the CIA, as an anticommunist journal, although Kristol did not know it at the time. While Kristol edited the journal, Himmelfarb returned to the Cambridge University library to undertake a study of Darwin.

By the time they returned to the United States in 1958, Himmelfarb occupied a curious position. She had two small children and two well-received books, and no academic position. In some ways this suited her perfectly. She could spend time with her children and have time for her research.

William McNeill was discharged from the army in 1946 and returned to Cornell where he finished his degree in 1947. In 1947 he was hired by his undergraduate alma mater, the University of Chicago, where he would teach until his retirement. The University of Chicago was once again a nerve center of higher education. The faculty now included a higher number of European refugees, many of them of extraordinary distinction. The influx of new faculty created a different order of culture and a new climate of opinion. The stimulating undergraduate courses in great books of the Western tradition continued along with the intense discussions among the faculty about whether these courses should be taught. The postwar students were excellent. McNeill learned to read German in order to acquire a deeper understanding of his subject material.[14]

McNeill's career also took several new directions. He had already written a book on contemporary Greece, *Greek Dilemma: War and Aftermath*, published in 1947, while he was still in the army. A follow-up volume appeared in 1948, written with his wife, Elizabeth Darbyshire McNeill, and Frank Smothers, as well as a handbook for a course in Western civilization. And McNeill had ideas for other books, including one on the wartime relations between the United States, Great Britain, and the Soviet Union. Fortunately, there was a great deal of grant support available for faculty research. In the 1950s McNeill had a Ford Foundation Grant for an entire year. He found, however, that with a whole year just to write, he became a bit isolated and lonely. Drawing from this experience, he was able a few years later to persuade the Rockefeller Foundation to spread out a subsequent grant over five years, so that he could teach for two quarters, then take two quarters off to write.

During this time McNeill also became aware of a deficiency in his training and that of most historians trained in the United States. The historical profession in the United States in the 1950s tended to be geared toward finding students fairly narrow dissertation topics based on original documents. They would turn the results into a book that would get them tenure and perhaps serve as the basis for a second book, which would allow them to get promoted to full professor. Thus, the profession tended to reward those who stayed close to their dissertation topics, resulting in the production of historians who are generally trained in fairly narrow specializations. McNeill was not comfortable with this progression. As someone who had always been attracted to grand thinkers, such as Toynbee, who tried to see the grand sweep of history, McNeill began to work on books that would also engage the big picture. In the tradition of Toynbee, he began to work on a study of the rise of the West, which would become his greatest book.

Others took up their first appointments. The University of Chicago had offered Edmund Morgan a job while he was still working in the radiation laboratory at MIT. Unable to accept the job at that point, Morgan told Chicago he would be interested when the war was over. In September 1945 he received a telegram from Chicago again offering the job, which he was delighted to accept.[15]

At Chicago he taught English composition and Social Science I, which was really American history. Teaching American history was easy, but the composition course was difficult to teach because, in Morgan's words, you can tell a class the rules of English composition in about an hour. The problem for the instructor is to get the students to apply the rules in actual practice. You can do it by meeting with them individually to go over their compositions, but to do that in class in Morgan's judgment was a waste of time. He could never figure how to fill up the time and would often wake up in the middle of the night wondering what he would do in class the next day.

The University of Chicago right after the war was an exciting place, full of discussion of great books and issues, and the meaning of a liberal education. It was, Morgan recalled, like "being sort of intellectually goosed every minute of the day," though there was never enough time to do anything about it. Morgan was often left intellectually exhausted, "like one of these pigs who's been put in a pen and jabbed with an electric prod until he goes crazy."

After a year at Chicago, Jim Hedges, the chair of the history department at Brown, called to ask Morgan if he would like to teach American colonial history at Brown. Morgan quickly said yes, and found Brown an ideal place to teach. Hedges and Henry Wriston, the president of the university, regarded their task as administrators to protect faculty from any outside interferences, including that of McCarthy, the trustees, or alumni. No one "so much as breathed at him" at Brown. Some pressures did exist. One alumnus reportedly threatened to withdraw a five-million-dollar donation unless a certain member of the philosophy department was fired. Wriston told the alumnus that it was none of his business what was taught in the philosophy department.

Morgan was on leave at the Huntington Library in San Marino, California, when his city upon a hill at Brown evaporated. Wriston had gotten a major corporate grant to develop a new curriculum. Under the new grant, each department was to offer a course in "The Identification and Criticism of Ideas." Hedges was not interested in having the department develop such a course, but a member of the department, seeking favor with Wriston, went to Wriston and volunteered to teach one of the courses. Hedges resigned on the spot as chair. Morgan, away in California, and the only faculty member uninvolved in the turmoil, got stuck with being chair upon his return. At the same time, his closest friend at Brown, Barnaby C. Keeney, was about to be named as Wriston's successor. Morgan was skeptical about being at a university where his best friend was the president. While he sat in the ruins of Brown ruminating on its decline and fall, Yale offered him a job as a full professor with the understanding that he would teach only early American history and nothing else. When he asked Hedges whether or not he should go, Hedges replied, "Brown is Brown, but Yale is Yale. You ought not to stay here. You ought to go on."

The fifties were an extremely productive time for Morgan. He edited the diary of the Puritan Michael Wigglesworth, which he published in 1951. In the next year he published the brief *Virginians at Home*, extending to Virginia the study of domestic life he had undertaken for the New England Puritans. In 1953 Morgan published one of his greatest books, *The Stamp Act Crisis: Prologue to Revolution*. Reflecting what would be a career-long interest in understanding the American Revolution, Morgan established the importance of the Stamp Act of 1765 in the Revolution's origins. When the British attempted to raise money to maintain their empire in the American colonies in the 1760s, they imposed through Parliament a new set of taxes on the colonies by requiring that certain documents be printed on stamped paper. In response the colonists argued that this was a violation of their rights as Englishmen. For Morgan this assertion was of supreme significance. The resort, he wrote, to "those magic words, 'rights of Englishmen,' which more than once had measured the tread of marching feet," was a crucial step. When the British defended the authority of Parliament, both sides embraced positions that could not be easily reconciled. The Stamp Act was thus a crucial prologue to revolution.

Edmund Morgan's most popular book, however, was published in 1958 and marked a return to the study of the Puritans. In his *The Puritan Dilemma: The Story of John Winthrop* Morgan tried to get inside the mind of a man usually regarded as the quintessential Puritan zealot. As Morgan's *The Puritan Family* tempered earlier views of the harshness of Puritan life, *The Story of John Winthrop* exercised a similarly tempering effect on the study of Winthrop. In addition to ranging widely through the social, religious, economic, and political life of the Massachusetts Bay Colony, Morgan demonstrated that Winthrop, far from being an intolerant bigot, was actually a moderating force in Bay Colony life, assailed more by extremists than by moderates. Moreover, *The Story of John Winthrop* was brief, elegantly, even poetically, written, making it a classroom favorite.

When he was released from service in 1946, Carl Schorske was over thirty, married, the father of two children, and without a Ph.D. Fortunately he quickly found what proved to be an ideal teaching post at Wesleyan University, where he stayed for fourteen years. At Wesleyan, President Victor Butterfield's imaginative recruitment and selection of faculty members fostered an atmosphere of multidisciplinary discussion and exploration. In retrospect Schorske recalled that only at a small, intimate college like Wesleyan could he have encountered the kind of openness and discussion among faculty that would allow him to move easily across disciplinary boundaries. Of all his mature experiences, teaching at Wesleyan probably had the greatest impact on the substance of his intellectual life and his understanding of what kind of historian he wanted to be.[16]

One example of an interdisciplinary epiphany came in 1952 when Schorske watched two of his radical friends, the Wesleyan classicist Norman O. Brown and the philosopher Herbert Marcuse collide happily with each other on the road from Marx to Freud. For Schorske, interdisciplinary discourse first came into focus in dealing with literature. When Schorske charged his Wesleyan supporters of the New Criticism with trying to read texts wrenched from the historical context in which they were conceived, they accused him of subverting a text by an excess of relativism. One friendly opponent echoed e. e. cummings as he inveighed against Schorske to "let the poem be." Despite occasional moments of rancor, Schorske learned from his friends in literature how to read in new ways and how a study of form and structure could reveal meanings invisible to those who were attentive mainly to ideas and context. From colleagues in architecture, painting, and other disciplines, he learned the basic techniques of analysis in those disciplines and how to apply them to his historical work.

Schorske's first scholarly work, however, did not incorporate his interdisciplinary insights. Before the war he had begun a study of the origins of German national socialism. After five years of toil, both as a student and as an OSS officer, he had tired of the subject. Like many of his contemporaries, including Peter Gay and Leonard Krieger, he was also interested in the failure of German democracy in the 1920s. Before World War I both German democrats and socialists had been welded into a single party committed to both socialism and democracy. The Weimar Republic had afforded them the opportunity to build a governing coalition. The coalition had of course failed. For Schorske the key questions were not only why it had failed, but why democracy and socialism appeared to be incompatible in Germany.

At the same time he undertook additional work on the issue of contemporary Germany for the Council on Foreign Relations. The members of the council's German study group, headed by Allan Dulles, were intelligent, influential members of America's business and political elite. The "German question" was of course critical to the postwar world. Should Germany be a buffer between Western Europe and the Soviet menace? Should it remain divided? Would the reunification of Germany allow it to rearm? In the council's deliberations Schorske steadily advocated a unified but permanently neutralized Germany. Although the council generously published his analysis of the German question, it rejected his recommendations.[17]

For his first two years at Wesleyan, Schorske had little awareness of the college's interdisciplinary possibilities. Like most veterans, he was just happy to resume academic life, and Wesleyan was teaming with students. The introductory course in Western civilization, which Schorske had taken at Columbia, had just been introduced at Wesleyan. Teaching four sections of the course, Schorske returned to academic life with a vengeance and was able to explore the material fully.

Others, who had begun their careers before the war, resumed them and took advantage of new opportunities. Gordon Craig, jettisoned by Yale after the beginning of the war, had already been offered a job by Raymond Sontag at Princeton and started teaching there in the fall of 1946 after his release from military service. For Craig Princeton immediately after the war was an enchanting place. The students were first-rate, and Joseph Strayer, then the chair of Princeton's history department, was building the department into one of the nation's best. By the late 1950s the department had more majors than any other Princeton department, and the department was packed with outstanding teachers, Strayer himself on medieval Europe, E. Harris Harbison on the Reformation, Eric Goldman on the recent history of the United States, and Craig on modern Germany.[18]

Craig thought Strayer was an excellent chair, willing to sacrifice his own career and work for the good of the department. Moreover, for Craig, the Princeton department lacked the starchiness that prevailed in the Yale history department before the war. At Yale the department had a weekly lunch together at Berkeley College. The center place at high table was reserved for the department chair, who would be flanked in equal balance right and left by the full professors, and then by the associate professors and assistant professors. Assistant professors did not address full professors by their first names, and the chair was a virtual czar.

Princeton was much more informal, and democratic faculty governance prevailed. Department members also saw a lot of each other socially. There were regular dinner parties and family get-togethers with occasionally raucous charade games, all of which contributed to a general sense of solidarity among department members. Strayer was a member of a poker club, which included Frank Craven, Julian Boyd, Jerome Blum, and Craig. Fierce debates over policies and personnel matters could occasionally erupt in the department, but in the end they came out friends. "You fight like tigers, but you respect each other," Julian Boyd once told Craig.

Like Carl Schorske, Gordon Craig was also interested in the historical context for the rise of Hitler. But where Schorske and others had tried to explain the failure of Weimar liberalism to deter the Nazis, Craig and others, such as George Mosse, examined the deeper roots of National Socialism. Craig was particularly interested in the military and diplomatic antecedents, particularly in questions that involved the role of Prussian army. The result of his inquiries was perhaps his greatest book, *The Politics of the Prussian Army*, published in 1955, and another book, *From Bismarck to Adenauer: Aspects of German Statecraft*, published in 1958.

Several historians moved up the career ladder by landing jobs at more prestigious universities. While Richard Hofstadter benefited by being surrounded by extraordinary young faculty members at Maryland, such as Kenneth Stampp, Frank Friedel, and C. Wright Mills, he found the teaching load oppressive and the administration tyrannical. The opportunity to return to Columbia was therefore welcome. Not only did Hofstadter relish the opportunity for less undergraduate and more graduate teaching, but he regarded New York City as far more intellectually stimulating than College Park and the Washington metropolitan area. Moreover, by 1948 Hofstadter had taken steps to rebuild his life following the death of his first wife. His *The American Political Tradition* was regarded in critical circles as a masterpiece of sweeping vision and critical imagination. He also married for the second time, to a young woman named Beatrice Kevitt. In 1952 she gave birth to Hofstadter's second child, a daughter named Sarah.[19]

In the early 1950s Hofstadter pursued a range of scholarly interests. The McCarthy hearings roused his sensitivities, and with Walter Metzger, a Columbia colleague, Hofstadter sought to place them in historical context.[20] Hofstadter's great achievement of the 1950s was *The Age of Reform*, for which he won the Pulitzer Prize in history for 1956. The book considered the dynamic of political and social reform in the United States from 1890 to the 1930s, focusing on the Progressive movement and on Franklin Roosevelt. Hofstadter found reform movements ambiguous, usually conservative in the sense that they were based on wide-eyed nostalgia for romanticized visions of the past. Hofstadter repeatedly stressed the wildly romantic views of the past on which many reform movements were based along with their class and material foundations. He concluded that the New Deal differed from earlier reform movements in that it was based upon pragmatism rather than nostalgia and was the first reform movement to have an urban base.

Kenneth Stampp also departed from Maryland, where he taught during the war. Relief from the Maryland's grinding teaching load was a primary consideration in his decision to leave. At Maryland he normally taught three large survey classes and upper division courses every semester, totaling several hundred students, for which he did all the grading. In 1946 John Hicks, a faculty member at Wisconsin who knew Stampp from graduate school, recommended him for a job at the University of California at Berkeley, which eventually offered Stampp the job. Even though Stampp disliked Maryland, he was at first undecided about whether to accept the offer. At the time he did not even know where Berkeley was and had to get out a map to find it, and the initial offer was only at the instructor level when Stampp was already an associate professor at Maryland. Moreover, Berkeley in the 1940s was not the academic Valhalla it later became. It was very strong in the physical sciences, but less distinguished in the humanities, and had yet to attract a national student body. Stampp decided only with reluctance to accept the offer. He never expected to stay very long at Berkeley; it was too far away from civil war archives. Indeed, when he told Richard Hofstadter about the offer, Hofstadter replied, "You're not going to take it, are you?" But Stampp accepted anyway. The teaching load at Berkeley was much less demanding than at Maryland, and Stampp unexpectedly fell in love with the bay area and the university. Better yet, he arrived in California at exactly the right time. The state prospered in the unprecedented postwar economic boom, and there were abundant funds available for higher education. In the 1950s the university and the history department got virtually everything they wanted. In 1949 Stampp received a handsome offer from the University of Illinois when James G. Randall, the noted Civil War historian, retired. Stampp was tempted by the Illinois job; a position there would have brought him closer to his archival materials. In the end Berkeley and the beauty of the bay area proved too compelling.[21]

Stampp began his career at Berkeley as an assistant professor, but his remarkable rate of publication allowed him to move quickly up. In 1949 his revised dissertation, the publication of which had been delayed by the war, appeared as *Indiana Politics during the Civil War*. In the next year his *And the War Came: The North and the Secession Crisis, 1860–1861* came out. In 1957, on the heels of his greatest triumph, *The Peculiar Institution*, which had been published in 1956, he became Morrison Professor of American History at Berkeley.

Still political, Stampp enthusiastically supported the 1948 presidential campaign of Henry Wallace, who presented himself as an alternative to the red-baiting of the major political parties. Such prominent historians as Ray Alan Billington, Curtis Nettels, and Paul Gates lent enthusiastic support to the Wallace campaign, though it later sputtered and Stampp became somewhat disillusioned. He and another young radical, Richard N. Current, were "among the millions of rats who deserted the sinking Wallace ship before the election." Stampp and Current voted for Farrell Dobbs and the Socialist Workers.[22] In 1952 Stampp voted for Adlai Stevenson, the first time he had ever voted for a candidate from a major party.

The Berkeley history department in the 1950s was in the midst of an exciting and painful transition. The department was divided into two factions. The first, known as the "Boltonians," were the followers of the longtime chair, Herbert Bolton. They had been hired by Bolton and had often, like Stampp, taken their Ph.D.'s at the University of Wisconsin, rather than Ivy League universities. They were interested in preserving as many of the old ways of the university and the history department as possible. The second group was the self-styled "Young Turks," led by a Harvard product, Carl Bridenbaugh. The goal of the "Young Turks," was to upgrade the scholarly reputation of the department by recruiting promising researchers, often with Ph.D.'s from Harvard. In Bridenbaugh's eyes the idea was to make Berkeley into Harvard.[23]

Stampp was a Bolton appointee, but he often sided with Bridenbaugh and the "Young Turks," particularly in the case of what was sometimes called the "Bouwsma Revolution," the two-year battle over the appointment of the Renaissance scholar William Bouwsma. The appointment of Bouwsma, a cutting-edge scholar of Renaissance thought and later president of the American Historical Association, was critical to the interests of the "Young Turks." Bouwsma was a Harvard Ph.D. teaching at the University of Illinois, who spent 1956–57 at Berkeley as a visiting faculty member. The "Young Turks" wanted to try to lure him to Berkeley, but his appointment was blocked by the Boltonian faction. Stampp supported Bouwsma's appointment, and helped the "Young Turks" cut a deal in which they agreed not to oppose the tenure bid of a faculty member from the "Boltonian" camp in exchange for Bouwsma's appointment.

Stampp and many of the "Young Turks" broke with Bridenbaugh, however, over Bridenbaugh's opposition to Thomas Kuhn, a historian and philosopher of science, who was seeking promotion to full professor in 1961. Kuhn was about to publish perhaps the most influential historical work of recent times, *The Structure of Scientific Revolutions*. Bridenbaugh, however, considered Kuhn's work too theoretical and opposed his promotion, which Stampp favored. After Bridenbaugh discovered Stampp's support for Kuhn, the two argued in Stampp's office. Unable to persuade Stampp to change his mind, Bridenbaugh stormed out of his office and never spoke to him again. Bridenbaugh soon departed Berkeley for Brown.

The murky waters of California politics, however, were a much greater danger in the 1950s than departmental turf wars. In the age of the cold war and McCarthy, colleges and universities were often under suspicion and targets for state legislatures. In the summer of 1949 Robert Gordon Sproul, the Berkeley chancellor, tried to take the heat off the university by having faculty sign a loyalty oath that was phrased in such a way that it would be impossible for a Communist to sign. In this way Sproul actually hoped to cut off political attacks. Teaching at the University of Wisconsin in the summer of 1949 Stampp, to his surprise, discovered that his standard letter of reappointment from Berkeley included the oath about which he had heard nothing but which he was required to sign. Stampp agonized over whether or not to sign it. In the end he recalled, "I had two small kids, and I just didn't want to get fired. So I signed it."[24]

The loyalty oath was discussed extensively in the history department and around the university. In the end, only one department member, the medievalist Ernst Kantorowicz, refused to sign, but landed on his feet by getting an appointment at the Institute for Advanced Study at Princeton. About twenty-five faculty members in other departments were fired for refusing to sign. Stampp helped organize a committee to raise money to assist the nonsigners, and he was responsible for collecting from the members of the history department. A year or two later, still troubled at the surrender of academic freedom, Stampp wrote to Sproul and withdrew his signature.

Vann Woodward was another scholar who moved up the academic ladder immediately after the war. After his release from military service in 1946, Woodward received a Guggenheim Fellowship and a job offer from the Johns Hopkins University in Baltimore, both of which he quickly accepted. The Hopkins offer was the best academic opportunity he had yet had. The chair of the Hopkins department had read his work, and Woodward was intrigued by the proximity to the Library of Congress and the possibilities such access held for his work. Hopkins had other charms. When he arrived, Woodward asked his chair what he should teach. The chair replied that his teaching depended upon what else he was doing. Woodward said that he was writing a book, and the chair suggested that Woodward offer a graduate seminar on the subject of his book and teach a section of the survey course.[25]

Living in Baltimore also enabled Woodward to meet one of Baltimore's famous sons and an icon the World War II generation, H.L. Mencken. Woodward had admired Mencken since his undergraduate days and shared many of his discontents with American culture. He met Mencken in 1947 and shared an enjoyable dinner with him.

His relatively light teaching load at Hopkins along with his Guggenheim fellowship enabled him to do a great deal of research, much of it archival and outside of the Baltimore-Washington area. During the years right after the war, Woodward wrote two of his greatest books, *Reunion and Reaction: The*

Compromise of 1877 and the End of Reconstruction and *Origins of the New South*, both published in 1951. In both of those books, Woodward built upon the foundations he had laid in his earlier book, *Tom Watson, Agrarian Rebel*. He took on a period, the post–Civil War era in the South, widely regarded as uninteresting by scholars, and was concerned to elucidate its complexity and significance. There can be little question of his success.

In the early 1950s Woodward was rewarded for his hard work with a stunning series of accolades. In 1952 *Origins of the New South* won the Bancroft Prize. In the same year he was elected president of the Southern Historical Association. Two years later, he received an award from the National Institute of Arts and Letters. In the same year, he served as Commonwealth Lecturer of London, and as James W. Richard Lecturer at the University of Virginia. In 1955 he served as Harmsworth Professor of American History at Oxford.

In the 1950s Woodward continued his commitment to academic freedom. When his friend and Hopkins colleague Owen Lattimore was targeted by the House Un-American Activities Committee for views about Asia that he had expressed in confidential discussion at the State Department, Woodward offered public support and helped persuade the academic community at Hopkins to rally around Lattimore and the principle of academic freedom.

Woodward also worked hard to remove existing barriers for black historians. At the 1949 meeting of the Southern Historical Association in Williamsburg, Virginia, Woodward helped get John Hope Franklin, then at Howard University, onto the program and into the banquet hall. In 1952 when he was president of the Southern Historical Association, a hotel in Knoxville, Tennessee, refused to serve black members, so Woodward canceled the banquet and moved it to another hotel out of town that did serve them. He also supplied Thurgood Marshall, then the chief counsel for the National Association for the Advancement of Colored People, with historical research, some of which Marshall used in arguing the *Brown v. Board of Education of Topeka, Kansas*.[26]

J.H. Hexter was one of the few who performed his military service while remaining at his prewar job at Queens College in New York City. After the war, like everyone else, he found classrooms overflowing with eager, ambitious returning veterans. For him an equally pressing question was what could be salvaged from the Guggenheim Fellowship that he had to abandon just before the beginning of the war. Where most of his generational cohort taught at prestigious universities, Hexter taught at an ethnic, urban, streetcar college that had much heavier teaching loads. Hexter therefore needed more than most of the others the release from teaching that a Guggenheim would allow. He approached Henry Ellen Moe, then the head of the Guggenheim Foundation, about renewing his grant, even though he had done virtually nothing on his original project, a study of the Interregnum period of British history, 1640–1660. Despite his meager productivity, he managed to wrangle another Guggenheim, this time to study the peculiar circumstances surrounding the consolidation of Burgundy in the late 1400s.[27]

Despite the best of intentions regarding the consolidation of Burgundy, Hexter soon veered off the intended path, reading in a variety of subjects, including the early articles of R.H. Tawney, who attributed the English Civil War of the 1640s to be a consequence of the rise of an acquisitive gentry that took power at the expense of the established aristocracy. Hexter had reservations about the idea of the gentry's rise, but from Tawney and others, he saw the importance of class and economic history and began to read extensively in that area. After his return to teaching, he published an article in 1948 based on that reading, "The Myth of the Middle Class in Tudor England." At the same time he was also a regular participant in the Columbia University seminar in the Renaissance, led by the intellectual historians Paul Oskar Kristeller and J.H. Randall. The seminar sent him veering onto another track. At the seminar other people presented papers, and Hexter, of a naturally critical caste of mind, often offered the most penetrating criticisms. One day after listening to Hexter badger the reader of one paper, Randall said to him, "Hexter, you've been critical of the others; now you do something." Hexter had been reading Thomas More's *Utopia* for its assessment of economic conditions in early modern England, so he asked Randall if he could present a paper on it. He went overtime delivering his first paper to the seminar, but the reception from the participants was enthusiastic enough that he was allowed to come back for another session. The exposure of his ideas to the Columbia seminar was invaluable, although the tables were now turned. Hexter, having been the seminar's most remorseless inquisitor, now became the subject of the inquisition. "The advantage," he wrote later, "of having one's favorite mistakes and illusions firmly knocked over the head in the relative privacy of the Paterno Library by critics at once profoundly learned, altogether friendly, fair, and well disposed, and entirely ruthless is immeasurable." In the end he presented three papers on *Utopia* to the seminar. When he had finished, Kristeller told him that his ideas on *Utopia* were good enough so that he should publish them, and the result was his second book, *More's Utopia: The Biography of an Idea*, published in 1952.[28]

For Hexter Queens was a special place. He met his wife there before the war; the students he taught there were the best he had. Fifty years later he and his wife still regularly returned to Queens to have a dinner and get-together with some of his favorite students and their spouses from the early years. But for all its charms, Queens had drawbacks, especially for someone who had scholarly aspirations. The fifteen-hour teaching load and the intense quality of teaching undertaken at Queens, left little time for scholarship, and Hexter had the domestic responsibilities that accompany four children. At the same time the Queens administration tended to regard scholars as troublemakers and was reluctant to recruit new faculty members with scholarly interests. Thus, in 1957, when he was offered a job at Washington University in St. Louis, Hexter was happy to take it.

At Washington, Hexter entered an entirely new atmosphere. He found himself happier "dealing with the crude middle western types" who administered Washington University. He also took a turn as department chair, where he endeavored to enhance the academic quality of the department by raising salaries, making paid leaves available for scholarly work, increasing the library budget, and removing untenured deadwood. His program as chair undoubtedly did not endear him to everyone, but he did have the support of the administration.[29]

Arthur Schlesinger's meteoric career resumed after the war. *The Age of Jackson* not only won for Schlesinger his first Pulitzer Prize, it also sold 90,000 copies, and established him as a major figure in American intellectual life. The Guggenheim Foundation awarded him a fellowship to begin a study of the Roosevelt years. He remained in Washington after the war and began to write for national magazine, seemingly ready for a career as a freelance writer. In the spring of 1946 he was offered a chance to join his father in the Harvard history department as an associate professor with tenure, even though he had only an A.B. degree from Harvard and slim teaching experience. He was twenty-eight years old.[30]

He soon became actively engaged in Democratic national politics, particularly eager to support policies consistent with the New Deal. Disappointed with Truman's disinclination to pursue such policies, he joined a brief, but abortive movement to draft Dwight Eisenhower as the Democratic candidate for president in 1948, which he later described as "the greatest mistake I ever made."

Despite his reservations about Truman's domestic policies, Schlesinger enthusiastically supported his foreign policy initiatives, especially those that seemed bent on containment of the Soviet Union. He passionately supported the Marshall Plan, and for a brief period in 1948 he was a special assistant to Averill Harriman to help oversee its implementation. Returning from Europe filled with optimism about the possibilities of rebuilding democratic institutions in Europe, he began *The Vital Center: The Politics of Freedom*, which established his reputation as "anti-Communist liberal." In *The Vital Center* Schlesinger expressed his distrust in the conservative impulse in American politics, associating it with the business community, which in his estimation had failed to demonstrate its capacity to govern. Nor did he place much faith in the Left. Indeed, in *The Vital Center* he delivered a searing attack on the Left and in particular against Communism. Within a few years, he was surprised to find himself derided by Senator McCarthy himself for being "soft on Communism." He replied by dismissing McCarthy as a "Joe-come-lately in the fight against communism."

Schlesinger continued his political activism in other ways. When Senator Robert A. Taft of Ohio charged that President Truman had no authority to send troops into Korea without congressional approval, Schlesinger responded with a lengthy exegesis on the numerous historical precedents for such an action, although during the Vietnam era, he would come to regret his position. In 1952 and 1956 he took leaves of absence from Harvard to serve as a speechwriter for the liberal intellectual's favorite candidate in the 1950s, Adlai Stevenson. John Kenneth Galbraith, a close friend and fellow Stevenson aide, recalled Schlesinger's remarkable affinity for the job. "Alone among all I've ever observed in this craft," Galbraith related, "he could remove his coat, address his typewriter and without resort to reference books, documents or pause for thought, produce an entire speech at one sitting. Within weeks he had achieved a perfect mastery of Stevenson's balanced sentences and could play perfectly to his delight in antonyms and frequent willingness to subordinate meaning to euphony."

Schlesinger told Felix Frankfurter that he had written *The Vital Center* to get his political ideas out of his system so that they would not infect his work on the New Deal. The study of Roosevelt and the New Deal was the historical project to which Schlesinger devoted himself in the 1950s. In 1957 he produced the first volume of his monumental study of the period, *The Crisis of the Old Order, 1919–1933*, followed in 1959 by a second volume, *The Coming of the New Deal*, and a third in 1960, *The Politics of Upheaval*.

Stephen B. Oates called *The Crisis of the Old Order* "the most perfectly sculptured work of historical art in this country, a book distinguished for its novelistic use of time, its symphonic organization, its vivid scenes and graphic vignettes, its telling quotations and dramatic narrative sweep." *The Crisis of the Old Order* won the Francis Parkman Award of the Society of American Historians and the Frederick Bancroft Prize granted by Columbia University. All three volumes were Book of the Month Club selections.

In Schlesinger's grand trilogy Roosevelt emerged as his shining paladin. While Roosevelt and the New Deal did not comprise a radical departure from earlier reform movements in Schlesinger's eyes, he repeatedly stressed Roosevelt's pragmatism and his concern to use government to alleviate suffering. To Schlesinger Roosevelt was the embodiment of the leader who succeeded by appealing to the hallowed vital center and who eschewed the dogmatism of the Right and the Left.

In Britain, the postwar world differed from that of the United States. While veterans returned happily from military service to resume their educations and careers and the specter of the Iron Curtain loomed large in political discussion, the economic picture was not as bright. Many other European countries, along with the United States, experienced unprecedented economic growth. For Britain the economic picture was mixed. On one hand, the war left the nation deeply in debt with a serious and debilitating "dollar gap." Shortages in several commodities, such as food and clothing, required rationing, even after wartime austerities. Moreover, immediately after the war, Winston Churchill, an exemplary war leader, was swept out of office, and the mantle of power handed over to the avowedly socialist government of Clement Attlee. Attlee proposed to operate certain industries, such as mining, electricity, and inland transport, as public corporations rather than private industries. The goal of these industries would now be public service rather than private profit. At about the same time the National Health Service Acts allowed all Britons, regardless of class or status to enjoy free medical and hospital care. Providers were paid by the government.

The effect of these reforms has been heavily debated. The economy continued to sputter, but this was in part because the Attlee government also had to contend with the debts that remained from the war and with other problems of postwar reconstruction. In any event it was not until the early 1950s that the economy began to recover, though that recovery was indeed formidable. In 1959 Harold Macmillan won a general election with the slogan that "you never had it so good."

Geoffrey Elton, released from the army in 1946, went at his first opportunity to the University of London to pay a call on Sir John Neale, the Elizabethan historian who in 1943 had invited Elton to become one of his research students in the unlikely event that Elton should survive the war. One morning, waiting outside of Neale's office, Elton encountered two of Neale's research students, who advised him not to work on parliaments or on Elizabeth, which were Neale's pet projects. So when Elton finally gained an audience with Neale, he told Neale that he wanted to work on Henry VIII. Neale agreed and sent Elton to the massive collection *The Letters and Papers of Henry VIII*. That, Elton recalled later, was the extent of his supervision from Neale.[31]

Trawling through the papers of Henry's reign, he noted with interest the profusion of papers and references to Thomas Cromwell, Henry's chief minister in the 1530s. Realizing that this meant that there would be sufficient material for a thesis, Elton plunged in wholeheartedly and completed his thesis in two years. In another year, he revised the thesis for publication and submitted it to the Cambridge University Press, which accepted it in 1950, although it was not published until 1953.

Word of its originality and interest circulated before its publication. In 1951 at the annual meeting of the Conference of Anglo-American Historians, an editor for Methuen approached another Tudor historian, Stanley T. Bindoff, about writing a textbook on the Tudors. Bindoff demurred and pointed the editor toward Elton, saying, "there's your man." Elton quickly came to terms with Methuen and composed the text of *England under the Tudors* in eighteen months, finishing it in 1953, and it was published in 1955.

After he was examined on his thesis, he got his first teaching appointment at Glasgow University in 1948, where he spent one year. He got a job at Cambridge when Attlee abolished university seats in Parliament. The abolition of university seats meant that the Clare College don and member of Parliament Kenneth Pickthorn would have to sacrifice either his seat in Parliament or his lectureship. He chose to give up his lectureship, and with Neale's help, Elton got Pickthorn's position at Clare.

J.H. Plumb returned to Cambridge after the war to resume his Ehrman Fellowship that had been suspended by the war. In 1946 he became a fellow at Christ's College, Cambridge, where he saw a chance to become the college's leading historian. By 1950 he had been appointed a university lecturer, a tutor of the college, and its director of studies in history.

But after the war Cambridge overflowed with undergraduates, and Plumb found himself teaching twenty hours a week, including subjects such as American history on which he knew nothing. Given a two-year appointment as a temporary university lecturer in 1947, he had to write forty lectures on eighteenth century politics for his first year and forty more for the second. During the war he usually worked a forty-hour week. From 1946 to 1948 he worked even harder, writing nearly 250,000 words of lectures and reading day and night to keep a step ahead of his pupils.

The hard work soon paid off. Allen Lane invited Plumb to write a short history of England in the eighteenth century for Penguin, and much of the lecture material compressed easily into the book. Plumb remembers vividly writing the last page at the home of Anthony Rothschild. He set his pen down and stretched back like a cat in satisfaction in the luxurious Chippendale chair in which he had been seated: it shattered. Rothschild barely batted an eyelash. "Don't worry," he informed the anguished Plumb, "Partridge will fix it." Once published, *England in the Eighteenth Century* received the approval of Sir George Clark, now Regius Professor of History at Cambridge, and cemented Plumb's standing at Cambridge.[32]

Following *England in the Eighteenth Century*, he wrote a political history of Leicestershire, his home county. But he had also decided to undertake a larger project that was to engage him for most of the next decade and a half, a life of Robert Walpole, where again much of the data he had acquired in writing up his eighteenth-century lectures would be useful. The first volume of his biography appeared in 1956, the second in 1960. In 1957 he was awarded a D.Litt.

At Oxford Lawrence Stone returned to Christ Church to resume his undergraduate studies, which had been interrupted by the war. Christ Church after the war was a different place from the staid, aristocratic college it had been before the war. Instead of its usual idle, privileged undergraduates, Christ Church after the war was swarming with flint-eyed, hardened veterans, determined to make up for lost time. Many of them also had difficulty adjusting to civilian life. There was great friction in the junior common room between those who had fought and those who had not. The dons, remembering what happened in 1918 when student veterans returned from World War I and inflicted serious damage to Christ Church's facilities with drunken, riotous parties, allowed returning veterans considerable latitude to come and go as they pleased, as long as they didn't "smash things."[33]

There was also a curious spirit of optimism. For many who returned from the war, there was a sense of confidence. They had survived the Great Depression and the menace of fascism. If these evils could be vanquished, perhaps all the problems of scholarship and even those of humanity would succumb before their steely determination. The optimism of historians was shared by people in other disciplines, though at times it could be somewhat dispiriting. Stone remembers a dinner with Peter Strawson, who became one of Oxford's most distinguished philosophers, where Strawson expressed his fear that he would have nothing to do by the time he reached middle age because all the problems of philosophy would be solved.

Despite the prevailing and infectious optimism, the postwar period was for Stone a difficult time, intellectually and emotionally. He had little money and his wife was in London. His tutors were sympathetic, but somewhat confused by the new temper of the times. When Stone asked one of his former tutors what he should do for his first essay, the tutor asked what he had written his last essay on before the war and told Stone to write another one on that topic. When Stone submitted the new essay, the tutor told him that the old one was much better. Stone did have a term as a pupil of Hugh Trevor-Roper, whom he admired greatly. Trevor-Roper was writing *The Last Days of Hitler*, and was already the subject of much admiration among Christ Church undergraduates, who included the future military historian Michael Howard. Stone worked hard to impress Trevor-Roper and thought he had succeeded.

Stone, like many veterans, found difficulty reentering academic life. Here Stone's old mentor, John Prestwich, came to his rescue and gave him the encouragement he needed to settle down. In June 1946 Stone took his schools, got a first, and soon received a research fellowship at University College. The research fellowship paid very little, but it gave him some sustenance while he tried to find a permanent job. The postwar job market in Britain was extremely tight. After three impoverished years at "the Univ," he landed his first permanent position at Wadham College, Oxford. At the time Wadham was poor and not particularly distinguished. But Maurice Bowra, its legendary warden, was determined to improve its reputation, and in the early fifties, Wadham was producing more than its share of first-class degrees. Producing top-notch students requires getting a lot more work out of the faculty, usually without much additional compensation. Stone remembers that the additional efforts he and others made on behalf of students at Wadham in the fifties were fun, and that he was "young and energetic, and one just did it." As the years passed, however, the burdens of excellence became increasingly onerous.

Stone pursued a variety of research paths in the late 1940s and early 1950s. One was frankly bizarre. In 1946, without a degree, any relevant course work, or having published a line in art history, he signed a contract to write a book on medieval English sculpture in a series on classic art edited by Sir Nikolaus Pevsner. This strange circumstance came about only through the sometimes odd bedfellows of publishing. Tom Kendrick, whom Pevsner wanted to write the book, wouldn't do it. Before the war Stone had worked briefly with Kendrick on a national survey of Anglo-Saxon sculpture. Kendrick recommended him to Pevsner, who reluctantly acquiesced, telling Stone, "I don't trust you at all, for you have absolutely no credentials for the job, but I don't see what else I can do."

Two other topics were more conventional. The first was a biography of Horatio Palavicino, a late-sixteenth-century entrepreneur, financier, diplomat, and espionage agent. His next topic was inspired by his admiration for the work of R.H. Tawney and in particular Tawney's ideas about the importance of the rise of the gentry. Stone elected to pursue the role of the aristocracy and in particular their financial condition.

As he studied the aristocracy, he, like Elton, encountered Thomas Cromwell, sometimes regarded as an early enemy of the aristocracy. For his work both on the aristocracy and on Thomas Cromwell, he discovered that he was trespassing on sacred grounds. He wrote an article about Cromwell's role, just as Geoffrey Elton was completing *The Tudor Revolution in Government*, and he published his article on the declining financial fortunes of the aristocracy just as his former tutor, Hugh Trevor-Roper, was reaching precisely the opposite conclusion.

After the war, Hugh Trevor-Roper returned to Oxford, first to his research fellowship at Merton College, and then to a teaching position as a "student" at Christ Church, his undergraduate college. Though students swarmed into Oxford and Christ Church after the war, Trevor-Roper managed to complete *The Last Days of Hitler* in 1946 and to enjoy the hat-in-the-air reception of the book when it appeared in 1947. An appointment as a university lecturer gave him some relief from tutoring, and he soon became a prominent and trenchant contributor to popular magazines and newspapers, usually as a book reviewer. While engagement with the popular press was generally scorned at Oxford, Trevor-Roper found it fun and profitable. Not infrequently he found himself in controversy, usually for scathing reviews of other people's works.[34]

After he finished *The Last Days of Hitler*, he returned to the field of early modern England, working on the papers of the Elizabethan financier Thomas Sutton. Examination of the Sutton papers compelled Trevor-Roper to confront the work of Tawney and the entire issue of the rise of the gentry. Up until this point Trevor-Roper was convinced that Tawney was right, and Tawney's ideas had underpinned Trevor-Roper's first book on Archbishop Laud.

Controversy continued to stalk him even at the moment of his greatest triumph. In 1957 he was appointed Regius Professor of History at Oxford, the highest honor Oxford can confer upon a historian. Unfortunately, Trevor-Roper's appointment came at the expense of A.J.P. Taylor, who, even Trevor-Roper conceded, was more qualified for the job. But realizing that it would be foolish to look a gift horse in the mouth, Trevor-Roper served as Regius Professor until 1980.

Richard Southern returned to his position as fellow and tutor at Balliol College after the war, although he now had a wife and child. The war had taken five years of his life, and he had vegetated as far as the study of medieval history was concerned. His interest in Anselm remained, and while there was a marvelous moment of exhilaration when he returned home, he felt, like many veterans, strangely detached and unfocused, as though he was locked in a dark house. Like Stone, he required outside inspiration, and it was his old éminence grise Powicke who provided the spark, inviting Southern to join his group of medievalists and to give a paper to that group in 1946. Joining the group helped Southern regain his focus and revived his interest in scholarship.[35]

Southern had to tutor and lecture as well. Balliol imposed a heavy teaching load on its faculty. Increasingly dissatisfied with the constitutional and political emphasis in medieval history, Southern wrote a series of lectures on the spiritual side of medieval life, based largely on his work on Anselm, Peter of Blois, and Lanfranc. At Powicke's suggestion he decided to turn the lectures into a book, and they proved to be the background for his greatest book, *The Making of the Middle Ages*, published in 1953. But the book was not completed without a strange twist of fate.

In 1949 Southern began to feel rocky. A vigorous man, he suddenly tired easily, and would wake up in the morning sweaty and exhausted. Alarmed, he saw a doctor, who diagnosed tuberculosis, still fatal in those days. Balliol was generous, keeping Southern's position secure and calling in the great expert on tuberculosis at the time, Geoffrey Marshall. If someone who contracts tuberculosis in the prime of life can be said to be lucky, Southern received a sudden stroke of luck. A wonder drug had just been discovered, although, even with it, recovery would take a year of rest. The drug itself was a double-edged sword. It cured his tuberculosis, but it had serious and, at the time, unknown side effects, and slowly robbed Southern of his hearing.

Southern was thus forced as if by arrest and incarceration to spend a year in a hospital room. He discovered that tuberculosis is not too debilitating unless you get up and try to move around. Confined to a hospital, he had a year without pupils, a year to do what he wanted at least intellectually, and he wrote most of *The Making*. Southern did have to contend with another terrifying force, almost as frightening as his disease. The nurse in his ward, Sister Barker, detested the slightest untidiness. Historical work requires a certain level of untidiness. Books, papers, pens, and notes are likely to be scattered everywhere. To continue his work Southern had to hide the forbidden tools of his trade under his blankets and pillows, even behind chamber pots, to avoid detection by the untidiness police. The writing went smoothly, since he already had the notes from his lectures as a base from which to proceed, and he was able to write roughly a chapter a month. By Easter 1950 he had four of a projected five chapters ready, but he couldn't figure out how to end it. Walking in the Oxford parks near his home, after his release from the hospital, he came up with the solution, a chapter on the transition from medieval epic to romance.

After the war Christopher Hill and Eric Hobsbawm came under the parallel influence of the Marxist Historians' Group. When the war ended Hobsbawm returned to Cambridge to finish his degree. In 1947 he became a lecturer at Birkbeck College, London, where he taught until 1982, except for a six-year stint, between 1949–1955, as a fellow of King's College, Cambridge.

By contrast Christopher Hill had a position as a fellow and tutor at Balliol to which he could return. Like many who returned as students, he had some difficulty adjusting to civilian life. When Paul Rolo, another Stuart historian, tutored at Balliol in 1947, he confessed to his students that he was still distracted from his tutoring by the effects of his military service. His pupils told him not to worry; the year before, they helped Christopher Hill get through the same difficulty.[36]

Hill and Hobsbawm were also young Marxist scholars looking for inspiration, and in the postwar era the world of Marxist scholars had changed. Before the war left-wing politics were *de rigeur.* There were Communist clubs at Oxford, such as the October Club, which many either joined or attended; Hobsbawm has remarked that at Cambridge in the thirties "an enormous number of the abler and livelier people, regardless of subject, were on the left. If you weren't, it was surprising." The postwar Britain, however, turned sharply anti-Marxist. The Iron Curtain had been erected; the Soviet totalitarian menace had been substituted for the Nazi totalitarian menace.[37]

Hill and Hobsbawm were fortunate in several respects. They both had jobs by 1947. Hobsbawm recalls that in 1948 a veil was drawn across English academic life. Those Marxists who were lucky enough to have a job before 1948 were on the whole able to stay. They might have been locked in the same job or not have gotten a promotion for ten or twelve more years, but they were usually able to stay in academic life. No Marxist, recalls Hobsbawm, who didn't have a job by 1948, "got a job for the next ten or eleven years.[38]

The other area in which Hobsbawm and Hill were fortunate was in their relationship to the Marxist Historians' Group, formed in early 1946 following a number of resolutions at the Communist Party Congress calling for increased educational programs, including the study of British history.

Sections devoted to particular periods were quickly established, with Christopher Hill taking charge of the Tudor and Stuart group, which included such scholars as Hobsbawm, Rodney Hilton, Victor Kiernan, George Thomson, Maurice Dobb, Leslie Morton, and Dona Torr.

Beginning in the fall of 1946, they met, normally on weekends, in the "dank, cold, and slightly foggy streets of Clerkenwell to Marx House, or the upper room of the Garibaldi Restaurant, Laystall Street." In addition to the London meetings, there were meetings in other parts of the country, special seminars and talks, and summer schools. Marxist historians discovered they were not alone and that they had a sense of shared purpose, roughly akin to the feeling experienced by those who attended the early meetings of the Berkshire Conference on Women's History in the United States in the 1970s. Membership in the group, for Hobsbawm, became "if not a way of life, then a small cause . . . a way of structuring leisure."[39]

The essence of the group was its passion and sense of intellectual excitement. The members, believed they were on the edge of a brave new world of historical truth, discarding the old liberal paradigms about Parliament and progress and rewriting the whole of British history in light of the insights provided by Marxist analysis. Unity and common goals did not mean unanimity. The meetings sometimes constituted a second Battle of Britain. "Few . . . hesitated to speak," recalled Hobsbawm; "even fewer to criticize, none to accept criticism." Certain subjects, such as the history of the party and the fairly recent history of Britain, too sensitive politically, were off-limits. For those with the fortitude to endure intense scrutiny before formidable antagonists, the results were gratifying. Before the early 1950s, Christopher Hill's published work consisted of a few articles and pamphlets. Following the stimulation of the group, he conceived and executed the writing of a multivolume history of the Church of England during the early modern period, the first volume of which, *Economic Problems of the Church*, was published in 1956. That was followed by another volume, *Society and Puritanism* and the *Intellectual Origins of the English Revolution*, along with an innovative and popular textbook, *A Century of Revolution*. Almost all of the ideas in these books were first tested on the Marxist Historians' Group.[40]

The effect of the group upon Eric Hobsbawm was similar. The Cold War, he believed, tended to isolate Marxist historians. By his involvement in the group Hobsbawm discovered that Marxist historians could be brought together. For Hobsbawm the works of Maurice Dobb were crucial. Dobb, as much as any historian, in his *Studies in the Development of Capitalism*, raised broad questions about the role of capitalism in English and European history. Dobb was particularly interested in the "transition question," the issue of how feudal Europe, dominated by landowning nobles and the church, was replaced by the dominance of entrepreneurial capitalism. Before the war Hobsbawm intended to work on agrarian problems in North Africa. But after the war, with a wife who worked and aroused by Dobb and the discussions of the Marxist Historians' Group, he turned to nineteenth-century labor movements, since he could now work on them in Britain. Much of Hobsbawm's earliest work, collected in *Labouring Men*, was done under the influence of Dobb and was first presented to the Marxist Historians' Group.

Another achievement of the Marxist Historians' Group was the creation of a journal, *Past and Present*, in 1952. In 1949 or early 1950 John Morris, a member of the Marxist Historians' Group, decided that there was a need for a journal that would convey the new findings and insights of the Marxist Historians' Group to the literate public and to the masses. Morris begged, cajoled, and harassed several members of the group to join the editorial board of his new journal, sometimes against their judgment. Morris also had to resolve several other quandaries. First, the journal, while springing from Marxist roots, had to engage non-Marxists as well. Second, while it was to be accessible to the interested public, its articles would be based on firm research and intellectual foundations. It had at once to sell history to the working class and to maintain its intellectual integrity.[41]

The journal was launched on the most tenuous foundations. There was little money and no staff. The editorial office was John Morris's private study. What kept it going was Morris's determination and his ability to secure the help of a group of bright and energetic individuals to act as editors, including Hill, Hobsbawm, Geoffrey Barraclough, A.H.M. Jones, and Gordon Chile. Service on the board was demanding. Members of the board were expected to read all submissions and participate in the collective discussion of them. In addition Morris sometimes asked board members to submit their own work.

At the outset Morris managed to snare over two hundred paid subscribers and subsequently discovered that production costs were relatively low. The original printers' estimate came to only £220 for one thousand copies of two issues. Eventually, it turned out that a sale of four hundred issues allowed the journal to break even.

Events in Poland and Hungary in 1956 severely tested the Marxist principles of several British historians. In that year members of the Polish Communist Party attempted to select their own prime minister instead of one approved by Moscow. Following their lead the Hungarian Communist Party attempted to demonstrate similar independence by forming a new ministry headed by Imre Nagy, who called for removal of Soviet troops from Hungary and Hungarian withdrawal from the Warsaw Pact. Nagy's intransigence was unacceptable to the Soviets. In November 1956 Soviet troops invaded Hungary, brutally crushed all resistance, deposed Nagy, who was later executed, and installed their own ruler.

The events of 1956 aroused a furious debate. For those who had previously defended Stalinist excesses and denounced American imperialism, the events of 1956 had a chilling effect. It was no longer possible to regard the Soviets as heroic defenders of freedom. Marxism might be salvaged but Stalinism was completely discredited. Several important figures in the Marxist historical community in Britain, such as E.P. Thompson, resigned from the party in protest. In 1957 Christopher Hill resigned from the British Communist Party because of its failure to differentiate itself from the Soviet Communist Party. For Eric Hobsbawm, the other great Marxist of the 1950s, however, the effect of 1956 was oddly liberating. He thought 1956 made little difference in his historical views and decided not to resign from the party. But he also believed that 1956 was ultimately liberating for Marxist historians because they no longer had to devote themselves to defending Stalin and the Soviet Union. Freed from this thankless task, they had more time to do history and were freer to explore twentieth-century topics. Both he and Hill published a great deal more in the decade after 1956 than they had in the decade before.

By 1958 *Past and Present*, begun in a spirit of enthusiasm and idealism, had fallen on hard times, in part because of its link to the Communist Party. To reduce the level of guilt by association, non-Marxists, such as Joan Thirsk, Lawrence Stone, and John Elliott were invited to join the editorial board, giving it a less sectarian composition. Stone made it clear that he was not interested in joining the editorial board of a Marxist journal, though he was willing to retain some of the board's traditions, such as democratic decision making and the readings of submissions by all members of the board. Not all *Past and Present*'s traditions remained sacred. A frightful row between Stone and the newcomers on one side and the founders of the journal on the other did erupt over the journal's subtitle, a "journal of scientific history," which could be seen as a flag word for Marxist analysis. After much heated discussion, the subtitle was changed to the more neutral "a journal of history." Over the years the editorial board of *Past and Present* engaged in many other acrimonious debates, particularly over which submissions were worthy of inclusion in the journal. In those debates, according to Stone and Elliott, the quality of the article was always the basis of the argument, never its ideology.[42]

Few will be surprised to discover that Richard Cobb pursued the least conventional course of action among the English historians following the end of the war. The others took the obvious steps to resume their careers, either teaching or returning to school to complete their education. In 1946 when Cobb returned to civilian life, he chose to stay in Paris. His life there was thoroughly Parisian and dissolute, spent mostly in the company of disreputable and alcoholic French friends. No doubt his dissolute life in part reflected the postwar confusion that veterans often experience. Cobb woke up most mornings in strange rooms where he amused himself by trying to determine from the quality of light in the room and the sounds from the street which part of Paris he had been ended up in the night before. From

1946 to 1948 he bounced erratically around France, usually drinking a great deal. He also devoted considerable time to shadowing a young woman with whom he had been briefly involved, but who had spurned his advances.[43]

During this time he also tried to pursue his own research, which gave him an excuse to stay in France. He had visited Georges Lefebrve, whom he had met before the war and who had given him his original research topic on the Hébertistes, on leave during the war in 1944 and 1945. After the war he decided to pick up on Hébertisme again. In 1947 he met another Marxist historian, Albert Soboul, who was working on the same subject. For a while they encountered each other suspiciously at the Bibliothèque Nationale, as they requested the same boxes of documents. Both came slowly to the conclusion that Hébertisme was not a viable topic. But, while in pursuit, each came across similar promising lines of inquiry: Soboul on the role of the forty-eight *sections* or districts of Paris during the French Revolution and the Parisian working class, or sansculottes generally, and Cobb on the individuals in those sections. Soboul was concerned to elucidate of the movement generally; Cobb, to explore the behavior of individuals.

Cobb was captivated by the human stories, usually the more sordid and dispiriting the better. At this point, he had no plan, no career goal. He simply enjoyed the research, wanted to stay in France, and was willing to be drawn along the byways and off-ramps of archival research in pursuit of a good story. The chance discovery of a crammed file folder or an extensive dossier of a revolutionary leader or an eyewitness account of a September massacre was likely to set him back for weeks. Occasionally he suspended the research to write up an article. He survived by teaching English to engineers, students, and airline hostesses, supplemented by occasional advances from his mother. During this time he came to his own view of the proper objects for historical research. He later wrote, "I have never understood history other than in terms of human relationships, and I have attempted to judge individuals on their own terms and from what they say about themselves in their own language."[44]

In 1948 Cobb became a minion of the Communist Party, when Soboul had persuaded the party to help support a group of promising *copains*. He dined with Soboul and other party operatives Monday through Friday, gave talks, and uttered the appropriate howls of outrage at the malignity of the United States and Great Britain. Being a creature of the party bred an unusual ambience, and Cobb never felt entirely certain that he belonged, well aware that he was a sponger. Soboul had decreed to his party colleagues that they must feed the English historian, recalled Cobb, and feed him they did. But if he felt out of place, Cobb did believe that much of the party line, especially regarding malevolent intentions of the United States, was convincing. When Stalin died, Cobb, like many of his party comrades, wept.

By the early 1950s he had acquired an extensive knowledge of French archival materials, published a series of articles and research notes, and prepared a doctoral thesis. The thesis was never submitted, although it was subsequently published as the two-volume *Les Armées Révolutionnaires.*

The period from 1945 to 1960 was crucial to the development of the World War II generation of historians. They were a generation in a hurry to restart their lives, begin their careers, get going with their research, and write their books. With a few exceptions, most of them either developed their most seminal ideas or wrote their greatest books during the 1950s, including Elton's *The Tudor Revolution in Government,* Stampp's *The Peculiar Institution,* Woodward's *Origins of the New South,* Southern's *The Making of the Middle Ages,* Handlin's *The Uprooted,* Craig's *The Politics of the Prussian Army,* Schlesinger's volumes on the New Deal, Boorstin's volumes on the pragmatic spirit of the United States, Plumb's biography of Walpole, and Cobb's studies of the French revolutionary poor.

Chapter 7

AT THE PINNACLE (MOSTLY)

※

For most of the World War II generation of historians the period between 1945 and 1960 represented the most intensive and productive period of their lives. They began their teaching careers; they did the reading and research that would form the basis for much of their future work, and several of them wrote their greatest books. During the 1960s and 1970s, most of them continued to work and most reaped the benefits of their earlier labor.

But the times had changed. World War II marked the triumph of their generation, and in John Kennedy's words, the passing of a torch "to a new generation of Americans, born in this century," steeled by the grim hardships of the Depression and sobered by the reality of war. The postwar expansion of the economy, a spree almost as gaudy as that described by Fitzgerald for the 1920s, and the "baby boom" population explosion of the 1950s contributed to an aura of triumph. Home and automobile ownership, electricity, modern conveniences, an interstate highway system, and mass-scale consumer culture transformed American life. Almost all of the World War II generation of historians lived in greater comfort and security than their parents and grandparents had.

Unprecedented prosperity and affluence, however, concealed disturbing social problems. Despite the emergence of a civil rights movement and the *Brown v. Board of Education* decision in the 1950s, segregationists still clung tenaciously to their divided society. Repulsive scenes with Southern governors defiantly standing outside the gates of state universities with armed troopers at their sides to repel the entry of black students and local police forces quelling demonstrators with attack dogs and electric cattle prods were grim reminders that equality in America was still a dream. In *The Other America* Michael Harrington reminded readers that prosperity had eluded millions of poor, white Americans as well as black. At the same time the increasing

American involvement in the war in Vietnam provoked howls of protest, particularly from college students who might themselves, along with friends or family, be called upon to fight.

As it turned out, the torch of protest had been passed to a new generation, but it was not the generation of which John Kennedy spoke; it was their children. Several years before the outbreak of student unrest, David Potter had warned of the dangers of having a large population of young people, generally raised in affluence and allowed an indulgent period of education and delaying of responsibility. Bruno Bettelheim warned that it was "unnatural to keep a young person in dependence for 20 years while attending school," and attributed the spirit of rebelliousness among young people in the 1960s to their having to wait "for things—for the real life to come." Affluence and the dramatic rise in American population in the 1950s led to the rise of the multiversity, which further delayed the onset of responsibility. In 1941 only two American institutions of higher education had more than twenty thousand students; in 1969 thirty-nine did. Even the radicals realized that they were a new generation. As the Port Huron statement, the most visible expression of their ideals, began, "We are the people of this generation, bred in at least modest comfort, housed now in universities looking uncomfortably to the world we inherit."[1]

While many of this group of historians had arrived at the pinnacle of their profession, others were in effect starting out. Anne Scott's career had been delayed by family commitments. When her husband took a new job in North Carolina, she found a part-time job in the history department of the University of North Carolina at Chapel Hill. Shortly after her appointment a department member asked her, the first and only woman in the department, to present a paper to a departmental seminar. Searching for a topic, Scott recalled the women she had discovered during her study of the Progressive movement. Additional research on Jane Addams convinced her that a paper on southern Progressive women was a worthy topic. As it turned out, she found not only a subject for the seminar but also one that would occupy her for much of the next decade.[2]

In 1960 Scott's husband was appointed to a Fulbright lectureship at the University of Bologna in Italy, and the family spent a year abroad. Life with three children in a city where no English was spoken, interspersed with excursions to the rest of Europe was an unforgettable experience. While abroad, she received a letter from a member of the Duke history department, asking if she would consider accepting an appointment at Duke as a part-time, temporary instructor while the department sought a suitable replacement. Before accepting, Scott asked if her Ph.D. and three years experience qualified her to be a part-time assistant professor rather than an instructor. With that point settled affirmatively, she began teaching at Duke in the fall of 1961. Her "temporary" position at Duke concluded with her retirement in 1992.

In short order other opportunities appeared. George Tindall invited her to give a paper on southern women at the fall meeting of the Southern Historical Association. She quickly agreed and wrote the paper while she endured the grind of first-year teaching. After a three-hour lunch with Oscar Handlin, she agreed to write a book about southern white women. Writing such a book was a bold undertaking. There was virtually no existing historiographical tradition on the history of southern women and no network of established scholars to provide guidance. But in a little more than a year Scott's life had changed dramatically. From a position on the margins of the profession, she was now teaching at a prestigious university, being invited to give papers at meetings, and being offered book contracts. She also began to see her research as more than something that could be picked up and set down in accordance with her family's needs.

Through it all she maintained an active life outside the university. Children, community, and friends were the common places to channel her energy. In 1963 Terry Sanford, the governor of North Carolina, appointed Scott to be the chair of a special Commission on the Status of Women. She also became involved in the civil rights movement, gaining an idea of what being a suffragette might have been like.

She was sustained by a variety of support networks. Her husband, a born parent, cared for the children when Scott disappeared on weekends for research trips or conferences. Oscar Handlin materialized regularly to keep her nose at the grindstone. Julia Spruill, a pioneer in the study of southern women and the author of the earlier *Women's Life and Work in the Southern Colonies*, took an early and sustaining interest in her work. Louise Young, a Washington friend, provided encouragement and a place to stay when Scott went to Washington.

In 1971 Scott published the fruits of her long labor, *The Southern Lady*. Among its many contributions to scholarship was the notion that the southern lady was generally not the coquettish Scarlet O'Hara of popular legend. Rather, in Scott's view, southern women were active contributors to southern economic life and responded with courage and determination to the deprivation of war. In 1996 *The Southern Lady* was reissued by the University of Virginia Press on the occasion of the twenty-fifth anniversary of its publication. In 1983 Scott's essays were collected and published by the University of Illinois Press as *Making the Invisible Woman Visible*.

The success of her work and *The Southern Lady* in particular brought her many accolades. In 1980 she was named W.K. Boyd Professor of History at Duke and served as department chair from 1981 to 1985. She was chosen president of the Organization of American Historians in 1983 and of the Southern Historical Association in 1989. She received numerous honorary degrees, from, among others, Lindenwood College in 1968, Queens College in 1985, Northwestern University in 1989, Radcliffe College in 1990, the University of the South in 1990, and Cornell College in 1991.

Like Anne Scott, Gertrude Himmelfarb delayed the beginning of her teaching career while she raised her family, though she was able to publish considerably as an independent scholar. In 1965 with children well into their teens she began her teaching career at Brooklyn College and the Graduate School of the City University of New York. She continued her prodigious rate of publication. *Victorian Minds* appeared in 1968, *On Liberty and Liberalism: The Case of John Stuart Mill* in 1974, *The Idea of Poverty* in 1984, *Marriage and Moral among the Victorians* in 1986, *The New History and the Old: Critical Essays and Reappraisals* in 1987, and *Poverty and Compassion: The Moral Imagination of the Late Victorians* in 1991. She was named Distinguished Professor of History at CUNY in 1978. In 1991 she delivered the Jefferson Lecture in the Humanities.

In contrast to Scott and Himmelfarb, dazzling success came to Barbara Tuchman in the 1960s. In the forties, while her children were young, being able to set aside time, close a door, and disappear into her work was difficult. As the children grew up, it became easier. In 1962 her third book, *The Guns of August,* became a best-seller and was awarded the Pulitzer Prize, followed in 1966 by *The Proud Tower: A Portrait of the World before the War.* Almost a decade after *The Guns of August,* she won a second Pulitzer Prize for *Stillwell and the American Experience in China,* which appeared in 1971. Then, with another radical shift of gears, she turned to the Middle Ages and wrote *A Distant Mirror,* a study of the cataclysmic century in which the Great Plague devastated Europe. "I had been thinking about the bomb," she explained later, "and I wanted to discover the result on society of the greatest recorded disaster we've ever had, the Black Death." In 1981 she published *Practicing History,* a collection of her essays and speeches, and in 1984, her *The March of Folly: From Troy to Vietnam* appeared, detailing examples of leaders who pursued policies that were virtually opposed to the self-interest of the body or state they represented. She died from complications following a stroke in 1989, shortly before her last book, *The First Salute: A View of the American Revolution,* appeared. Arthur Schlesinger Jr., Vann Woodward, John Hope Franklin, and Daniel Boorstin are perhaps the only historians of our time who have received comparable renown. In addition to her two Pulitzer Prizes, Tuchman received a Gold Medal from the American Academy of Arts and Sciences in 1978, a Regent Medal of Excellence from the University of the State of New York, and honorary degrees from, among others, Yale, Columbia, New York University, Harvard, and Mount Holyoke. In 1980 she delivered the Jefferson Lecture in the Humanities.[3]

Several historians made significant career changes, and there was a small, but significant, generational convergence at the history department at Yale University. In 1963 J.H. Hexter, then at Washington University in St. Louis, received an offer from Yale. Usually a decisive person who made up his mind on any issue in five minutes or less, Hexter deliberated inconclusively for months over the Yale offer. He found Washington University a splendid place to work, but Yale was one of the greatest universities in the world with a special library strength in his chosen field of English history. It also offered deliverance from a career-long identity crisis. Hexter had spent most of his career teaching at institutions with names that bred confusion. He taught for eighteen years at Queens College on Long Island, but his friends from other parts of the country persistently confused Queens College with the Queen's University in Ontario, Canada, or the Queens College in North Carolina. Confusion continued to reign when he went to Washington University in St. Louis, which was just as persistently confused with the University of Washington in Seattle. For Hexter one of the charms of Yale was that no one would confuse Yale with some other college. "When you tell someone you are at Yale," he wrote triumphantly in 1983, "they do not ask: 'Wherezat? In Lost Nation, Iowa?' or 'In Painted Post, New York?' or 'In Cambridge, Mass?'"[4]

A more compelling reason for going to Yale was the exceptional quality of the faculty in the history department, which included Edmund Morgan, Vann Woodward, John Morton Blum, and R.R. Palmer. For Hexter they all behaved like gentlemen and scholars, even if they did not always agree. The quality of the department was largely the work of its chair in the late fifties and early sixties, George Pierson. Before World War II the Yale history department had been excellent, but by the 1950s it had become highly inbred. At the time of Edmund Morgan's arrival at Yale in 1955 there were only two or three members of the department who did not hold Ph.D.'s from Yale. Pierson was himself the bluest of the Old Blues, but was determined to build up the department. He wanted to hire the best faculty, including Jews and those who did not possess a Yale pedigree, significant departures from customary practice. Under his leadership most of the stalwarts of the Yale department of the sixties and seventies were hired, including Vann Woodward, Hexter, and John Morton Blum.

Teaching loads were deliciously generous. Hexter and Woodward taught primarily graduate students; Morgan taught five hours a week. For Morgan, the most important benefit that Yale offered came when he and John Blum convinced Kingman Brewster, Yale's president in the 1960s, to offer productive faculty a semester off every three years.

Given this generosity, most continued their remarkable productivity. Among Morgan's achievements during this period were *The Gentle Puritan: A Life of Ezra Stiles* (1962), *Visible Saints: The History of a Puritan Idea* (1963), *Roger Williams: Church and the State* (1967), *The Challenge of the American Revolution* (1976), and *The Genius of George Washington* (1980). But Morgan also produced his greatest and most ambitious book, *American Slavery, American Freedom: The Ordeal of Colonial Virginia*, in 1975, after initial soundings into the subject appeared in two 1971 essays, "The Labor Problem at

Jamestown, 1607–1618" and "The First American Boom: Virginia 1618–1630." In these essays and in *American Slavery, American Freedom,* Morgan explored the great American paradox, that as white Americans increasingly embraced notions of liberty and equality for themselves, they imposed legal servitude and enslavement upon black Americans. Morgan also found time to write books and pamphlets for general audiences. He was a coauthor, along with John Blum, Willie Lee Rose, Arthur Schlesinger Jr., and Vann Woodward, of the immensely popular textbook *The National Experience.* In 1969 he wrote a pamphlet introduction to the three accounts of Paul Revere's ride and a book for junior high school students, *So What about History?* describing the nature of historical studies. He composed the text of the pamphlet in about a week, but spent two years gathering seventy-four photographs, prints, and drawings for illustrations. In 1988 he published *Inventing the People: The Rise of Popular Sovereignty in England and America,* and he has completed a manuscript on church and state relations in early America, though he is reluctant to publish it because he fears that it is "too damn dull."[5]

He also received a variety of awards and honors. In 1970 he was the Commonwealth Lecturer at the University of London, where he had been a student more than thirty years before. In 1971 he was elected president of the Organization of American Historians. He has had honorary degrees conferred upon him from, among others, Brown, Rutgers, William and Mary, and Williams College, and has received numerous other tributes, including an award for scholarly distinction from the American Historical Association.

The heroic phase of Vann Woodward's historical writing came in the 1950s with the publication of *Reunion and Reaction, Origins of the New South, The Strange Career of Jim Crow,* and the essays published in 1960 in *The Burden of Southern History.* For most of the rest of his career, he defended his carefully constructed edifice of southern history from a new generation of students, many of whom had tested Woodward's grand hypotheses on particular areas. In essays and as his books came out in new editions Woodward modified and adapted his views in light of new research, but remained convinced of the general truth of the conclusions he reached earlier. Like Morgan, he enjoyed a position at the pinnacle of the profession. He contributed frequently to the *New York Review of Books* and served as president of both the Organization of American Historians and the American Historical Association in 1969. In 1978 he gave the Jefferson Lecture in the Humanities at the Library of Congress. In 1982 he received a Pulitzer Prize for his editing of the Civil War journal of Mary Boykin Chestnut, a South Carolina intellectual with a keen eye for the nuances of life inside the Confederacy. The Chestnut journal represented a triumph in historical editing. There were in effect two versions, an original and an edition revised by Chestnut later, together totaling approximately three quarters of a million words, all written in an idiosyncratic hand. Woodward recognized that both the original and revised versions were valuable, and his principal editorial task was to combine them in a way that revealed the insights in both versions, along with identifying the hundreds of persons referred to in the journal. In 1985 Woodward published a retrospective account of his life and work, *Thinking Back: The Perils of Writing History*, in which he combined an account of his life and intellectual development with comments on the survival of his works and criticisms directed at them. He has also undertaken the task of general editor of the projected eleven-volume Oxford History of the United States.[6]

For Jack Hexter the article rather than the book was his preferred form of expression, and, in his hands, combat. From 1961 to 1979 his essays appeared in three main collections, *Reappraisals in History: New Views on History and Society in Early Modern Europe, Doing History*, and *On Historians: Reappraisals of Some of the Masters of Modern History*. In these essays he often appeared as an enfant terrible, highly critical of his fellow historians, and using words like a club to bludgeon his victims. He was particularly skilled at trying to get into the mind of the historian under scrutiny, such as in his essays on Christopher Hill, John Pocock, and Fernand Braudel, who remarked with astonishment after reading Hexter's essay on him, "how is it possible that, without knowing me, you have seen me with such exactitude . . . it is marvelous. In each case, it is absolutely successful." Hexter also persuaded the National Endowment for the Humanities to establish the Yale Center for Parliamentary History. With Hexter as director, the center began transcribing and publishing the diaries kept by members of the English Parliament in the 1620s. In 1978 Hexter retired from Yale to return to Washington University (in St. Louis) as Distinguished Historian in Residence where he helped found and raise money for a new center, the Center for Freedom.[7]

Life in the Yale department was not entirely milk and honey. The department was superb, but not cohesive. While there was a weekly lunch at one of the colleges, the faculty normally had little contact with each other. Faculty offices were dispersed widely across the campus and the most productive scholars did their work at home. Moreover, most new appointees were informed at the time of their appointments that they were not likely to be granted tenure. This frank assessment of their prospects was intended to relieve some of the pressure on junior faculty, but it often backfired. Despite the grim prospects for tenure, most of the new assistant professors persisted in the belief that they might be the visible saints worthy of election to Yale's high church, the effect of which was to make them even more anxiety-ridden. Moreover, the senior faculty tended to shun the junior faculty since friendship with the latter was not likely to last.

The most controversial of the junior faculty members who were denied tenure was Staughton Lynd, a radical historian and the author of several well-received books, including *Class Conflict, Slavery and the United States Constitution* and *Intellectual Origins of American Radicalism*. He was also a left-wing activist, serving as director of the Freedom Schools for black children in Mississippi and chairing the committee that organized the first major anti-Vietnam War march on Washington. In 1965, while holding his Yale appointment, Lynd traveled to Vietnam with Tom Hayden and Herbert Aptheker in defiance of a State Department ban. When, despite his generally favorable reviews, Yale rejected his bid for tenure in 1968, Lynd told the *New York Times* that the rejection was in part political, a retribution exacted for his radical politics. The case attracted national attention, and Morgan and Woodward responded by insisting that the department's decision on Lynd was based entirely on academic considerations. Lynd merited tenure at most institutions; Yale's standards were higher. It is hard to believe that two men with the left-wing backgrounds of Morgan and Woodward based their decision concerning Lynd's tenure on politics, but eight years later Woodward led the fight to prevent another historian who made the trip to North Vietnam, Herbert Aptheker, from teaching a one-time, one-term course at Yale on W.E.B. DuBois, one of the founders of black history. Aptheker was a radical historian, who despite an important book on black slave rebellions, had never held a major university appointment. The effort to prevent Aptheker from teaching at Yale inspired another leading radical historian, Jesse Lemisch, to write an essay for the *Radical History Review*, "If Howard Cosell Can Teach at Yale, Why Can't Herbert Aptheker?" A resolution calling upon the Organization of American Historians to investigate the Aptheker case passed in a mail ballot, but died when Yale cited its policy of refusing to divulge the reasons behind appointments.[8]

The department was also visited by tragedy. In 1970 Vann Woodward's only child, Peter, not yet thirty, died of cancer. At roughly the same time, Woodward lost two other close friends, Richard Hofstadter and David Potter, also to cancer. In 1982, his wife of forty years, Glenn, died. In the face of tragedy, Hexter recalled that "Vann was very stoical." A few years before the death of Glenn Woodward, Edmund Morgan's wife and collaborator, Helen M. Morgan, died. In 1983 Morgan remarried.

A second, but smaller, generational convergence of historians occurred at Princeton. By the 1960s the formidable Princeton department of the 1950s was crumbling. Strayer had retired as chair. Robert R. Palmer left to become Dean of the Faculty of Arts and Sciences at Washington University in 1963. Early modern history was in particularly perilous condition. Elmer Beller was on the verge of retirement, and E. Harris Harbison was in the early stages of an illness that would take his life in another year. It was left to Jerome Blum to rebuild the department. One of his first moves was to entice Lawrence Stone away from Oxford.

Stone's dissatisfaction with Oxford had been mounting for some time. After a decade of teaching at Wadham College, he had tired of Oxford's impenetrable curricular emphasis on English political and constitutional history and of the relentless burden of tutorial teaching. He and his colleagues raised Wadham's standing immeasurably in the fifties, but "no one rewarded or thanked us," he recalled more in puzzlement than anger. While in Princeton as a visiting fellow at the Institute of Advanced Study, a short distance from the university, Stone discovered a new world of historical scholarship far beyond the narrow confines of English constitutional and political history, as well as a new interdisciplinary world, promising new approaches and insights for historical study, which was also foreign to Oxford.

While at the Institute Stone met most of the members of the Princeton history department, which offered him a job. Robert R. Palmer's decision to leave Princeton left the Dodge chair of history vacant, and one member of the department suggested that because of "Englishmen's fondness for titles," the special distinction of the Dodge chair might help persuade Stone to accept their offer. Stone had already made it clear that his salary had to be high enough to permit annual research trips to England. He also requested more money to improve the library's holdings in English history, and he asked for a house with at least five bedrooms. The last request was the most challenging. But the administration managed to find Stone a large house next door to Arthur Link.[9]

Princeton offered many advantages. Stone had more time to himself and more flexibility about what he would teach. In contrast to endless battles over curriculum at Oxford, in the spring of his second year at Princeton, Stone went to Blum with a proposal to teach a new course that would combine history, sociology, and anthropology. Blum told him to go ahead and try it and not to worry if it didn't work. Princeton also offered a sabbatical leave every four years. The benefits of Princeton were enough to keep him there until his retirement in 1989, despite offers from Nottingham, Pittsburgh, Johns Hopkins, the University of California at Los Angeles, Yale (in 1969 and 1976), Edinburgh, and the Massachusetts Institute of Technology.

Stone had barely arrived at Princeton when the department received an unprecedented windfall. A Princeton graduate named Shelby Cullom Davis donated 5.2 million dollars to the Princeton history department toward the goal of the making the department the best in world. With the department generally depleted, it fell largely to Stone to decide how to spend the money. Stone decided first of all that under no circumstances should the money be spent on a building. Instead, he spent the money to advance the department closer to the cutting edge of historical study, creating the Shelby Cullom Davis Center for Historical Studies. Stone became its first director in 1968. Each year the Davis Center uses its resources to bring in four or five outside scholars to Princeton to stimulate intellectual exchange.[10]

The primary medium of exchange was the Davis Seminar, which continues to meet most Friday mornings in the Firestone Library. At the seminar one of the visiting scholars or another invitee or on occasion a member of the Princeton history department presents a paper, which usually summarizes work in progress and is subjected to the criticism of the audience. The seminar soon developed an aura of mortal combat where many a scholar found himself transformed into a wounded and hunted animal, hounded remorselessly by a pack of merciless wild dogs. Stone himself set the aggressive tone. Following a paper by the director of a lavishly funded social history project that had produced few publishable results, Stone asked him if he did not feel like the last dinosaur, "devouring all of the remaining provender that might otherwise sustain dozens of smaller but better conceived studies." Not all of Stone's ambushes succeeded, even though he did not shrink before the great and near great of the profession. When the social historian E.P. Thompson, whose status had reached near deification, delivered a paper that attacked the ruling oligarchies of eighteenth-century England, Stone rose to deliver a counterattack. Quoting a string of derisive terms that Thompson had employed to describe Sir Robert Walpole and the ruling elite, Stone asked, "Is this history? Is this kind of language, even helpful, much less objective?" Thompson was barely fazed. "Why Lawrence," he replied in mock indignation, "a new deity has recently been erected in the land, and it is called 'political stability.' When someone creates new gods, the only proper response is—blasphemy."[11]

Part of the edge that the Friday seminar acquired was derived from Stone's determination to confront the so-called "new history." For all its excellence the Princeton department of the 1950s tended to focus on fairly traditional political and intellectual history. Moreover, there was little archival work being undertaken. "Not one person, either faculty or graduate student, was engaged in archival research when I arrived at Princeton," Stone recalled.

The "new history" was largely the creation of two French professors, Marc Bloch and Lucien Febvre, who admonished historians to look beyond what they considered largely ephemeral political and diplomatic events, to the larger variables, such as demography, climate, geography, and *mentalité*, which in their judgment did more to shape human behavior. Toward that goal the Davis seminar advanced such themes as the history of the family, popular culture, education, political power and ideology, war and society, charity and welfare, and the transmission of culture.

At the core of the new history was the assimilation of history and cultural anthropology. Several members of the Princeton department, such as Natalie Zemon Davis and Robert Darnton, inspired in part by the work of the anthropologist Clifford Geertz, employed the techniques of cultural anthropology in their work. Their findings often seemed to lend credence to left-wing approaches to history. Natalie Davis's work placed many civic riots in the sixteenth century, not as unruly behavior, but as subtle protests. This apparent sympathy with the Left led Norman Cantor, a historian at New

York University who had been one of Strayer's graduate students in the old regime at Princeton, to publish several articles in the 1980s on what he perceived as the leftist takeover of the academy. Prominent among his examples of leftist dominance, was Lawrence Stone and the Davis Center.[12]

Stone's scholarship flourished at Princeton. He had just arrived when his masterpiece, *The Crisis of the Aristocracy, 1558–1641*, appeared. In 1972 he published the controversial *The Causes of the English Revolution, 1529–1642*, followed by *Family and Fortune: Studies in Aristocratic Finance in the 16th and 17th Centuries* in 1973. His next project began under difficult and unusual circumstances. In 1973 he suffered a mild heart attack and was confined to a hospital for six weeks. With nothing to do for such an extended period of time, except read and sleep, he "instructed" his wife to remove from the university library shelves all English collections of family letters, autobiographies, advice books, journals, etc., from the sixteenth, seventeenth, and eighteenth centuries, and to bring them to his bedside along with a substantial supply of paper. Thus equipped, he immersed himself the source materials of the early modern English family, emerging from confinement six weeks later with almost enough material to write a book.[13] With that book completed, he returned, along with his wife, Jeanne Fawtier Stone, to a long-standing project on social mobility in England, which resulted in *An Open Elite? England, 1540–1880* in 1984. In 1981 his essays were collected and published as *The Past and the Present*. In recent years he has published a series of volumes on divorce.

One of Stone's triumphs as chair was to recruit Carl Schorske from the University of California at Berkeley, for which he had left Wesleyan in 1960. In 1959, while on leave at the Institute for Advanced Study in the Behavioral Sciences at Stanford, a friend at Berkeley asked him to take over his course in intellectual history for two weeks. Schorske was delighted to discover that the class, which enrolled over three hundred students, exuded a spirit of engagement and intellectual energy that he had never encountered before. He was quickly gripped by a sense that Berkeley was the place where he wanted to teach. Strangely, he had spurned an earlier offer. Now, four years later, he called another friend to find out if the offer was still open. To his amazement, it was.[14]

Harvard gave him a vocation. Wesleyan sharpened his interdisciplinary sense. Berkeley placed him in the epicenter of the crisis of the American university in the 1960s. Lingering fears of Communism, the civil rights movement, the war in Vietnam, all tested, among other things, the commitment of the American university to academic freedom. In 1964 the history department invited Herbert Aptheker, a self-proclaimed Marxist historian with impressive scholarly credentials, to speak at a departmental colloquium. When the university administration refused to fund his appearance, the department raised its own money and took the colloquium off campus.

Student unrest sliced the campus apart.[15] Schorske became involved on the Emergency Executive Committee of the Academic Senate and as the chancellor's officer for educational development. Strange bedfellows appeared everywhere. The Berkeley history department was deeply divided on how the crisis should be handled, and many of the Academic Senate's more persuasive speakers were drawn from its ranks. Yet, even though history colleagues might oppose each other on the Academic Senate, they might reunite in department deliberation. Professional courtesy and collegiality prevailed amidst deep division, unlike other Berkeley departments, such as politics and sociology, where methodological divisions often collided head-on with political divisions and where collegiality vanished. Schorske also found stability in his classes, which remained eager and engaged throughout the controversy.

Schorske accepted the Princeton offer in order to rescue his scholarly work. He loved Berkeley, but the students and the student unrest sapped too much of his energy, and his research had been seriously neglected. The Princeton appointment included a three-year, half-time fellowship at the Institute for Advanced Study. The change in position again affected his intellectual direction. At Princeton his vocation shifted away from history to the humanities as a whole.

Stone and Schorske were also involved in the worst moment in recent years for the Princeton history department, the dispute over the scholarship over one of the department's young assistant professors, David Abraham. Abraham was recommended for tenure by the history department, primarily on the basis of his book *The Collapse of the Weimar Republic*, only to have his bid rejected by the university administration. At about the same time, several scholars outside Princeton raised questions concerning the integrity of Abraham's scholarship in *The Collapse of the Weimar Republic*. With a virulence unusual even for the historical profession, those critics denounced Abraham for misquoting, misciting, misusing, and even deliberately falsifying documents. The most damning and repeated charge was that Abraham's errors had been used to buttress an argument that could not stand without them. Abraham, however, refused to go quietly. While he acknowledged and apologized for many of his errors, he denied that there was a pattern to them or that his overall thesis was damaged by their correction.[16]

Several members of the Princeton history department, including Stone and Schorske, rose to Abraham's defense. Natalie Davis compared the attack on Abraham to McCarthyite attacks on Communists in the 1950s. Stone defended Abraham in terms of the general messiness of life. "When you work in the archives," he said, "you're far from home, you're bored, you're in a hurry, you're scribbling like crazy. You're bound to make mistakes. I don't believe any scholar in the Western world has impeccable footnotes." Schorske was offended by the incivility of the attack and what he regarded as a sad confusion on the part of Abraham's critics between "facticity" and historical truth. "The defects in David's book are glaring and inexcusable," he argued, "but they are remediable and without any substantial impact on the unfolding economic and political analysis. When all the errors are corrected, the argument will stand exactly; the historical configuration will not change; the interpretative logic of the book will be upheld." Another member of the department, Arno Mayer, suspected a more subtle motivation. Abraham's critics, he declared, were really "trying to get at the Princeton history department—because of what Stone does, what Natalie Davis does, what Carl Schorske does, and so on. Those who have been attacking are very old-fashioned political historians and are resentful that they have been, how should I say, passed by."[17]

Apart from Yale and Princeton, several other historians made career changes. In 1960, on the crest of his Pulitzer Prize–winning work on Roosevelt, Arthur Schlesinger Jr. reentered politics, willing to work for "any two-legged liberal mammal who could defeat Richard Nixon." He finally selected John F. Kennedy, though Schlesinger's wife remained loyal to the traditional liberal champion of the Democratic party in 1950s, Adlai Stevenson.[18]

Without realizing it at first, Schlesinger and Kennedy may have been attracted to each other because they had much in common. Born one year apart, Harvard undergraduates in the 1930s, authors of Pulitzer Prize–winning books, veterans of World War II, Kennedy and Schlesinger were virtually poster children for their generation. Schlesinger was also looking for a more active role in the formation of public policy and had in the past complained of "being upstairs writing the speeches while the political decisions were being taken elsewhere." When Kennedy offered him a position as a special assistant to the president, he took a leave of absence from Harvard to take it. His new assignment, if somewhat nebulous, took him into many new areas, including liaison to the United States ambassador to the United Nations and policy advisor on Latin American affairs. Schlesinger was perhaps most valuable as an informal liaison between the Kennedy administration and the nation's university and cultural communities. As such, he was often the subject of conservative criticism. In the face of one barrage of criticism, he offered to resign. Kennedy dismissed his offer. "Don't worry about it," the president told Schlesinger, "all they are doing is shooting at me through you." Schlesinger eventually resigned from Harvard to continue working in Washington after his leave of absence expired in 1962.

Schlesinger was having dinner with John Kenneth Galbraith and Katherine Graham when he heard the news of Kennedy's assassination. The news was particularly jolting to Schlesinger, who revered Kennedy. He accepted Lyndon Johnson's request to remain on the White House staff, but the magic was gone. He resigned in 1964 and remained in Washington to write a personal memoir of the Kennedy years. After the Bay of Pigs fiasco,

Kennedy asked Schlesinger to keep a journal. "You can be damn sure that the CIA. has its record and the Joint Chiefs theirs," Kennedy asserted. "We'd better make sure we have a record over here."

With stunning speed, at one stretch producing 420 manuscript pages in a month, Schlesinger produced *A Thousand Days: John F. Kennedy in the White House*, which was serialized in *Life* magazine. *A Thousand Days* sparked more controversy, especially with the revelation that Kennedy was particularly disappointed in the performance of Secretary of State Dean Rusk, who was still serving in the Johnson administration. But in 1966 *A Thousand Days* was awarded a Pulitzer Prize for history and biography.

In the same year Schlesinger returned to academic life, accepting a fellowship at the Institute for Advanced Study in Princeton, and, shortly afterward, becoming Albert Schweitzer Professor of Humanities at CUNY. The chair included a salary of $30,000 combined with a minimal teaching load and a $70,000 stipend for staff, research, conferences, and other expenses. The CUNY offer provided a breathtaking opportunity to pursue his own research and writing. His wife remained in Washington, and Schlesinger became known as something of a man about town in New York, occasionally spotted at the city's more fashionable nightspots, and giving an interview to *Playboy* magazine. Eventually he and wife divorced in 1968. Schlesinger remarried in 1970.

In New York his life took two other directions. First, he became a constituent and friend of another Kennedy, New York's senator Robert Kennedy. Second, he became engaged in the debate about the Vietnam War. As early as 1965 he opposed the American involvement in Vietnam, and in 1967 he published *The Bitter Heritage: Vietnam and American Democracy, 1941–1966*. Despite his opposition to the war, Schlesinger was hard-pressed to defend himself from the charge that American involvement in Vietnam was an outgrowth of the anticommunist legacy he himself had nurtured in the 1950s and that his critique of American foreign policy did not go far enough.

At the same time the history of American foreign policy was reevaluated by left-wing historians, among them William Appleman Williams, Gabriel Kolko, and Gar Alperovitz, who not only denounced American foreign policy as imperialist, but blamed the beginning of the cold war on American policy makers. These officials, claimed the New Left revisionists, blinded by their hatred and irrational fears of Communist aggression, confused the Soviet desire for security and internal rebuilding with expansionism, thereby pushing the world to the edge of destruction.

For a while these arguments seemed to have swept all before them. For these radical historians American policy in Vietnam was not an aberration in American foreign policy, but the extension of a tradition of self-interest, often conceived from incorrect or irrational fears. Such arguments struck at the core of Schlesinger's political philosophy, and he attempted to rebut the revisionists in popular journals. He also gave his imprimatur to what appeared to be a mortal blow delivered to the revisionists, Robert J. Maddox's *The New Left and the Origins of the Cold War*. In this book Maddox, who had begun as a student of Williams at Wisconsin, but had twice failed his comprehensive exams, examined the way seven New Left scholars had treated a critical, four-month period in 1945 and uncovered many serious discrepancies between what was said in the documents and what appeared on the pages of the revisionists' books.

Those who believed that the New Left view of the cold war and American foreign policy was too extreme bored in for the kill. Schlesinger and Oscar Handlin believed that Maddox had proven his case and that revisionist history on the origins of the cold war had been thoroughly discredited. When other reviewers were not as impressed, seeing Maddox as more pedantic than substantive, Handlin charged them with "betraying the profession." In the end the most persuasive work on the origins of the cold war, John Lewis Gaddis's *The United States and the Origins of the Cold War*, while assigning primary responsibility to the Soviets, made substantial concessions to the revisionists.[19]

In the debate over the origins of the cold war, Schlesinger found, like many of his generation, his centrist point of view under assault. Like many American liberals, he saw errors on both sides, but still adhered to the anticommunist viewpoint he had repeatedly expressed after World War II. The cold war was in his judgment and that of most of his generation, "the brave and essential response of free men to Communist aggression." For the revisionists, it was this kind of knee-jerk, anti-Sovietism that blinded American policymakers from the reality that the Soviets were principally concerned with security and internal reconstruction rather than expansion and global dominance.

In 1973 Schlesinger published *The Imperial Presidency*, which condemned what he argued was Richard Nixon's attempt to highjack the presidency from the control of Congress and the people. In 1979 Schlesinger's *Robert Kennedy and His Times* won for him a second National Book Award. The assassination of Robert Kennedy in 1968 had been as personally devastating to Schlesinger as that of John Kennedy. When he heard the news of Robert Kennedy's assassination, he was preparing a commencement address at CUNY. Abandoning his original text, he delivered instead a scathing address on "The Politics of Violence," in which he bitterly denounced the American people as "the most frightening people on earth." In his biography of Robert Kennedy he posed a sharp contrast between the Kennedy brothers: "John Kennedy was a realist disguised as a romantic; Robert Kennedy, a romantic stubbornly disguised as a realist."

In recent years Schlesinger published *The Cycles of American History* (1986), a collection of essays in which he argued, along lines similar to his father, that there are boom and reform cycles in American history. Periods of economic boom, for example, tend to lead to the concentration of wealth in the hands of the few and a general inattention to the problems of the poor. The triumph of business is usually followed by a period of reform, of which the Progressive movement and the New Deal are the most obvious examples, where the excesses of rampant free enterprise are redressed. In 1991 Schlesinger tackled the burning issue of multiculturalism in *The Disuniting of America*. While he claimed to welcome the increasing historical attention to the role and achievements of previously subordinated groups in America history, such as women, Hispanics, black Americans, Native Americans, he warned that the obsession with the cult of race, gender, and ethnicity had a price. In contrast with the New Deal liberalism he consistently admired, multicultural politics created a culture of complaint in which political resources were distributed in accordance with which groups could present the most abrasive case for victimization.

In the 1960s Daniel Boorstin also received many awards and made a career change. Having taught at the University of Chicago since 1944, he was appointed to the Morton Professorship of History, and in 1968 he was designated a distinguished service professor at Chicago, the university's highest honor. In 1968 he was awarded an honorary doctorate from Cambridge University. In 1969, he decided to leave Chicago when he was appointed director of the National Museum of History and Technology of the Smithsonian Institution in Washington. In 1975 President Gerald Ford appointed Boorstin Librarian of Congress, though he was not a professional librarian.[20]

For most of the sixties and early seventies, he continued work on his great trilogy of American experience. *The Americans: The National Experience*, for which he was awarded the Francis Parkman Prize, appeared in 1965, and *The Americans: The Democratic Experience*, which won the Pulitzer Prize for history, appeared in 1973. Boorstin continued to stress the idiosyncratic, adaptive features of American society. By the time of the second volume he had clearly been influenced by his work at National Museum of History and Technology at the Smithsonian, as he added more emphasis on technology, exploration, and inventions, an interest that persisted through such later works as *The Exploring Spirit: America and the World, Then and Now*; *The Discoverers*; and *The Creators*.

But no historian moved around as much as John Hope Franklin. In 1964 after eight years at Brooklyn College he went to the University of Chicago. The move to Chicago was prompted by his desire to teach graduate students. There were many topics that aroused his curiosity, far more than he could explore himself.

Before he left for Chicago he took part in the 1963 freedom march from Selma, Alabama, to Montgomery. Twice before, marchers had been turned back by state troopers. This time they were determined not to be denied, but an undercurrent of tension and fear swept through the marchers. They were expected to be brave and unbowed, but as they marched, they were clearly watched and stalked by disapproving spectators. They did not know what the most disgruntled might do or when they might do it. Nearly one hundred historians participated in the march, and it was more unnerving when someone suggested they all be pushed to the front ranks.

In 1976 Franklin was invited to give the Jefferson Lecture. The invitation posed a bleak irony. Jefferson, the mythic champion of American freedom, said nothing in the Declaration of Independence about the injustice of the slave trade or the need of freedom for black people, and while he deplored slavery in his later writing, he continued to live off slave labor. In his lecture Franklin exposed these contradictions in Jefferson's life. Other historians knew of them, apologized for them. Franklin did not.

Franklin retired from Chicago in 1980, spent two years at the National Humanities Center, and in 1982 became James B. Duke Professor of History at Duke and later a professor of legal history at the Duke University Law School. In 1996 he was awarded the Presidential Medal of Freedom from President Clinton, and he had received 105 honorary degrees and served as president of the main historical associations in the United States, the American Historical Association, the Organization of American Historians, and the Southern Historical Association.

Several others remained at the institutions where they had established themselves. During the 1960s and 1970s Oscar Handlin remained at Harvard and like many of the others, garnered high hosannas for his work. At Harvard he became Charles Warren Professor of American History and director of the Warren Center for Studies in American History in 1965. In 1973 he was chosen Carl Pforzheimer University Professor. In 1979 he was named director of the Harvard University Library. Outside of Harvard, he was awarded honorary degrees by Colby College, Hebrew Union College, Northern Michigan University, Oakland University, Seton Hall, Brooklyn College, and Boston College. In 1972–73 he served as Harmsworth Professor of American History at Oxford. In 1973 he became a trustee of the American Academy of Arts and Sciences.[21]

He also continued his Olympian rate of scholarly production. Working as usual with his wife and collaborator, Mary Flug Handlin, Handlin produced in the 1960s a study of civil rights, a book on the characteristics and meaning of liberty in American life and a popular history of the American people, stressing ethnicity and internal migration in American history rather than politics and great men. A book of his poetry appeared in 1977. Of particular interest to the Handlins were questions of education, university life, and student unrest. In *Facing Life: Youth and the Family in American History*, the Handlins wrote a history of adolescence, reaching some harsh conclusions concerning what they regarded as the affluent, spoiled brat radicals of the 1960s, who denounced the material wealth of the United States but who continued to enjoy the luxuries it produced.

Mary Flug Handlin died in 1976, and Handlin remarried a year later. In 1979 he published *Truth in History*, a collection of his essays, in which he professed a profound disillusionment with the historical profession. He even said that, given the chance, he might choose another profession. For so renowned a scholar, holding a position at the pinnacle of his profession, such alienation was astonishing. The roots of his disillusionment were many. First, he deplored what he regarded as a steady erosion of standards and collegiality in the profession. Describing the first meeting of the American Historical Association he attended in 1936, Handlin recalled the cordiality of the older members, such as Howard K. Beale, Paul Lewinson, Eugene Anderson, and Hans Rosenberg, who made him feel that he was part of a community of scholars who shared a willingness to assist each other in the search for historical truth. The idea of shared enterprise eroded slowly over the years. AHA meetings increasingly became arenas for individual advancement and partisan causes. By the late 1960s the tightly knit community of scholars Handlin encountered in 1936 had been torn asunder by historical fads and ideologically rigid men and women eager to use the association to advance their own agendas. Hiring quotas, requests to consider candidates for association office on the basis of race, gender, and ethnicity, scheduling association meetings only in states that had ratified the equal rights amendment, overspecialization, and antiquarianism all contributed to the erosion of the historical community that had initially attracted him to the profession. Handlin was also distressed in 1970 when David Hackett Fischer, a historian at Brandeis University, published *Historians' Fallacies*, a book about the flawed methodologies employed by some historians. Fischer examined a vast range of historical writing and discovered some egregious violations of the most elementary norms of historical evidence, even by some of the most celebrated members of the profession. Handlin was stunned to find himself included in places on Fischer's roster of errant scholars.[22]

The debate over the origins of the cold war was perhaps the final blow. Like Schlesinger, Handlin viewed the cold war as complex, but on balance, the product of Soviet aggression. He therefore welcomed Maddox's expose of the factual errors made by New Left historians. But what truly outraged him was not so much the errors exposed by Maddox, but the response of the historical profession to Maddox's book. Handlin believed that by the standards of the historical profession, reviewers were compelled to recognize that the errors discovered by Maddox discredited the revisionist point of view. Many of the reviewers of Maddox's book, however, particularly those on the Left, scrambled to defend the revisionists. The defenders of revisionism usually argued that the mistakes identified by Maddox were inconsequential, or even if they were consequential, nevertheless did not damage the broader interpretation of American culpability in cold war origins. For Handlin the defense of revisionism meant that books were no longer to be reviewed on merit; they would be praised or denigrated as representatives of a school or interpretation, in Handlin's eyes the final abdication of professional responsibility.[23]

Kenneth Stampp remained at Berkeley for the rest of his career. Following his acclaimed work on slavery, a new book, *The Era of Reconstruction*, published in 1965, offered a fresh theoretical perspective, on the Reconstruction. In the era of the civil rights movement, Stampp enjoyed an enormous national and international reputation. He delivered dozens of lectures and was a visiting professor at Harvard and Colgate. In 1960 he was Commonwealth Lecturer at the University of London, and a year later he served as Harmsworth Professor at Oxford. In 1977 he was elected president of the Organization of American Historians. He received numerous awards and citations, including an American Historical Association award for scholarly distinction.[24] In 1980 his essays were collected and published as *The Imperiled Union: Essays on the Background of the Civil War*. In 1990 he published *America in 1857*, explaining why the American Civil War became all but inevitable by the end of 1857.

His stay at Oxford had important personal implications for his life. Recently divorced from his first wife, he met Isabel Macartney-Filgate, a medical social worker, while in Oxford. They married even before he left Oxford, and their marriage survived until her death in 1996.

Like Schorske, Stampp was frustrated by student unrest at Berkeley. Still a radical at heart, he was quite sympathetic to the free speech movement, believing that university authorities were foolish to deny the students the right to have political meetings. He devoted a great deal of time to service on committees dealing with student concerns. But he slowly became disillusioned with the students, when having secured free speech for themselves, they tried to deny it to others. Students objected to having Arthur Goldberg speak at Berkeley because he was in favor of the Vietnam War. In the face of student objections Goldberg could come to Berkeley only as part of a debate with a radical professor. In the end Stampp came to wish that he had not wasted so much time with student issues.

Equally distressing was the attitude of black militants. The success of *The Peculiar Institution* had not only won Stampp renown as a historian, but had made him a prophet in his own time. Year after year Stampp was asked to speak at Negro History Week at Berkeley and to lecture on black history and race relations at other campuses. *The Peculiar Institution* had been praised by black historians as well as white. Yet by the end of the 1960s, Stampp and his book were attacked by younger blacks. At a 1969 conference at Wayne State University on the "Black Man in America," Stampp was informed by blacks that, as a white man, he had no right to write *The Peculiar Institution.* The fact that other white historians faced the same indictment did not make it easier to accept.[25]

For William McNeill the 1960s were a happy harmonic convergence. Since his magical encounter with Toynbee at Cornell just before World War II, he nursed an ambition to write a history of the world. He found two colleagues at Chicago, Donald Lach, a history colleague interested in the impact of China upon Europe, and Marshall Hodgson, a student of Islamic languages, who had similar interests and ambitions. Hodgson in particular shared McNeill's desire to write a history of the world, but died before he began the project. The two worked in close concert. Collaboration with Hodgson was essential for McNeill to write his greatest book, *The Rise of the West,* published in 1963, for which he received the National Book Award.[26]

The Rise of the West combined a stunning global vision with wide learning spread across millennia. The book vaulted onto national best-seller lists when it received a rave, front-page review from Hugh Trevor-Roper in the *New York Times Book Review.* Trevor-Roper certainly recognized a great book when he saw one, but in *The Rise of the West,* McNeill proposed a version of historical development much different from that of Toynbee, whom Trevor-Roper despised and whose *A Study of History* Trevor-Roper thrashed in an earlier review. Trevor-Roper's review of *The Rise of the West* was at least in part a device for Trevor-Roper to continue his attack on Toynbee, but McNeill was nonetheless the prime beneficiary.

The response of his Chicago colleagues to McNeill's global vision was varied. Most were encouraging in general terms. But outside of Lach and Hodgson, none of McNeill's colleagues had much interest in what he was doing. While they congratulated him on the great success of *The Rise of the West,* McNeill doubts that any of them actually read it, although he concedes that, "well, it was eight hundred pages."

From 1961 to 1967 he served as chair of the Chicago history department. His goal as chair was to develop a systematic and linguistically competent investigation of all the great cultures of the world. In his six years at chair the Chicago department managed to have at least two persons with linguistic competence in the study of all the major cultural regions of the world except Africa. This impetus, however successful, had some disastrous consequences, which McNeill had not anticipated. With the professoriat spread diffusely over different regional and linguistic specialties, the department lost much of the sense of shared enterprise and common ground it possessed when it was comprised primarily of American and European historians.

From 1971 to 1978 McNeill served as the editor of the *Journal of Modern History.* The position placed him even more on the cutting edge of scholarship and also gave him a sense of the enormous power wielded by the editor of that journal, since as editor he could shape what was published in it by commissioning articles and, indirectly, by selecting the people to review submissions. Among the high points of his editorial tenure were two issues that he commissioned specially, one on Fernand Braudel, the other on A.J.P. Taylor, both with the goal of trying to connect the relationship between their lives and their work. Braudel was initially reluctant to contribute, though he eventually did so on the urging of his wife. The Braudel issue also contained a stimulating critical assessment of his work by J.H. Hexter. McNeill thought the Braudel issue was the best one he produced as editor. The Taylor issue commanded as much attention, but was less successful. Taylor produced a typically perverse essay, arguing for the importance of accident in life and history; the supplementary pieces were dense. McNeill concluded that the Taylor issue was a dud.[27]

A multitude of honors came McNeill's way. Following his tenure as chair, he was, like Boorstin, appointed a distinguished service professor at Chicago. He lectured in universities in Europe and Australia and was awarded numerous honorary degrees. In 1985 he served as president of the American Historical Association. He continued to publish prodigiously. *Plagues and Peoples*, published in 1976, brought many of the ideas first developed in *The Rise of the West* to a popular audience. Other books, such as *Venice: The Hinge of Europe* (1974), *The Pursuit of Power* (1982), *Europe's Steppe Frontier* (1964), a biography of Toynbee, published in 1989, and, most recently, *Marching in Time* (1994), reflect his remarkable range of interests and voluminous reading.

Two members of the World War II generation died at the peak of their careers. Between 1970 and 1971, cancer claimed both Richard Hofstadter and David Potter. By the 1960s Hofstadter stood at the summit of the historical profession. In 1964 he received his second Pulitzer Prize for *Anti-Intellectualism in American Life*, a book that reflected Hofstadter's long-standing interest in the extent to which American life was shaped by anti-intellectual attitudes. He was awarded prestigious guest lectureships at Berkeley, Harvard, and other American universities, and held such coveted positions as Pitt Professor at Cambridge and as a visiting senior fellow at Princeton. In 1959 he was appointed to the De Witt Clinton Chair of American history at Columbia.[28]

In the last years of his life, Hofstadter continued to work with the disciplined intensity that had characterized his entire professional career. Between 1968 and his death in 1970, he published two books, *The Progressive Historians: Turner, Beard, and Parrington* (1968) and *The Idea of a Party System: The Rise of Legitimate Opposition in the United States, 1780–1840* (1969). He had also written several chapters of another project on a completely different project, a projected three-volume work on *America at 1750: A Social Project*, which he referred to as "Hofstadter's folly."

He wrote his first great book in a darkened hospital sickroom while his first wife battled cancer. Now, weakened by disease and wracked by pain, he struggled with *America at 1750* in his own hospital sickroom, continuing to work and talk about future books even as his condition worsened. He died 24 October 1970.

Like Hofstadter, David Potter lost a battle with cancer. Unlike Hofstadter, he did not go out in a blaze of glory. In his later life he suffered grievously both personally and professionally. His first marriage ended in divorce after six years. In 1960 he decided to leave Yale for Stanford, a decision that opened the door for Vann Woodward to come to Yale. Potter had been at Yale for eighteen years and felt underappreciated there. Still, the decision to leave was agonizing. Edmund Morgan stayed up most of the night talking with Potter the night before he left.[29]

At Stanford, Potter was a success as a teacher, winning Stanford's Dinkelspiel Award for distinguished teaching in 1968. But his problems persisted. He overcommitted himself to publishers and lecture tours, promising far more than he could deliver. In 1968 his second wife committed suicide. Shortly after her suicide he discovered he was desperately ill with cancer.[30]

Gordon Craig, who had recently arrived at Stanford after his own departure from Princeton, remembers the tragic story. Craig and other faculty members gave parties and organized bird watching trips to help Potter keep his mind off his troubles. Potter responded by taking treatments for his cancer and maintaining a fierce sense of professionalism. He once flew back to Stanford to attend an Academic Senate meeting after receiving treatment for his cancer. The disease could not be arrested, and in the end he went quickly. He died in Palo Alto on February 18, 1971. "He was the wisest man I ever knew," Edmund Morgan remarked in tribute. In 1977, his last manuscript, *The Impending Crisis*, completed and edited by his Stanford colleague and friend, Don Fehrenbacher, was published and awarded a Pulitzer Prize.

Gordon Craig's years at Stanford were happier than Potter's. He had strong emotional ties to Princeton, and his wife had founded a nursery school there. But, after more than twenty years at Princeton, he itched for a change, tired of seeing the same cars parked outside at every dinner party. Princeton bred too much familiarity. Craig had already rejected several opportunities to leave. He could have gone to Berkeley when his mentor Sontag retired, and he was offered a position as department chair at the University of Washington in Seattle. The chance to go to Stanford came one night with a phone call from Gordon Wright, the Stanford chair. The Stanford offer was tempting in part because Craig could go there as the J.E. Wallace Sterling Professor of History, and because it afforded him his first opportunity to teach German history. In all his years at Princeton Craig had never taught German history; he had always taught diplomatic history.[31]

While his experience at Stanford was a happy one, Craig saw a vast difference between Stanford and Princeton. At Princeton there was a great deal of socialization and a sense of solidarity among the department and commitment to students and the university. These things existed at Stanford, but not to the extent that they did in Princeton. There was certainly less friendship among the Stanford history faculty, since many of them lived in San Francisco, and came to campus only to teach classes and fled back to the city as quickly as possible.

Like the others, Craig continued to work steadily. In 1966, several of his essays were collected and published as *War, Politics, and Diplomacy*. In 1978 *Germany, 1866–1945* appeared, followed by *The Germans* in 1982 and, with Alexander George, *Force and Statecraft* in 1983. In 1982 he served as president of the American Historical Association.

In Britain many of the World War II generation of historians capped their careers by becoming heads of Oxbridge colleges. Richard Southern and Christopher Hill, fellows of Balliol College since the 1930s, assumed the presidencies of Oxford colleges. In 1965 Christopher Hill was elected Master of Balliol College, the institution he had attended as an undergraduate and served as a fellow since 1938. He had acquired an exalted reputation at Balliol. Richard Cobb, a fellow of the college, due to a garbled telephone message, referred to Hill as "Supergod," and the name caught on. Maurice Keen, another history colleague, urged Hill to stand for the mastership even though he knew Hill would propose many measures that Keen would detest. The assumption of the Balliol mastership was a curious paradox. Hill was the most prominent Marxist in Oxford but now stood at the pinnacle of the Oxford establishment, a circumstance as incongruous as a vagrant becoming a CEO. In the 1960s many of the same social forces that had been exerting pressures on American universities invaded the sheltered spires of Oxford. Many hallowed Oxford traditions, such as the refusal to admit women to the traditionally men's colleges, came under ferocious assault. Students also objected to rules requiring formal dress on so many occasions, to rules against having women in their rooms, and to curfews. At Balliol Hill sided with students on almost every issue, advocating the admission of women, reducing the number of college occasions requiring formal dress, and favoring a greater degree of student freedom and autonomy. In 1968 his radical principles were put to their severest test. Student unrest at Oxford generally and at Balliol particularly erupted over opposition to American involvement in the Vietnam War and student right of access to their academic records and files. Again, Hill sided with the radicals, offending some of the Balliol and Oxford old guard who wanted him to assume a firmer line.[32]

Hill made other contributions to Balliol during his time as Master. Because of his personal charm and amiability, the senior common room at Balliol became more open and friendly. Not surprisingly Balliol undergraduates discovered a more accommodating and accessible Master than Balliol pupils had previously experienced. Fears that prevailed at the time of his election that he would neglect older fellows and abolish all the revered traditions, proved to be false. Hill even devoted considerable effort to fund-raising, even though he found that aspect of his job difficult and distasteful.

Despite the enormous demands on his time as Master of Balliol, Hill continued his staggering rate of scholarly productivity. *Intellectual Origins of the English Revolution* appeared in 1965, *Reformation to Industrial Revolution* in 1967, *God's Englishman* in 1970, *The World Turned Upside Down* in 1972, *Milton and the English Revolution* in 1978, and *Milton and Some Contemporaries* in 1984. In 1984 the first volume of his collected essays appeared, with succeeding volumes appearing in 1986. *A Turbulent, Seditious, and Factious People: John Bunyan and his Church* appeared in 1988, *A Nation of Change and Novelty* in 1990, and shortly after he turned eighty years old, *The English Bible and the Seventeenth Century Revolution* in 1993, with no end in sight.

Hill's Balliol colleague Richard Southern also became the head of an Oxford college, serving as president of St. John's College from 1969 to 1981. Southern received several other honors before ascending to St. John's presidency. In 1961 he was elected Chichele Professor of History at All Souls College, Oxford. His professorship provided relief from his heavy Balliol teaching load, and under it, Southern entered the most productive period of his scholarly career, writing or editing works such as *Western Views of Islam in the Middle Ages* (1962), *Eadmer's Vita Anselmi* (1963), *St. Anselm and his Biographer* (1963), and, with Dom F.S. Schmitt, OSB, *Memorials of St. Anselm* (1969). Southern also wrote most of *Western Society and the Church in the Middle Ages*, published in 1970. In 1968 Southern was a visiting professor at Berkeley, and he lectured widely in Britain, the United States, and Australia.

In 1969 he assumed the presidency of St. John's College, Oxford. Southern's goals as president of St. John's were different from Hill's as Master of Balliol.[33] The student revolution had eased somewhat by the time of his appointment. St. John's was a rich and beautifully appointed college, but lacked the intellectual power and reputation of the top Oxford colleges. Southern exhibited considerable interest in maintaining and improving the college buildings, especially the college chapel. But his main goal was to advance the college's academic reputation by expending greater efforts to recruit academically top-notch pupils and preparing them more thoroughly for Schools, while encouraging faculty research. At one point Southern assembled St. John's pupils and scolded them for their poor performance. He also made St. John's the first Oxford college to house all its pupils in college to encourage more diligent study. College presidents represent their institutions to the public, and Southern was a superb speaker at dinners and college gatherings, very much at ease with the fund-raising and glad-handing required of college presidents. He also took a personal interest in the members of the college staff at St. John's and was in turn beloved by them.

In later life honors continued to come Southern's way. He received honorary degrees from several universities, and from 1968 to 1972 served as president of the Royal Historical Society. He was knighted in 1974. In 1989, very deaf and in retirement, he was awarded a $60,000, all-European humanities prize. To the surprise of many, he donated the entire award to a small Oxford women's college to support a position in medieval history. Southern's generosity was in part a repayment of one of his principal intellectual debts. He offered it in the name of Vivian Galbraith, his favorite tutor at Balliol in the 1930s, whose daughter was now the head of the college.[34] After retirement he continued to publish. In 1986 he published *Robert Grosseteste: The Growth of an English Mind in Medieval Europe.* The title was significant. Grosseteste, the greatest of the English medieval scientists, had previously been regarded as the product of continental training. Southern demonstrated that Grosseteste was the product of an insular, English tradition, more humanistic than scholastic. Well into his eighties, he continued to work and has recently published *Scholastic Humanism and the Unification of Europe* (1995), the first volume of a projected series on scholastic humanism. In this work Southern has been particularly concerned to show how the development of academic learning even in the Middle Ages was subject to the demands of practical politics.

Balliol's tradition of combining scholarly productivity with dedication to teaching was continued by Richard Cobb, who was elected a fellow and tutor of the college in 1962. Like the others, he received many honors and awards in the 1960s and 1970s. He became a fellow of the British Academy in 1967 and delivered the Raleigh Lecture in 1974. In 1974 he was elected to a chair of modern history, which necessitated his removal from Balliol to Worcester College, Oxford. He was a visiting professor at the College de France in 1971 and Zaharoff Lecturer at Oxford in 1974, and received honorary fellowships from Balliol in 1977 and Merton, his undergraduate college, in 1979.

Like the others, Cobb maintained an impressive level of scholarly productivity, publishing *The Police and the People* (1970), *Reactions to the French Revolution* (1972), and *The Streets of Paris* (1980). His great work, *The People's Armies,* published in French in 1955, finally appeared in English in 1987. Cobb also produced a popular and captivating series of semiautobiographical volumes, including *A Second Identity* (1969), *People and Places* (1985), *Something to Hold Onto* (1988), and *Still Life: Sketches of a Tunbridge Wells Boyhood* (1993). A full-scale autobiography, *The End of the Line,* was published posthumously in 1997.

Cobb was also as great a personality as a historian, regaling his confidants at Oxford high tables with uproarious stories of his exploits. Restless by nature, Cobb rarely went gently into the night. While married with a family, he was definitely not a pipe and slippers man. His stories usually centered around some Olympian drinking bout, conducted through several pubs and establishments, and concluding in the wee hours of the morning.

He was on occasion even drunk when it came time for him to receive awards. Health problems related in part to his gargantuan alcoholic consumption required hospitalization in the last years, and a visitor heard a nurse remark to him, tongue deeply in cheek, "Richard, you must try to drink more."[35]

At Oriel College, Hugh Trevor-Roper continued as Regius Professor at Oxford, and was created Lord Dacre of Glanton in 1979. He continued to publish at a remarkable rate. *The Rise of Christian Europe* appeared in 1965, though it was subjected to a vicious review by Bruce McFarlane. Other books included *The Philby Affair* (1969), *The Plunder of the Arts in the Seventeenth Century* (1970), *Princes and Artists: Patronage and Ideology in Four Habsburg Courts, 1517–1633* (1976), and *The Hermit of Peking* (1977), a study of Sir Edmund Backhouse, a relatively obscure manuscript collector, small-time confidence man, and pornographer, who lived in China in the early twentieth century. Trevor-Roper's strength as a scholar was as an essayist, and he published several volumes of essays, including *The Crisis of the Seventeenth Century* (1967), *Renaissance Essays* (1985), *Catholicism, Anglicans, and Puritans: Seventeenth Century Essays* (1987), and *From Counter Reformation to Glorious Revolution* (1992).

Trevor-Roper also stubbed his toe on more than one occasion.[36] In 1983 he prematurely and incorrectly pronounced a bundle of documents thought to be the diaries of Adolf Hitler as authentic. And a few years before, in 1980, he was offered a position as Master of Peterhouse, Cambridge. Out of the blue, the phone rang one day with Peterhouse authorities offering him the job, which he accepted in part because he would be forced to retire against his wishes at Oxford at sixty-seven, and in part because his wife was charmed by the Master's lodgings at Peterhouse.

But instead of being a place to round off his career, Peterhouse proved to be a snake pit. One observer remarked, "they think they are getting a Tory, and [Trevor-Roper] is a Whig." Trevor-Roper likened Peterhouse at the time to a nineteenth-century British colony with lavish feasts, opulent living, and appointments made through a vast network of patronage rather than merit. If Peterhouse resembled a nineteenth-century colony, Trevor-Roper may have ruled it like a colonial governor. There were cries of tyranny among the Peterhouse dons when Trevor-Roper tried to introduce such things as open advertisements for tutorial positions. Much to his dismay, he found himself opposed by the conservatives who favored his appointment. He was relieved to step down in 1987 and retire to a rambling former rectory a few miles outside Oxford.

Geoffrey Elton also endured some unpleasant moments in Cambridge, although he did move steadily through the ranks. A fellow of Clare College since 1954, he was promoted to reader in Tudor studies in 1963, a position he held until 1967. He believed that the *Past and Present* debate over his *The Tudor Revolution in Government* had damaged his standing in Cambridge and that it had been designed to do so. In 1967 he was a candidate for the Regius Professorship in history along with John Plumb, though the position went instead to a compromise candidate, Owen Chadwick. In 1967 Elton did receive a chair in English history, where he chose the title of professor of constitutional history, in defiance of current historical fashion. In 1983 Elton succeeded Chadwick as Regius Professor of Modern History at Cambridge and remained there until his retirement in 1988. The appointment elicited a broad range of reaction. The *Guardian* deplored Elton as "the current spokesman of Tory history" and "a favorite of Thatcher's England." At the same time John Kenyon hailed Elton's appointment and matched him with Lewis Namier as the greatest British historians of the twentieth century.[37]

The Regius Professorship was only the most prestigious of many other honors garnered by Elton. He was elected a fellow of the British Academy in 1967 and president of the Royal Historical Society in 1972. He received honorary degrees from Glasgow (1979), Newcastle (1981), Bristol (1981), and London (1984). He was also awarded visiting professorships in the United States at Pittsburgh in 1963, Colorado in 1967, and Minnesota in 1976. He gave the Ford Lectures at Oxford in 1972, which were published as *Policy and Police: The Enforcement of the Reformation in the Age of Thomas Cromwell*. In 1986 he received a knighthood.

By the late 1980s several of his favorite and most debilitating habits began to catch up with him. He lived his life in flagrant disregard of conventional health practices as well as historical fashion, chain-smoking unfiltered Camel cigarettes, and drinking heavily, with Jack Daniels and Glenfiddich whiskies as particular favorites. By the early nineties he had lost much of the drive and demonic energy that had propelled him in his early career. Pupils who had known him during the earlier stages of his career noticed a visible physical and intellectual deterioration. His valedictory lecture at Cambridge, delivered to a full house, began in a rambling, incoherent way. With about ten minutes to go, he suddenly snapped out of it, and concluded with what one observer called "pure Gold."

Like several of the Oxford men, J.H. Plumb accepted the leadership of an Oxbridge college, becoming Master of Christ's College, Cambridge, in 1978, where he had been a fellow since 1946.[38] After his monumental work on Walpole, Plumb's career had taken a fresh turn in the 1960s, when he began to devote himself to writing books, including *The Crisis in the Humanities* (1964), *The Italian Renaissance* (1965), *Royal Heritage: The Treasures of the British Crown* (1977), *Georgian Delights* (1980), and *Royal Heritage: The Reign of Elizabeth II* (1981), designed to reach a popular audience. In 1987 and 1988, two volumes of his collected essays were published. As of 1997, his books had sold over three million copies, netting him more than a quarter of a million pounds in royalties.

In 1970 he provoked a controversy with the publication of *The Death of the Past*. Plumb began the book by distinguishing between "history" and the "past." Plumb reserved the past for events that can be used to explain and justify the present and the future. History is the attempt to determine what actually happened. History remains vital; the past is dying. Britain's decline as a world power and increasingly rapid technological change have combined to render the past obsolete. The past no longer helps explain the present, much less the future. Overly pedantic and specialized studies have severed the public from its interest in the past. To rescue it, historians must resist the temptation to write specialized studies and return to writing history for the general public. The new history of the past, according to Plumb, would not be a garish popularization designed to win back readers; it would reveal the lessons of human success in all their complexity.[39]

Plumb's love affair with America continued. In 1958–59 Richard Hofstadter arrived in Cambridge as Pitt Professor of American History. Plumb soon met both Hofstadter and his wife and became convinced that Hofstadter was going to be the outstanding historian of his generation and arranged a meeting between Hofstadter and the elderly George Macaulay Trevelyan. Hofstadter persuaded Plumb to come to Columbia for a term the following year. After seeing Plumb in action, Columbia proposed an arrangement by which Plumb might teach at both universities. The details accompanying the arrangement could not be worked out, but Plumb did manage to attach himself to *American Heritage*, a new popular history magazine.

Between 1961 and 1977 he returned again and again to the United States, mostly to lecture. By 1997 he had visited every state except three. Most distinguished academics who visit the United States confine themselves to elite universities and metropolitan areas, but Plumb went virtually everywhere, from Omaha, Nebraska, to Nagadochees, Texas, to Farmington, Maine. His most memorable experience occurred at Phillips University in Enid, Oklahoma. He arrived in Enid in ninety-five degree heat and was taken to a massively air-conditioned Chinese restaurant where the temperature dropped twenty-five degrees and where he dined on "egg rolls which tasted as if they had been cooked in diesel oil." He then discovered he was giving an after dinner speech not a lecture and that the unair-conditioned banquet hall was filled with characters out of a Zane Grey novel, wearing cowboy boots and Stetson hats. He ate his dinner in a growing pool of perspiration and realized that the decent people who filled the audience were probably not ready for a heavy-duty lecture on the growth of political stability in the eighteenth century. Casting aside his notes, he ad-libbed for fifty minutes on George III and the American Revolution, finishing, still somewhat damp from perspiration, to enthusiastic applause. He was quickly borne away to a reception in the house of a faculty member who possessed striking art and superb drinks and where the evening concluded with a lively discussion of the modern novel. At his motel the next morning he got a first-class breakfast at 6.30 (impossible in England), and his hostess from the previous night appeared, ready to make a 200–mile drive to Tulsa to see that he caught his plane.[40]

By this time he had also entered the ranks of American East Coast intellectual elite, when he began to review books for the *New York Review of Books* and to do a monthly column, usually about books, for the *Saturday Review*. He also renewed an earlier friendship with Daniel Patrick Moynihan, later a United States senator, whom he had known during Moynihan's days as a student at the London School of Economics. Moynihan and his wife had a vast circle of friends, especially New York intellectuals, like Arthur Schlesinger Jr., Gertrude Himmelfarb and Irving Kristol, Lionel and Diana Trilling, and the sociologists, Daniel Bell and Nathan Glazer. Associating with them gave Plumb access to high-level discussions of politics and social policy. He became particularly interested in slavery and the civil rights movement, and when Eugene Genovese spent a year in Cambridge at Pitt Professor, Plumb befriended Genovese and his wife, Elizabeth Fox-Genovese. With regular transatlantic jet service increasingly available in the 1960s, Plumb spent more and more time in the States and eventually became better known and more highly regarded in the States than in England.

By the 1970s Plumb began to be bored by academic life in England. As a professor he had to set on the Faculty Board for endless debates about tripos reform, particularly between Geoffrey Elton and Moses Finley, who never agreed about anything, except the design of the appalling History Faculty Building. Tired of the constant clashes and able to live from his own writing, Plumb retired in 1974.

Honors as well as wealth were his in the 1960s and 1970s. In 1965–66 he gave the Ford Lectures at Oxford, on the subject of the growth of political stability in England, 1675–1725, for which the ideas had been rattling around in his head since the late forties. Like Elton, he failed to win the Regius Professorship at Cambridge in 1967. But like Elton, he had a professorship created for him, and he served as Professor of Modern History at Cambridge from 1966 to 1974. In 1968 he was elected a fellow of the British Academy, and in 1982 he received a knighthood.

In 1978 he was appointed Master of Christ's College, a position in which he served until 1982. During his mastership, he made a concerted effort to stir up the college by appointing able faculty members, including the playwright Harold Pinter, and the psychologist Jonathan Miller, and by introducing a lecture series. A confirmed bachelor, he recalled that the period of his mastership was the only time in his life that he ever wanted a wife, due to the enormous amount of entertaining he was required to do with no staff to provide assistance.

Another Cambridge man, Eric Hobsbawm, did not enter administration.[41] Instead he continued his career at Birkbeck College, London, and his prodigious rate of publication. He produced several seminal studies of the British working class and social protest, including *Primitive Rebels* (1959), *Captain Swing,* with George Rude (1968), and *Bandits* (1969). But his major work involved the grand synthesis involved in several major works written for a popular audience, including *The Age of Revolution, 1789–1848* (1963), *The Age of Capital, 1848–1875* (1975), *The Age of Empire* (1987), and most recently, *The Age of Extremes* (1994). Hobsbawm also wrote extensively on jazz under the pseudonym of Francis Newton. In 1976 he was elected a fellow of the British Academy.

The years from about 1960 to 1980 saw the members of this generation reach the academic and intellectual summit. For the most part, they stood at the pinnacle of American and British intellectual life, holding top positions at prestigious universities, receiving distinguished visiting chairs and lecture invitations at home and abroad, reviewing new books in cutting-edge journals and the popular press, deciding much of what got into print and who got the most coveted jobs, and receiving money as well as acclaim for their books. There were of course a few potholes in the road. Being at the top also made them more visible targets. Even those who were themselves radical found themselves under attack in the changing mood of the sixties.

Chapter 8

TEACHING

𝔚

While the World War II generation of historians earned renown through their scholarship, it was teaching that kept food on the table, especially during the early stages of their careers. Teaching has become a controversial issue in modern higher education. Many have argued that the quality and amount of teaching in American universities has been sacrificed at the altar of research. It would be hard to apply that criticism to the World War II generation. Most taught enormous numbers of students and considered themselves dedicated teachers, achieving almost as much renown for their teaching as for their scholarship. "There is nothing more stimulating than teaching bright, inquisitive undergraduates," wrote John Hope Franklin as he surveyed his career.[1] Carl Schorske's finest book, *Fin-de-Siècle Vienna*, emerged in part from a long reflection on the best way to convey intellectual and cultural history to undergraduates.[2]

Ironically, the World War II generation encountered its finest students for the most part at the beginning of their teaching careers. Almost all of the World War II generation cite the veterans who returned to school right after World War II as the best group of students they ever taught. J.H. Hexter taught at Queens College from 1939 to 1957 and this experience was the best for him in terms of students, even though he subsequently taught at Washington University in St. Louis and at Yale. Hexter's students were primarily first- or second-generation Americans, perhaps half from Eastern European, Jewish families, the others a mixture of German, Irish, and a smattering of other nationalities. Their politics, especially the young Jews, were strongly leftist, even veering toward Moscow. Conservatism was regarded as a mild disorder that would eventually pass by graduation.[3]

Unlike most of his contemporaries, Hexter never lectured. Queens expected Socratic teaching, and in any event, the purpose of teaching for

Hexter was to make students think by reading great texts and being challenged to confront the ideas contained in them: "a bloody hard way to teach," he remembered later. Hexter feared that he was a terrible teacher at first, but he got better. Recalling the introductory course in Western civilization he taught at Queens, Hexter described an example of the way his teaching worked at its best, though he attributed whatever success he enjoyed as a teacher to his subject. For his Western civilization class, he normally used the section of Aristotle's *Politics* that contains the famous defense of slavery. Explaining to the students that their first task was to understand the argument and the logic behind it, Hexter took them through each step in Aristotle's argument, where Aristotle discusses how some human beings are brighter, more talented than others, some are capable of governing, while others through a variety of defects are incapable of being governed. In Hexter's relation there was a critical moment in the process when Aristotle's dialectical ambush unfolds. Accept a lengthy exposition of premises about the inferiority of some people or about how some people are not capable of self-governance, and Aristotle snares you in a shrewdly laid trap. Even if you feel passionately that slavery is unjust and cruel, you can't escape Aristotle's logical conclusion. For Hexter, it was a particularly poignant moment in the educational process. "Those terribly bright and touchingly humane argumentative radical [no punctuation in Hexter] youngsters were up against the fact that intellectually Aristotle had argued them into a justification of human bondage," he wrote later. At this point in the discussion Hexter assured the students that he knew they were not bigots or apologists for slavery, but if they did not like the trap into which they had been snared, it was up to them to fight their way out. After another quarter of an hour, these young people, Hexter noted, "the brightest and best I ever taught, were still unsuccessfully struggling against the silken bonds of reason they had let Aristotle trap them with. . . . It was a dramatic lesson in humility . . . ; now suddenly they found themselves eyeball to eyeball with a tough Greek kid 2300 years old who that far back had anticipated all the moves they tried to make, and kept them blocked into an intellectual position they found intolerable. They were licked."

Hexter practiced this method through textbooks as well. In the 1960s he was editor in chief for a volume titled *Traditions of the Western World* that contained selections or "snippets" from the major texts of Western civilization. Ordinarily, such collections include introductions by the editor that at some point state in a couple of sentences the general meaning or drift of each selection. That was too easy for Hexter. The *Traditions of the Western World*, J.H. Hexter, editor, did not provide such introductions. The student, however, did not have to begin in the dark. Hexter's introduction did include several questions to provide initial guidance and prevent total bewilderment.

Hexter also applied unorthodox methods to what became his favorite course, that on the writing of history. After he had left Queens for Washington University in St. Louis, the chair at Washington University, Richard Wade, a historian of slavery, decided the department needed to have a course taught in the writing of history and said, "Hexter, you write good history, you teach it." Hexter taught the course by selecting a problem in seventeenth-century history, assembling the relevant primary documents, telling the students "to go make like historians," and admonishing them to confine themselves to the assembled sources and not to consult secondary works. After the initial panic among the students, Hexter found that this method was a good way of getting students to analyze documents for themselves and reach their own conclusions.

Oscar Handlin often followed similar methods.[4] When he started teaching at Harvard in 1939, no one told him what to do, and he often taught in areas, such as Greek history, in which he had no background. Handlin equated teaching with learning and, like Hexter, took pains not to direct students toward his answers. He refused to recommend dissertation topics for graduate students. In tutorials and small groups he considered listening to be the most effective way of teaching and in his small group discussions and seminars long periods of silence could pass as he waited, seemingly impervious to the nervous hush, for students to respond. Handlin's approach varied from class to class, and his presentation depended upon his sense of a particular class at a particular moment. He therefore never gave the same lecture twice and never stayed wedded to the explication of a particular text.

Many can testify to the effectiveness of these occasionally exasperating methods. In the Handlin seminar that Richard Bushman took, students were assigned to read on a particular theme and one student raised questions for discussion. Near the end of the class, Handlin, after being virtually silent the entire period, summarized the drift of the discussion and raised new questions, which the students then had to sort out for themselves. In retrospect, Bushman recalled, the point was less to find the answer than to make the journey, to learn to frame good questions. Handlin preferred specific rather than cloudy, general questions. The classic Handlin question, students joked, concerned why railroads went east and west when north-south lines made more money.

In student eyes Handlin's methods were also applied to lectures, which often conveyed surprisingly little conventional information. It was not necessary, according to Bushman, to take copious notes, although that did not mean that Handlin's lectures were shallow. Handlin's skill lay in evoking an image or explaining a general pattern. Students also chafed but profited under Handlin's goading. He was not shy about goading his students to produce. Women whose work was interrupted by marriage and children were not immune. His admonition to Anne Scott has already been reported. "Glad to hear the baby arrived safely. Are you back at work?" he wrote to her. Though an occasionally intimidating presence, Handlin, like many of the teachers described here, would go to remarkable lengths to help students, a concern that did not end at graduation. Handlin was always ready with advice about jobs, fellowships, and publishing to his students long after they had left Harvard.

At the same time, Handlin made little attempt to curry favor with students, eschewing visual aids and showmanship, all of which seemed to him to divert attention from the central goal. He also tried to avoid offering courses that were required so that the students who took his courses were registered because they wanted to take them, not because they were compelled to. During the 1970 student strike at Harvard, one of the strike leaders even attended Handlin's class on the day of the strike. Handlin of course was conducting class despite the strike. In 1963 when the enrollment in his American social history class surpassed the four-hundred mark, Handlin ceased to offer it, fearing that students might be taking it out of habit or reputation. Thereafter, he chose subjects for courses not likely to attract big crowds; he insisted on a year's commitment from the students, and offered his courses at an hour that required students either to skip or postpone their lunch.

A Handlin examination stressed summation and thinking rather than replication of factual material. Early in his teaching career, "cram schools" still existed in Cambridge to help the recalcitrant students acquire enough information to pass their finals, no matter how dilatory their attendance and study had been. Many Harvard faculty were offended by the presence of "cram schools," and developed a variety of arcane devices to thwart them. Handlin did not share their views. If the "cram schools" could help students learn, what was the problem? In any case factual details alone would not be enough unless the student could relate them to a larger theme.

Sadly, Handlin came away from his career in the classroom as disillusioned with teaching as he was with the profession. Again, many things contributed to his disillusionment. The need to teach with an eye fixed on enrollment figures, the harsh reality of grade inflation, and lightened reading assignments to achieve popularity were all part of his dissatisfaction. Handlin was saddened, when as part of a hallowed tradition, he attended the last lecture of a retiring faculty member, once one of the Harvard department's most popular teachers. Surveying the lecture hall, Handlin saw indolent students munching doughnuts and sipping Cokes, reading newspapers, ignoring the closing of the curtain on a part of life, doubtless unaware of the poignance of what was transpiring.

Handlin was forced to conclude that teaching had lost the meaning he once attributed to it. "I could teach but no longer learn," he concluded sadly. Even more discouraging was the fate of graduate teaching. While generally gratified by the number and quality of his graduate students, Handlin detected a malaise among them beginning in the mid-1960s. Graduate students came to Harvard supremely gifted and qualified, with impressive test scores and golden recommendations. But to Handlin they seemed to believe that they knew it all and did not have to work. "Take it essay" was the standard greeting of Handlin's last graduate student, who all often followed his own advice.

Anne Scott, a Handlin student, employed many of his methods, though she did not take Handlin's graduate seminars and saw him in action only as a lecturer.[5] She was most influenced by her father, himself a college professor. Her father's method of teaching both in the classroom and at the family dinner table was Socratic; you were expected to have opinions and to be able to defend them. As a teacher, Scott's methods were also Socratic; she believed people learn best what they learn for themselves, not what they are told. In her classes, graduate and undergraduate, she assigned a great deal of reading, much of it from primary sources, and led discussions on it. Students were told not to come to class unless they had read the assignments and that they couldn't pass unless they came to class. At the beginning of class, therefore, she started right in on the material, and any student in class was fair game for her interrogation.

She also required a great deal of writing and was famous for covering student work in red ink. Her favorite and most revealing assignment was a term paper in which she asked students in her women's history courses to explore the history of the last three generations of women in their own families. In many cases students discovered numerous trials and triumphs of the women in their families of which they had been completely unaware. More than one student told Scott that writing the paper was the greatest experience of their undergraduate days, and Scott still receives at least one query a year from faculty members at other institutions about incorporating this assignment into their own courses.

Several members of this group of historians began teaching at the University of Chicago in the 1940s. Anyone who taught at the Chicago in those days could not escape engagement with the great texts. Under the dynamic leadership of Robert Maynard Hutchens in the 1930s, Chicago developed a series of interdisciplinary courses based on the reading of great texts and their dissection in small group discussions. Immediately after the war, William McNeill returned to Cornell to complete his Ph.D., but in 1947 accepted an opportunity to return to Chicago, his alma mater.

McNeill was soon immersed in undergraduate teaching at Hutchens College, of the University of Chicago, one of Hutchens's pet projects. Hutchens wanted truth, garnered from the great texts, but did not see history as one of the more promising paths to the truth. It was nonetheless a heady time to begin a teaching career. The faculty involved came from a variety of disciplines, and many were European refugees who had escaped from Germany or Italy before the war. They brought a new climate of opinion to the teaching of Western civilization. McNeill found it very valuable and learned to read German while teaching the course, at the same time savoring the chance to work out in his own mind the formative ideas of the great texts. "There is no better way to exercise your brain," he remarked later.[6]

McNeill occasionally reproved himself over his teaching. The success of the Chicago Western civilization course depended upon eliciting student discussion and opinion. Unlike Hexter and Handlin, McNeill sometimes lacked the patience to tolerate long silences and feared that he injected himself into the discussions too often, instead of letting students work out the solutions.

Daniel Boorstin also spent most of his teaching career at the University of Chicago.[7] By the sixties he was teaching almost entirely graduate students. Students in his classes often had the sense of watching a genius at work. "Boorstin was the smartest man I ever met," recalled Richard Beeman, a Boorstin graduate student at Chicago in the mid-sixties. The vastness of Boorstin's learning and the agility of his mind were both thrilling and terrifying to students, and some tried, usually without success, to emulate his style. While some were intimidated by his brilliance, he was remarkably open to questions and new ideas. His goal seemed to be to invite students to think about the process of doing history. If a student said something that impressed him, he would take out a pad of paper and write it down, which would be flattering to the student, but he also made it clear when he had lost interest.

John Alexander, while not a Boorstin student, witnessed a firsthand example of Boorstin's openness and intellectual honesty. Taking Boorstin's course in eighteenth-century American intellectual history, Alexander was asked on the final examination to write a critique of either Vernon Parrington's *Main Currents of American Thought* or Boorstin's own prize-winning *The Americans: The Colonial Experience.* Alexander was aware through the graduate student grapevine what his choices would be for the final and had actually lain in ambush for the question on *The Colonial Experience* all semester. He had decided that while the book was brilliant and exciting, it was also based on a highly selective reading of the evidence. Taking his graduate school future in hand, he chose to critique *The Colonial Experience* and turned in a savage attack, fully expecting Boorstin to exact a brutal retribution. To his surprise, Boorstin praised his essay, gave him a grade of "A-," and invited Alexander to stop by his office to talk about it.

Boorstin took his responsibilities to graduate students seriously. Students often went to Chicago having been dazzled by his books, and Boorstin made many efforts to accommodate them. He threw elegant parties for them at which there would be other people of interest and at which he was an unfailingly gracious host. He was a conscientious supervisor of dissertations, reading student work carefully and offering valuable suggestions about style and content. Like most of the others of this generation, his interest in students did not stop at the completion of the degree. He wrote letters on their behalf and guided them to job leads.

Boorstin's teaching sometimes closely paralleled his own work. He talked in class about the things that presently engaged him and as in his own work, had little use for debates with other historians. In discussing books, students were rarely asked to summarize the book's arguments or determine where the book fit into historical debates. Instead, Boorstin tossed out general comments about the books usually designed to make students think about how that book could be used to deepen historical understanding and assist students in arriving at their own conclusions.

Edmund Morgan was also teaching at University of Chicago right after World War II. He had been offered the job earlier, but was still working at the radiation laboratory and could not accept the position at Chicago until after the war. When the war was over, he sent them a telegram asking if they were still interested, and they were. In September 1945 he began teaching a compulsory course in social science, which turned out to be an American history survey, and a course in English composition.[8]

Like most postwar students, Chicago students were highly motivated, Morgan remembered. Of the two classes he taught, English composition was by far the most difficult. From Morgan's point of view, everything you can tell students about composition can be conveyed in about an hour. The trick is getting them to do it. Getting them to do it is best done through individual meeting and consultation, but there are limits to what one can do in teaching composition by standing in front of a class every day. Morgan found himself searching for things to do in the class, often waking up at night wondering what he would do in class the next day.

The social science class was basically an American history survey, based on an anthology of documents later published in two volumes as *The People Shall Judge*. Morgan found this class more interesting, but it was nevertheless a basic course, and he didn't have the opportunity to teach upper-division courses. His teaching at Chicago was nonetheless stimulating. There were perpetual discussions among the faculty about teaching and what a liberal education should be.

When Morgan moved to Brown in 1946, the nature of his teaching changed. He did more lecturing at Brown, and he came to prefer lecturing to discussion. Lecture classes were easier to predict, though Morgan invited his students to ask questions at any point. But Brown was different from Chicago, and he found little willingness to interrupt and discuss at Brown, attributing this unwillingness to the fact that Brown was coeducational and neither the men nor the women wanted to make fools of themselves in front of the other. Under these circumstances his move to Yale in 1955 brought a conspicuous change to his teaching. Yale was all-male, full of privileged young men fairly certain, in Morgan's view, that they would be running the world in a few years. They had no reservations about challenging him, which he found refreshing. But as the character of Yale changed in the 1960s, the nature of his teaching changed, too. Yale became coeducational, and began admitting increasing numbers of public school students along with the usual complement of private school graduates. Teaching at Yale reverted to that of Brown. Fewer and fewer Yale students were as confident of their place in the world as their immediate predecessors had been, and undergraduate teaching particularly was less invigorating.

John Hope Franklin came to Chicago later than the others. After years of undergraduate teaching at several institutions, he became interested in working with graduate students, partly because no matter how hard he worked he could not investigate all the topics that interested him regarding the history of slavery, free blacks, and the Reconstruction Era. Undergraduate teaching remained one of his loves. Undergraduates also offer their own idiosyncracies, sometimes peculiar to their institutions. Franklin was puzzled when one of his Howard students complained that Franklin's demanding syllabus did not take into the fact that black people were only eighty-five years removed from slavery. Franklin was intrigued when a Brooklyn undergraduate asked him to suggest some additional books to read since the student had read everything on the syllabus. He was delighted when, having absentmindedly scheduled a class on a legal holiday, his Chicago students came anyway. And he was amused, while teaching at the Duke Law School, that his students requested that a working dinner at his house be changed because it conflicted with a Duke-Virginia basketball game.[9]

One episode demonstrates Franklin's commitment to students and also allowed him to savor an irony that must have been especially sweet. In the spring of 1939 Franklin arrived in Raleigh, North Carolina, to do work in the North Carolina state archives, only to be informed by the director that there were no research facilities set aside for African Americans to use. When Franklin's face registered disappointment, the director, a Yale Ph.D., suggested that if Franklin would wait a week, he would make some arrangements. After managing to get the waiting period reduced to several days instead of a week, Franklin was allowed to work in a small, private room with a table and chair. He was also given the keys to the manuscript collection to avoid the embarrassment of requiring white assistants deliver manuscripts to a black man. This arrangement, however, lasted only two weeks. White researchers, outraged at such blatant discrimination, demanded their own keys to the manuscript collection. Rather than submit to their demands, the director simply took Franklin's keys and ordered the assistants to serve him.

A quarter century later, Franklin took ten of his graduate students to Raleigh for a two-week stint in the archives. The trip represented first of all an intense commitment to students on Franklin's part. The trip was two weeks long, and Franklin was always available to talk in the evenings. Second, Franklin received a very different welcome at the state archives than the one he had received in 1939. He was no longer an obscure African American historian trying to work in the segregated South; he was now a distinguished historian at the University of Chicago returning to a South that had changed greatly since 1939. The director of the archives was the same man who had been director in 1939, and he now treated Franklin like visiting royalty, welcoming him with open arms, asking him to give a talk, and arranging for the governor of North Carolina to meet him.[10]

Gordon Craig also admired the postwar generation of students. Returning from the Pacific in late 1945, Craig found his classes full of veterans taking notes furiously, often with their pregnant wives sitting next to them. As a teacher, Craig was known as a showman, capable of packing a lecture hall with rapt students, but he thought the keys to teaching were relatively simple. The Princeton department of the 1940s and 1950s was renowned for its superb teaching. There were the spellbinders like Craig, Harris "Jinks" Harbison, and Eric Goldman who played to standing room audiences, but also lower-key but equally effective teachers like Joseph Strayer, the long-time chair.[11] Craig later recalled, "we talked a lot about teaching at Princeton, and it was important to Joe Strayer. I asked Ray Sontag about what you have to do to become a good teacher. He said you have to like students and you have to be interested in what you are doing. I don't think you need anything else besides a brain." Craig excelled in both lectures and the Princeton preceptorial or small group teaching, but he recalled that he "enjoyed lecturing the most," attributing part of his success to the fact he "couldn't go wrong with Bismarck and Frederick the Great as [his] subjects."

Arthur Schlesinger Jr. was another spellbinding lecturer. His courses enticed the largest audiences at Harvard, often standing room only.[12] He, too, admired the postwar generation of students, who, he thought, were willing to work harder and were vastly superior to the Brahmins who populated Harvard in the thirties. By the mid-1950s Schlesinger decided that he preferred to write history rather than teach it, and he resigned from Harvard to serve in the Kennedy administration. When he returned to teaching, it was in an appointment that limited his teaching to graduate students, although he continued to teach right up to his retirement in 1995 at 78.

Teaching for Carl Schorske was different at each of the institutions where he taught.[13] But his teaching was grounded in the conviction that there are some universal principles that apply to good teaching anywhere. Students, for Schorske, are good if you treat them like adults, and if you can engage them. At Wesleyan he taught small classes where it was often possible to know the students quite well. They could often be engaged by assigning them texts that corresponded with their personal beliefs. Schorske might assign, for example, Protestant students readings from Luther and Calvin and Catholic students readings from Loyola. Both groups could also be assigned secondary sources sympathetic to their positions. He also engaged students by giving them a chance to think, preferring to hand out examination questions in advance. "Do your thinking at home; do your writing here," he told them.

In the late forties and early fifties Wesleyan was also trying to implement a new core curriculum much like the great books of the Western world sequence that Schorske had taken as an undergraduate at Columbia. This meant that the faculty from different disciplines argued over what should be included in the curriculum and that the societal tensions of the 1950s, including the cold war, Henry Wallace's candidacy for president, and McCarthyism, often spilled over into the faculty debates and the classroom.

The move to Berkeley in 1959 changed the nature of Schorske's teaching from small group seminars to large lecture courses. As a lecturer, Schorske did not require students to attend, believing that it was his job as a teacher to make them want to come. When he realized that students in the sixties were hungry for discussion and dialogue, he used his graduate assistants to teach small discussion sections. The graduate assistants were allowed to choose a special topic related to the course and develop readings and assignments that would allow the undergraduates to see the basic course material from another angle. His graduate students proved to be extremely creative in their choice of topics. In one small group that Schorske particularly admired, one of his teaching assistants organized discussions around the theme of "The Costs of Freedom." Schorske considered this to be his most successful experiment in teaching.

Teaching changed again upon his arrival at Princeton. The need to find innovative ways to engage students in small groups was not necessary at Princeton because the preceptorial system already utilized them. One of the interesting wrinkles of that system was that members of the faculty actually served as teaching assistants in courses taught by other faculty members, even outside their regular fields. "Why not?" thought Schorske, "I can read a text in medieval history as well one from the nineteenth."

Princeton's other gift to Schorske's teaching was the creation of an interdisciplinary program in European Cultural Studies in which Schorske taught. The program included faculty members from various Princeton disciplines and from the Institute for Advanced Studies and allowed students to pursue problems in European history of almost any nature. This kind of interdisciplinary study would not have been possible at any of Schorske's institutions at the times he taught there.

At Maryland right after World War II Kenneth Stampp was being crushed under a heavy teaching load, teaching three large surveys in American history each semester along with an upper-division course and doing his own grading.[14] A chance to escape to the University of California at Berkeley in 1946 enabled him to reduce his load to one survey and one upper-division class. Stampp was a popular lecturer, attracting 500–700 students to his American survey, but after four years at Maryland and fourteen more at Berkeley, he grew a bit tired of lecturing. His graduate seminar became his favorite course. Stampp held his seminars at his house and particularly enjoyed trying to create a family atmosphere, getting to know his students personally, and even hearing about their problems, however intimate.

David Potter was another popular lecturer, playing to packed houses and winning Stanford University's prestigious Dinkelspiel Award for exceptional teaching. Colleagues and students noticed several intriguing paradoxes about Potter's teaching. Many of this generation's popular teachers were showmen, who made it a point to entertain as well as instruct. Potter, equally popular, eschewed showmanship, lecturing without playing to the crowd. Yet, by an intimate and reflective tone that seemed to be welcoming students to share with him the joy of historical discovery, Potter could hold a lecture hall of three hundred students in suspense for an entire period. Gordon Craig, who taught with Potter at Stanford, thought that the keys to his success in the classroom were his sense of humor, his way of talking directly to students as if telling a story, and his way of addressing students on their level. Potter's eyes were also slightly crossed, giving him a curious, quizzical look when he spoke, which, Craig believes, made it hard it to look away from him.[15]

Another paradox was that in his personal demeanor, Potter at times could be stern and intimidating. But when students came to see him, no matter how busy he was, he immediately brightened, ready to assist in any way he could for as long as it took to help. When the student left, Potter could return immediately to his more forbidding side. While Potter gave immensely of himself to students, he could be very tough on them. An intrinsically conservative man, Potter was appalled when students tried to close down Stanford to protest the Vietnam War. When they tried to enforce the closure by blocking his way to class, he bulled his way through them and conducted class anyway.

Several members of this group were at their best in the instruction of graduate students. Eric Foner believes that Richard Hofstadter was not a particularly good undergraduate teacher at Columbia. Hofstadter lacked the love of the classroom required of the truly great instructor and was particularly uncomfortable giving lectures. At times Hofstadter seemed almost to go out of his way to make his lectures dull, perhaps to scare away the droves of students eager to seek his wisdom. But there was a Jekyll and Hyde quality to his teaching. In graduate seminars, Hofstadter, as if transformed by magic, became a different teacher. In those classes his strengths as a teacher, which included his erudition, openness, and breadth of vision, were more readily apparent.[16]

Most of Vann Woodward's teaching involved upper-level undergraduates and graduate students. Success at this level of teaching is harder to measure than in introductory courses. But one measure of success in Woodward's teaching is undeniable. "I have on my shelf forty dissertations which have been published," he said in December 1995; "there may yet be more."[17]

Virtually every American college teacher encountered an abrupt and radical change in atmosphere and students in the 1960s, especially at elite universities. For the most part of the twentieth century American college students have been apathetic politically. But the 1960s brought a new period of political awareness. Universities expanded rapidly as the baby boom generation began to enter college in the early and mid-1960s. High school guidance counselors made presentations showing how much one's income would go up with a college education, and the university changed from training small groups of elites to the megaversity, cramming as many students as possible into its halls. Class sizes shot up, the size of the bureaucracy multiplied, and the university became increasingly impersonal.

The 1960s were also a time of political unrest. The civil rights movement and growing concern with the expanding conflict in Vietnam combined with dissatisfaction with the American emphasis on material values and success, to create unprecedented levels of political activism. Many students remained untouched by politics, but others marched for civil rights, demonstrated against the Vietnam War, and demanded radical change in American society and university life.

By the late 1960s, protest centered around the Vietnam War. Certainly self-interest played an undeniable part in the intensity of the protest. The war was initially fought with volunteers, usually recruited from the lower echelons of American society. College students could initially obtain deferments. But as the war continued to expand, the possibility increased that college students would face the draft. Later the draft lottery removed the student deferment, forcing all students to confront the reality that they or their brothers, friends, and relatives might be serving in Vietnam.

Protesting students often sought to make the university a vehicle for their dissatisfaction, since many, especially elite, universities had investments in companies that were profiting from the war. Thomas Barnes, a historian serving in the Dean of Students' Office at Berkeley in the mid-1960s, remembers the campus "blanketed with tear gas and a full-scale battle raged between a thousand insurrectionists and half as many police, with a hundred casualties."[18]

The World War II generation of historians had a variety of responses to student unrest. At Yale student protest was particularly bitter, and three historians of this group were in the middle. J.H. Hexter, at this time a liberal Democrat, thought entry of politics into academic life was "disgusting," remarking later that "what I did was to act as if it wasn't there. I had no trouble with students in the sixties. I didn't suspend expectations. I made no concessions. I thought it was nonsense."[19]

Neither Edmund Morgan and Vann Woodward, both at Yale with a stronger radical heritage than Hexter, encountered problems either. The student rebels, Morgan recalled, "were a tame group, contemptuous of the value of early American history. But they challenged the sociologists." Vann Woodward thought that the Yale students of the 1960s were of extremely high quality, comparable to the postwar veterans of the late 1940s. Three of them, he recalls, won Pulitzer Prizes. Woodward recalled few problems with radical students. "I had considered myself a leftist," he remembered, "I could sympathize."[20]

The political situation may have been a bit more tense at Stanford, where students tried to shut the university to protest the war. David Potter's reaction to students' attempt to prevent him from conducting his class has already been noted. Gordon Craig was in Germany during the worst part of the trouble, which spared him from having to deal with the greatest tension. Upon his return to teaching, Craig at first opposed student behavior and supported the generally conservative approach espoused by his friend David Potter. "It struck me as foolish, " he said. "The university was not a tool to stop the war." Craig continued to get along well with students, though, like Hexter, he brooked no nonsense from them. At one point he spoke in favor of the war. When the war continued, however, Craig eventually changed his mind and began public opposition to it.[21]

Tensions also ran high at Columbia, and Richard Hofstadter, another intrinsically conservative man, found himself under the gun. Mark Naison, a graduate student of Hofstadter's, was scheduled to take his comprehensive exams during the middle of the Columbia student strike of 1968. On the day in question, a battle raged across the campus. Naison's examination began amidst the sounds of breaking furniture, shouts of rage, fragments of falling plaster, and chants of "Shut it down." Naison noticed the behavior of Hofstadter and the other Columbia faculty involved was curious. Normally Pd.D. oral exams are intended to be rigorous and to test the candidate's mettle and intellectual depth. But Naison sensed that rather than testing him or even resenting him, they were more interested in their own performance than in his. Their goal that day was not to examine him, but to see if they could maintain their own dignity and sense of decorum, which they did, even though they were aware that Naison supported everything that was "happening in that bldg, from the breaking of furniture to the slugging of professors." At the conclusion of his examination, Naison, in suit and tie, "leading rh, dwight miner, equally attired, out of an occupied building in front of 2000 people," raised his fist in triumph, "feeling at once overjoyed at having the whole fucking mess over with, and guilty at deserting my brothers inside . . . SCHIZOPHRENIA! You better believe it."[22]

Hofstadter was accorded a rare honor during the troubles, perhaps indicative of his stature at Columbia. Hofstadter had managed a balance of

genuine concern for the students and firm commitment to the academic freedom and opposition to the threat to academic freedom that the student strikes
posed. In June of 1968 he was invited to give the commencement address at
Columbia, the first time that a faculty member rather than the president,
had been so honored. Hofstadter's address, not surprisingly, acknowledged
the validity of student concerns, but admonished them to remember the university as an institution committed to certain core values of "freedom, rationality, inquiry and discussion" and to keep in mind the possibility that even
the most zealous reformers might be mistaken.[23]

Daniel Boorstin was perhaps the historian most affected by student
radicalism of the sixties. In several ways he was the most vulnerable to student hostility. He was embarrassed by his brief membership in the Communist Party in the thirties, he had named names to the House Un-American
Activities Committee in the fifties, and he had written books celebrating
American greatness. All of these things were now quite unfashionable. More
recently he was blamed by students for the failure of radical historian Jesse
Lemisch to get tenure at Chicago, and he often appeared aloof. In short he
seemed to epitomize to students the establishment they despised. Students
disrupted his classes and left anti-Boorstin slogans and pronouncements in
classrooms. Disgusted by student insolence and the coarsening of discourse
in the halls of learning, Boorstin left teaching in 1968 to accept a position as
director of the National Museum of History and Technology of the
Smithsonian Institution in Washington.[24]

It appears that the Oxford contingent of the World War II generation
of historians also excelled at teaching and research, especially those at Balliol
College. For nearly a quarter century, with an interruption for World War
II, Balliol history undergraduates were treated to a teaching team of Christopher Hill and Richard Southern, and an overlap with others such as A.B.
Rodger and later, Richard Cobb. In 1961 Richard Southern was appointed
Chichele Professor of History at All Souls College, Oxford, and in 1965
Christopher Hill became Master of Balliol. But from 1937 to 1961 they
formed an electrifying pedagogical combination, like Miller and Matthiessen
at Harvard, heady wine for Balliol undergraduates. Maurice Keen remembers Southern as the major inspiration for his life. Keith Thomas remembers
Southern as a dedicated tutor and captivating lecturer who got better as he
got older. Hill's style was more laconic, and his tutorials were often punctu-
ated by long periods of silence, but he operated through indefinite but per-
ceptible magnetism.[25]

Hugh Stretton, who graduated from Balliol in 1948, remembers the
high quality of teaching vividly: "Richard Southern dispensed a bewitching
mixture of astringency and kindness. . . . A.B. Rodger bent his decanal rules
very tolerantly to returned soldiers. Christopher Hill seemed to be a man for
all seasons, a helpful human being without any barriers. All four were mar-

velously accessible. To pupils wanting their time or company they never appeared too busy, bored, important, or condescending. From affectionate interest as well as duty the college did seem to exist for its undergraduates, as its rhetoric alleged."[26]

Balliol is perhaps Oxford's most egalitarian and academically powerful college. Where other Oxford colleges devoted a considerable portion of their resources to gracious in-college living, the consensus at Balliol favored, according to Stretton, "low-living and high thinking." Rooms were rearranged to sleep 250 where 150 had slept before. Endowment and academic income were apportioned to scholarly uses, rather than expended for claret, beer parties, and central heating. As much teaching as possible should be done by the fellows of the college rather than by lecturers and part-time faculty, and the teaching hours of the fellows should be high. Scholarships should go primarily to the most academically qualified, and the college must capture the most first-class awards in the various Oxford examinations.

As a tutor, Christopher Hill embodied most of Balliol's goals, but he was also something else, the most conspicuous and distinguished Marxist at Oxford. The first thing Maurice Keen, coming up to Balliol in 1954, noticed about Hill was a bright red tie, the only outward sign of his Communist party membership. Others found Hill most impressive in tutorials, but Keen did not. Keen recalls Hill, laconic and withdrawn, curled up in a big, curiously shaped armchair. If someone said something very Royalist in an essay on the English Revolution, he might suddenly be aroused from his languor, but Keen believes that Hill's gift as a teacher was his vast knowledge of history, which enabled him to send students to precisely the right book that would make the subject come alive for them.[27]

Keith Thomas also recalls the laconic style and a "jolly long pause" that followed the reading of an essay during which he might not say a word until the college bells tolled and Hill would set the topic for next the essay. Hill clearly saw the purpose of instruction as the learning of history for its own sake. Thomas remembers Hill's becoming quite cross, "which he seldom did," when a pupil asked if a topic would help him prepare for his examinations. "You are here to learn," Hill informed the pupil. By contrast Thomas's tutorials with Southern often went on beyond the tolling of the college bells, and Southern, an enchanting conversationalist, would discourse on all the issues raised by Thomas's essay.

Ved Mehta, a blind pupil and native of India, who came up to Balliol in the 1950s, found a shy, and utterly humane man. Mehta first met Hill at the Balliol ritual known oddly as "handshaking," though no handshaking actually took place, where the tutors comment on a pupil's progress in the presence of the master. Sometimes called "collections" in other Oxford colleges, it is an ordeal for most pupils. Mehta's experience was worse because he went in actually expecting to shake hands, though no one did, and he could hardly hear a word anyone said in the cavernous room in which the handshaking was held. He was about to leave the room, feeling like a character from Kafka, when Christopher Hill jumped up to open the door for him and assure him that almost no one understands anything said in that particular room. This was exactly what Mehta, totally disconcerted by the event, needed to hear. But a moment later Mehta was again disconcerted when he extended his hand to Hill and received only a little finger in return.[28]

Mehta ended up going to Hill for several terms, climbing to the top of Staircase XIX before he knocked on the door. "Come in," Hill would call, with the emphasis on the "come." Hill's rooms were often cold and damp, but immense and piled with books. The most prominent object in the room was a large portrait of Oliver Cromwell. Mehta would find Hill in tweed coat and slacks, sitting in a wing chair, his feet tucked under him, seeming more like an older graduate student than a great historian. When Mehta addressed Hill as "sir," Hill replied, "Please not sir, just Christopher." Mehta and his tutorial partners took turns reading essays, and Hill listened intently, although he rarely commented directly on the essay. If he asked for a source on a point of which he was unaware, Mehta believed that meant Hill had been quite impressed. Hill seldom corrected anything a student said, although he might shift in his chair and ask, "That's not really an answer, is it?" or "Come on, what about this and so?" He never advanced his own views, preferring to play devil's advocate, only asking questions. If students tried to incorporate interpretations from Hill's own books into their essays, he would challenge them even more vigorously and with such conviction that it would be hard to believe he himself had ever entertained such views. He sought consistently to bring out the best in his pupils. When he discovered Mehta's interest in *Paradise Lost* he assigned Milton's disillusionment with the Puritan revolution as the subject of Mehta's next essay.[29] Hill was unusual among Oxford, even Balliol, dons at the time for his egalitarian views. He was free of any kind of racial prejudice and, according to Mehta, "was so far ahead of his time that he treated women no differently than men, without a hint of condescension."[30]

Teaching of course has many dimensions, and Hill reached his pupils in many ways. On Monday evenings he and wife, Bridget Hill, opened his college rooms and provided a barrel of beer to all comers, as a way of getting people who read history at Balliol to meet each other. Hill's parties attracted consistently large crowds, and Hill could often be found engaged in deep discussion with anyone who wished to talk with him. These parties and the atmosphere he created, unique in Maurice Keen's lengthy time as a pupil and tutor at Balliol, were one of the reasons why Hill became a lifelong guide and advisor of so many historians, even those who were not seventeenth-century specialists or Marxists.

Hill's parties did have one odd rule. If a student took a pint glass before his third year, he would be mildly scolded. It was surprising that so committed an egalitarian as Christopher Hill would bother about such a trivial rite of passage. It had nothing to do with quantity. First- and second-year pupils could refill their half-pint glasses as often as needed. When Hill became the senior tutor after Southern's departure to All Souls in 1961, Maurice Keen, by then a colleague, saw Hill at his best, taking immense pains to help anyone in difficulty, possessing the ability to stand apart from his own prejudices, when dealing with people or approaching issues, and his ability to be independent, wise, and fair. Not only did Hill's seventeenth-century pupils find him a powerful stimulus, but his influence has been acknowledged by pupils in other fields. Rhys Isaacs, in his book on the transformation of eighteenth-century Virginia, acknowledged his gratitude to both Hill and Southern.[31]

Mehta was also enchanted by Southern. Initially interested in the Middle Ages, Mehta would enter Southern's rooms at Balliol to find him buried in the dense monastic chronicles that formed the source material for Southern's work. Southern would immediately suspend his work in them and welcome Mehta into his room. Southern decided to tutor Mehta individually, and since Mehta could not read his own essay, Southern would have to read it himself. At one point he read one of Mehta's sentences aloud. The experience of having one of his sentences read back to him by one of the world's great medievalists was "devastating" to Mehta. In Southern's plumy Oxford tones, his sentences sometimes sounded like total gibberish. When Mehta once ventured that he feared his whole essay was bad, Southern laughed kindly and said, "I don't like 'motivation' in this sentence. It sounds like jargon. And don't you think it's jarring to come upon it in a discussion of the sixth century?" Mehta asked if 'impulse' was better. Southern agreed, and then asked a series of questions about the substance of Mehta's essay, which had been about Saxon migrations to England. Had Mehta been right to assume that between a half a million and a million Saxons had crossed over to England? How many ships did he think would be required for such an operation? Where could the invaders have gotten the lumber to build their ships? How long did he think it took them to build each ship? How long would it take them to make a crossing? What would be the rate of increase in the Saxon population once they reached Britain?

Mehta tried to respond, but Southern easily deflected his answers, usually referring to a source among the volumes of books stacked on his large desk, and reading aloud the pertinent point, but always in the spirit of sharing information rather than correction. Southern invariably knew which book to consult and went right to the particular page on which the passage in question would be found. When Mehta's first tutorial with Southern was over, Southern remarked kindly, "by the way, you don't have to exhibit your reading in your essay. It should just be a point of departure." Mehta left feeling at once exhilarated and depressed. It was exhilarating to be the presence of as great a scholar as Southern, but depressing to think of how far he had to go.[32]

Southern was notorious for his absentmindedness, and Mehta saw this side of Southern firsthand. One afternoon before he had elected to read history, he encountered Southern in the Balliol quad and asked about the possibilities of concentrating on history. Southern talked at length with Mehta and offered encouragement. When they had finished talking, Southern asked, "By the way, Mr. Mehta, which direction was I coming from?" Mehta replied that he was coming from the senior common room. "Very good," Southern replied, "then I've had my lunch."

Mehta sometimes had back-to-back tutorials with Hill and Southern, and the contrast was striking. Hill's rooms were damp and cold. Southern's rooms, in a new part of the college, were warm and snug. Hill's style was secular; Southern's clerical. Mehta thought it was like going from one chamber of a Turkish bath to another. Mehta wrote a series of essays for Southern, sometimes writing two a week to make up for lost time. Southern was always buried in a book at the time of Mehta's arrival, but would respond upon hearing Mehta's knock, "Oh, Mr. Mehta, do come in. Have you got an essay?" Southern usually seemed surprised that Mehta always did. While Mehta stood in awe of Southern, especially of his massive learning and saintly presence, sometimes becoming completely tongued-tied in that presence, he began to have doubts about medieval history, although they had nothing to do with Southern. Mehta's grasp of Latin was insufficient; the period was too remote, the sources too intractable. When he expressed his doubts to Southern, Southern explained that studying at Oxford was like joining the church: "You know that the university has been here for centuries and that countless generations of undergraduates have benefited from studying here. You have to take it on faith that since the system worked for them it will work for you."[33]

Not everyone's experience was quite as positive. In 1954 Norman Cantor arrived in Balliol from Princeton as a Rhodes Scholar.[34] He had read Southern's masterpiece, *The Making of the Middle Ages*, and believed that it offered the prospect of a new approach in medieval history where ideas could be taken seriously as social and cultural forces. He therefore looked forward to working with Southern and was delighted when a card from Southern arrived at his rooms in Oriel College inviting him to tea. But Cantor and Southern did not connect. According to Cantor, Southern thought Cantor was a pupil of another medievalist, Ernst Kantorowicz, whom he disliked, and Southern did not like Cantor's proposed topic of research on the investiture controversies of the eleventh and twelfth centuries. "I am only paid fifteen pounds a year to supervise you," Cantor reported that Southern told him. "It's hardly worth my while." Cantor was crushed. It was like being scorned by your greatest hero. But seeing the disappointment plainly visible on Cantor's face, Southern made a suggestion. "Write me an essay on St. Anselm of Canterbury, then I will decide whether I should supervise you." Still shaken, Cantor returned to Oriel, cried for an hour, and the following afternoon wrote a thirty-page essay on Anselm, on whom he had already devoted considerable study. Two days later he heard from Southern, who informed him that Cantor had it all wrong about Anselm, that he really didn't understand him, but Southern was nevertheless impressed, informing Cantor, "it is remarkable that you could have done all this work so fast. So I will take you on as a student."

Relations between the two eventually improved. In two terms at Oxford Cantor met with Southern six times, mostly to take long walks in the university park near Southern's house in Oxford where they argued incessantly about the medieval church. While Cantor stressed the unsavory politics and corruption that often poisoned the activities of the medieval church, Southern emphasized its devotional and intellectual side.

While leaving Oxford with a residual bitterness that Southern had not shown him more kindness and was unwilling to lead a following of faithful acolytes, Cantor nevertheless owed Southern a substantial debt and conceded to Southern a number of estimable virtues. Cantor wrote his popular *Medieval History: The Life and Death of a Civilization* largely as an extension of his Oxford park debates with Southern. In retrospect Cantor came to admit that Southern was "seventy-five percent correct" in his views about the church and acknowledged Southern's brilliance as both a tutorial instructor and university lecturer.

Richard Cobb was also a popular Balliol tutor who had yet another approach to teaching. Cobb taught by the force of his personality. If you were his pupil, he wanted to eat, drink, read, and talk with you and take it all very seriously. If you were indulgent of him and willing to be enveloped by him, he could teach you without your realizing that you were being taught. He was popular with students, who once ran him for master. Fortunately, they did not succeed, sparing Balliol an unmitigated disaster. In the end he became somewhat disillusioned by the students. After lunch one afternoon in the early seventies he observed students preparing for a demonstration and suggested to a friend that they go and support them. The students, however, were surly and in the 75–yard walk back to his rooms Cobb became a conservative.[35]

At Christ Church, Hugh Trevor-Roper took pains with his tutorial pupils. Like most tutors, he enjoyed teaching the able pupils and found the dolts less stimulating. He could often be intimidating, even with the better pupils. He loomed large over his pupils, sitting in a high chair, and made it clear when he was bored. His appointment as a university lecturer reduced the time he spent as a tutor, and he enjoyed lecturing and was determined to be good at it, which, he said, made it hard work. Many remember him as a superb lecturer. Michael Howard thought that Trevor-Roper's inaugural lecture as Regius Professor was the best he had ever heard.[36]

At Wadham in the 1950s Lawrence Stone was already fashioning his own legend.[37] After beginning his teaching career as a lecturer at University College in 1948, he moved to Wadham as a fellow in 1950. Wadham in the 1950s was lively and intellectually vibrant college, famous for its characters, especially its acid-tongued warden, Sir Maurice Bowra. Bowra's bons mots were to be savored, wrote Julian Mitchell, unless you were their target. Stone soon emerged as a formidable character of his own, although as Mitchell has observed, the myth was often better than the reality. Stone was known for his war experience, and "a whiff of the depth charge hung about him still," wrote Mitchell. His myth came, thought Mitchell, from his war record and from his role in that brutal scholarly equivalent of jungle warfare, the Gentry Controversy.

It also concerned attitude. Many things set Stone apart from the typical Oxford don. He drove an Allard, a rare and fast sports car suited to his independent and impetuous personality. Even his rooms seemed distinct from the rest of the college, at the top of the narrow staircase over the college's main gate. More strikingly, Stone regularly used vernacular language in tutorials to make points, and he occasionally stomped about his room, seemingly at odds with the Oxford ideal of genteel erudition, sometimes brandishing a squash raquet for which pupils had to be wary. And his judgments were spectacularly swift and usually severe. When one undergraduate attempted to emulate Stone by describing John Dudley, the first duke of Northumberland, as a fascist beast, Stone thought for only a brief moment before replying that Northumberland was not a fascist beast at all, but a bloody shit, not at all the same thing. The speed of judgment, Julian Mitchell recalled, was even more impressive than the judgment itself. Pupils finishing their essays were often greeted with an incredulous, "Is that all?"

Mitchell later took part in a program of sketches put on by the Wadham Amateur Dramatic Society, in which Michael Barnes, a history graduate with a physical resemblance to Stone, played a history tutor. Mitchell played the part of an undergraduate who read an essay on Thomas Cromwell which consisted of one magnificently simple and incontestable sentence, "Henry VIII came to the throne in 1509," which Mitchell was to read as though it came from a tablet. Then Barnes, who had been peering out the window through a cardboard tube, turned to him and sneered, "Is that all?" which brought the house down because it so perfectly caught Stone in the essence of his myth.

C.S.L. Davies, who was taught by Stone as both an undergraduate and research student at Wadham, found truth in both the myth and the reality. As a tutor, Davies recalled, Stone was not a fearsome tyrant, a veritable Grendel on the prowl for fresh victims, but he "would challenge the logic of our arguments, demand evidence for unsubstantiated statements, and express his amazement at any suggestion that public life might be conducted on any but the lowest principles. Above all, he would try to provoke us to fight back." For those who expected their resistance to result in dismemberment or humiliation, the results were sometimes surprising. A couple of jabs in response to a Stone query, Davies recalls, were often "enough to send Lawrence scuttling back to his corner."

For all his passion and intensity about his own work, Stone had not the least desire to create a school nor did he demand that students echo his wisdom, even on the Gentry Controversy. For undergraduates, he provided an up-to-date and realistic reading list, but left it to students to work out their own interpretations, provided they could defend their point of view. For research students, though there were only a few at Wadham in the 1950s, Stone made little attempt to influence what they wrote and was willing to let students make their own mistakes, largely confining his criticism of their written work to style and internal logic. He insisted, however, on one iron-clad requirement: his students must produce one thesis chapter per term. His Wadham teaching load, usually heavy and varying between fourteen and twenty hours a week, was never sacrificed to research, even during the period when Stone was working on his masterpiece, *The Crisis of the Aristocracy*, although he benefited from the willingness of his colleague, A.F. "Pat" Thompson, to deal with the crises of youth. But like the Oxford dons most devoted to students, he cared deeply about the college's performance in examinations, although by the late 1950s he was becoming increasing frustrated by the heavy load and Oxford's emphasis on traditional constitutional history, which he described as "sterile."

Moving to Princeton in 1963, Stone developed a lecture course eventually titled, "The First Road to Modernization: England, 1470–1690," and encountered women in the classroom. In the 1960s Princeton was being dragged kicking and screaming into the admission of women, who could enter graduate programs with faculty approval. Miriam Slater was one of the first women in the Princeton history program. Not only had Stone allowed her admission, but he took her seriously as a scholar. During breaks in his graduate seminar, he would talk informally with the students. This often resulted in a graduate school ritual in which particularly the male students descended on Stone, assuming positions of dominance around him and trying hard to score points with him or gauge their status in the seminar. When Slater felt excluded and too intimidated to join in the ritual, Stone deliberately sat down next to her during break times, sending a clear message that he would not allow women to be marginalized, years before the women's movement began at Princeton.

Slater found Stone stimulating in a variety of ways. She considered him superb in the seminar, massively erudite, yet friendly and approachable, assisted by a sense of humor. As a married student with small children, living outside of town, she was cut off from normal graduate student camaraderie. Stone assisted by encouraging her to call him, at home or at the office, if she had an idea she wished to discuss. It soon became clear that the invitation was genuine, and Slater discovered that her phone conversations were an intellectual "lifeline" she badly needed. As the parent of small children, she often had responsibilities other students did not. It is not at all unusual today for parents to bring their children to class and to faculty offices, but it was unusual in the 1960s. When Slater could not find a sitter and was compelled to take her children along to Stone's office, Stone never raised an eyebrow, though others did. Another couple arrived in Oxford, where Stone and his family spent their summers even after they moved to Princeton, with a croupy baby. The Stones invited them to stay at their house, cranky baby and all. Graduate students, their spouses and children were also regular guests at Stone's house. When Slater's husband became seriously ill in the summer of 1970, she called Stone, then in England, to tell him her thesis work would be delayed. He told her not to worry at all, that he would return to Princeton shortly, that she could call him again collect if he could help in any way, and offered to lend her money. When he returned to Princeton, he called and invited her to lunch. Slater remembers this as an act of kindness, allowing her relief from the trial of caring for her husband and allowing her to begin thinking about her future anew.

Yet Stone was by no means an easy advisor. There were moments when he could be as intimidating as a ticking bomb. Slater remembers wanting to crawl out of his office when he had finished assessing a part of her work, although it was only a slight comfort to her to recall that this treatment was not reserved for mere underlings, like graduate students. It was not for nothing that someone, most likely a graduate student, once affixed a hand-lettered sign on Stone's office door, reading *Lorenzo Il Magnifico*.

David Cannadine once pointed out that Lawrence Stone and Geoffrey Elton, so often at each other's throats, failed to realize how much they had in common. Cannadine was probably referring to their scholarly activities, but the analogy could be pushed much further, to include their teaching. Through their scholarly work, both acquired reputations as enfants terribles, reducing anyone who crossed them to hash and having no patience for incompetence. But the myth did not always correspond to reality.[38]

For undergraduates at Clare College, Cambridge, Elton offered a workable syllabus, generous supervision time, and a glass of sherry. His pupils were expected to read. At one point an irate university librarian called Elton to complain that his pupils were actually checking books out of the library. Elton congratulated him on being helpful.

But Elton was at his best as a supervisor of graduate students. He had accepted eighty, and two-thirds received their degrees. Elton offered encouragement to all, even an American who planned to take a Cambridge degree, requiring only a thesis, as a way to evade language requirements and comprehensive exams. Instead, he was handed a plea roll from the Public Record Office and was expected to make sense of it. He was soon on a plane back to the States. Research students received the benefits of Elton's lively seminars, which not only were full of students working on similar topics, but were attended by distinguished senior scholars as well.

Like Stone, Elton was capable of enormous kindness to his students and to anyone with an interest in Tudor history, whether they were his pupils or not. Many an American arrived in Cambridge to find themselves relegated to a tiny bed-sitter with no heat, bedding, or utensils. Elton often met incoming students at their lodgings or on at least one occasion, right at the train station, inviting them immediately to dinner at his Cambridge home. Dazed students would often leave this initial visit to the Elton household laden with pillows, blankets, sheets, pots, pans, knives, forks, and sometimes, a dissertation topic.

Teaching does not end in the classroom or with the completion of the degree, nor is it confined to one's own pupils. Elton's engagement as a teacher extended well beyond his own pupils and to subjects in which he was not personally interested. Steven Ellis remembers vividly the importance of the encouragement and enthusiasm with which Elton received his early research on early Tudor Ireland, then thought to be a topic of little interest. Christopher Haigh treasures a stack of letters he received from Elton regarding his work on the English Reformation, although religion is not central to Elton's own work. On Sunday evenings during term time at his home, Elton and his wife, Sheila Lambert, herself a historian, opened their home at 30 Millington Road in Cambridge to all comers for beer and conversation. They were particularly generous to visiting Americans, occasionally the target of some scorn in Britain. Some think that Elton's kindness to nomadic academics resulted from his seeing in them something of himself when he came to Britain in 1939, a stranger in a strange land. The Eltons served regular Thanksgiving and Christmas dinners for homesick Americans and stranded students, also treating American visitors to guest accommodations, walks on the Cam, evening pints at a local pub, and other aspects of local color.

J.H. Plumb liked the face-to-face aspect of tutorial teaching, where pupils were not just faces in a classroom and he could get to know them personally.[39] Although some of his former pupils might dispute his claim, Plumb conducted his teaching on the principle that one just can't pull apart a pupil's essay and writing style in front of tutorial partners.

Plumb believed that when he took on able students he took them for life. Nowhere can his commitment to students be seen better than in his reaction to the news that his pupil Simon Schama, whom Plumb regarded as uncommonly able, had received a second-class degree. First, Plumb drove immediately to London to console the shaken Schama. Then, believing that Schama had been victimized by Plumb's political enemies, he took steps to improve the integrity of the examination process. While Schama had received superior marks on the majority of his examination papers, he had been given low marks on three papers by one examiner, Brian Wormald. Wormald's marks had cost him his first. Along with Wormald, Plumb blamed Geoffrey Elton, who as head of the History Faculty Board, should have insisted upon a second reading of Schama's papers. "I took the faculty by its neck," he recalled later. "It was an outrage. From then on I insisted that examination papers be submitted anonymously and double read by different examiners, so that being a member of Christ's College was not harmful."

Plumb was also a superb lecturer, but lecturing filled him with anxiety. For years, he was unable to sleep the night before a lecture, tossing and turning anxiously until four or five in the morning. The tension would vanish by the time he took the podium, but the nights were agonizing. Fortunately, by the time he delivered the Ford Lectures at Oxford in the 1967, he had gotten over his anxiety.

His final Cambridge lecture was a grand spectacle. The lecture hall was filled to capacity with undergraduates and members of the faculty, many of whom had arrived early to secure a good seat. Those who arrived late were either turned away or allowed to sit on the floor at Plumb's feet, allowing him to remark that he had never seen so many distinguished backsides together on the floor at the same time. The lecture concluded with deafening applause, the popping of champagne corks, and an impromptu party, at which Plumb could be seen brandishing a magnum of Louis Roederer. As Neil McKendrick remarked, "Obviously Jack was delighted with the reception; it suited both his nature and his expectation to go out with a bang, not a whimper."

Daniel Boorstin at the University of Chicago
(Courtesy University of Chicago News)

Richard Cobb around 1970
(Courtesy of Balliol College)

Gordon Craig in the 1980s
(Courtesy of Gordon Craig)

John Hope Franklin in the 1950s
(Courtesy of Archives and Special Collections Division of the Brooklyn
College Library, CUNY)

Oscar Handlin in 1971
(Courtesy of Oscar Handlin)

J.H. Hexter at Yale around 1975
(Courtesy of Yale University)

Christopher Hill around 1970
(Courtesy of Balliol College)

Gertrude Himmelfarb around 1980
(City University Graduate Center)

E.J. Hobsbawm about 1995

Richard Hofstadter in the 1950s
(Courtesy of Columbia University Archives
and Columbiana Library)

William McNeill around 1980
(Courtesy University of Chicago News)

Edmund S. Morgan, ca. 1950

Sir John Plumb in his rooms at Christ's College, Cambridge, 1996
(Photo by the author)

David M. Potter in the 1960s
(Courtesy of Stanford University News Service)

Arthur Schlesinger Jr. in the mid-1990s
(Copyright Dominique Nabokov)

Professor Carl Schorske, Professor of History,
Emeritus, Princeton University
(Photograph by Mary Cross, May 2000)

Anne Firor Scott, 1990 (Courtesy of Anne Scott)

Sir Richard Southern shortly after receiving his Knighthood in 1971
(Courtesy Newsquest [Oxfordshire] Ltd.)

Kenneth M. Stampp around 1980
(Courtesy of Kenneth Stampp)

Lawrence Stone around the
time of his arrival at Princeton
(Photo by Orren Jack Turner)
(Courtesy of Jeanne
C. Fawtier Stone)

Hugh Trevor-Roper about the
time of the Gentry Controversy
(Lord Dacre of Glauton) (Courtesy
of Lord Dacre of Glauton)

Barbara Tuchman around 1980
(Courtesy of the National Archives)

C. Vann Woodward in the early 1980s
(Courtesy of Yale University)

Part Two

The first section of this book presented biographical information on its subjects. The second section seeks to assess their work. I hope that it will be clear to the reader that it is impossible to cover everything these historians wrote and still keep the book to a manageable length. Their production is Olympian by any standard. I cannot imagine that anyone wants me to inspect all of it. Instead, I have selected aspects of their work that seemed to me to be the most important or in some cases unremarked upon. For the purpose of analyzing their scholarship, I divided my cohort into four groups: cultural critics, controversialists (meaning primarily those historians who were involved in the Gentry Controversy of the 1950s), archivalists, and lastly, those who wrote works of synthesis, utilized printed primary sources or engaged in some combination of the two approaches or who defied categorization.

I am aware of the dangers of such an approach. Several could fit easily into more than one category. I placed Arthur Schlesinger Jr. among the cultural critics, for example, even though he could have been included in every other category except the Gentry Controversy. And given his taste for controversy, I am surprised he didn't somehow find his way into that one. Edmund Morgan was the next hardest to classify. He doesn't completely fit the category of synthesizer, but he doesn't really fit as a cultural critic or archival historian either. The one historian I allowed in multiple categories was Lawrence Stone, whom I considered as an archival historian and as a participant in the Gentry Controversy.

Chapter 9

THE CULTURAL CRITICS

♈

Between 1831 and 1832 the French aristocrat Alexis de Tocqueville took a trip across America and eventually wrote a book, *Democracy in America*, about his experience. Tocqueville's book remains a penetrating analysis of the American character, containing a remarkable range of insights. Tocqueville informed skeptical Europeans that America is not a reflection of Europe in its infancy; it is the European future. Democracy, individualism and rejection of aristocratic tradition comprise the prime components of the new America and the brave new world of the future for which Europeans should be prepared. In some ways Tocqueville's analysis of early America emerged from fairly conventional assumptions that a nineteenth-century European aristocrat might make about society. America, Tocqueville observed, lacked a landowning aristocracy, an established church, and time-tested traditions to guide them in the creation of a new society. Instead, Americans constructed their own society as they went along.[1]

Tocqueville did not particularly welcome the American influence on the future. In one of the most arresting passages in *Democracy in America*, he claimed that while there was freedom of speech and of the press in America, there was no free thought. Too many aspects of American life, he thought, must be diluted for mass consumption. Freedom of expression or democracy itself in Tocqueville's judgment meant very little because the majority will not tolerate divergent or eccentric opinion and because complex ideas must be simplified for the masses.[2]

Tocqueville was by no means the first to discern the existence of a distinctly American character, but he did advance the most perceptive analysis of it, and he had several successors. Perhaps the most famous of these was Frederick Jackson Turner, whose paper on "The Significance of the Frontier in American History," first delivered in 1893, may be the single most discussed piece of writing on American history. Building upon the foundations laid by Tocqueville in many ways, Turner argued that a distinctively American character emerged as Americans moved westward. The America of the eastern seaboard was settled by Europeans and remained European in its values and outlook. But as Americans moved westward, they settled new territories and created new sets of values. The American of the frontier, according to Turner, was pragmatic, equalitarian, individualist, anti-intellectual, and democratic, and hence decisively different from his European ancestor.[3]

The America of the 1950s called for a fresh analysis of the American character. The twin demons of Depression and fascist dictatorship had been vanquished. The American Century approached its zenith. At the same time Americans faced the daunting challenge of resisting the new and ominous Communist menace. How had we gotten where we were? Were we up to the challenges of the postwar world? First, sociologists and, later, historians offered a series of answers that seized the public imagination. In 1950 a group of sociologists, David Riesman, Reuel Denny, and Nathan Glaser, published *The Lonely Crowd: A Study of the Changing American Character*, which became a rousing best-seller, and Riesman found himself on the cover of *Time* magazine. In 1951 C. Wright Mills published *White Collar*, and in 1956 *The Power Elite*.[4]

The conclusions of the sociologists were not uplifting. Riesman, Denny, and Glaser called attention to the emergence of a conformist culture in the United States. They argued that in the nineteenth century most Americans possessed a sense of "inner-direction," a fierce trust in themselves and their own ability to determine their values. By the middle of the twentieth century, however, the research of Riesman, Denny, and Glaser revealed an anxiety-ridden, conformist nation, dominated by peer group pressures and conformity, slouching uncomfortably toward a Bethlehem it was no longer sure existed. The authors of *The Lonely Crowd* concluded that in the twentieth century the tendencies that Tocqueville identified a century before in *Democracy in America* had emerged in depressing profusion.[5]

In *White Collar* Mills criticized the increasing power of a new affluent class of middle managers, bureaucrats, and salaried employees. Like the authors of *The Lonely Crowd*, Mills described this group of Americans as rudderless and adrift, severed from the sense of mission and purpose inherent in its Calvinist past and lacking pride in craftsmanship and productivity, with no moral compass to guide them. In *The Power Elite* Mills saw the management of the country turned over largely to another morally and spiritually bankrupt group, an upper class of technicians, experts, military commanders, and corporate executives, who had realized the mutual benefits that could accrue from a marriage between military and industrial power.[6]

Historians also confronted the question of the American character and America's future in the postwar world, and those who excelled at it received more attention from the public than those who slaved away in archives. The historians who aspired to be the culture czars of the 1950s were of necessity different from other historians. Eschewing archives and specialized research, the cultural critics undertook the understanding of the sweep of American history. Archival research was too specific. The cultural critics generally depended upon printed sources and they incorporated the smaller-scale studies of other historians to construct their own, larger vision of the past. Their work could be done in a reasonably well-endowed university library, because its success depended upon the breadth of their reading and their ability to think and synthesize.

They also operated in concert with several earlier traditions of American historiography. First, American historians from Parkman to Turner and Beard offered interpretations of the grand sweep of American history and Olympian pronouncements on the best and worst elements of it. Second, Progressive historians emphasized conflict. Conflicts occurred in American history in bewildering profusion, between regions, classes, generalized areas such as the city and the frontier, and ideologies. Conflicts were usually based upon economic considerations. The historians who emerged in the United States in the 1950s as cultural critics shared the Progressive interest in the grand sweep of American history and Olympian pronouncements on it. But while they shared the Progressive interest in the grand sweep of American history, they rejected the progressive emphasis on conflict.

The historians who achieved distinction as cultural critics in the 1950s included such distinguished scholars as David Potter, Daniel Boorstin, Richard Hofstadter, and Arthur Schlesinger Jr. As a group, they have several things in common. They wrote history as much to comment on the present as to understand the past. All of them engaged Progressive historiography. Finally, central to their understanding of America in the post–World War II period was their consideration of Tocqueville's analysis of the American character or their assessment of a combination of Tocqueville, Turner, and the early national period of American history.

Daniel Boorstin was perhaps the most prolific of the historians who emerged in the 1950s as cultural critics. An earlier book, *The Lost World of Thomas Jefferson*, established Boorstin's reputation as a sensitive interpreter of American thought. He suggested that Jefferson's contribution to early American history was not, as some thought, as the embodiment of the ideals of the European Enlightenment. For Boorstin the key to understanding Jefferson was grasping his practical, pragmatic approach to problems. Early America was mixture of culture and barbarism, and Jefferson as a frontier farmer and planter, had a foot in both cultures. Boorstin suggested that the true Jeffersonian legacy rested with the idea that the survival of the republic depended not upon philosophical speculation, but recognition of the unique problems posed by the realities of a New World environment and finding practical, pragmatic solutions to them.[7]

The theme of pragmatism, originally conceived in *The Lost World of Thomas Jefferson*, was developed on a grander scale in Boorstin's next and most important book, *The Genius of American Politics*. Its stated purpose was to explain why the United States has never produced a political philosopher or political theory comparable in quality to those produced in Europe. But Boorstin ended up offering an assessment of the American character along with his ideas about the absence of political theory in America, and he introduced a new concept, "givenness," to explain them. By "givenness" Boorstin meant that certain aspects of American history were determined by immutable facts of geography and history, such as America's isolation from the rest of the world and its immense natural resources. "Givenness" especially helped explain American exceptionalism, why America had developed differently from Europe and why the American experience was not likely to be repeated. Moreover, linked with economic abundance and natural resources, "givenness" dictated an American consensus whereby most Americans were in general agreement about the direction and values of the nation. Like Tocqueville, Boorstin understood America as the exception to the ordinary flow of world history, in contrast to a Europe buried in a bitter and superfluous ideological discourse, wisely eschewed by most Americans. America, according to Boorstin, was founded by an unrevolutionary "revolution without dogma," and even the Civil War did not lead to any substantive overhaul of society or institutions.[8]

In a remarkable series of books, including *The Americans: The Colonial Experience, The Americans: The National Experience,* and *The Americans: The Democratic Experience,* Boorstin elaborated on the themes developed in *The Genius of American Politics.* Displaying a particular gift for amassing carefully sifted facts and for citing the telling example, Boorstin delighted in repeatedly exposing the non-European elements of American society and culture and extolling the virtues of innovators, boosters, and inventors. One innovator admired by Boorstin was Frederick Tudor of Boston, the "Ice King," who refused to be denied in his efforts to discover how to ship ice to Europe and Asia. Boorstin also admired the boosters who by canny promotion helped turn wilderness into civil society, and the inventors who produced such things as condensed milk and the Pullman car. All of the volumes in the series won coveted prizes. *The Colonial Experience* won the Bancroft Prize in 1959. *The National Experience* received the Parkman Prize in 1966. *The Democratic Experience* was awarded the Pulitzer Prize in 1974.

Boorstin has sometimes been classified as part of the "consensus" school of American historians, who, led by Louis Hartz, have stressed the continuity of the American experience and the general agreement of Americans about values. And indeed, before the work of Hartz and Boorstin, the debate on the American character had focused on the dreary, Prufrocklike threnodies of the sociologists about the ominous signs of conformity in American culture.

In the hands of Hartz and Boorstin, the debate was extended to a discussion over the existence and meaning of an American consensus. Boorstin is also sometimes charged with being an unabashed booster of America.[9] There is some validity to this charge, given Boorstin's faith in the business community, but it is worth noting that *The Genius of American Politics* contained some criticisms of the American character. In his main theme, for example, Boorstin emphatically denied that the American people possessed any special virtue; the success of America was attributable to circumstances, not character. The rest of the book was also laced with criticism of a number of attitudes prevalent in America in the 1950s. Boorstin was particularly annoyed by those who criticized beliefs and behaviors as "unAmerican." "Who would think," he asked, "of using the word 'un-Italian' or 'un-French' as we use 'unAmerican.'" Boorstin contrasted Americans who think the Constitution represents the unfolding of ultimate political truth with the English. "No sensible Briton," Boorstin contended, "would ever assert that his history is the unfolding of truth implicit in the Magna Carta and the Bill of Rights." Nor, Boorstin added, would an Englishman have been disturbed by the suggestion that medieval barons had a personal interest in extracting from King John the concessions written into Magna Carta. But Americans are offended by the idea that self-interest played an essential role in the framing of the Constitution.[10]

It is possible to see several powerful intellectual influences in Boorstin's work. The first are Tocqueville and Turner. Like Tocqueville, Boorstin based his conclusions primarily on his study of early America, and he stressed American exceptionalism and the pragmatic strains of the American character. Boorstin has been called "Tocqueville redivivus," even though he admired American exceptionalism and pragmatism much more than Tocqueville did.[11] Boorstin also quoted Turner with approval, citing the famous passage in "The Significance of the Frontier" where Turner asserted that "American democracy was born of no theorist's dream. . . . It came out of the American forest, and it gained new strength each time it touched a new frontier."[12] Second, there is the subtle undercurrent in Boorstin's work of Edward Gibbon, the eighteenth-century author of *The Decline and Fall of the Roman Empire*. Boorstin wrote a Bowdoin Prize essay on Gibbon, "Unspoken Limitations of History," as a Harvard undergraduate in the 1930s, and the idea for *The Genius of American Politics* came to him while he traveled in Italy in the early fifties with his family and he sat, like Gibbon, ruminating amidst the ruins of Rome.[13] Several other similarities may be noted. Gibbon's book was as much about the eighteenth century as it was about the Roman Empire, a moral homily for his own time. Boorstin's book was as much about the twentieth century as it was about early America. In *The Genius of American Politics* Boorstin essentially stood Gibbon on his head. In *The Decline and Fall of the Roman Empire* Gibbon described the torpor and stagnation that led to the fall of the Roman Empire; in *The Genius of American Politics* Boorstin described the vitality and élan that sustained American civilization.

The Genius of American Politics also bears marks of having been composed in the face of the totalitarian menace. The book, remarked Boorstin, speaks "to those who think we should try to compete with the Russians in a war of philosophy." Boorstin denounced almost anything even mildly ideological from the French Revolution to Communism and Nazism. "For the first time in modern history," he contended, "and to an extent not true even in the age of the French Revolution, Europe has become the noisy champion of man's power to make over his culture at will. Communism is, in one sense the extravagances of the French Revolution rewritten on the Gargantuan scale and acting with the terrifying efficiency of the twentieth century. People all over Europe have been accustomed since the 18th century, to the notion that man can better his condition by trying to remake his institutions in some colossal image. Fascism and naziism [*sic*] proposed this, and so does Communism. Europe has not yet realized that the remedy it seeks is itself a disease."[14]

The Genius of American Politics was published in 1953, and one year later David Potter reached similar conclusions in several respects, but also departed from Boorstin on several others. After an early career devoted primarily to the study of the American Civil War period, Potter published *People of Plenty: Economic Abundance and the American Character* in 1954.[15] The book was based on the Walgreen Lectures that Potter delivered at the University of Chicago in 1950. In its theme and interdisciplinary orientation, it marked a significant departure from his earlier work, which had established him as a superlative, if fairly conventional, historian of sectional conflict. Preparing his lectures on the American character, Potter borrowed deeply and heavily from social science, including sociology, cultural anthropology, and psychology. Indeed, an early draft of *People of Plenty* received a long and searching criticism from David Riesman, the principal author of *The Lonely Crowd*.[16]

Like Boorstin, Potter asserted that the American character was defined primarily by accidental and immutable forces, which were, in Potter's judgment, the abundance of land and natural resources in America. Like "givenness," "abundance" could be linked to a number of American developments. Humorously, Potter described the sizable role abundance has played in defining American practices in such unexpected realms as the rearing of young children. The luxury of bottle feeding, Potter noted, requires several processes, including refrigeration, heating, sterilization, and temperature control, which are only attainable in an advanced and affluent society. Powerful furnaces keep children warm enough to make the swaddling practices of earlier eras unnecessary. Disposable diapers, washing machines, and diaper services relieve parents from the tedious physical burdens of child rearing. Instead, they can spend their time, as parents did in the fifties, agonizing over their children's intellectual and social development.[17]

But *People of Plenty* of course contained more profound ideas. Like Boorstin, Potter was not afraid to puncture some American myths in order to develop his broader themes. American society in the 1950s congratulated itself on its classless nature, social mobility, and democracy, which most Americans assumed were the product of their superior national character. According to Potter, these virtues are the product of abundance, without which most Americans would be consigned, as is most of the rest of the world, to heavy labor, subsistence living, and reduced freedoms. Less abundant societies require a work force relegated primarily to subsistence agriculture; less abundant societies cannot permit freedom of opportunity, widespread competition for the few desirable positions, excessive leisure, extended periods of education, or the granting of extensive freedom to its peoples. The principles of participatory democracy, which Americans tend to regard as a universal political truth that only we have had the genius and selflessness to embrace, are thus not universal. They are the direct consequence of our unique abundance.[18]

Like Boorstin, Potter therefore perceived America's key institutions to be the product of immutable, even "given" factors, though he would never have pronounced upon the "genius" of American politics. And, like Boorstin, he also accepted the theme of a general continuity of American history, though he did not necessarily admire it. The continuity in American history, Potter argued, derives from the American tendency to bypass critical problems rather than to solve them. In the last decades of the nineteenth century, for example, the country faced the dual crisis of a shortage of gold bullion and the formidable power of monopolists like John D. Rockefeller. Both problems would have required significant legislation and sacrifice to solve, and despite massive hue and cry, they were never really addressed. In effect, however, they eventually solved themselves, without direct action, through the discovery of gold in Alaska and the discovery of oil in the Southwest, which undermined Rockefeller's control of the market.[19]

Potter concluded with a consideration of Turner and the frontier hypothesis. While recognizing "The Significance of the Frontier in American History" as a turning point in American historical writing, Potter criticized Turner for his vague and protean definition of the frontier. At times Turner treated the frontier as a specific region and at others, as a generalized concept. But more seriously, contended Potter, Turner persistently confused the frontier with abundance. The American character, Potter noted, did not change when the frontier closed. Instead, the same pragmatic strains of character and behavior persisted, suggesting to Potter that the frontier was not the principal explanatory force. Abundance, however, has continued well beyond the end of the frontier. In an earlier phase of American history, Potter concluded, the frontier was simply the most accessible form of abundance.[20]

The success of *People of Plenty* was both a blessing and a curse to Potter.

On one hand it established him as a penetrating and sensitive critic of the American scene, injecting new life into his career. A wave of honors came his way. On the other hand, he was deluged with invitations to deliver lectures and contribute to books related to his new eminence as a student of the American character. Potter refused only a few of these invitations, and soon found himself deeply overcommitted. Like Turner, Potter labored mightily, but found himself hard-pressed to honor his commitments. In 1951 he signed a contract with Harper's to write a volume on the coming of the Civil War for the New American Nation Series. At his death in 1971 the Harper book remained unfinished, despite Potter's best intentions, frequent promises to his editor, and stern admonitions to himself.[21]

One of the honors that Potter derived from the Civil War volume was an invitation to give the University of London's Commonwealth Fund Lectures in 1961, which were posthumously published as *Freedom and Its Limitations in American Life* and which afforded him the opportunity to return to consideration of the American character. In these lectures Potter, echoing Tocqueville and Riesman, contended that Americans are not as free as they think they are, and that the freedoms Americans do enjoy have come at a prohibitive cost. Potter conceded that Americans have achieved freedom from overt coercion by kings and landowning classes, in such forms as arbitrary arrest and seizure and suppression of ideas, to a greater extent than any other country in the world. He concluded that Americans in 1776 acquiesced in the creation of a society in which people applied a minimum of force to each other. But in 1776, he contended, Americans also agreed that all men were created equal, and the two propositions were not entirely compatible. Potter suggested that equality of opportunity led to a society without fixed status, which meant America was deprived of people sufficiently elite to defy authority. To Potter the dearth of elite leadership meant that the individual tended to comply with the expectations of the majority. "One began with freedom," Potter concluded, "and ended with conformity." In his last lecture Potter described the power of mass advertising to coerce subtly the American consumer into conforming to societal norms. To Potter the greatest threat to American freedom came not from totalitarian powers or seductive ideologies; it came from forces within American society itself. "Eternal vigilance remains the price of liberty," Potter concluded, "but the first person to watch is oneself."[22]

Here it was possible to see the influence of Tocqueville and of *The Lonely Crowd* on Potter's work. Both works, cited by Potter in *Freedom and Its Limitations on American Life* emphasized the dangers of conformity in American life. Like the authors of *The Lonely Crowd* Potter deplored the mass consumer value system seemingly driving American society. Like Tocqueville, Potter saw conformity as a trade-off or consequence of the acceptance of democratic institutions.

The consensus school is sometimes linked with Richard Hofstadter, and he has much in common with Potter and Boorstin. Hofstadter and Boorstin were drawn toward the Communist Party in the 1930s, but both quickly became disillusioned with it.[23] Neither spent much time with archival materials. Both relied upon prodigious reading, formidable intelligence, and an individual willingness to live poised on an intellectual abyss by interpreting history on a grand scale. "I had the courage to write *The American Political Tradition*," the controversial book that brought him professional acclaim and a mass audience, Hofstadter once said, "Now I'm not sure I have the courage to see it to publication."[24]

But Hofstadter's consensus, emerging through several books, is very different from Boorstin's. And like Boorstin's, his later work often echoed themes developed years, even decades, before. After the publication of his first book, *Social Darwinism and American Thought* in 1944, Hofstadter wrote *The American Political Tradition*, published in 1948. *The American Political Tradition* was a bold expedition into the study of American leadership, consisting of essays on leading American political figures from the founding fathers through Franklin Roosevelt. Hofstadter included three non-presidents, the abolitionist Wendell Phillips, the slavery apologist John C. Calhoun, and the populist William Jennings Bryan, as well as chapters on the founding fathers and the great entrepreneurs of the late nineteenth century. Hofstadter's conclusions about America's leaders were almost as depressing as the sociologists' lamentations about America. Part of the dreary undertone of *The American Political Tradition* may be attributed to the circumstances behind its composition. In 1944 Hofstadter's first wife, Felice Swados, was diagnosed with cancer and died after suffering grievously, in July 1945. Hofstadter, according to Alfred Kazin, began to write *The American Political Tradition* "on a pad in her darkened sickroom; he could not see the first words, but he finished the book."[25] While no one can know the precise effect of Felice's death on *The American Political Tradition*, it is clear that Hofstadter could not have been in a particularly hopeful mood as he wrote the book, and in the book itself, he expressed dislike for almost everyone he discussed, with the exception of Wendell Phillips, the abolitionist. Even such icons of American politics as Thomas Jefferson, Andrew Jackson, and Woodrow Wilson were placed under Hofstadter's remorseless scrutiny in an unflattering light.

Hofstadter echoed Beard's suspicion of the founding fathers, seeing them as economic realists, whose opposition to democracy stemmed from their need to protect their property and security from the swinish masses. Hofstadter presented Jefferson as a condescending aristocrat and pragmatist rather than a man of the people or a man of ideological principles. In this sense his vision of Jefferson as a pragmatist was similar to Boorstin's, except that Hofstadter inveighed against it. Jefferson, Hofstadter thought, lent himself too readily to partisan politics, and the only group in which he had any faith were gentlemen farmers like himself. Hofstadter quoted approvingly Alexander Hamilton's assessment that Jefferson would be "as likely as any man I know to temporize—to calculate what will be likely to promote his own reputation and advantage."[26] Andrew Jackson, like Jefferson, sometimes regarded as a man of the people, was to Hofstadter, an unprincipled rogue who did what was politically expedient. Theodore Roosevelt, the supposed Progressive reformer and enemy of the trusts, was to Hofstadter, mostly bark, with little bite. "There was," wrote Hofstadter, "a hundred times more noise than accomplishment."[27] Even Franklin Roosevelt, the creator of the working-class safety net, could not escape Hofstadter's critical eye. Writing about Hofstadter, whom he had befriended in the 1930's, Alfred Kazin recalled that "we were obsessed with Roosevelt," whom he described as "our great non-hero." For Hofstadter, Roosevelt was slippery and nonintellectual. Hofstadter reserved a special venom for William Jennings Bryan, describing the "torpor" of Bryan's mind and his "inability to hold to any intellectual principle." Hofstadter found one remark particularly indicative of Bryan's vacuousness. When asked about the issue of free silver, Bryan replied, "the people of Nebraska are for free silver. I am for free silver. I will look up the arguments later."[28] But as critical as he was of the superficial nature of those who were supposedly reformers, Hofstadter had not relented in his condemnation of the business barons. "Exploiting workers and milking farmers, bribing congressmen, buying legislatures, spying upon competitors, hiring armed guards, dynamiting property, using threats and intrigue and force," Hofstadter wrote in his chapter "The Spoilsmen," "they made a mockery of the ideals of the simple gentry who imagined that the nation's development could take place with dignity and restraint under the regime of laissez-faire."[29]

The sole figure to emerge unscathed from *The American Political Tradition* was the abolitionist Wendell Phillips. Phillips was usually dismissed as a zealot whose irrational crusade against slavery contributed to the polarization of opinion that led to the Civil War. But in Hofstadter's treatment, Phillips comes off as a man possessing the kinds of principles and backbone that other more celebrated politicians lacked. Hofstadter seemed to prefer the visionary utopian, like Phillips, who would not be swayed, to the pragmatist and compromiser.

In later life Hofstadter complained that he had been unfairly lumped into the consensus school of Boorstin, and he attributed the label to the hastily written introduction to *The American Political Tradition* that he had composed at the request of his publisher. In this introduction Hofstadter alluded to such things as "shared beliefs," "the economic virtues of capitalist culture," and a "unity of cultural and political tradition, upon which American civilization has stood."[30]

There was thus some reason to place Hofstadter with the consensus school, although not in the sense of what is normally meant by the term.

Unlike Boorstin, Hofstadter did not celebrate American achievement; he deplored it.[31] In particular he was appalled by the pragmatism and lack of principled commitment on the part of American leaders. *The American Political Tradition* is an account of principled politicians veering off-track as they surrender their beliefs to popular enthusiasm. Determination to resist the temptation to succumb to the popular will was the reason that Hofstadter particularly admired Phillips, an abolitionist who refused to compromise. Nor was Hofstadter inclined, as Boorstin was, to extol the virtues of individualism. Americans may have agreed on the virtues of individualist competition, but Hofstadter denied that the products of individualism were entirely admirable.

The ghost of Charles Beard lurked in many sections of *The American Political Tradition*, as it did over so much twentieth-century American historiography. In fact much of Hofstadter's work from *The American Political Tradition* to *The Age of Reform* to *The Progressive Historians* can be interpreted as the continuing evolution of his position on Beard and the Progressive historians. Beard stressed the primacy of economic motivation in American history, a view Hofstadter had found compelling as a student, once remarking that "Beard was really *the* exciting influence on me."[32] But in the late 1940s and early 1950s, he was working his way toward a new synthesis. In his first book, *Social Darwinism in American Thought*, he traced the power of an idea, the Darwinian "survival of the fittest." His second book, *The American Political Tradition*, while it follows several Beardian strains, is the beginning of Hofstadter's attempt to stake out some new ground, making ideas, though not always those of intellectuals and political leaders, a force in their own right.[33]

The principal actors in *The American Political Tradition* are all men with ideas. But with the exception of Phillips, they allow their ideas to be perverted as they come into contact with mass consumption and political reality. The ideas as they are initially conceived do not reflect economic reality, nor are they based on economic considerations, nor are they modified in light of new economic realities. Rather, they are diluted and modified according to political necessity.

In this theme there was nonetheless the beginning of an interpretation propounding an American consensus, but as it turned out, this consensus was in Hofstadter's judgment a reprehensible one, and one that would not emerge fully formed in his mind until a few years later. After Hofstadter finished *The American Political Tradition* he undertook an intensive program of interdisciplinary reading, especially in the fields of sociology, psychology, and literary criticism. He was fortunate that several leading figures in other disciplines were his colleagues at Columbia. These included the literary critic Lionel Trilling, the sociologist Robert K. Merton, and another sociologist, C. Wright Mills, whom Hofstadter had also known when both were at the University of Maryland.

Another influence came from Karl Mannheim, whose book *Ideology and Utopia* became central to Hofstadter's work in the 1950s. Where conventional Marxist thinking reduced ideology to mere "superstructure," the reflection of economic realities, Mannheim sought to refine the concept by showing the way its influence could appear in other ways. Ideology, for Mannheim, could develop from specific day-to-day experiences and from self-perceptions that did not necessarily correspond to economic realities.[34]

The influence of Mannheim provided Hofstadter with several of the final nails for Beard's coffin. Where Beard had described the political motivation of groups and individuals primarily through their personal finances and economic circumstances, Hofstadter explained their behavior with the use of new tools, drawn from his interdisciplinary reading, to explain other aspects of motivation, including status, myth, transference, conspiracy, and alienation. Under Mannheim's influence, Hofstadter began to see "status politics" as having as much explanatory force as economic motivation.[35]

Hofstadter further distanced himself from Beard in a 1952 article in which he examined the politics surrounding the American acquisition of the Philippines. Where the Progressives would have attributed the clamor for war to the economic interests, the business leaders who ultimately profited from the war had originally opposed it, while few of the original war hawks had an economic stake in the outcome. The real source of the expansion fever, according to Hofstadter, was a "psychic crisis" in the 1980s, attributable to a barrage of fears, including anxieties about the expansion of business and the end of the frontier. The war in the Philippines served as an outlet for the discharge of these fears and anxieties. While its proponents defended it with principled arguments, these arguments only served to mask its psychic function. For Hofstadter, Daniel Joseph Singal has concluded, "the irrational needs of the psyche, even more than the calculated pursuit of profits, supplied the key to an understanding of the Gilded Age."[36]

The insights Hofstadter received from his interdisciplinary reading along with his rapidly growing dissatisfaction with Charles Beard stand at the core of his best book, *The Age of Reform*, published in 1955, for which he won a Pulitzer Prize. In his introduction he thanked Mills and Riesman, and the book is infused with sociological explanations, particularly in terms of how groups develop their ideas from idealized visions of the past. In *The Age of Reform* Hofstadter investigated the reform impulse in American history from the 1890s through the New Deal, with particular attention to the populists. It was here, with the help of his interdisciplinary reading, that Hofstadter finally exorcised the ghost of Beard. Where earlier scholars, especially the Progressive historians, admired the grassroots, back-to-the-people style of populist agitators, Hofstadter took a very dim view of populism. In *The Age of Reform* Hofstadter portrayed the populists as anti-Semitic bigots, who clung to an irrational, mythic view of themselves as self-reliant farmers, at a time when the world had moved into the industrial age and who embraced conspiracy as an explanation for the forces that threatened them.

While Hofstadter had shed Beard, he was still a child of Mencken, another of his early idols. Hofstadter, like Mencken, lived in fear of the "boobus Americanus," who Hofstadter feared was not only bigoted and ignorant, but used numerical superiority to intimidate spineless politicians into doing the will of the masses. Arthur Schlesinger Jr. has emphasized the fact that Hofstadter was one of the first major American historians to emerge from the cultural life of New York City, and this fact, according to Schlesinger, accounts in significant measure for the character and direction of his work.[37] Moreover, as an academic who received his first full-time job at CCNY after forty teachers had been fired or forced to resign after a legislative committee investigated subversive influences within the city colleges and as a man who had lived through the McCarthy era, Hofstadter had more reason than most to fear popular government and to long for a principled leader.[38]

Hofstadter was particularly critical of those who deified rural America, and he devoted the opening chapter of *The Age of Reform* to shattering the myth of yeoman farmer of the early republic, a myth that was in large measure the creation of another of Hofstadter's favorite non-heroes, Jefferson. Here Hofstadter engaged Tocqueville and Turner, arguing that between 1815 and 1860, the character of American agriculture changed and the ideal of the self-reliant farmer canonized by Turner disappeared. Moreover, cheap land and easy profit encouraged extensive speculation in land and shoddy cultivation. The early-nineteenth-century farmer directed most of his energy toward the acquisition of more land and profit and the development of other businesses rather than to the thoughtful or innovative cultivation of the land he held. The yeoman farmer of earlier days was replaced by a debt-ridden, land speculating farmer-entrepreneur.[39]

The rejection of the agrarian myth was consistent with Hofstadter's general hostility toward rural America. The characters in *The American Political Tradition* who aroused his greatest scorn, Jefferson, Jackson, Bryan, and Hoover, were rural. The lone hero in the book was Wendell Phillips, a Bostonian. Moreover, other parts of *The Age of Reform* are loaded with additional hostility toward rural America. For farmers, Hofstadter suggested, "it was bewildering and irritating to think of the great contrast between the verbal deference paid them by almost everyone and of the real status and real economic position in which he found himself." At the same time, many rural supporters of Populism, noted Hofstadter, believed that there was an East-Coast, big-city conspiracy against them. The willingness to explain things by conspiracy, suggested Hofstadter, "frequently occurs when political and social antagonisms are steep. Certain audiences are especially susceptible to it, particularly, I believe, those who have attained only a low level of education, whose access to information is poor, who are so completely shut out from access to the centers of power . . . [that] when conspiracies do not exist, it is necessary for those who think in this fashion to invent them." In these assertions Hofstadter described what he called the "rural mind," which, he contended, when confronted with immigrants and the city, often responded with shock. Even the hostility shown toward immigrants, according to Hofstadter, was the result of small-town people who had moved to big cities.[40] Hofstadter's distaste for rural America culminated in *Anti-Intellectualism in American Life*, published in 1963, in which he bemoaned a persistent opposition in American life toward creativity and independent thought, which he again traced to the ignorant, particularly the Southern and Midwestern masses. Hofstadter appeared not to notice that possessing the education and erudition that rural Americans so manifestly lacked, he subscribed to his own version of conspiracy, this one emanating from the rural masses.[41]

Hofstadter nevertheless had succeeded in finding a way to reduce the power of economic motivation in historical analysis and advance the power of ideas. But he feared that the wrong ideas exercised most of the power, and he was suspicious of the lower-class bigotry and paranoia that controlled politicians in a democratic society, causing them to lurch from one demagogue to another. In his stress on the tyranny that could be imposed by the rural masses, Hofstadter departed from Boorstin's consensus and shared a Tocquevillian vision of America with Potter, since both of them believed that the most disturbing of Tocqueville's predictions had come true.

Arthur Schlesinger Jr. also emerged in the aftermath of World War II as a leading critic of American culture. Different from Boorstin and Hofstadter in that he was also an archival historian, Schlesinger wrote even more extensively than they for the journals of the Eastern intellectual establishment, was active in politics, and could have made a living solely by his writing. Schlesinger's father was a Progressive historian, and his father's legacy as well as the legacy of the Progressive historians looms over him, as it did for Hofstadter.[42] Schlesinger's first great book, *The Age of Jackson*, contained what was in large measure an essentially Beardian message, that the business community, rapacious and without redeeming conscience, could not be trusted to govern. But there was a guarded optimism in *The Age of Jackson*. Schlesinger was by no means naive concerning politicians, but he saw Jackson as the shining paladin of the working class, who was willing to summon the power and resources of government to protect the common citizen from the dangers that arise from the concentration of power in the hands of the few. Schlesinger noted that Jackson recognized the importance of trade and industry, but rejected the Jeffersonian antipathy toward state power by promoting democratic government as a bulwark against the excesses of capitalism.[43]

In *The Age of Jackson* Schlesinger was also compelled to confront Turner and the frontier hypothesis. Where Turner had regarded Jackson as the archetypal new American created by the frontier and emphasized the frontier roots of Jackson's policies, Schlesinger contended that Jacksonian democracy should be understood as a problem of classes, not sections, and emphasized the Eastern roots of key Jacksonian ideas. Where Turner had stressed Jackson's experience on the frontier, Schlesinger paid scant attention to that phase of Jackson's career. At the heart of *The Age of Jackson* is Schlesinger's detailed examination of Jackson's attack on the Second Bank of the United States, which Schlesinger perceived as the darkling plain on which Jackson waged his war against business.[44]

Following World War II Schlesinger moved away from Jacksonian America to the study of contemporary politics. As he contemplated writing a book on the New Deal, he began to write *The Vital Center: The Politics of Freedom*, which he described as a political tract, written to get his political views out of the way so that they would not infect the New Deal book.[45]

The Vital Center is therefore in essence a statement of Schlesinger's political views after World War II, building upon ideas initially developed in *The Age of Jackson*. It is also very much a generational text. Schlesinger, born in 1917, heard as a boy at school Franklin Roosevelt's inaugural address in 1933, his first exposure to the power of liberal ideas. His political views were shaped by the events of the 1930s, particularly over the issue of how a compassionate human being should try to address the mass suffering occasioned by massive economic collapse. Fascism demonstrated to Schlesinger the evils of totalitarian solutions and demonstrated to him that people could be easily duped. Stalin and the Soviet Union taught him that evil could exist on the Left, while Roosevelt and the New Deal endowed him with a guarded optimism about the possibilities of reform government, an attitude confirmed by his research on Jackson.[46]

Schlesinger discovered a philosophy that combined his political optimism with his general skepticism about human nature in the works of Reinhold Niebuhr. Niebuhr proposed a nonideological liberalism that conceded the essential depravity of humanity, but rejected totalitarian solutions for restraining it. Instead, Niebuhr argued that democratic government, however imperfect, remained the best vehicle to protect people from exploitation. Democratic government also provided the best opportunity to arrive at solutions selected on the basis of their efficacy, not their ideology.[47] A liberalism based on pragmatic principles, with no illusions about the virtues of humanity exercised a powerful appeal to Schlesinger. In the last chapter of *The Age of Jackson*, he called for essentially the same thing, "an earnest, pragmatic attempt to wrestle with new problems as they come, without being enslaved by a theory of the past, or by a theory of the future."[48]

With his political baggage supposedly out of the way, Schlesinger turned to the writing of a history of the New Deal. But to a certain extent the political baggage remained. Schlesinger emphasized that the New Deal did not signify a radical departure in American politics, and in his rendering Roosevelt emerged as a pragmatic champion who succeeded by locating the "vital center." Roosevelt at once prevented rapacious capitalists from devouring the system, but at the same time resisted the pressures from the Left to overhaul the system completely. In Schlesinger's hands Roosevelt bore an uncanny resemblance to Jackson.[49]

It is now possible to propose some connections between the various forms of cultural criticism advanced by historians in the late 1940s and 1950s. Somewhat different fates have befallen each scholar. Intellectuals, like Samuel Smiles or William Gilmore Sims, who advocate optimistic, boosterish visions, tend to be less enduring and more harshly regarded by posterity than those, like Carlyle or Marx, who express more despairing views of society and convey a more powerful sense of social injustice. Boorstin's reputation perhaps suffered the most on this score. A nation of shared values could be defended in the 1950s, but only if one left out women, blacks, and the poor, and Boorstin's view of American history took scant account of these groups. By the 1960s, when the lid blew off American society, it was no longer possible to see a national consensus, only a deeply cleaved and hostile society. Historians condemned Boorstin roundly.[50] On one count, however, Boorstin could claim vindication. If they were anything, the sixties in the United States were an age of ideology, that divisive impulse that Boorstin had always deplored as the root of all political evil. Looking at the upheavals of the sixties, Boorstin could argue that he was correct in his disdain for solutions depending upon ideological underpinnings. When ideology entered American life, it destroyed the pragmatic spirit of an earlier America and replaced it with reactions conditioned by a priori ideologies.

Arthur Schlesinger Jr. was subjected to similar hostility from the Left. Even though he opposed the Vietnam War and was one of Richard Nixon's most relentless critics, he remained a centrist. In the 1960s the Left did not seek truth in the center. Truth was to be found on the extremes, and Schlesinger did not follow them to the extremes. Moreover, subsequent students of the New Deal, generally on the Left, saw Roosevelt as driven by socioeconomic forces rather than mastering them as Schlesinger would have it. At the same time, they believed Roosevelt did not go far enough to eradicate all of the nation's social and racial problems.[51]

Potter and Hofstadter died tragically, within a year of each other. Potter died with much of his work unfinished, which perhaps impaired his reputation. By contrast Hofstadter's reputation soared.[52] His sad, early death at the height of his powers certainly contributed to the elevation of his reputation. But both the Right and the Left could take some solace from his historical vision. Hofstadter's fundamental distrust of authority, the business community, and people in power appealed to the Left. But his essential conservatism and his antipathy toward popular movements were embraced by the Right.

There are some interesting similarities and differences in the group. By stressing a pragmatic approach to politics based upon nonideological foundations, Schlesinger has much in common with Boorstin, who admired similar things. For Schlesinger Roosevelt succeeded because he dealt flexibly with issues, eschewing abstractions and dogmatism, and Boorstin admired people with similar adaptability. Both historians perceive a consensus or a vital center keeping America on focus. Schlesinger parts company with Boorstin in his persisting suspicion of the business community and by embracing what he would regard as the tough-minded liberalism of Niebuhr.

Hofstadter and Potter may be seen to a certain extent as a matched pair in opposition to Boorstin and Schlesinger. For Hofstadter there is an American consensus, but it is an invidious one. For Schlesinger politicians err when they ignore the vital center; for Hofstadter they err when succumb to it. Potter did not scorn the common man with the ferocity of Hofstadter, but he clearly feared the conformist, sheeplike majority, which lacked an elite to guide them.

The four do have several things in common. The first is that their works to a certain extent are meditations on a combination of Tocqueville, the early national period in American history, and Frederick Jackson Turner. Boorstin's first serious work of history was on Jefferson; Schlesinger's first book was on the Jacksonian Orestes A. Brownson, and his first great book was *The Age of Jackson*. While Hofstadter ranged widely over the entire compass of American history, his chapters demolishing myths about Jefferson and Jackson in *The American Political Tradition* along with his chapter on Wendell Phillips were crucial to the overall argument of the book. At the same time in his assault on the agrarian myth in early America in *The Age of Reform*, he echoed Tocqueville while rejecting Turner. Potter, himself a historian of early-nineteenth-century America, consciously applied a Tocquevillian analysis to contemporary problems in both *People of Plenty* and *Freedom and Its Limitations in American Life*.

There are clear generational undertones in their work. In *The Age of Reform* Hofstadter referred to "the concentration camps, the Nuremburg Laws, Guernica, the Moscow trials," from which postwar Americans were induced into having a false sense of superiority over the rest of the world. Schlesinger introduced *The Vital Center* by observing that "western man in the middle of the twentieth century is tense, uncertain, adrift. We look upon our epoch as a time of troubles, an age of anxiety. The grounds of our civilization, of our certitude, are breaking up under our feet, and familiar ideas and institutions vanish as we reach for them, like shadows in the falling dusk."[53] The most powerful themes in Boorstin's *The Genius of American Politics* and Schlesinger's *The Vital Center* serve to remind Americans how they have avoided ideological excess. Hofstadter, alienated in ways that Boorstin and Schlesinger were not, was also influenced by the temper of his time, referring in *The American Political Tradition* to his reluctance to add to an American postwar frenzy of "hero-worship and self-congratulation," a sentiment with which Potter clearly concurred, though less stridently.[54]

The historian as cultural critic was not new in the 1950s; Progressive historians like Beard and Carl Becker wrote history with an eye on the present. In the 1950s a number of distinguished historians continued to use their work on the past to understand the present. Arthur Schlesinger opened *The Age of Jackson* by declaring that we do not know how American democracy will meet the perplexities of the postwar world, "but this we do know, that, if it is to remain a democracy, its moods, methods and purposes will bear a vital relation to its attack on similar (if less intense) crises of its past."[55] In the 1960s Hofstadter remarked that all his books had "begun with a concern about some present reality. . . . I still write history out of my engagement with the present." *The American Political Tradition* and *The Age of Reform*, he conceded, "refract the experiences of the Depression era and the New Deal."[56] Justifying his departure from writing traditional history to studying the contemporary American character in the introduction to *People of Plenty*, David Potter argued that history was the discipline that did not shrink from tackling the most profound problems of society and "never held itself aloof from life." Moreover, Potter asserted, in a democracy history was the discipline best positioned to provide the ordinary people with sound information for dealing with public affairs.[57]

There is even a sense in which the histories of several of them were debates about which Americans should be admired. In the past twenty or thirty years, historians have tended to eschew the selection of historical figures as heroes or villains. But with the exception of Potter, such designations were central to the work of this group. Boorstin's heroes were the pragmatists, the seekers. Schlesinger's heroes were Jackson and Roosevelt. Hofstadter was better on villains, and he concentrated on the spineless, the unprincipled, and the anti-Semitic.

The tendency toward cultural criticism reached its pinnacle in the 1960s, but seems less visible today. Recent historians, with a few exceptions, tend to shrink from grand interpretations of the past or from using history to speculate about American culture, and appear to have less faith in the efficacy of the entire enterprise. Writing in 1987 Theodore S. Hamerow detected a "growing recognition that scholarship can offer no guarantees for the solution of social problems," so that today we have to recognize history as "irrelevant." Hamerow also spoke of the profound doubts of historians that the discipline has anything to offer "for the education of the citizen, the conduct of the government, or the guidance of the community."[58] Yet the strain of cultural criticism in historical writing does persist, particularly among members of this generation who are still alive and active. Arthur Schlesinger remains in the front lines of the culture wars. In the 1980s the culture wars were less about an American character and more about multiculturalism, the degree to which courses in the histories and cultures of non-white, non-male groups should be included in college curriculums. In *The Disuniting of America*, published in 1991, Schlesinger tackled this question from his liberal centrist perspective. Once the archvillain of the Marxists, he became the target of the multiculturalists. He welcomed the long-overdue drive to recognize the role and achievements of previously subordinated and ignored groups in American society, such as women, Hispanics, black Americans, Indians, and others. But, Schlesinger warned, the cult of race, women, and ethnicity had a price. In contrast with New Deal liberalism, which aspired, he thought, to unite disadvantaged groups with universal reforms, multicultural politics promote groups demanding individual benefits and created a culture of complaint in which political resources were dispensed in terms of which groups could present the loudest case for victimization. Identity groups in the eighties often bypassed normal democratic channels and advanced their cases by exerting pressures on courts and bureaucracies.

In conclusion Schlesinger returned to his emphasis on the vital center. Instead of a nation of individuals exercising free choice, America was now a nation of identity groups demanding equal and sometimes extravagant attention to their problems and histories. In *The Disuniting of America* Schlesinger proposed that it would be a distortion of history to abandon traditional histories of Western culture to accommodate those who want history to be taught as the history of identity groups. "It may be too bad," Schlesinger asserted, "that dead white European males have played so large a role in shaping our culture. But that's the way it is. One cannot erase history." Moreover, too much emphasis on identity group history threatened the vital center that in Schlesinger's judgment had sustained America. "Will the center hold?" Schlesinger asked, "or will the melting pot yield to the Tower of Babel?"

Gertrude Himmelfarb developed similar themes in her work in the 1980s and 1990s. Early in her career, she wrote books deflating the reputations of traditional Victorian heroes such as Charles Darwin and John Stuart Mill, and exalting the ideas of more realistic thinkers like Thomas Malthus and Edmund Burke.[59] In the 1980s, however, she transformed herself from a traditional intellectual historian to a cultural critic. The first step in this transformation was the publication of a book of critical essays on historians and what she contended was an unfortunate left-wing influence in recent historical writing. In these essays, collected and published in 1987 as *The New History and the Old*, she defended traditional political and intellectual history from the psychohistorians, the Marxists, social historians, and the *Annalistes*, sometimes known as the "new historians."

She emphasized that her objection was not to the new history, much of which she admired, but to the dominant role it has assumed in the discipline, the extravagant claims made by some of its practitioners, and distortion of the historical truth by ignoring other aspects of history. Social historians often assert that the history of high politics is irrelevant to ordinary citizens, who are more interested in feeding and clothing themselves, making a living, raising children and surviving to care about politics. In some cases the new social historians asserted that the amusements of the masses were more suggestive than their political leaders. Himmmelfarb quoted a remark by the late Warren Susman that Mickey Mouse may be more important to understanding the cultural history of the 1930s than Franklin Roosevelt. Attending a session on new directions in historical writing at a historical meeting, she heard a young historian describe his study of a single New England village, the purpose of which was to provide an in-depth analysis of the inhabitants' occupations, incomes, family and sexual relations, habits, attitudes, and social relations. When he finished, Himmelfarb asked him what bearing his study had on the most momentous political event in early America, the founding of the American republic. The historian conceded that from his work in parish registers, wills, deeds, and court rolls he could not "get at" the founding of the republic. But he denied that the event was as important as Himmelfarb believed. What was more important in his judgment was understanding the lives of ordinary people, the subject of the "new history." He was not impressed by her reply, which asserted that the founding of the republic, in essence the creation of a new society, had profoundly to affect even those elements of society most disconnected from politics. Neglect of its role, suggested Himmelfarb, amounted to a distortion of history.[60]

By the late 1980s she emerged as a torchbearer for the right-wing and used her historical writing to support right-wing ideas. In *The Demoralization of Society: From Victorian Virtues to Modern Values*, published in 1994 she contrasted the Victorian concepts of virtue, hard work, self-reliance, cleanliness, patriotism with twentieth-century relativist values. She connected the decline in poverty, illegitimacy, and crime that took place in nineteenth-century England to the infamous New Poor Law of 1834, which distinguished between the "deserving" and "undeserving" poor. For those who were poor but working, the law prescribed an income supplement; for the "undeserving" poor, it created the workhouse system described by Dickens in *Oliver Twist*. Himmelfarb argued that the system was not as odious as it is commonly portrayed and was the result of a conscious moral decision to discourage dependency and preserve the dignity of the poor. She further inveighed against the contemporary fear of attaching "stigmas" to people for fear of reducing their self-esteem. Stigmas, she wrote, are the corollaries of values and society needs the importance of social sanctions that discourage certain kinds of behaviors and encourage others. This idea was quickly appropriated by contemporary conservatives. Newt Gingrich praised Himmelfarb for helping "to establish shame as a means of enforcing proper behavior."[61]

Himmelfarb was unusual among the cultural critics in that the others considered here were American historians and used their study of American history as a foundation for their cultural criticism. Himmelfarb was unique in that she used her knowledge of nineteenth-century England as the foundation for her analysis of twentieth-century America. In 1994 she returned to her role as a cultural critic. Her book *On Looking into the Abyss: Untimely Thoughts on Culture and Society* attacked the multicultural and deconstructionist camps in the university. The book was dedicated to the memory of Lionel Trilling and took its title from a line in Trilling's *On the Teaching of Modern Literature*. In his most famous work, *The Liberal Imagination*, Trilling, like Arthur Schlesinger Jr., had rejected the idea that truth lies at the extremes, particularly on the leftist extreme. Trilling pleaded for a literary imagination that would display sensitivity to the variations and complexity of literature, and he condemned left-wing critics for abandoning the true spirit of liberalism by being too rigid, even Stalinist, in their approach to literature.[62]

Himmelfarb used Trilling's position as a point of departure to attack, among other things, the rigidity of poststructuralist literary theories. These theories come in many shapes and manifestations, but several core ideas may be identified, the most contentious of which is that there is no connection between the text and outside social or political realities, that there is in essence no reality except the text. Moreover, texts naturally subvert themselves since a positive statement cannot exist within the text without a negative corollary implied. Thus, by itself the text has no meaning. A critic who advances his own interpretation thus fails to recognize that there is no external reality outside the text and no internal meaning within it. To insist that the text means one thing and not another is to commit an act of intellectual tyranny.

The leading practitioners of poststructuralist criticism seemed to delight in being outrageous. Literature was now to be professed and not read. Reading works of theory became more important than reading works of literature. Jonathan Culler argued that interpreting particular works was subordinate to theoretical work. Stanley Fish made the claim, later retracted, that "the demise of objectivity relieves me of the obligation to be right . . . and demands only that I be interesting."[63]

The ideas of poststructuralist critics had chilling implications for history, and Himmelfarb offered a plea for their rejection based on several of her established principles. She noted some of the outrageous statements made by poststructuralists, insisted upon a connection between ideas and reality, and noted that historians had long been aware of the fallibilities of their disciplines. It was not a hot flash, she observed, to suggest, for example, that source materials used by most historians have flaws or that objectivity is an illusion. Himmelfarb also saw problems when a leading a feminist historian declared that poststructuralism created a base for the creation of a feminist history, based upon feminist political goals. Two other historians noted that the practice of feminist history might necessitate concealing the theories on which this history is based for political reasons. While they advised against such deception, they sympathized with those did conceal elements of their work that might damage the feminist cause. In response Himmelfarb reiterated the criticism she advanced of the social historians, that their methods distort history. If a feminist historian can distort history in the interest of political truth and political correctness, she asked, what is to stop other historians from distorting history on behalf of their groups in ways that might marginalize women? Historians of white men, long accused of ignoring or marginalizing women and disadvantaged groups, would now have a justification for their emphases.[64]

Himmelfarb occupies an unusual place in the pantheon of historians who lead double lives as social critics. A conservative, she might be expected to have the most in common with Richard Hofstadter, who became increasingly conservative as he grew older. But Hofstadter's conservatism and much of his historical writing was based on the idea that Americans have no idea how flawed their history and their great leaders are, nor are they aware of the dangers posed by the ignorance and anti-intellectualism of the masses. Himmelfarb is not an alienated conservative in the sense of the 1950s conservatism exemplified by Hofstadter, but one in tune with more recent developments in the conservative movement, who believes that Americans have been too disparaging about their past and in their zeal to criticize America, have forgotten the things that made the country great and have clutched extremist ideologies that take them still farther from the past. In this sense she has the most in common with Arthur Schlesinger Jr., a liberal and a political and intellectual historian, who also deplores aspects of the perceived left-wing takeover of the academy and urges a moderate course.

Chapter 10

THE CONTROVERSIALISTS

※

Controversy was often the preferred form of intellectual engagement for the World War II generation of historians. Almost all of them became entangled in it at some point, and several seemed to thrive on it. By far the most notorious controversy waged by the historians of this generation was the Gentry Controversy of the 1940s and 1950s. The Gentry Controversy involved four members of the generation, Lawrence Stone, Hugh Trevor-Roper, Christopher Hill, and J.H. Hexter, and was conducted in the classic slash and burn style of English historiography. As it turned out, for several of the participants, the Gentry Controversy was only the first eruption in a career of controversies.

The English Revolution of the 1640s continues to be one of the most debated events in world history.[1] It was largely a parliamentary rebellion against the policies pursued in the 1630s by Charles I and his advisors. The Gentry Controversy focused on the extent to which the English Revolution resulted from changes in the structure of society rather than from political and religious issues. In the early twentieth century Samuel Rawson Gardiner's multivolume history of England between 1603 and 1656 emphasized a heroic constitutional struggle between king and Parliament for political and religious liberties. The finest early practitioner of what came to be called the "Whig Interpretation," Gardiner possessed a remarkable mastery of source materials and a gift for political narrative. But his account and those of several others, while shrewd and illuminating on many matters, were naive on others. They assumed, for example, that Parliament represented the people, and they viewed the Revolution as an attempt by Parliament to liberate all the people from the tyranny of Charles I. In fact Parliament often proved less interested in the people and more tyrannous than Charles.[2]

In 1941 R.H. Tawney published two articles that proposed an exciting new interpretation of these events. Far from being a struggle over political and constitutional liberties, the English Revolution was, according to Tawney, a class struggle. During the century before 1640 a new class of rising gentry began to threaten the dominance of the traditional landowning class. By enterprise and adaptability, this new class replaced the old one as the economically dominant class, and its members embraced Puritanism as the ideology of enterprise. The English Revolution, according to Tawney, reflected the gentry's demand for political power commensurate with its economic power. The platitudes expounded by parliamentary speakers about liberty and freedom were smokescreens to disguise their class and economic self-interest. Tawney supported his arguments with comments from contemporary observers about the rise of the gentry and two sets of statistics. The first set purported to indicate a substantial decline in the landholdings of aristocrats in comparison with the gentry. The second set was intended to demonstrate a shift from the ownership of large estates toward ownership of smaller estates.[3]

Tawney's work, as we have seen, collided with traditional historiography like a high-speed car smash. Tawney appeared to have demonstrated that there was a connection between political change and social change and to have taken into account the possible roles of class and economic motivation. Even non-Marxists were dazzled by the force of his arguments. Lawrence Stone was inspired by Tawney's work to investigate the fortunes of the English aristocracy. J.H. Hexter wrote in 1978 that when he published his *The Reign of King Pym*, in 1940, he was "probably the last historian concerned with seventeenth century England to write a book in the naive (but not English) Whig tradition of political history before Tawney buried it under 'The Rise of the Gentry' and 'Harrington's Interpretation of His Age.'" Hugh Trevor-Roper once remarked, "until I did my own research I thought Tawney was right," and he later christened the period from 1540 to 1640 as "Tawney's Century."[4]

Briefly relegated to obscurity by World War II, Tawney's arguments at first received little direct criticism from scholars. And in 1948 Lawrence Stone seemed to clinch Tawney's argument by publishing an article that supported Tawney's claim that the English aristocracy was in decline in the century before the English Revolution. Where Tawney cited inept management as the prime cause of the aristocracy's decline, Stone emphasized the extravagant life styles and indebtedness of the aristocrats as the cause of the decline. Stone also deployed a new battery of statistics, designed to show that "two-thirds of the earls and barons were thus swiftly approaching or poised on the brink of financial ruin in the last few years of Queen Elizabeth."[5]

Three years later, Stone's article was subjected to unexpectedly fierce criticism by Hugh Trevor-Roper. Trevor-Roper challenged virtually everything about Stone's argument, exposing a number of serious errors. Trevor-Roper demonstrated, for example, that several of Stone's claims for the massive indebtedness of the aristocracy resulted from misreadings and misquotations of the evidence. More seriously, according to Trevor-Roper, Stone failed to recognize that his principal source of evidence, the documents in the Public Record Office called Recognizances for Debt on Statute Staple, were not lists of aristocratic debts. The Recognizances for Debt were records of bonds, the purpose of which was to give security to the lender for a much greater sum than the loan itself, usually twice the loan amount. Thus, by using the bonds to gauge indebtedness, Stone greatly exaggerated the extent of aristo-cratic indebtedness. After reviewing several other errors, Trevor-Roper con-tended that Stone's article was based upon "demonstrably inaccurate figures, in whose support he has felt obliged to misquote literary sources." Stone's portrait of a declining aristocracy might have pleased King James I, con-cluded Trevor-Roper acidly, but "it can hardly satisfy anyone else."[6]

There were a number of curiosities in the attack. Seldom has any scholar been attacked as remorselessly as Trevor-Roper attacked Stone. The strength of Trevor-Roper's piece lay in its pitiless recitation of error after error on Stone's part, truly Pelion piled upon Ossa. But strangely, Stone had been Trevor-Roper's pupil as an undergraduate at Christ Church, and the two of them had studied the Recognizances for Debt on Statute Staple during that time. A year later, Stone replied to Trevor-Roper's article, withdrawing slightly from some of his more extreme claims, but with some new statistics defend-ing his general arguments. He conceded that he had in several instances exaggerated the extent of noble indebtedness, but contended that a high level of noble indebtedness still existed. And according to Stone, Trevor-Roper was guilty of several errors of his own. In his critique he had on several occa-sions appeared to score points by showing that Stone had confused different generations of nobility. In several of these instances Stone had not ascribed circumstances to a particular noble, but only to the family.[7] Stone concluded with the statement that the issues raised in the Gentry Controversy would be settled on the basis of detailed research not by the "fierce polemical style" displayed by Trevor-Roper. That suggestion was certainly true, but here Stone learned a hard lesson of academic controversy. In controversy as in war a devastating first strike is usually lethal. The advantage almost inevitably goes to the offense, since the attacker can appear, as Trevor-Roper did, objective, virtuous, and incredulous at the amount and nature of error. By contrast the person under attack usually appears defensive and self-serving, even when they have valid points to make.

In 1953, in a lengthier work, Trevor-Roper dismissed Stone's reply in a footnote and unleashed an all-out assault on Tawney and his notion of the rise of the gentry. Tawney, according to Trevor-Roper, got it all wrong, and he launched into a critique of Tawney's methods and statistics. He noted that where Tawney had reckoned aristocratic wealth by counting the number of manors held by aristocrats, a manor was not a unit of wealth. The amount of

land, the number of tenants living on it, the payments and services exacted
from the tenants, the value and extent of the demesne land were all subject to
the widest possible variation. Here Trevor-Roper was observing what John
Cooper put more trenchantly a few years later when he remarked, "The
counting of manors seems to have effects dangerously similar to the counting of sheep. It introduces us to a dream world in which, as in our own dreams,
reality may not be entirely absent, but appearances are often deceptive."[8]

Trevor-Roper further emphasized that while Tawney's definition of an
aristocratic landowner was fairly narrow and amounted to about sixty families, his definition of gentry was as broad as the Grand Canyon. For example,
new persons added to the peerage were excluded from Tawney's definition of
aristocrat on the grounds that they were in all likelihood "risen gentry." But
the flaw in this reasoning was quickly exposed by Trevor-Roper. If Tawney
counted only the old landowners as "aristocracy," he thus excluded new and
almost by definition thriving landowners from his analysis, thereby exaggerating the financial predicament of the aristocracy.

Having wreaked havoc on Tawney's basic argument, Trevor-Roper
proceeded to expound an alternative interpretation of the gentry's situation
between 1540 and 1640. The gentry, he suggested, could not be seen as a
unified class. Those attached to the king's court held vastly different interests from those in the country whose income came largely or solely from
land. Nor could they all be seen as rising. In fact, far from rising, the rural or
country gentry, which Trevor-Roper termed the "mere gentry," were in an
economic free fall of their own. To Trevor-Roper, the mere gentry consisted
of small or middling landowners, who found it difficult to contend with the
pressures of mounting inflation, had few other sources of income, and found
their accustomed lifestyles slipping away. As their wealth and income fell,
other sectors of the gentry rose, especially the "court" gentry who had access
to royal favor and profitable office. Suffering economically and denied royal
favor, the mere gentry blamed the court for their plight and decided to challenge the king and court in 1640. When they failed to achieve redress through
Parliament, they resorted to military confrontation in which they defeated
the king and emerged as the most radical leaders of the New Model Army
and the Independent Party.

But having humbled the king and established church, the victorious
mere gentry were obliged to devise a new system to put in their place. In this
endeavor the mere gentry proved singularly inept. "None climbs so high,"
Trevor-Roper quoted Oliver Cromwell as saying, "as he who knows not
whither he is going." Searching desperately for a solution, they executed the
king, abolished the House of Lords, purged and re-purged the City, eliminated wardships and purveyance, abolished the centralized church, and established their own gentry republic to ensure preservation of their own
liberties and power.

But it was all an illusion. The gentry republic collapsed. The political vacuousness and incapacity of the mere gentry were demonstrated repeatedly in the 1650s. No agreement could be reached on forming an acceptable government nor could they contrive an acceptable church settlement. All they achieved in the 1650s was confusion, endless debate, and higher taxes. In the end they were forced to turn to Oliver Cromwell and military rule to save them from anarchy and popular revolution.

At first Trevor-Roper seemed to have delivered a knockout blow to the concept of the rising gentry. So skilled and savage was his demolition of Tawney's interpretation that it was possible to wonder how any sensible person could have subscribed to it. And Trevor-Roper was able to demolish it without falling victim to the unsophisticated assumptions of earlier accounts. Politics in his rendering did reflect social and economic realities, but it was the social and economic reality of declining gentry, not rising capitalism. "Political history is often a commentary, a corrective and clarifying commentary, on social history, and as such cannot be divorced from it," Trevor-Roper concluded.[9] His interpretation also allowed considerable room for the role of human initiative, or in this case the lack of it, on the part of the mere gentry. Tawney tried to defend himself from Trevor-Roper's onslaught, but by then in his seventies, he was not prepared for the level of work and intellectual energy necessary to take up the fight.

But if Trevor-Roper had destroyed Tawney's argument, it did not mean that his own position was impervious to criticism. Over the next few years other historians began to chip away at Trevor-Roper's argument and its evidential base. Christopher Hill entered the debate by pointing out a number of definitional problems, particularly with the mere gentry. Could the mere gentry be equated with the small gentry? Were the mere gentry the same as the declining gentry and were they all declining? Was it correct to assume that profit could not be made from agriculture or that it could be made at court? Were all the parliamentary radicals and Independents gentry? Hill and others were able to cite examples that showed the answer to each of these questions should be "no."[10]

In 1958 J.H. Hexter attacked both the rising and declining gentry theses in an article appearing in the popular journal *Encounter*, which was at the time financed by the Central Intelligence Agency to combat Communism. Hexter argued that both the rising and declining gentry frameworks were misleading and that both Tawney and Trevor-Roper had ideological axes to grind. Tawney, Hexter argued, was committed to a Marxist model and was determined to fit the rise of the gentry into his preconceived, Marxist view. Similarly, said Hexter, Trevor-Roper was just as duped by economic motivation. By appearing to argue that economic deprivation and court status were the sole motivational factors among the gentry, Trevor-Roper reduced politics to a simple struggle between the political ins and outs. Hexter himself contended that as the military power of the aristocracy declined so did their political power. The result was a shift in power away from the House of Lords where the aristocrats sat, toward the House of Commons, where inability to solve political and religious questions, rather than class struggle or economic transformation, triggered the Revolution.[11]

Perhaps the most interesting response to the Gentry Controversy was that of Lawrence Stone. His original article on the decline of the Elizabethan aristocracy had crashed and burned in the face of Trevor-Roper's assault, an assault that might have daunted a lesser man. Stone did defend himself in the pages of the *Economic History Review*, but he also embarked on another quest. What had become clear by the mid-fifties was that the leading figures in the Gentry Controversy had constructed their positions from rather narrow evidential bases. What was needed was a massive assault on the surviving records, economic and personal, of the landed classes of the period, and an examination of the footnotes showed that no one had done very much work on these lines.[12]

As it turned out, Stone was the historian willing to dig the most deeply into these sources, and here he entered the controversy at a fortuitous moment. Immediately after World War II, precisely the material necessary for the study of landowning finances was becoming available, especially in county record offices, under the auspices of the National Register of Archives, and in private houses. Seizing the opportunity provided by this outpouring of resources, Stone undertook a massive study of aristocratic life and finances in the century before the outbreak of the English Civil War, in effect a *histoire totale* of the aristocracy. The result of his work, more than fifteen years in the making, was *The Crisis of the Aristocracy, 1558–1641*, published in 1965.[13]

In writing a total history of the English aristocracy, Stone was influenced by several new trends both in and apart from the discipline of history. The first influence was the French *Annales* School of historians, which introduced the concept of *mentalité*, or mental world, to the study of social groups. Where earlier historians might have been content to examine the aristocracy's political behavior, Stone, under the influence of the *Annalistes*, tried to illuminate every aspect of aristocratic behavior, including wealth, social status, political and economic power, lifestyles, value systems, education, and family structure.

The study of concepts like lifestyle and status required insights from other disciplines, like sociology, and in the early 1950s Stone read extensively in that discipline. In this endeavor Stone had to overcome the constricting effects of an Oxford education. At Oxford it was perfectly possible to win a first-class degree without studying much history besides English constitutional history or reading much in any field beyond history. Stone did not discover Max Weber until he began to work on the aristocracy, and Weber's influence is evident throughout *The Crisis of the Aristocracy*. Stone did little with Weber's famous suggestion of a link between Protestantism and capitalism, but Weber's subtle distinction between class and status and his insistence on the relationship between ideas and ideology to social and political change became cornerstones of his research.

Stone was also influenced by the so-called quantitative revolution, by which historians tried to avoid resting their arguments on supposedly "impressionistic" data, whereby they would base their narratives on the comments of a few contemporary observers. Quantification seemingly involved more intellectual rigor than traditional history. Historians often used language that implied numerical comparisons, such as that a class was rising or falling or a political group was seizing or relinquishing legislative power. Under the rigor of quantification, they would be expected to provide some quantifiable evidence for their claims. In *The Crisis of the Aristocracy* Stone made considerable and effective use of statistics to demonstrate several of his key propositions, especially in one of his key contentions when he argued that the early Stuarts had demeaned the stature of the aristocracy by creating dozens of new peers, a process that Stone described as the "inflation of honors."[14]

Based on the remarkable archival odyssey described in the next chapter, Stone produced a detailed study of the English aristocracy in the century before the English Revolution. At the outset of his research he believed that the aristocracy in 1640 was on the verge of collapse from the tidal wave advance of the gentry, a clear instance of the Marxist transition from feudalism to capitalism. It soon became clear to him that this assumption was false; the aristocracy was not poised on the precipice of ruin in 1640. But at the same time Stone found support for his original argument, savaged by Trevor-Roper, that the aristocracy had undergone a financial crisis in the late sixteenth century. The Elizabethan aristocracy had endured such a crisis, but had survived it. Stone also demonstrated that the Revolution was not made, as Trevor-Roper contended, by desperate gentry shut out from court wealth, but by some of the most distinguished landowning families.[15]

But settling the old scores with Trevor-Roper was only part of *The Crisis of the Aristocracy*. Stone's consideration of the total environment and especially the mentalité of the aristocracy enabled him to discern a malaise deeper than economic decline. The real crisis of the aristocracy was diminution of its prestige and confidence whereby the middle classes no longer deferred to the power and majesty of the big landowners. Stone attributed the decline in public regard for the aristocracy to a decline in landed wealth and particularly to the "inflation of honors," whereby James and Charles almost indiscriminately created new peers, which in turn reduced the respect accorded them. In Stone's view the recovery of the aristocracy left the king and his ministers in a dangerously exposed position when they began to implement controversial political and religious policies in the 1630s.

The Crisis of the Aristocracy was accorded the highest praise of the profession, with terms like "masterpiece," "landmark," "magisterial," and "seminal," being tossed around liberally in the reviews. Given the character of the historical profession and the field in early modern English history, it has been subjected to criticism, but nothing approaching the kind of criticism leveled at his original article. More than any other work inspired by the Gentry Controversy, with the possible exception of Hexter's "Storm over the Gentry," *The Crisis of the Aristocracy* survived historical scrutiny. It took more than fifteen years, but for Stone redemption was his.[16]

But Trevor-Roper was not finished with the English Revolution. In the early 1960s even before the publication of *The Crisis of the Aristocracy*, he tried to revive his arguments about the English Revolution by use of the comparative method. Surveying the entire European scene, he noted that England was not the only country faced with political insurrection in the mid-seventeenth century. Spain, France, and the Netherlands experienced similar difficulties. Trevor-Roper was not the first to notice this "general crisis of the seventeenth century," but he offered a new and distinctive view of that crisis, one that echoed his earlier position on the English gentry. In Trevor-Roper's view this crisis was not merely a crisis in politics or in economic production; it was a crisis in "the relations between society and the state."

Under the stress of war, budgetary shortfall, and economic slump, the monarchies of seventeenth-century Europe struggled desperately to find new ways of raising revenue. One of the safest ways to do this was to create more governmental offices, which since they had to be purchased by their holder, became a tempting source for easy revenue. The holder received a small salary, in return for which he was entitled to exact fees for his services, influence, and favor. State churches solved their financial problems with comparable strategies. Thus, while the expansion of officeholding benefited the king and established church, it threatened particularly the mere gentry and their continental equivalents who, already pressed by inflation, paid ever larger sums to support the bureaucracies and now faced a new swarm of bureaucrats eager to take their money. From the backbenchers of the English Parliament to the Cortes of Castille, from the work of Francis Bacon to the *Testament Politique* of Richelieu, the voices of the oppressed throughout Europe cried out for emancipation from the parasitical burden of government and for the reduction of fees and offices. Trevor-Roper's essay sparked a spirited debate in *Past and Present*, the journal in which the piece first appeared. In 1969 Perez Zagorin presented a detailed case for the applicability of Trevor-Roper's thesis to the English Revolution as one that resulted from a clash between court and country, an indication that his argument had gained some acceptance. But not everyone was convinced. Trevor-Roper found himself taxed with the criticism that England's bureaucracy was far less developed than its continental counterparts and that the parliamentary opponents of royal policy were in fact anti-court and anti-centralization.[17]

The discipline of history has been noted for acerbic disputes and personal vitriol often over trivial matters, and these disputes often seem more intemperate and overheated than those conducted in other disciplines. But the Gentry Controversy stands almost in a league of its own even in the context of historical disputes. It attracted enormous attention and was conducted first in the hot specialist journal of the time, the *Economic History Review*, and later in popular readership journals, such as *Encounter*, in which the participants continued to denounce each other. In retrospect, Lawrence Stone, in his recollection of the controversy, suggested that among the reasons for the attention attracted by the Gentry Controversy could be included the total lack of common ground in the debate, the impressive stylistic gifts of the various combatants, their ability to deal in bold, conceptual generalizations about the past, and the chilling tenacity with which the combatants conducted the battle. "An erring colleague is not an Amalekite to be smitten hip and thigh," Stone quoted the mortally wounded R.H. Tawney as he tried to recover from Trevor-Roper's assault.[18]

But another element that rendered the debate so acerbic was that the Gentry Controversy can be regarded as an extension of the 1930s debates on the social efficacy and value of Marxist doctrine. It cannot be entirely accidental that the leading participants in this debate, with the exception of Tawney, were part of the World War II generation of historians and that almost all of them had some level of confrontation with Marxist theory. Moreover, in the 1950s, history could be seen as a battleground on which the value of Marxism could be debated. If Marxist interpretations of history could be seen as correct, it lent some credence to the idea that Marx's ideas about how society should be organized were correct. Those historians on the left, like Hill and Stone, found Tawney's work inspirational; those farther to the right, like Trevor-Roper and Hexter, found it false and misleading.

In retrospect the Gentry Controversy had no winners in the sense of any of the participants being able to win a consensus for their views. Stone's depiction of the aristocracy won wide acceptance, but he did not address the gentry issue directly. At the end of the day the attempt to weld a social dimension onto a Whiggish political framework failed, largely because the evidence was patchy and contradictory. There was evidence to indicate that the gentry was rising, but also evidence that the gentry was declining. In the absence of convincing documentation, the participants had little choice but to employ vague terminology and resort to rhetorical fireworks. Theory sometimes became more compelling than evidence.

In the early 1970s, in *The Causes of the English Revolution, 1529–1642*, Lawrence Stone tried to reform some of the old battle lines. He conceded that the class-war theory of the Marxists had limited applicability to the English Revolution and that none of the usual polarities such as rising/declining gentry, rising/declining aristocracy, feudal/bourgeoisie, rural/urban, rich/

poor made much sense. But he proposed to replace the old class warfare explanation with a new theory, borrowed from the social sciences, called "multiple dysfunction," by which a social dimension for the Revolution could be retained.

"New social forces were emerging," Stone wrote in an oft-quoted passage, "new political relationships were forming and new intellectual currents were flowing, but neither the secular government nor the Church was demonstrating an ability to adapt to new circumstances. Thanks to the growth of the national product, the changing distribution of wealth, the spread of higher education, the decline of aristocratic political dominance of local affairs, the formulation of new religious and secular ideas, and the consolidation of new administrative organizations in the century after 1540, there appeared a growing body of men of substance, rich property owners, professionals, and merchants. These men—the leading figures among the county squirearchy, the successful London lawyers, the more eminent Puritan divines, and the urban patriciates that dominated the cities—were steadily enlarging their numbers, their social and economic weight, and their political independence. Behind them loomed far larger numbers of yeomen and artisans, the respectable, industrious, literate, Bible-reading, God-fearing lower middle class, many of whose aspirations these leaders shared, represented and articulated."[19]

The foregoing passage had the effect of creating a historical explanation designed to blend together the most prominent social forces in Stuart England and make them agents in the same process. This was in many ways a shrewd strategy, since it spared Stone the risk of having to defend one component as the principal cause, which was where he and Tawney had gotten into trouble over the gentry. But Stone added another twist. The multiply dysfunctional society did not necessarily guarantee rebellion. In Stone's view the response of established institutions and their leaders is crucial.[20] In *The Causes of the English Revolution* Stone examined the key institutions of English government and the country's leaders and pronounced them wretchedly inadequate to deal with the nation's problems.

He solved the problem of the Revolution's origins by the use of a multitiered model of causation, derived in part from structure/conjuncture theory of the *Annales* School. Stone distinguished first what he called "preconditions," those long-term structural problems, economic, social, political, and religious, that stretched back into the sixteenth century. The preconditions of the English Revolution of 1640 included such things as the financial weakness of English state, religious instability, economic growth, social change, and the appearance of new ideas and values.

Stone's preconditions reflected the long-term problems in English society. They were necessary for the Revolution to occur, but they could not by themselves cause it. At this point Stone turned to an examination of what he called "precipitants," in which he examined the reactions of people in power to dealing with the problems of society in the decade or so before the outbreak of civil war in 1642. During the 1630s Charles I and his Archbishop of Canterbury, William Laud, tried to implement policies to harass and persecute Puritans, to rule and tax without Parliament, and to extend the power of the Church of England to Scotland. The new policies, however, backfired. Harassing Puritans and governing without Parliament helped create a firm and principled opposition to Charles, and the attempt to extend the English Church to Scotland sparked a rebellion that left Charles defeated and deeply in debt. As Stone concluded, "by the autumn of 1640 the folly, obstinacy, and misjudgment of Charles and Laud had brought the English government to its knees."[21]

To get from the failure of Charles and Laud in the 1630s to the outbreak of civil war in 1642, Stone turned to what he called triggers, those immediate policies and events that made the possibility of revolution into a probability. The most powerful trigger was the outbreak of a rebellion in Ireland in the fall of 1641. By this time Charles had summoned Parliament in order to raise money and had made significant concessions to them. But at the same time he had also displayed his own capacity for duplicity and untrustworthiness. The Irish Rebellion was a unique and disquieting event. Perhaps nothing terrified seventeenth-century Englishmen more than the thought of barbarous Irish Catholics butchering supposedly innocent English settlers in Ireland. There was an immediate need to raise an army to subdue the Irish Rebellion, but legally, only the king was entitled to do so. Parliament, however, was unwilling to entrust the command of an army to Charles, who then decided that control of the army was the one of his prerogative rights that he would not surrender. Parliament's distrust of Charles and Charles's unwillingness to prove his trustworthiness left king and Parliament at a standoff. While the Revolution had far more profound causes, the immediate outbreak of hostilities resulted from the deadlock between Charles and Parliament over control of the army.

The foregoing summary does not do justice to the power and scope of *The Causes of the English Revolution*. Stone's erudition and grasp of subject were impressive, as he distilled a quarter century of his own study and research, voluminous literature, and ideas from other disciplines into a bold new interpretation. The problem of keeping up with all literature about English history from 1529 to 1642 alone was staggering. Stone might have reasonably expected *The Causes of the English Revolution* to receive accolades comparable to those he received for *The Crisis of the Aristocracy*. But while many reviewers were impressed, *Causes* instead led to the creation of a new interpretation of the Revolution, now called revisionism.

In the mid-1960s Geoffrey Elton had already published an essay denying that there were long-term social causes to the Revolution, in effect a first blast of the trumpet against the importance of social-change explanations.

And in 1973 he published a review of *Causes* that could be seen as a second call for a new interpretation. Elton criticized Stone's use of social science terminology, such as the term "multiple dysfunction," noting its excessively elastic quality. He wondered also about how prudent it was for Stone to trace the causes of a rebellion that began in 1642 back to 1529, arguing that the sixteenth century needed to be studied on its own terms, not as the prehistory of the English Revolution. Elton concluded that *Causes* was little more than the old Whig interpretation, presented in sociological and political science dress.[22]

Elton's criticism reflected primarily his own peculiar outlook on history, scornful of interdisciplinary study, promoting the centrality of the Tudors, and insisting that the 1530s was the critical period in English history. If he could reduce the importance of the 1640s, it would serve to elevate the importance of the 1530s.

But other critics voiced similar concerns, and the storm over *Causes* encouraged the birth of a new perspective on the Revolution called revisionism.[23] Denying the importance of long-term social causes and issues of political principle, and stressing the ineptitude of those in power, the revisionists regarded not just Stone but the entire generation of historians who proceeded them as "Old Hat," though there was an even "older hat" quality to their own work.[24] In their judgment the importance of establishing a careful chronology of political events again exceeded the study of the social and economic context of those events. It seemed to some in part a return to the narrative studies of the late nineteenth and early twentieth centuries.

But in one sense Hugh Trevor-Roper might have been the historian who best survived the revisionist onslaught. While the revisionists dismissed Trevor-Roper's revolution of the declining mere gentry, several of Trevor-Roper's other ideas became incorporated into their mantra. Trevor-Roper, for example, stressed the problems generated by the intense struggle for political office, the stubborn provinciality of the gentry, their resentment of outside intrusion, and their almost total lack of principled motivation. The anti–big government spirit of Trevor-Roper's work also fit neatly with the "government is bloated and incompetent" spirit of the late seventies and early eighties, which seemed to underscore at least some of the revisionist revolt.

Trevor-Roper also survived the Gentry Controversy with his reputation high. While few agreed with his conception of a general crisis of the seventeenth century, his essay on the subject revealed him at his elegant and erudite best. It was clear that in writing history Trevor-Roper eschewed traditional narrative approaches and preferred to consider a particular historical problem. The problem that intrigued him the most was the dynamism between social, established institutions and the individuals caught up by them. Moreover, in his essay, Trevor-Roper soared majestically over the deplorable

English historical tradition of insularity. With a command of foreign languages that few historians could match, Trevor-Roper mastered the necessary literature in French, Spanish, German, and Dutch, and glided smoothly through developments across Europe. Specialists could carp about minor errors in their particular fields, but no one could rival his Olympian perspective.

The essay on the general crisis was also an example of Trevor-Roper's mastery not only of the essay form, but also of the thought-provoking essay. The subject of a "general crisis of the seventeenth century," clearly cried out for book-length treatment, which some people believe Trevor-Roper undertook but decided not to publish. He elected instead to present it at considerable intellectual risk in a highly distilled and condensed form. In this he laid himself open to specialist criticism, which he got, but in return he increased dramatically the scope of the debate. *Past and Present*, the journal that published his initial essay, eventually published an entire volume on the controversy that included Trevor-Roper's original essay and responses from other historians.[25]

Another example of Trevor-Roper's mastery of the bold, interpretative essay was his examination of the great witch hunts of the sixteenth and seventeenth centuries. Against historians who thought that the persecution of witches reflected the delusions of the persecutors, Trevor-Roper insisted that witch hunting was the product of social and economic circumstances, which created an almost McCarthylike hysteria. The first context for understanding the witch hunts was the Reformation. While witches had been persecuted during the Middle Ages, the high point of the witch hunts came between 1590 and 1640 after the Reformation had been established on firm foundations. The leading figures of the Reformation rejected the more tolerant position of Erasmian humanism. And while inherently conservative, they were also evangelical, likely to see the hand of the devil in all things, and intolerant when they encountered opposition, a pattern repeated by Catholic missionaries a generation later. The 1590s, moreover, were times of inflation, high employment, agricultural failure, and economic decline.

The social tensions created by evangelical preaching and economic deprivation resembled earlier persecutions of Jews in the need of the instigators for finding someone to blame. Where Jews had been the usual targets for such bigotry, during the witch hunts they were replaced as targets by old, poor, powerless women. For Trevor-Roper these contexts explained why witch hunting was most intense in the remote mountainous region of the Alps and Pyrenees, where the population was the most ignorant and susceptible to the efforts of the witch hunters.

The witch hunts, then, for Trevor-Roper, were not a delusion; they were a clash of ignorant armies in the high mountains. Trevor-Roper easily demonstrated that in the case of the reformers a little knowledge was a dangerous thing. The witch hunters who saw themselves as enlightened were every bit as bigoted as the mountain people they sought to enlighten. Trevor-Roper reserved a special place of honor, however, for the men of reason and tolerance, such as Johan Weyer, who spoke out against the madness of the hunts, but he was forced to concede the powerlessness of reason in the face of such colossal ignorance and bigotry.

Like his essays on the gentry and the general crisis, Trevor-Roper turned out to be incorrect about the witch hunts. The specter of a recent irrational elite, the Nazis, perhaps influenced Trevor-Roper to emphasize irrationality in an earlier elite. At the same time he believed that witch trials were common in late medieval Europe and that the sixteenth-century appearance of witch hunting was an extension and magnification of the earlier phenomenon. Thus, he paid little attention to important differences between the late medieval and early modern manifestations of witch hunting. Moreover, witch hunting was not confined to the mountains, and, in a remarkable book, Keith Thomas challenged Trevor-Roper's view of the context and irrationality of the hunts. In his *Religion and the Decline of Magic* Thomas tried to demonstrate that witchcraft beliefs were not private delusions, generated by situations of stress, but were anchored in a culturally acceptable view of reality. Witches were not the only ones believed to be capable of magic, nor did magic always have to have an evil intent. Everywhere in Europe, wizards, cunning men, conjurers, astrologers, and others attempted to manipulate the universe in some way. They tried to heal the sick, control the elements, inspire love, and predict the future, thus possessing many of the same powers as the witch.[26]

Thomas also detected an important psychological subtlety. Accusers were almost always of a higher social standing than the accused, and virtually every charge of witchcraft was proceeded by a request for charity. A beggar or poor person would approach a well-to-do household for assistance, would be refused, and leave muttering some sort of malediction. Subsequently something would happen in the well-to-do household, crop failure, illness, even death. Householders, feeling guilty at their lack of Christian charity, felt responsible for the tragedy, but projected their guilt onto the charity-seeker. She was the malevolent force who caused the damage, and if she was the devil's agent, she should have been refused.

Thomas's work offered a psychological dimension that went beyond Trevor-Roper's analysis. But the value of Trevor-Roper's work was only partly in providing the answers; most often the value of his work was to present a bold, new interpretation that would suggest new lines of inquiry, in this case the social and economic context of the witch hunts. In his inaugural lecture delivered at Oxford in 1957 when he assumed the Regius Professorship, he made this point himself, remarking that "in humane studies there are times when a new error is more life-giving than an old truth, a fertile error than a sterile accuracy."[27]

More visibly, Trevor-Roper had emerged by the late 1950s as the Lord High Executioner of English history, his critiques of Stone and Tawney having become classics in the literature of historical controversy. In 1957 Trevor-Roper trained his arsenal at another inviting target, Arnold Toynbee.[28] Toynbee had devoted most of his adult life to a multivolume work, *A Study of History*, in which he examined the rise and fall of a score of civilizations, going back to Mesopotamia. *A Study of History* was the product of massive reading and monstrous energy. After the completion of ten volumes Toynbee was prepared to advance some tentative conclusions. Progress, he contended, occurs in societies that have religious unity and creative minorities. Civilizations collapse in the face of religious divisions and complacent majorities. Western Civilization, the sole survivor of advancing civilizations, was itself teetering of the brink of collapse since the Reformation. For Toynbee, even though Western civilization staggered feebly onward, the laws of history demanded its inevitable collapse. Only one thing can save Western civilization from itself. Human beings, according to Toynbee, do have the will power to change and recover their religious unity, and refashion a creative minority by which they can redeem themselves.

While *A Study of History* was immensely popular, Toynbee was sailing blithely alone at the helm of a historical Titanic. Even though his conclusions were modest, he took a substantial risk by advancing them. To range widely over millennia was to invite specialist criticism. To offer a grand theory was to invite nihilist reaction. To suggest that the pre-Reformation world dominated by the Roman Catholic Church was better than the modern, pluralist world and that the Reformation was a step in the decline of the Western world, was to invite denominational outrage.

Even though Toynbee was clearly courting disaster, Trevor-Roper's response was extreme by almost any standard. He responded by calling Toynbee a prophet, comparing him to Hitler, and deploring the messianic quality of Toynbee's work. In satire as bitter as anything Swift ever wrote, Trevor-Roper transported himself to the centenary of Toynbee's birth (A.T. 100) and described a vision of eager acolytes reading the Old Testament (the first six volumes of *A Study of History*) and the New Testament (the final four volumes) and reciting Toynbeesque litanies.

Almost immediately Trevor-Roper found himself again immersed in controversy. His essay on Toynbee appeared just as he was being appointed Regius Professor of History at Oxford, an appointment swathed in even more controversy. In 1957, following the retirement of V.H. Galbraith, the position of Regius Professor of History at Oxford University became open. The Regius Professor is the head of the History School at Oxford. Appointments to the position are made by the prime minister himself and are among the most coveted academic honors in Britain.[29]

If scholarly productivity had been the only criterion for the appointment, Alan Taylor, a Magdalen College don, was the obvious candidate. Not only had he published prolifically, but he was also one of Oxford's most popular lecturers and a conscientious college tutor. Taylor was thus the immediate front runner for the position. By contrast, Trevor-Roper was considered a dark horse. His scholarly production was modest by comparison, although he was eight years younger, and, while he was a good lecturer, he could not match Taylor's magic in the lecture hall. But the Regius Professorship is a highly political appointment, and in the 1956–57 the political winds, once favorable to Alan Taylor, began to blow in Trevor-Roper's direction. At one point Anthony Eden, then prime minister, was prepared to accept the recommendation of Oxford's vice-chancellor, Alic Smith, that Taylor was the Oxford history faculty's preferred candidate. But the political winds of the late fifties in England changed like the winds in the English Channel at the approach of the Spanish Armada. Both Eden and Smith were forced to resign in 1957 on the grounds of ill health, and they were replaced by Harold MacMillan as prime minister and J.C. Masterman as vice-chancellor of Oxford. Masterman was a classic member of the Oxford establishment with close personal ties to Trevor-Roper. Trevor-Roper had been Masterman's pupil as an undergraduate at Christ Church, and both were members of the informal Oxford group, "The Club," which included such other quintessential Oxford figures as Isaiah Berlin and John Sparrow, and which exercised enormous influence on Oxford appointments. Alan Taylor was unequivocally not a member of the club. His scholarly productivity alone was enough to arouse the ire of his fellow dons. But he also wrote extensively for popular magazines and newspapers and appeared frequently on television and generally scorned the reclusive, high-table lifestyle of an Oxford don.

Masterman quickly informed MacMillan that the appointment of the Regius Professor must be reconsidered. MacMillan consulted his friend, the Manchester historian Sir Lewis Namier, who stirred the pot further. Namier was an old friend of Alan Taylor's and a specialist in the history of eighteenth-century England. Taylor and Namier had taught together at Manchester in the 1930s. But they were also quite different in temperament. Namier was plodding and methodical; his books were magisterial in scholarship, but dense and prolix. Not surprisingly, Namier was highly scornful of writing that appealed to a popular audience. By contrast Taylor was incisive and mercurial, a classic quick study. It was said at Oxford that Taylor read and reviewed a book every morning before breakfast, which he took at eight o'clock. He then worked at his documents, in five languages, until midafternoon, at which time he was ready to see pupils.[30] Taylor also thrived on controversy and relished the spotlight, often seeming to delight in taking deliberately outrageous positions, qualities that seemed unbecoming to Namier.

What happened next is unclear. Namier appears to have given

MacMillan a list of four names, with comments on each. It is not clear whether Taylor's name was on the list. Taylor himself claims that Namier was prepared to recommend him, on the condition that Taylor "give up all this nonsense about appearing on television and writing for the *Sunday Express*." While the Taylor account is not entirely reliable, it does fit with some of the facts. Taylor did not surrender his public persona. Namier did include on his list Dame Lucy Sutherland, his former pupil and Principal of Lady Margaret Hall, an Oxford women's college, and she was offered the position. Sutherland was a reputable scholar, but was by no means in Taylor's class. She declined the position, however, when it became clear that she would have to give up her position as Principal at Lady Margaret Hall. The chair was then offered to Trevor-Roper, who accepted.

The storm over the regius chair was almost as wild as the storm over the gentry, and once again Trevor-Roper was in the eye of it. Taylor was bitterly disappointed and broke with Namier over what he believed was Namier's betrayal. Many observers saw Trevor-Roper's appointment as a typical example of the politics and pettiness of Oxford in which an obviously superior candidate in terms of publication was rejected in favor of a more politically astute and connected candidate. There is some truth to this. In terms of publication of international renown, Taylor was the superior candidate. But with his extensive publications and popular journalism, Taylor appeared to thumb his nose at other Oxford dons, which had manifest risks. Busy with his own work, Taylor devoted little time to cultivating the friends and allies he needed. He also threatened others by his success and popularity, thereby appearing to be fatally innocent about the realities of the Oxford political world. Trevor-Roper by contrast moved easily in the highest Oxford circles and was connected to high places through his friendships in the Club and his marriage to the daughter of Field Marshall Haig, the World War I general. Trevor-Roper behaved gallantly with the news of his appointment, explaining that he remained "stubborn in his belief that Alan Taylor should have had the position." He was not, however, about to look a gift horse in the mouth. In any event, the night after the appointment, Namier dined with Trevor-Roper in Christ Church Hall.

But this is only part of the story of the controversy surrounding the appointment. Trevor-Roper aroused some of the same antagonisms that Alan Taylor did. Trevor-Roper had also published more than the typical Oxford history don and also engaged in popular journalism. But it should not come as a shock to anyone that the Regius Professor appointment turned out to be political. In the 1920s Stanley Baldwin appointed F.M. Powicke as Regius Professor at Oxford, even when Powicke had been undistinguished during his time at Oxford, when Baldwin read one of Powicke's essays on religion. V.H. Galbraith had been appointed with minimal publications in 1947, primarily because Clement Atlee wanted someone politically sympathetic to his socialist reforms. And despite the anti-Taylor sentiment in Oxford, the critical wind did not blow entirely from Oxford. The winds of fortune that blew control of the appointment out of the hands of Anthony Eden and Alic Smith and into the hands of Harold MacMillan and J.C. Masterman were the critical points where Taylor lost out.

Trevor-Roper's appointment was controversial in other respects. His scorched-earth style of writing history raised some doubts regarding how he would behave as Regius Professor, a position requiring a certain gravity. Referring to Trevor-Roper's attack on Toynbee, the *London Observer* expressed some concerns about Trevor-Roper and "the influence of a man capable of writing a considered article with such elaborate violence and hatred." At about the same time Harold Nicolson remarked that Trevor-Roper lacked "the daring scope of Toynbee, the majesty of Namier, the incisive wit of A.J.P. Taylor, the taste of Miss Wedgwood, the humanity of Trevelyan, or the charm and modesty of Dr. A.L. Rowse. . . . Among the strings of his lute there is a wire of hate which is apt to twang suddenly with the rasp of a banjo."[31]

Securely ensconced in the most prestigious academic position in England, Trevor-Roper might have been expected to mellow. But in 1961 another fat target appeared within range of his ordnance. In that year, his former rival for the Regius chair, Alan Taylor, also with a highly refined taste for academic combat, published his most controversial book, *The Origins of the Second World War. Origins* slammed into the English historical world like a shell from a German 88–caliber howitzer. In the book Taylor challenged the almost universal wisdom that Hitler and his henchmen from the first had a calculated plan for territorial expansion of Germany that led inevitably to World War II. Instead, Taylor argued, there was no plan and World War II resulted from a series of diplomatic blunders. Hitler was by no means a demented lunatic; he was an ordinary statesman running a clever bluff, using his opponents' reluctance to wage war as an opportunity to take what they were willing to give him. The invasion of Poland was a mistake, an aberration from the pattern of Hitler's earlier diplomacy.[32]

This was the kind of argument in which Taylor delighted. At a time when most historians liked to advance carefully constructed theses that fit into some broad historical scheme, Taylor generally denied pattern or order in historical events and processes. He often asserted that historical developments were the result of blunders and accidents rather than human intervention. At the same time, arguing that Hitler was not a madman, Taylor challenged many people's most cherished assumptions about an event that still aroused fierce passions. If Hitler was a madman, World War II was an aberration, not likely to recur. If he was not, it was a tragedy that could recur. Taylor also delivered a favorable view on Neville Chamberlain, who had appeased Hitler at the Munich conference and was generally regarded as a fool for thinking that he had bought "peace in our time." According to Taylor,

Chamberlain, by conceding the Sudetenland to Hitler, had learned the great lesson of World War I, where millions of people had died fighting over a dispute that began in an obscure Balkan country that no one cared anything about and unexpectedly had escalated into a major conflict.

Here was a historian who was almost the exact polar opposite from Toynbee. Where Toynbee swallowed huge hunks of history to advance grand theses about the meaning of human existence, Taylor generally denied any grand meaning to events. He was therefore a much more elusive target. But Trevor-Roper was not deterred. He accused Taylor of using the origins of World War II as a stick to beat his former colleague and antagonist over the regius appointment, Lewis Namier, a Polish Jew who was fanatical in his hatred of Germany. At the same time Trevor-Roper also accused Taylor of being interested primarily in the "laying of banana skins to disconcert the gravity and upset the balance of the orthodox," and denying that history has any meaning, seeming to believe that history's sole purpose is to amuse. For Taylor, according to Trevor-Roper, history had no more right to a place in education than "the blowing of soap bubbles or other forms of innocent recreation."

Within a few months, in the pages of *Encounter*, Taylor responded in kind with a brief essay titled, "How to Quote—Exercises for Beginners." Taylor's response consisted of two columns of passages, one from Taylor's text, juxtaposed against how Trevor-Roper had summarized or quoted it. Taylor concluded that Trevor-Roper had exaggerated many of his claims and portrayed unfairly several of Taylor's arguments in the *Origins*. He concluded with the sardonic quip, "The Regius Professor's methods might do harm to his reputation as a serious historian, if he had one."[33]

The debate over *Origins* replicated many of the patterns revealed by the Gentry Controversy. The lines of dispute were fundamental. There was no obvious middle ground. The conduct of the debate seemed to resemble two boys settling a dispute in a nasty schoolyard scrap. Taylor and Trevor-Roper even engaged in a testy debate on the BBC, in which Taylor repeatedly referred to Trevor-Roper as "Hughie," and Trevor-Roper referred to Taylor as "Taylor," even though in personal life they were on a first-name basis.

Once again, the debate called the value and purpose of professional history into question. Two able and respected historians had reached completely opposite conclusions, leading some to wonder if history could produce convincing answers to major questions about the past. But debate was central to Hugh Trevor-Roper's essence as a historian, and his career is primarily the story of his involvement in them. In addition to his tilts with Tawney, Stone, Toynbee, and Taylor, he launched missiles at E.H. Carr and Christopher Hill and became involved in controversies over the Kennedy Assassination and the Cambridge spy ring that included Kim Philby. Even in retirement, Trevor-Roper found himself in the swirl of controversy when he prematurely and incorrectly pronounced the Hitler diaries to be genuine.[34]

Shortly after Trevor-Roper's appointment as Regius Professor, Ved Mehta, who had read history at Balliol, and later wrote extensively for the *New Yorker*, sought out Trevor-Roper to discuss his views on history. Mehta found Trevor-Roper at work in the History Faculty Library on Merton Street in Oxford. His view of the Lord High Executioner was not favorable. Mehta described Trevor-Roper as a young gentleman, with a "voice as bleak as the winter wind from the open window beside his desk, and he had no time for pleasantries." Mehta felt as though he was in the lion's den. Trevor-Roper finally showed a small spark of interest when Mehta mentioned Taylor, sitting up like "a sullen country squire might when he is asked to talk about his grouse shooting." Trevor-Roper described Taylor's *Origins* as a document, "albeit a worthless one." When asked if he admired any twentieth-century British historians, Trevor-Roper replied, "not really," although he did express admiration for Edward Gibbon, the eighteenth-century author of *The Decline and Fall of the Roman Empire* and one or two French historians in this century, though he did not name them. When Mehta suggested that Trevor-Roper had often dismissed historians in terms of their personalities and then asked Trevor-Roper if there were any personal details that might throw any light on him and his way of writing history, Trevor-Roper again replied, "not really."[35]

But if Mehta could not coax any grand statements about history out of Trevor-Roper, it was not because Trevor-Roper did not have them. Admittedly those views were elusive. Trevor-Roper as a historian appeared at first glance to be best understood as a clever nominalist and committed controversialist, indiscriminately hacking up the arguments of others as it amused him. But over the years it became clear that this view of his work was woefully inadequate. Subsequent works revealed that Trevor-Roper had a sweeping and principled view of history, and that the targets of his criticisms were usually those who held views at variance with it.

Trevor-Roper's view of history had three main components, all closely linked. The first was anti-Marxism. Trevor-Roper insisted his opposition to the Marxist point of view was not instinctive or political, but was the product of his own investigations. He rejected Marxism because he failed to find convincing evidence for the critical links in the argument, particularly as presented by Tawney. There was, in Trevor-Roper's judgment, simply not enough evidence to prove the supposed link between Puritanism and capitalism, or that the period between 1540 and 1640 was a period of general prosperity, or that the gentry was rising, or that the English Revolution facilitated the triumph of the bourgeoisie. But if Trevor-Roper rejected Marxist views, he was manifestly not blind to the power of economic motivations, though principally on the part the disgruntled outs of the political world.

Second, Trevor-Roper championed those who fought for intellectual freedom against prevailing currents of repression, and he believed in slow, torturous, but eventual intellectual progress. He deplored fanaticism and irrationality as the enemies of progress, particularly as embodied in totalitarian institutions, like Nazi Germany, the Catholic Church, and the Inquisition. He disliked historical actors who could be described as religious fanatics, such as Archbishop Laud, the subject of his first book, along with witch hunters and Jesuits. He admired humanist champions of rationality, such as Erasmus, Montaigne, or Bacon, who pleaded for reason and tolerance against the current of repression and fanaticism. Someone, like Laud, who wished to return the church to an imagined medieval purity, or Toynbee, who believed the Reformation destroyed a desirable religious unity, offended him. And he was powerfully attracted to the Enlightenment as the scourge of the Catholic Church and religious fanaticism and as an engine for social and religious freedom.

Trevor-Roper had little faith in governments to facilitate progress. Seventeenth-century governments, in his view, did little except expand and extort more money from their subjects. "By the seventeenth century," he wrote in "The General Crisis of the Seventeenth Century," "the Renaissance Courts had grown so great, had consumed so much in 'waste,' and had sent their multiplying suckers so deep into the body of society, that they could flourish for a limited time, and only in a time, too, of expanding general prosperity. When that prosperity failed, the monstrous parasite was bound to falter."[36] Nor did social forces drive progress. Intellectual progress, for Trevor-Roper, came from heroic initiatives of individuals with the courage to rage against the forces of ignorance and fanaticism. Trevor-Roper's oft-stated admiration for Gibbon and Burckhardt can be attributed in part to the same point of view; Gibbon believed that the coming of Christianity destroyed the superior civilization of the Romans and plunged Europe into a millennium of darkness. Burckhardt saw the Renaissance as a bridge between the world of medieval superstition and the modern scientific world. In this sense, moreover, for Trevor-Roper, it was perfectly acceptable for the historian to throw off the mantle of dispassionate narrative and take sides to designate heroes and villains.

A third pillar of Trevor-Roper's historical vision, again closely linked to the first two, was his hostility for Hitler and the Nazis. Of his generation of historians he was the one most affected in his work by the war and the events leading up to it. If the history of the early modern period was his beloved ancestral home, the history of Germany was his charming summer retreat. Not only were the Nazis irrational and totalitarian, but he never doubted that Hitler represented the ultimate evil, and he despised the Western powers for their failure to stand up to him. Hence when Taylor argued that Hitler was an ordinary statesman without a plan who stumbled by happenstance onto the notion that he could exploit the fears of Western leaders, he, too, trampled on one of Trevor-Roper's most cherished tenets.

The historical viewpoint of J.H. Hexter has some similarities with that of Trevor-Roper. Both appeared early in their careers to be gifted intellectual saboteurs, with special affinities for vivid prose and a bullfighter's instinct for the kill. The strength of both men lay in their abilities as essayists. At various times, Hexter published essays that denounced theories of new monarchy, the Tudor middle class, the rise of the gentry, historical relativism, and near the end of his career, revisionism.

But like Trevor-Roper, Hexter was much more than an icy hatchet man. When his first set of collected essays was published in 1961 as *Reappraisals in History*, Hexter, too, demonstrated that his view of history was both consistent and principled. He rejected economic determinism as essential to understanding early modern England. He was uniformly skeptical of any arguments for great trends, unifying principles, or all-embracing constructions. Much of his criticism of other historians concerned their sloppy use of language. Heaven help the careless scholar who bandied about such nebulous terms as "factors in modern history," the "middle class," or "gentry" without defining the terms precisely. Hexter himself was an able and exacting stylist for whom the failure to find the mot juste could be as damaging as insufficient research. Virtually all of Hexter's work was written to challenge an accepted idea.[37]

While he was invariably at his best using another historian's work as a point of departure, Hexter did have positive viewpoints about the nature of history. The first was the belief that there is truth in history, not adamant, unassailable truth, but truth nonetheless. Many of the historians of his generation accepted the principle of historical relativism, that there is no ultimate historical truth. Each generation writes its history anew, and that historical judgment, ultimately, is in the hands of the individual historian, who is a prisoner of his own upbringing and prejudices. In various places Hexter tilted with this position for much of his career. If relativism was right, history was not only nebulous and inexact, but pointless, merely the construction of a usable past from generation to generation. Perhaps Hexter's firmest argument against historical relativism came in a remark he made in regard to Lawrence Stone. In *The Causes of the English Revolution*, Stone commented that one of the lessons of the Gentry Controversy seemed to be that each participant assumed the stance closest to his personal view. Then he went a step further, remarking that "in the final analysis the imposition of a rank order of importance depends not on objective and testable criteria, but on the judgment, sensibility, or bias of that historian." If this were true, Hexter replied, there would be "no difference between a historian who alleged that the Japanese attack on Pearl Harbor was of high importance in accounting for the entry of the United States into World War II and the historian who denied this, asserting the greater importance of the conjunction of Mars and Saturn in the house of Leo." For Hexter there were real and verifiable historical truths; he did not find them very often, but they were there.[38]

The controversy over revisionism was a second place where Hexter took a positive stand on what he believed to be valid and reasonable. In two lengthy review articles on revisionism, he still preferred to present his work as critiques of others' ideas, and his invective had not lost its edge. One of the revisionists had argued that opposition to royal policy in early Stuart England was led by a group of "Livian Republicans," aristocrats, who, steeped in the study of Roman historian Titus Livy, used Livy's ideas to lead England into rebellion. After checking the article's footnotes and finding little to corroborate them, Hexter concluded that it "was possible that in early seventeenth century England the men who opposed the king's actions were Livian republicans. It is also possible that they were defenders of an imaginary ancient constitution. And it is even possible that they were Mahayana Buddhists. Unfortunately, on the evidence provided by Farnell, it is not possible to tell which, if any, of the three they were. It is perhaps unnecessary to chase further after the ephemeral phantasms of Farnell's overheated historical imagination."[39]

Hexter also insisted, as he had in 1958, that the English Revolution concerned liberty and rule of law and that any account of the onset of that Revolution that does not fix its attention firmly on king and Parliament firmly locked in combat against each other amounts to being in a "dark house at midnight looking for a cat that is not there." The question central to the Revolution and ignored by the revisionists, according to Hexter was this: "Is England to be a land where the law rules or is England to be a land of the lawless?"[40]

Moreover, according to Hexter, the revisionists were led astray by their acceptance of anachronistic assumptions about the world. Irritated by the revisionists' dismissal of the role of ideas in the English Revolution, Hexter claimed that the revisionists had assumed an intellectual stance appropriate to the 1930s, where the notion that ideas merely reflect existing economic and social realities was widely accepted. By the mid-1970s, he contended, there was plenty of evidence that political ideas could inspire peoples in Eastern Europe, Africa, and Asia to resist tyranny and oppression, regardless of economic and social conditions.[41]

But the most notorious of his later controversies was his attack on Christopher Hill in 1975. A conflict between the two historians was perhaps inevitable. After the two had combined to raise the most telling objections to Trevor-Roper's conception of the decline of the gentry, any vestige of similarity vanished. Since the 1930s Hill had been working to apply Marxist theory to the English seventeenth century; Hexter emerged as its most formidable opponent.

By the 1970s Hill's work had undergone several shifts in perspective.

The first phase of his historical writing was crudely Marxist. In 1940, disgusted with the outbreak of a war that he believed would result in a senseless waste of lives, he published an essay that presented the English Revolution as "a class war in which the despotism of Charles I was defended by the reactionary forces of the established church and conservative landlords. Parliament beat the king because it had the enthusiastic support of trading and industrial classes."[42]

After the war he received renewed inspiration from the Marxist Historians' Group. With their encouragement and criticism, he entered a second phase of historical writing as he modified his earlier views and turned out the massive body of work that would make him famous. While he did not publish a major book until he was forty-four, his rate of productivity in the years that followed was breathtaking. Between 1956 and 1975, he published ten books, most of which dealt with seventeenth-century England, focusing principally on the meaning of the English Revolution, ideas in social and economic context, the relationship between religion and society, and radicalism. Partly through their sheer volume and stunning erudition, Hill's books established a modified Marxist interpretation of the English Revolution, roughly equivalent to Albert Soboul's "revolutionary catechism" of the French Revolution. "Christopher Hill," wrote his former pupil, Sir Keith Thomas, "must have read more of the literature written in and about the English seventeenth century than any man who ever lived."[43]

In this second phase of his historical writing, Hill displayed a particular sensitivity for understanding Puritanism and the social bases of religion. In *The Economic Problems of the Church*, published in 1956, Hill examined the Church of England's response to the financial pressures it faced in the late sixteenth and early seventeenth centuries. He sought to demonstrate that the church's attempts to solve its financial pressures alienated it from the laity. As the church's property diminished over the course of the sixteenth century, the clergy, from the lowliest parish priest to the mightiest bishop, and the church itself were left impoverished. As they made increasing fiscal demands on the laity, the laity turned away from the church, blaming the clergy, especially the episcopate. Thus, the economic problems of the Church of England contributed mightily to the weakness of Charles I's government in 1640 and explained why some people for nonreligious reasons would be offended by church policies.[44]

In 1964 Hill followed up *The Economic Problems of the Church* with an equally important and closely related book, *Society and Puritanism in Pre-Revolutionary England*, which he told friends, perhaps tongue in cheek, he wrote with notes left over from *The Economic Problems of the Church*. In *Society and Puritanism* he sought the reasons why people would be attracted to Puritanism for nonreligious reasons. Some of those attractions were economic, but for Hill, perhaps the most compelling factors for the spread of Puritanism were social. Puritanism afforded an opportunity for the establishment of a Puritan New Jerusalem, a godly, orderly, hierarchical community, based upon Calvinist teaching. By appealing to a popular desire for order and stability in a time of confusion and disorder, Puritanism addressed the needs of all classes, but primarily those of the "industrious" sort of people.[45]

In this endeavor he bowed before one of his own and his generation's most cherished articles of faith, that the stated motivations of historical actors are often divorced from their real motivations. Hill's Puritans thought they were responding to the doctrinal message of Puritan preaching; in reality Puritanism addressed needs that were far more deeply embedded in society than any of them realized.

One of the early criticisms of Marxist history was that it attributed historical change to agents, such as the bourgeoisie and emerging capitalists, who had no idea that they were part of the process and never intended to build the capitalist society they were supposed to be creating. In the second phase of his historical writing Hill's contribution to the Marxist interpretation of the English Revolution was to show how the Revolution could have social and economic bases even if contemporaries were unaware of them and to leave considerable room for individual initiatives and ideas.

The breakdown of English society in the 1640s, he contended, was not brought about by the bourgeoisie, nor was it their intention to make a revolution. But in the 1640s, faced with the centralizing tendencies of Charles's government and divided elites, the "industrious sorts of people" joined the opposition to Charles and Laud and were able to get the groups competing for their military support to take up their issues. The prerogative courts and the regulatory agencies of government were quickly eliminated, clearing the way for the more acquisitive society that followed.

It is hard now to keep in mind how exciting the ideas in Hill's work initially seemed. Building from a Tawneyesque base, Hill added an entirely new dimension to the study of Puritanism as a social force and several aspects of his work endured. While his Marxism was denounced by the revisionists, part of his work escaped their fury. He is perhaps the father of the "clash of cultures" aspect of revisionism, and the revisionists repeatedly stressed the revolutionary spirit of Puritanism over the importance of political ideas.

Hill's view of the Revolution became increasingly complex. By the sixties he no longer accepted his own earlier view of an outright class war; he recognized that England was no longer feudal in 1640, and he insisted on the role of ideas in transforming society. By the time of the publication of *The Century of Revolution* in 1961, Hill had also perceived a far more profound revolution than the political one he had initially comprehended. He now saw a midcentury revolution in literature and arts as well as politics and economic life. And he had not retreated from the notion that the English Revolution set in motion the eventual bourgeoisie shift of English society and laid the groundwork for Britain's subsequent emergence as a modern capitalist state.[46]

But Hill's work in its second phase posed two problems. The first problem was his dependence on printed primary sources. He seemed to know all of them and to have studied them carefully, but they represented only materials in print, not those buried in manuscripts.[47] The other problem was that he was chasing ephemeral motivations, unknown even to the people they were acting upon and by their nature hard to document. Hill was able to demonstrate repeatedly how points of doctrine in Puritan sermons could have multiple meanings and how those meanings could have economic and social attractions for their auditors. What was harder to show was if and how these ideas actually reached their audience and how the audience itself responded. Hill could cite what dozens of Puritan preachers said; he could only rarely cite what merchants or artisans said in response to what they had heard.

His interest in the unconscious motivation and the development of ideas sometimes forced him to argue from connection, that if two persons had the same ideas and could have had some contact, one might have gotten the ideas from the other. In his *Intellectual Origins of the English Revolution*, first presented as the Ford Lectures at Oxford, he tried to connect Puritanism with the scientific spirit. Both, he argued, were the ideologies of forward-looking men in the seventeenth century and were derived from the same source, the drive for freedom and the desire to create a new science, a new philosophy, and a new political system. Almost immediately he found himself in a bunker surrounded by hostile scholars flinging hand grenades at him. Trying to link Puritans with Francis Bacon aroused the ire of Hugh Trevor-Roper, for example, who claimed that Hill missed the fundamental point of difference between the two: Puritanism was inherently repressive; science was inherently liberating.[48]

The difficulty of argument by connection also aroused Hexter's ire a few years later. Purporting to review Hill's first volume of collected essays called *Change and Continuity in Seventeenth Century England*, Hexter assailed Hill's methods and in effect his entire contribution to seventeenth-century historiography. Hill stood accused of tailoring his evidence to fit a preconceived model, being unable to recognize, much less deal with, contradictory evidence and failing to honor the professional historian's duty to police himself by recognizing the limitations of his thesis.[49]

At the core of the turmoil was Hill's position on the emergence of a capitalist society in seventeenth-century England. In *Change and Continuity* Hill considered one aspect of that tradition, namely, the relationship between Protestantism and the rise of capitalism. This is of course hallowed historical ground, where such historians as Tawney and the sociologist Max

Weber had argued that Protestant ideas had in them the spirit of capitalist free enterprise and that a connection, if only tenuous, exists between Reformation theology and the growth of capitalism. This argument has been criticized on the grounds that capitalism is neither a product of the Reformation era nor an exclusively Protestant phenomenon. It is medieval, if not ancient, in origin and was practiced by Catholics such as the Medicis of Florence as well as Protestant Englishmen.

In his essay "Protestantism and the Rise of Capitalism," Hill began by stating these limitations and then advancing his own revision. He contended that a by-product, though not necessarily an intent, of Puritan preaching was an increase in confidence in one's conscience. If a man could find religious truth without priestly guidance, this would encourage him to practice self-reliance in secular affairs.[50]

Hexter criticized Hill's position on evidential grounds. First, he examined the treatises of the four preachers on which Hill based his argument. For Hill's position to obtain, asserted Hexter, the men should have preached to bourgeois congregations. Hexter claimed, however, that their audience was more likely composed poor people and university folk, as opposed to a bourgeois audience, though he admits that it is impossible to know the exact composition of each man's congregation. More seriously, Hexter suggested that there are passages in the sermons that do not reveal any affinity with capitalist tendencies and significant portions of the sermons that have absolutely nothing to do with capitalism. Hill, said Hexter, neglected to cite these, thereby misleading the reader. The neglected sections indicate that these men were not giving encouragement to capitalism as Hill would have us believe. Their intent, as always, said Hexter, was to "bring Christian teaching to bear on their flocks."

Hexter suggested that Hill was an insidious combination of two historical tendencies. The first of these he called "source-mining," the second he called "lumping." Source-miners, according to Hexter, raid the sources for information about particular items of historical importance, in this case, evidence of Puritan preachers encouraging capitalism. Lumpers, in Hexterese, attempt to box history in tidy parcels and delight in finding great patterns and themes. In Hill's hands these two tendencies combined with disastrous results. Clearly Hill was both a source-miner and a lumper. With his boundless knowledge of the sources, he was certain to find plenty of examples of Puritan preachers encouraging capitalism. With his tendency to lump, he would wedge his evidence into a Marxist model and fail to recognize contradictory evidence. Hexter concluded that by citing mainly the evidence that seemed to support his case and not noting contradictory evidence, Hill had created a way of doing history in which people never get in the way, and he had in so doing "failed his colleagues."[51]

Hexter's review provoked another controversy. But if the Gentry Controversy was a ten on the controversy scale, this one was closer to a two. Hexter was both right and wrong. Hill often did seem to pick out the elements from Puritan sermons and literature that seemed to support his interpretation. On the other hand, Hexter drastically oversimplified the nature of Hill's contribution to scholarship. No one can read *Society and Puritanism* without a sense that fierce spiritual and religious convictions formed the base of Puritan conviction. Nor can anyone read Hill without a sense that ideas are a force in their own right and not the mere reflection of economics.[52]

It is difficult to sort out all of the hidden agendas at work in the Hexter-Hill controversy. There were first of all cavernous differences between the two men as historians. Hill was a Marxist; Hexter was Marxism's most conspicuous opponent. Hill tried to develop big themes in his work; Hexter usually tried to shoot them down. Hill's métier was the book; Hexter's was the essay. Hexter's style was flashy and occasionally indulgent; Hill's was spare and workmanlike.

But two other agendas are worth attention, although like aspects of Christopher Hill's work, they amount to a search for the unverifiable. In several senses both men were refighting the Gentry Controversy, and during that time Hexter, usually the source of vitriol, had himself been scorched by Hill's pen. In the exchange of letters in *Encounter* that followed Hexter's "Storm over the Gentry," there appeared a letter from Christopher Hill. Hill's letter began by stating that in his analysis of the Gentry Controversy Hexter had been "less than fair to Professor Tawney. It is—how shall we put it?—disingenuous to describe as 'Tawneyese' a Marxist use of the word *feudal* which Professor Tawney has specifically disavowed. Professor Hexter summarizes accurately enough various criticism of Tawney's thesis made by other historians, sometimes remembering to acknowledge his sources." After a further discussion of other problems in Hexter's article, Hill continued, "Professor Hexter offers two suggestions of his own. First, so important that he italicizes it, the discovery that in the decades before the Civil War, '*the magnates do not directly control arms and men the way they once did.*' This is true, and was new when Professor Tawney pointed it out forty-six years ago in *The Agrarian Problem of the Sixteenth Century*." Hill concluded that "if Professor Hexter had a better grasp of Professor Tawney's achievement his criticisms of one of our greatest living historians would be impertinent, as it is they seem to me irrelevant."[53]

A second agenda is also ephemeral. In the late 1950s J.H. Hexter, despite the writing of two books and several seminal articles, had been stuck with a heavy teaching load at Queens College, where there was little administrative interest in research. In 1958 he left Queens to become the chair at Washington University in St. Louis, where his circumstances improved, but Washington University at that time was not the elite institution it soon became. Hexter's career prospects were stalled until Peter Laslett, a young

English historian, undertook the task of collecting Hexter's essays and find-ing a publisher for them. In 1961 Laslett persuaded the Northwestern Uni-versity Press to publish them as *Reappraisals in History*. Hexter's best work was in his essays, and their publication helped land him the job at Yale in 1964.[54]

At about the same time Laslett published *The World We Have Lost*, an anti-Marxist social history of seventeenth-century England, which was sub-jected to a scathing review by Christopher Hill. After a lengthy recitation of Laslett's errors, which included mistakes on several elementary matters, such as the date of the Short Parliament, Hill concluded that he hoped to end more in sorrow than in anger: "but the most serious accusation against [Laslett] is sheer ignorance. It is bad not to know that the Short Parliament met in 1640, but it is worse, in an author who takes it upon himself to rebuke others, to be ignorant of the most important sociological history written in England and the USA in the last twenty-five years."[55] Thus, Hexter did have several axes he could have been grinding as he wrote his review of *Change and Continuity*, trying to avenge both himself and Laslett. We will never know for certain whether either or both of these agendas affected Hexter, though it is hard to believe that they did not have at least some motivational force.[56]

A third phase in Hill's career began with the publication of one of his most successful and popular books, *The World Turned Upside Down* in 1974. By this time he had begun to move away from the origins of the Revolution to its later development. He had always contended that there were two po-litical revolutions in the 1640s. The first was the one that overthrew Charles I and his ministers. That revolution was a success in a political sense. The second revolution occurred when the poor and middle classes, having helped defeat the king, rebelled upon the realization that the upper classes had little intention of compensating them for the role they played in that defeat. This second revolution failed, but it produced a torrent of radical ideas, which Hill tried to consider in *The World Turned Upside Down*. The frightening nature of these ideas, which included universal suffrage, redistribution of the land, and free love among others, reunited the divided upper classes in their fear of the ignorant masses and were thus instrumental in the Restoration.[57] Hill's colossal output continues well into his retirement. It is possible to ar-gue that there is a fourth phase to Hill's career in which to a certain extent he has returned to his first love, literature, by writing books on Milton, Marvell, and Bunyan.

As Peter Lake has suggested, the various controversies in which histo-rians of early modern England engaged between 1950 and 1975 were cen-tered on some form of modernization theory.[58] Whatever their ideological sympathies, most of them agreed that in 1500 England was not a capitalist or a modern political state; by 1800 it was. Hill saw the modern state emerging from the mid-seventeenth-century revolution that reduced the repressiveness of church and state in order to facilitate the growth of capitalism. Lawrence Stone's view was similar. Twice in the seventeenth century the English landed elite went to war to preserve their perceived version of a balanced constitution, rule of law, their right to consent to taxation, and the protection of their church from popery. In 1688 their victory was decisive. The Crown was never again granted sufficient revenue to function without Parliament. By 1720 England was a country run by and for the landed elite, the mercantile and banking elite, and the Protestant establishment. Hexter believed that the modern state was the product of the struggle for political and religious liberties. Hugh Trevor-Roper believed that modernism represented the triumph of rationality against the repressive forces of religion and ignorance.

There is another related and undeniable thread linking the work of the members of this generation. In the 1930s, all of them had or began an engagement with Marxism, the results of which helped determine the nature of their future work. Half a century later that engagement had not subsided. Most of Christopher Hill's best work came from the inspiration of Marxism, while much of the best work of Hugh Trevor-Roper and J.H. Hexter was concerned to refute it. While Lawrence Stone was never a Marxist, most of his career has been spent exploring ways to find the proper balance between social, intellectual, political, and economic variables.

Like the biblical preacher in Jerusalem, in the 1930s four young scholars came to the study of history determined to seek and search out wisdom concerning all things that were done under the early Stuarts. One found that there was something new under the sun. Three found a crooked thing that could not be made straight.

Chapter 11

THE ARCHIVAL REVOLUTION

♨

Most mornings in the summer when I have the chance to pursue my own research in England, I make my way from my room in a small hotel in central London near the British Library eastward down High Holborn Street toward the Public Record Office on Chancery Lane. I seldom mind the walk, and I stop for tea and newspapers along the way. There is a moment, as I turn off Holborn onto Chancery Lane, where the Public Record Office flashes into view for an instant and then is obscured by other buildings as the road twists in another direction. The Public Record Office on Chancery Lane (there is another branch for more modern documents near Kew Gardens in southwest London) is to some a rather hideous hulk, a manifestation of the worst excesses of late Victorian architecture, but to me and to many others, it is a temple. Its closure and the removal of most of its records to Kew is a minor tragedy, wrenching away another place with the weight of history.

The mystique of the Public Record Office for me derives in part from the fact that every time I walk down Chancery Lane toward it, I am conscious that this is a path walked by almost everyone who has worked in those periods of English history before 1750. I have a particular sense that this is the same journey made by the young Geoffrey Elton as a research student in the late 1940s and many times later. Elton, along with several others of this generational cohort, English and American, elevated archival research to the highest form of the historian's art. Before Elton's death in 1994, when I entered the Round Room of the PRO to read manuscripts, I always looked around carefully, thinking that I might see him. I never did, although I was not disappointed one morning to spot Hugh Trevor-Roper at work.

The Public Record Office, created in 1838 by an act of Parliament, links together several generations of British historians, primarily medievalists. Before the transfer of manuscripts to Kew, one could usually see a medievalist studying his tax records and plea rolls, cumbersome documents, which have to be read on special readers, set up like easels. But beyond the medievalists, Geoffrey Elton, a student of the reign of Henry VIII, is the man most responsible for the romance of the Public Record Office for early modernists. Henry VIII's reign left a remarkable body of documents, and beginning in the 1860s a squad of scholars transcribed the original documents from sixteenth century hand into a readable script. They also provided concise summaries of each document, which were eventually published as the *Letters and Papers of Henry VIII.* On one level it was a surpassing triumph in historical record editing. The publication of the summaries enabled scholars, especially Americans, to use the records without having to go to the PRO, and provided a uniform body of evidence. Legal scholars, such as Maitland and Pickthorn, had used manuscripts in their work. But A.F. Pollard, the czar of early Tudor historians and the author of the most highly regarded biography of Henry VIII to appear until the late 1960s, relied entirely upon the printed letters and rarely if ever visited the Public Record Office to consult the originals.[1]

Geoffrey Elton was a pupil of Pollard's student, J.E. Neale, who specialized in the study of Elizabeth and her parliaments. Warned by Neale's other pupils not to work on Elizabeth and already dissatisfied with Neale's seeming compulsion to make Elizabeth the source of almost everything that was good about England, Elton decided to work on the early Tudors. Neale's only advice was to suggest that Elton go sample the *Letters and Papers.* As he scanned the sections on the 1530s, Elton noticed the name Thomas Cromwell leaping off page after page of the records, and he realized that he had discovered his subject.

Not content with the summaries provided in the *Letters and Papers,* Elton went to the Public Record Office to study the originals and discovered a number of interesting things. First, he found that the *Letters and Papers* were riddled with errors: errors in transcription, errors in dating, and errors in attribution. Second, the documents themselves often contained much more than what was recorded in the transcriptions. Many small turns of phrase and particular words of critical importance were omitted or misdeciphered. Elton also discovered that there were other document classifications bearing on Henry VIII's reign unexamined and untranscribed by the editors of the *Letters and Papers.* Elton soon came to know the records better than the PRO's record keepers themselves. For several months in 1947–48 he made the trek every day to the Public Record Office, stopping punctually at three o'clock in the afternoon to watch cricket.

The result of Elton's labor was a book titled *The Tudor Revolution in Government,* published in 1953. In *The Tudor Revolution in Government* Elton contended that the 1530s marked a sharp divide in English history. Earlier historians, such as Pollard, had already argued that Henry VIII's break with the Roman Catholic Church was a critical step in the creation of a sovereign English state, but Elton pushed the argument much farther. In the 1530s, he asserted, Henry's leading minister, Thomas Cromwell, effected a number of administrative changes that signaled a transition from medieval "household" methods of government to a modern "bureaucratic" government. Elton regarded this transition as the most significant change in English government between the Norman Conquest and the Victorians. In the king's marriage crisis, Cromwell recognized the opportunity not only to break away from the Catholic Church but to create a new national sovereign state by establishing the sovereignty of king-in-Parliament, an efficient bureaucracy, and the supreme law of the land embodied in statutes approved by Parliament. If Elton was right, the medieval development of the English constitution, the reign of Elizabeth, and even the English Civil War were less important than the 1530s in the development of the English state and no single individual was more important than Thomas Cromwell.[2]

Equally important was the intellectual attitude proudly paraded on nearly every page of *The Tudor Revolution*. The book was the product of detailed research in archives, and the interpretation advanced in it was derived almost entirely from the empirical data assembled. It also rode resolutely against the currents of the times. In the age of the Gentry Controversy and Marxist analysis, historians increasingly chose to study social groups and economic forces, and eagerly sought insight from social science theory. By contrast Elton defiantly eschewed it all, choosing to study an administrative process far removed from class structure, and portrayed himself as a fierce opponent of preconceived hypotheses, theory, and interdisciplinary approaches. For Elton the study of history began with the need to understand the most fundamental truth in historical procedure, that it is necessary to start with a question and evidence, not from teleological assumptions and theories. The historical truth comes from documents not theory. "We historians are firmly bound by the authority of our sources and by no other authority, human or divine," he once said.[3]

It is a curiosity of *The Tudor Revolution in Government* that it was a broad theme approached in a narrow manner. The emergence of the modern state is an important topic in European history to which a vast amount of study has been devoted. Yet the time period and evidentiary base for *The Tudor Revolution in Government* was extremely narrow, covering mainly the early 1530s. Most historians at that time preferred large subjects, such as the Protestant Reformation or the French Revolution and wrote for general audiences. *The Tudor Revolution in Government*, however, was almost antiquarian in its approach, an administrative history of the early 1530s, based on the study of minutiae within rather arcane records.

While Elton published widely on a number of subjects, *The Tudor Revolution in Government* was his favored child, and he spent much of the rest of his life defending it. Perhaps no scholar has ever held so fiercely to a position taken at the beginning of his or her career. Part of Elton's genius may be seen in the remarkable manner with which he defended, revised, and reformulated the ideas in *The Tudor Revolution* over the next forty years. In the remarkable textbook, *England under the Tudors*, published in 1955, Elton distilled the ideas in *The Tudor Revolution in Government* into a textbook chapter, and continued to publish articles sharpening the argument. In the 1990s he was still defending his position.[4]

By designating the 1530s as the pivotal point in the development of English government, Elton placed himself in a particularly exposed position. His arguments in *The Tudor Revolution in Government* were likely to be challenged by medievalists who believed the critical developments occurred earlier and from Elizabethan specialists who might continue to see Elizabeth as the key figure in modern government. In 1963 the Oxford journal *Past and Present* published critiques by the medievalist Gerald Harriss and the Elizabethan specialist Penry Williams, which challenged Elton precisely along these lines, along with Elton's defense against their charges. While Elton, a Cambridge don, acquitted himself well during the debate, he came to believe that the controversy was an Oxford plot against him and that it impeded unnecessarily his career at Cambridge.[5]

By the 1970s Elton developed some new ideas about Thomas Cromwell. In *Policy and Police* (1972) he set out to demonstrate that Cromwell was not a despot. In *Reform and Renewal* (1973) he tried to show that Cromwell's vision extended to economic and social policy as well. But an offer from the Harvard University Press to write a new textbook on the early Tudors for a series in English history afforded him the opportunity to reconsider the original arguments of *The Tudor Revolution in Government* in light of new research.[6]

Reform and Reformation, published in 1977, contained substantial modifications in the original thesis. While none of his critics had succeeded in convincing Elton that Cromwell was not the architect and engineer of the Tudor Revolution, it was a different Cromwell who appeared in the pages of *Reform and Reformation*. While Elton had originally viewed Cromwell as a visionary with a secular cast of mind, by 1977 he regarded Cromwell as an evangelical Protestant, with an enthusiasm for the reform of society as well as government. The secular man who seized the opportunity of the king's marital problems to create the sovereign English state was now replaced by the visionary who wished to revitalize and reform society and government. At the same time, Elton also had to incorporate the findings of one of his research students, David Starkey, into his overall argument. Starkey had discovered the existence of a new aspect of early Tudor governance, the Privy Chamber, a key aspect of English government in the 1530s, which, with Cromwell's connivance, operated like the medieval household.[7]

As he reconsidered his position on Cromwell, Elton followed several important rules of survival in academic combat. By all means insist on your position. Do not ignore or surrender to your critics. Keep answering them, which will keep your name in the forefront of learned journals. People not familiar with the technical details will assume that as long as you persist in defending yourself some of the substance of your argument must remain. Eventually you and your position become one and the same; you will yourself become the issue. Journal editors will ask you to review the important new books that you can assess in terms of how well they complement your own work; publishers will ask you for new textbooks which you can utilize to keep your ideas alive. To these rules Elton added a subtle refinement: when you are boxed in, admit minor mistakes and occasional exaggerations, but in the end insist that the "substance" or "essentials" of your original argument remain. As Elton wrote in the preface to a new edition of *Reform and Reformation*, "I should think it distressing if twenty-five years of constant activity (by myself as well as so many others) had not made me alter many parts of the story, but for myself I incline to the view that in essentials the forecast written in 1953 differs little from the retrospect concluded in 1976."[8]

The problem for Elton with trying to incorporate the findings of David Starkey into *Reform and Reformation* was that Starkey's findings were incompatible with Elton's core thesis. Elton saw a "modern" government under the design of Cromwell and Cromwell's status as the supremely pragmatic and rational man directing it. Starkey saw the survival of medieval forms of government into the 1530s and the importance of faction in driving the politics. Starkey's argument required refutation rather than incorporation.

The debate as it evolved in the late 1970s and 1980s, displayed Geoffrey Elton at his best and worst. In many cases his most profound critics were his own students. Elton had supervised, encouraged, and approved the dissertation on which David Starkey advanced his ideas about the king's Privy Chamber. Another one of Elton's students, John Guy, denied the centrality of the 1530s and the originality of Cromwell. Guy argued that earlier figures, such as Thomas Wolsey, had attempted Cromwellian reforms in the 1520s and that earlier thinkers, such as Christopher St. German, devised the policies later enacted by Cromwell. Another student, Brendan Bradshaw, challenged, on a friendly basis, Elton's antipathy for Sir Thomas More, who usually aroused more admiration from scholars than Cromwell. So there was no requirement that Elton's pupils were expected to echo his wisdom. Indeed, Elton seemed to welcome dissent. On the other hand, he remained tenaciously territorial about *The Tudor Revolution*. There was no problem with Starkey when Starkey published some of his findings in a couple of obscure journals, but when Starkey went forward more publicly, an ugly feud erupted, which did not flatter either man. At the same time, when Elton's old opponent Penry Williams published his own synthesis, *The Tudor Regime* in 1979, Elton wrote a brutal review in the *Times Literary Supplement*, which flayed

Williams for making a number of minor errors. Elton did not acknowledge that *The Tudor Regime* proposed a different and, to many Tudor specialists, more convincing interpretation of Tudor politics than *The Tudor Revolution in Government*. In contrast to Elton's stress on the rational, pragmatic reform of government in the 1530s, Williams stressed the persistence of faction, corruption, and patronage as wheels of Tudor government, a view with which most historians would concur.[9]

The rationality and pragmatism of Cromwell's approach to politics, were central to Elton's understanding of the 1530s, and he made no secret of his admiration for Cromwell the man as well as the politician. He appeared to be pleased when people suggested that he wanted to be Thomas Cromwell, and he seemed to be a biographer who had fallen in love with his subject. In several respects *The Tudor Revolution in Government* was also very much a product of the time of its composition and of its author's experience. It is not hard to see why anyone in the Western world in the 1940s and 1950s, especially a Jewish refugee from Hitler, would praise rationality and pragmatism in government and why Elton would admire those who eschew theory. Ironically, Elton turned Cromwell into what he had always despised his mentor Neale for doing with Elizabeth, the creator of everything.

While Elton became the torchbearer for archival history, he was by no means its progenitor. Medievalists had examined the development of the medieval state through its bureaucratic records, and S.R. Gardiner used manuscripts for his histories of the Stuarts. The use of manuscripts was also central to the work of the two historians Lewis Namier and Charles Beard who are in many ways the intellectual fathers of the World War II generation, and the two men are connected intellectually. Namier was a Gallician Jew whose family emigrated to England. After receiving a first-class degree from Balliol College in 1911, Namier began to study the eighteenth-century English Parliament. Before Namier, historians focused primarily on newspapers, printed memoirs, and official parliamentary records, which caused them to focus on the public pronouncements and beliefs of leading political figures. Partly under the influence of Beard, Namier came to reject this analysis.[10]

Early in his career Namier visited the United States and become familiar with the work of Beard and other Progressive historians. Beard and the Progressives believed that true political reality could never be discerned from official and public accounts. They sought the inside story and the reality behind the public accounts. In Beard's most famous and controversial book, *The Economic Origins of the American Constitution*, published in 1912, he rejected the idea that the development of the American Constitution represented the triumph of an epochal American struggle for liberty. For Beard it was the product of a series of backroom deals by which various interest groups got the political system they wanted and could control, with only an occasional nod to altruism and principle.

Namier's work embodied these strictures. Not content with official records, Namier visited the great houses of the English aristocracy to consult the surviving records. He was able to produce dozens of painstaking, detailed, individual biographies of major and minor parliamentary figures. In the work that resulted from these painstaking investigations, Namier described an ugly, sordid world of eighteenth-century politics, where most of the leaders were more interested in local politics and self-aggrandizement than national interests.

The Tudor Revolution fit, but only partially, into this framework. Geoffrey Elton did not see the development of modern government as the product of accidental, self-interested forces, nor did he see it as particularly sordid; he saw it emanating from the vision of a politician of genius, Thomas Cromwell. But he did see manuscript materials as the path to the truth, and he did see behind-the-scenes politics as more important than parliamentary maneuvers. The Tudor Revolution is in one sense a Namierite book: an antiquarian investigation of a fairly narrow subject, based upon archival materials, but one that turned out to have enormous implications.

Elton was not the only historian seeking to approach questions more scientifically and willing to propose a wide-ranging new interpretation. Ironically, at the about the same time, Lawrence Stone was engaged in a similar manuscript journey. Stone and Elton were in any case two unlikely bedfellows. Stone had the temerity to publish an early article on Thomas Cromwell, and he derived insight from other social science disciplines and methodologies; Elton despised theory.[11] But in the late 1940s and early 1950s they were both pursuing a similar research path.

In the late 1940s Lawrence Stone was still trying to pick himself up after having collided with the historical blitzkrieg known as Hugh Trevor-Roper and Gentry Controversy. Probably no historian, much less one at such an early stage in his career, has been subjected to such a devastating attack on his work. After Trevor-Roper's assault on his methods and findings in the *Economic History Review*, Stone had several choices. He could have fled from the historical stage or found another topic to work on. As we have seen, he chose another course.

While both Stone and Trevor-Roper used archival materials in their early research into the Tudor and Stuart aristocracy and gentry, they relied primarily on records available in public repositories, such as the British Museum and the Public Record Office. Stone increased the stakes. At about this time a new set of records was becoming available. Before the twentieth century most of the records needed to study the early modern aristocracy lay unknown and uncatalogued in the great estate houses of England. As the power and prestige of the aristocracy declined, aristocrats opened up not only their homes but their archives to qualified persons or placed them for examination in local record offices.

Willing to explore this mass of information and only mildly intimidated by Trevor-Roper's assault, Stone decided, as we have seen, to conduct a large-scale investigation into the economic might, social status, political power, lifestyle, value system, education, and family structure of the English aristocracy in the century before the outbreak of the English Civil War. The book was in effect a *histoire totale* of the English aristocracy, a subject on which he spent much of his scholarly life.[12] For the next fifteen years Stone enjoyed "the dizzy excitement of turning over and reading in archive rooms, cellars, and attics great masses of papers which no one had ever examined before."[13]

The condition of the archive varied considerably from estate to estate, ranging from the orderly and even lovingly catalogued to the supremely chaotic. At one great house the late duke had devoted his life to sorting and cataloging his family papers. During his last illness he asked to be taken down to the archive room so he could die amid his papers. His son was dissolute and did not even bother to return Stone's phone calls regarding the family papers. By chance one of Stone's calls was answered by an aged nanny who gave Stone access to a superbly ordered room.[14]

In another house Stone worked over the family records in a frigid room in the depths of winter, bundled in blankets and great coat, while at the other end of the room two elderly servants sat beside a small fire polishing silver and gossiping maliciously about the owners of the estate. When the chill became too much, Stone would huddle around the fire with the servants, and the thought struck him that this was a scene that could have occurred in the seventeenth century.[15]

At another house the owner led Stone up a flight of creaking stairs, thrust the key into the lock, and turned it. Nothing happened. Stone and the owner then forced the door open and found a great sea of parchment covering the entire floor, three feet high in some places. The only way to enter the room was to walk on the pile of scattered and bundled papers, and, as Stone entered, treading as lightly as possible, the seals and crumbling parchment cracked and crunched under his feet.[16]

Occasionally the owner of the house would invite Stone to lunch, which would be the occasion for an oft-repeated scene that could have come from the novels of Evelyn Waugh. Stone would be summoned to an elegant dining room, replete with magnificent art on the walls and superb wine, but soured by food so unpalatable that Stone often had to struggle to eat it, sometimes after service by a confused and drunken butler.[17]

In addition to entering the debate on the English Revolution, in *The Crisis of the Aristocracy* Stone also entered the debate over the development of the early modern state, in which, oddly enough, he found himself holding a position similar to Geoffrey Elton's. In the chapter on "Power" Stone described the process by which the Tudors gradually wrenched military power from the aristocracy and claimed a royal monopoly on violence both public and private. During the Middle Ages the English Crown had been compelled to depend upon the system of maintenance by which nobles built up large retinues. These retinues spared the Crown the expense of supporting a standing army, but left it in a dangerously exposed position when nobles could summon greater resources than the Crown. The War of the Roses in the mid-fifteenth century appeared to reflect the worst excesses of the system. Several members of the titular nobility could muster larger armies than the king, and they saw no reason why they should respect his authority. At the same time violence appeared to be an endemic part of society. Aristocratic ideals of honor encouraged aristocrats to engage in personal violence in order to defend their reputations and honor.

According to Stone, over the course of the sixteenth century, the Tudors gradually rid England of the monopoly that the aristocratic classes had established over violence, both individual and collective. The Tudors crushed powerful regional nobles, such as the duke of Buckingham, and were stingy about creating new ones. They further reduced the power of the nobility by creating new institutions, such as the Commission of Array, to take responsibility for military service. Through the Commission of Array, local officials trained what amounted to a militia, which meant that it was no longer controlled by the landowners. By 1600 the Crown had established itself as the central authority in England.[18]

In arguing for the early modern foundations of the modern state, Stone faced some of the same criticisms that Elton did, particularly from medievalists. In the early 1950s the Oxford medievalist K.B. McFarlane exploded the idea of a rebellious and contrary nobility precisely for the period, the fifteenth century, during which they seemed the most rebellious. McFarlane described a failure of nerve about the Yorkist nobility, arguing that the interests of king and noble were compatible. A few years later, after McFarlane had taken the violence out of the Lancastrian age, Lawrence Stone was putting it back into the Elizabethan age. The weight of recent scholarship has been more with McFarlane than with Stone.[19]

The work of J.H. Plumb has many similarities with that of Lawrence Stone. Both were concerned to understand the connection between politics and social and economic transformation, and both undertook extensive work in archives. In 1936 after finishing his Ph.D. at Cambridge, Plumb decided to try to publish what he regarded as its most significant discovery. This discovery was that, contrary to virtually all established authority, the Convention Parliament that followed the Glorious Revolution of 1688 was not dominated by Whigs; it contained a balance of Whigs and Tories. In conducting his research Plumb had followed the research obiter dicta of Namier, laboriously tracking down the political affiliations and votes of each member.[20]

World War II interrupted his work, and following the war, he returned to Cambridge and to a heavy teaching load. Among his duties was to teach a special subject on Sir Robert Walpole, the early-eighteenth-century minister. Plumb estimates that during the summers of 1946 and 1947 he wrote nearly 250,000 words of lectures on Walpole and other eighteenth-century subjects trying to keep up with his teaching. There was no time for archival research, but in 1946 he agreed to write a short history of eighteenth-century Britain for Penguin. The work he had undertaken for his teaching provided him with a firm base for the book, which he finished in 1948. After finishing a history of his home county of Leicestershire for the Victoria County History, he decided to write a biography of Walpole.

Walpole was one of the many great paradoxes in the history of England in eighteenth century. Coarse, corrupt, profane, Walpole was probably a despicable human being, seemingly unsuited to lead an England that had been plagued by a century of civil unrest and still seemed torn by political division. But Walpole soon won the confidence of the new king, George I, and under Walpole's leadership England entered an unexpected period of political stability.[21]

Plumb's interest in Walpole had first been aroused by sitting beneath his picture, which hangs over the high table at King's, during many silent dinners as a junior fellow. That interest brought Plumb, like Lawrence Stone, research adventures that ranged from the awful to the sublime. The sublime was reserved for his visit to Houghton, the magnificent house built by Walpole, then owned by the Marquess and Marchioness of Cholmondeley, who provided superb hospitality and an ideal environment for work. The awful was working on the Churchill papers at Blenheim. Accompanied by a bright undergraduate, Neil McKendrick, Plumb spent three bitter January days there in the frigid cellar that passed as the archive room, wrapped in the royal standard for warmth. When McKendrick, encouraged by Plumb's panache, reached for a similar sustenance, Plumb ordered him to desist and to continue copying documents. "Youth will keep you warm, McKendrick," he snapped.[22]

If many suspected that Geoffrey Elton wanted to be Thomas Cromwell, there were no such suspicions that Plumb wanted to be Walpole. An opinionated and intimidating bachelor don, with a taste for fine wine, porcelain, and great art, Plumb was not to be confused with Walpole, a coarse, backslapping man of the people. In his biography Plumb was able to demolish several myths about his subject. Earlier accounts stressed the ease with which Walpole dominated the feckless early Hanoverian kings, like Richelieu dominating Louis XIII. They also regarded Walpole as a financial wizard. Plumb certainly recognized Walpole's estimable political gifts, but he demonstrated that his triumphs did not come easily. Considerable tact and skill were required on his part to deal with the Hanoverian kings. More importantly, work in Walpole's correspondence with Robert Jacombe, Walpole's financial advisor, revealed that Walpole was not a financial wizard. He did not, for example, foresee the South Sea Bubble crisis and had invested heavily in that shady venture. But he was able to keep his wits about him at the height of the crisis and find solutions.

As he worked on Walpole, Plumb became drawn to the larger problem of political stability. Historians have referred to the "general crisis of the seventeenth century." In England there were revolutions in 1640 and 1688, and an explosion of fierce religious and ideological passions. By the time of Walpole these passions appear to have evaporated and an age of political stability begun. How was such stability, rare not only in England but in Europe and the world, achieved? As he worked on Walpole, Plumb began to formulate an answer, which he wrote up as *The Growth of Political Stability in England, 1675–1725*. The first draft of *The Growth of Political Stability* was written in 1949, but not published until 1967, after Plumb had presented the work as the Ford Lectures at Oxford.[23]

By political stability Plumb meant the acceptance by society of its political institutions and those classes of men and officials who control them. Not only is political stability a relatively rare phenomenon historically, but England's prospects in the seventeenth century for achieving it were slim. In the seventeenth century, as we have seen, men killed, tortured, and executed each other over politics. By 1688 conspiracy and rebellion, treason and plot, torture and execution were part of the history and experience of several generations of English men and women.

To make matters worse, several other developments seemed to portend more instability. The main force in the creation of instability was Parliament. Its control of money made its management essential, but reformed or unreformed, no one seemed able to manage it. When people assemble, they love to complain, especially about those in authority. Moreover, from the backbenches to the country estates of the landowners, to the pubs and taverns of London, the truculence of Parliament was not feared but welcomed.

Population growth also seemed to foreshadow difficulty. Growth in population increased the size of the electorate, and deep political divisions, which Plumb called "the rage of party," led to increasing competition for seats in Parliament. The need to be prepared for war led to higher taxes, mounting public credit, the expansion of the bureaucracy, a dramatic increase in the number of people wanting positions in government, and the prevalence of corruption, all of which inflamed the squirearchy.

The situation seemed to amount to aimlessly tossing matches into an ammunition dump. One would eventually cause an explosion. Disaster was staved off only by circumstances and Walpole's political skills. The growth of population, seemingly dangerous, also led to an expansion of business and commercial activity that enriched the merchant and banking community and allowed Walpole to keep taxes low. Walpole thwarted the Tory opposition by denouncing them as Jacobites as successfully as McCarthy denounced his opponents as Communists. No one understood the political value of Jacobitism better than Walpole, who used it to destroy not only the Tory Party but the party rage that had demonized English politics for the previous century. In its place Walpole offered single-party government, commercial expansion, lower taxes for landowners, peace, and the corrosion of principle.[24]

Plumb's work contains numerous similarities to Lawrence Stone's. Both began with concerted efforts in archives: Stone on the aristocracy, Plumb on Walpole. Both moved on to present sweeping syntheses that went beyond the original scope of their archival work, Stone's *The Causes of the English Revolution, 1529–1642*, and Plumb's *The Growth of Political Stability in England, 1675–1725*. Both were concerned to connect political change with social change. Stone believed that social tensions led to the English Revolution; Plumb believed that the closing of these rifts led to the Walpolian oligarchy. Both were also concerned, contrary to the Marxists, to reintroduce the role of ideas into history.

Both historians also triggered a reaction. For Stone, it came in the full-scale assault from the regiment of revisionists; for Plumb, the reaction came on two fronts, first, from E.P. Thompson, and, second, from Jonathan Clark. In *Whigs and Hunters*, published in 1975, Thompson, the most famous radical historian of his time, focused on a single act of Parliament, the notorious Black Act of 1723, which created fifty new capital offenses, all concerning threats to property. Where Plumb celebrated the stability and prosperity of England under Walpole, Thompson argued that the Black Act revealed Walpole's total lack of sympathy with the lower classes and was just another tool for patrician dominance. The political life of England in the early eighteenth century resembled, in Thompson's memorable phrase, a "banana republic." In conclusion Thompson deplored Walpole's achievement. "I am at a loss to know," he remarked, "who . . . benefitted from Walpole's administration . . . beyond the circle of Walpole's own creatures."[25]

In a series of books and articles, Clark attacked both Plumb and Stone by denying the efficacy of social-change explanations for the eighteenth century.[26] Clark's alternative to social-change explanations was presented in *English Society, 1688–1832*, published in 1984, in which he argued that practically nothing changed in England between 1688 and 1832. England was as much a stagnant Old Regime as France, although Clark preferred the term "confessional state," to indicate the significance of religion in England. Religion more than any other factor determined political affiliations and ideas. The Church of England was the cornerstone of the confessional state, and those who wished to practice other faiths were excluded from key avenues of power within society. But many were prepared to pay the price for worshiping outside the Church of England, and religious diversity, or "heresy" in Clark's view, rather than social change, was the chief destabilizing force undermining England's Old Regime, which was not really dismantled until the repeal of the Test and Corporation Acts in 1828 and Catholic emancipation in 1829.[27]

Clark's dissatisfaction was not of course solely with Plumb, but with the explanatory framework that tried to connect social and political change, of which Plumb was the principal eighteenth-century exemplar. In turn Clark's work has come under fire, primarily for oversimplifying the arguments of others and for not defining the key phrase of "confessional state."[28] But the historical debate involving Plumb, Thompson, and Clark should not obscure the point that Plumb was first of all an archival historian.

The manuscript revolution was not confined to Great Britain. At about the same time, Kenneth Stampp was applying the same principles to the study of American slavery. The prevailing view of slavery in the early 1950s had been established by Ulrich B. Phillips in 1918. A native Southerner teaching at Yale, Phillips contended that slavery was at its core a benevolent institution, sustained by kindly masters at a personal sacrifice to support in benign fashion a black population incapable of supporting itself. Based on extensive archival research, Phillips's work was not without value. But it also reflected Phillips' assumption that blacks were inherently inferior. Phillips therefore had no interest in studying how the institution of slavery affected black people and even less interest in the darker side of the institution: whippings, beatings, sexual exploitation, and other brutalities associated with it.[29]

By the 1940s some challenges to Phillips' work had appeared. By that time a black tradition existed in historical writing on slavery that included W.E.B. DuBois and Carter G. Woodson. At the same time a new generation of white scholars began to take up the issue. In 1943 Herbert Aptheker argued in *American Negro Slave Revolts*, that slaves were not always the submissive, Sambos depicted by Phillips. A year later Gunnar Mrydal published *An American Dilemma*, which raised questions about the racist nature of American society by contrasting the freedoms and affluence enjoyed by white Americans against the humiliations and prejudices endured by black Americans. In the same year Richard Hofstadter published an article in the *Journal of Negro History*, "U.B. Phillips and the Plantation Legend," in which Hofstadter criticized Phillips for relying on the records of slaveowners for his point of view and for letting his entire account be determined by racist assumptions. In conclusion Hofstadter called for a new history of slavery, based on interdisciplinary approaches and written in large measure from the point of view of the slaves. In 1947 John Hope Franklin published a history of black Americans, *From Slavery to Freedom*. While Franklin throughout his career denied that he was a "Negro historian," he insisted in *From Slavery to Freedom* that American history was incomplete until the history of black Americans was integrated into the mainstream of historical writing.[30]

It remained for someone to tie these different threads of interpretation together. And it was also clear that anyone who wished to try to tie them together or challenge Phillips's interpretation was going to have to match his work in archives. Here Stampp began an odyssey resembling that of the English historians, especially Lawrence Stone. He had established an impressive reputation as a historian with two earlier books, *Indiana Politics During the Civil War,* a revised version of his Wisconsin dissertation, and *And the War Came: The North and the Secession Crisis, 1860–1861.* Moreover, he was already delivering lectures to his classes and leading discussions in his graduate seminar where he expressed his dissatisfaction with Phillips's work. In 1948 one of his seminar students, listening to Stampp inveigh against Phillips and describe the need for a better book on slavery, said to him, "Why don't you write it?" In 1952–53 with the help of a grant from the Guggenheim Foundation, Stampp then began a remarkable voyage of discovery through southern record offices and university libraries in Alabama, Kentucky, Louisiana, Maryland, North Carolina, South Carolina, and Virginia. In these libraries and archives Stampp gathered evidence from a variety of records, including plantation records, census reports, writings of former slaves, and papers and records of slaveholding families. The result was a searching critique of the Phillips interpretation in a 1952 article in the *American Historical Review* and, later, the appearance of Stampp's celebrated book, *The Peculiar Institution: Slavery in the Ante-Bellum South,* first published in 1956.[31]

The Peculiar Institution remains one of the most remarkable books ever written by a historian, boasting a range of virtues, including concise, readable prose and understated passion. But the characteristic that made *The Peculiar Institution* so compelling was its relentless challenge to Phillips as the established deity and its articulation of a fresh and for a time, utterly convincing new interpretation. In *The Peculiar Institution* Stampp shattered myth after myth about American slavery. Challenging Phillips's contention that slavery rescued black Africans from their supposedly primitive and backward culture and endowed them with the benefits of education and Christianity, Stampp asserted that slavery wrenched the slave from "his native culture and gave him, in exchange, little more than a vocational education."[32] Stampp pointed out that contrary to public opinion in the 1950s, the typical slaveowner was not a big plantation owner, like Gerald O'Hara in *Gone with the Wind;* he was a hard-bitten, small farmer, holding five or fewer slaves. Nor were the masters the kindly father figures of popular imagination, and he stressed brutal and frightening foundations, including beatings, rape, and whippings, underlying the system. Stampp also insisted that slavery was profitable. Owners received at least reasonable compensation for their investment, and only the most incompetent owners failed to realize a profit.[33]

Moreover, Stampp made no pretense of neutrality. Not only dissatisfied with Phillips's interpretation, he was also disgusted with contemporary American attitudes toward race relations, and influenced by the civil rights movement, Stampp had several times expressed his position. In 1946 he told his mentor Hesseltine that had he been alive during the Civil War, he would have been an abolitionist and Radical Republican, and his only criticism of the Radicals was that they weren't radical enough, at least so far as the Southern problem was concerned.[34] It is perhaps difficult to recognize now what a powerful statement Stampp was making not only in *The Peculiar Institution*, but also with the famous sentence in his preface to the book in which he wrote, "I have assumed that Negroes *are*, after all, only white men with black skins, nothing more, nothing less."[35]

Stampp also staked out a clear position on the issue of historical relativism, siding clearly with Becker and Beard on the idea that history is changeable, being written and rewritten by each succeeding generation. It was perhaps fortunate that Stampp embraced this view, since his work was revised by succeeding generations. At first the response was largely celebratory. At the time of the publication of *The Peculiar Institution*, many young scholars, such as David Brion Davis and John Blassingame, found it not simply a great book, but a personal revelation, one that opened their eyes to entirely new ways of thinking. Some doubts, however, were also raised. Hesseltine, himself a Southerner, published a churlish review in the *Milwaukee Journal*, Stampp's hometown newspaper, where Stampp's friends and relatives would be sure to see it. Stanley Elkins wondered whether Stampp's picture of slaves ground into submission by malevolent masters reduced them to childlike, obedient Sambos, to which Stampp responded that Sambo behavior was simply one of many masks slaves adopted in order to survive. Others argued that Stampp's arguments rested more with moral indignation than evidence and that there was little in Stampp that one could not find in the arguments of the Abolitionists.[36]

To argue that Stampp's work rested primarily upon moral outrage missed the greatness of *The Peculiar Institution*. Published amid the excitement generated by the Brown v. Board of Education decision, the Montgomery bus boycott, and the publication of Vann Woodward's *The Strange Career of Jim Crow*, there was unquestionably a political and moral message to *The Peculiar Institution*. But it was not a jeremiad. The book was written in a tone of controlled passion, but the key to its success was that it was based upon Stampp's detailed archival research, and his critical insights came from that research. For example, before undertaking his archival journey, Stampp accepted the traditional view about the economics of slavery by which most historians believed that slave labor was not profitable. Investment in slaves was risky, and since slaves had no incentive to work efficiently, they were lazy and indolent. But when Stampp studied the business records of slaveholders, he found a great deal of information that contradicted the traditional view. While profits fluctuated with the rise and decline in the prices of Southern staple crops, the average investor in slave labor made a good profit, as good as or better than he could have reasonably been expected to make from other kinds of investment with comparable risks. By judicious use of various incentives, both positive and negative, Southern planters managed to turn slavery into an efficient and productive labor system.[37] More importantly, while Stampp was clearly not the first to work in archival evidence, *The Peculiar Institution* established an implicit precedent in slavery studies. Following Stampp it would be extremely difficult for those who wanted to say something valuable about slavery to work primarily from printed sources. They would have to visit the archives.

One of the historians to undertake this task was Eugene Genovese, and Genovese's work resulted in the most profound criticism of Stampp and a debate between the two that continued into the 1990s, with neither man feeling vanquished. Genovese, born in 1930, belonged to a succeeding generation of historians, and he was highly influenced by the ideas of the Italian Marxist, Antonio Gramsci and Gramsci's concept of hegemony. By hegemony Gramsci meant the various means, not always economic or coercive, by which a group or a class achieves and maintains dominance over a society and culture. In his own work Genovese defended Phillips's account of the economics of slavery over Stampp's and, in his greatest book, *Roll, Jordan, Roll: The World the Slaves Made*, stressed the autonomy and resourcefulness of slave culture. More controversially, Genovese contended that the motivation for slavery came not from desire for profits and nor was its survival based on coercion, but from a Gramscian struggle for hegemony by which slaves and masters battled to control and accommodate each other, developing what Genovese called a "mutually paternalistic" relationship. While the masters profoundly controlled and circumscribed the world of the slaves, they and the slaves inhabited the same world and their lives were so closely entwined that neither group could express even the simplest human feelings without reference to the other. While coercion explained part of the submission of slaves to the system, there was a wealth of behaviors that coercion did not explain. Genovese cited, for example, many instances of slaves refusing to be whipped and not being punished for their refusal, of masters being stricken with grief at the illness or death of a favored slave, and black slaves defending a white woman from the advances of a drunken Union soldier on the streets of Charleston, South Carolina. Far from crushing their bondsmen into demeaning submission, masters, according to Genovese, came to depend upon the slaves as much as the slaves depended upon masters. Slaves, for example, managed to elevate the custom of receiving pay for Sunday work into something approaching a right. Genovese further contended that the slaves were able to construct an alternative life within slavery into which whites could not intrude. The key to this alternative life was religion, which came to serve as a source of unity and consolation to the slaves.[38]

Genovese and Stampp both found themselves buffeted by changing times. Where in the fifties Stampp was welcomed as a herald of a new world of racial equality and regularly asked to speak at Negro History Week observances, by the 1970s he was denounced to his face by black militants who insisted that he, as a white man, had no right to write a book on slavery. Genovese, once the Marxist darling of the Left, found himself by the eighties denounced by the extreme Left when he criticized multiculturalism and political correctness. Both men found their books relegated to the category of historical writing reserved for books that come to be described as groundbreaking at the time of their publication but can no longer be accepted without qualification.[39]

The work of C. Vann Woodward has many interesting parallels with Stampp's. While Woodward and Stampp approached Southern history from different perspectives, they shared a passion for social justice and opposition to segregation, and their work was deliberately constructed to present a message for the present. In a series of works, beginning with *Tom Watson, Agrarian Rebel*, published in 1938, through *The Strange Career of Jim Crow*, published in 1955, Woodward strove to "indicate that things have not always been the same in the South" and to show that the "the belief that [Southern racial policies] are immutable and unchangeable is not supported by history."[40]

In the late thirties after the publication of *Tom Watson, Agrarian Rebel*, Woodward cast around for a new subject, giving serious thought to writing a biography of the socialist Eugene Debs, but deciding against the project when it became clear that Debs's papers would not be available for years. Within a few months, however, Woodward received a letter from Charles Ramsdell, editor of a projected series on the history of the South, who invited him to write the volume on the New South. Like Elton writing *England under the Tudors*, Woodward, barely thirty, was quite young for the job of writing a work of synthesis, which would normally have gone to a senior historian. As it turned out, one senior historian, Benjamin Kendrick, had been offered the job and turned it down, though he recommended Woodward.[41]

Ironically, twelve years would pass and several other books would be written before the New South volume appeared. World War II of course accounted for most of the delay, and changing jobs several times for another part. The change that landed him at the Johns Hopkins University was fortuitous because it gave him easy access to the Library of Congress, and he benefited from Hopkins's generous policies regarding teaching load and research leaves. Yet another reason for the delay concerned discoveries Woodward made in the course of his research. The editors of the series chose the dates for Woodward's volume as 1877–1913. The beginning date was clearly selected because it marked the end of Reconstruction and the beginning of a new era.

The traditional account of the end of Reconstruction gave pride of place to a bargain, supposedly cut at the Wormley House Conference, between Republican friends of Rutherford B. Hayes, who had won a narrow but disputed victory in the election of 1876, and Southern Democrats prepared to contest his election. According to the traditional account, Hayes's friends agreed to abandon the two remaining Republican state governments in the South and promise to refrain from the use of force to protect freedmen in return for the peaceful inauguration of Hayes.

Understanding the Compromise of 1877 was essential to Woodward's work, but as he began to examine the documents in a variety of archives, some unexpected complications began to arise. Why was there so much fevered correspondence from California and Texas, from chambers of commerce, boards of trade, cotton exchanges, and railroad companies? Why were cabinet members and Supreme Court justices corresponding with railroad barons? Was it coincidence that elaborate compromises between Union Pacific and South Pacific and between Central Pacific and Union Pacific coincided with the compromise between North and South? What was all the rhetoric about "the Road to India" or "a Railroad to Mexico" about? Why did the participants who wrote memoirs about the compromise call their works a "Secret History" or an "Inside History?" And why did they often hint at dark secrets by saying things like, "I want to say things I cannot write."[42]

Confronted with this complex body of information, Woodward began to think of himself as a detective, and the Wormley House Conference was the crime scene. The historian's job would be to reconstruct what happened at the conference and what led up to it. The evidence Woodward accumulated in the archives served as clues; those who left written records were his witnesses and in some cases his suspects. It was not until the summer of 1949, when his research had taken him to several Midwestern repositories, including one in Fremont, Ohio, and the Iowa State Historical Society in Des Moines, that the answer began to emerge. But while he had initially envisioned that his research on the Compromise of 1877 would comprise the first chapter in his New South volume, the story had become too prolix; it would require a separate book, which was published in 1951 as *Reunion and Reaction: The Compromise of 1877 and the End of Reconstruction.*

In Woodward's investigation the decisions that emerged from the Wormley Conference were not the part of a last-minute, smoke-filled room deal; rather, they were the result of a series of negotiations and bargains struck in the preceding months between Northern Republicans and Southern Democrats. The Wormley House Conference was what would be described today as a "media event," staged to conceal the sordid nature of the bargain. By 1877 faced with the possibility of Southern resistance to further attempts to advance the station of the freedmen, Northern leaders decided to abandon them, to preserve peace along with their economic growth, and to throw in attractive railroad routes to sweeten the deal for the South. The Wormley Conference was designed to present the deal in noble terms, portraying it as necessary to rescue the South from "the tyrannical heel of the carpetbagger."[43]

Like Stampp, Woodward was profoundly influenced by Charles Beard, and Beard's influence is readily apparent in *Reunion and Reaction*. Like Beard's interpretation of the Constitution, Woodward's interpretation of the end of Reconstruction emphasized the backroom deals by which the compromise was constructed and the totally sordid nature of the process. Altruism and humane consideration vanished; economic reality was everything.

Reunion and Reaction can stand alone as a historical tour de force, a model of intricate detective work to reveal the sleazy foundations of the decisions announced at the Wormley Conference. But the book may be best understood as a prologue to Woodward's masterpiece, *Origins of the New South*, also published in 1951, and for which he was awarded the Bancroft Prize in 1952. In many ways *Origins* was an extension of ideas Woodward first developed in *Tom Watson, Agrarian Rebel*, now painted on a much broader canvas and supported by the extensive archival research he had undertaken since the end of the war.

Among the unusual features of Woodward's work was that he devoted his career to studying a period of Southern history that most historians regarded as romanceless. "How can you possibly write so long a book," a friend asked him half in jest as they sat on the steps of the Library of Congress late one afternoon, "about a period in which nothing happened?"[44] Compared with the staggering shelf space reserved for books on slavery, the Confederacy, the Civil War, and the Reconstruction, the bibliography for the period of Woodward's interest, the post-Reconstruction South, was depressingly thin and unsophisticated. It was no small part of his achievement that he took a seemingly mundane period and endowed it with considerable significance. Moreover, the history of the South before Woodward approached it was littered with clichés, regardless of what period one studied. The "Old South," the "New South," the "land of cavaliers," and the "Solid South," were all phrases used to understand Southern history with easy generalization rather than serious historical study.

In the first chapters of *Origins* Woodward described the interests of Southern leaders, called Redeemers, who controlled Southern governments after the end of Reconstruction. Their interests had usually been assumed to be identical with those of the prewar plantation aristocracy. Woodward, however, showed how much more complex their interests were and how far they actually were from representing the old planting aristocracy. "In the main," Woodward wrote, "they were of middle-class, industrial, capitalistic outlook, with little but nominal connection with the old planter regime."[45] In this sense the Redeemers were as corrupt and predatory as the Carpetbaggers they despised, and they represented a sharp break from the continuity of aristocratic dominance in the Southern past. The immediate legacy of the

Reconstruction in his view lay in the fraud, infighting, embezzlement, corruption, gerrymandering, land scandals, and massive self-interest employed by the Redeemers to cement their position in the postwar world. Most despicable was the common practice of leasing state prisons and convicts to favored politicians for exploitation as a private labor force. Racial loyalties and political solidarity meant nothing to the rapacious Redeemers, who instead created third-party rebellions and bitter economic hostilities.

In succeeding chapters Woodward's relentless demolition of orthodox opinion on the post-Reconstruction South continued. One of the most pernicious myths about the South concerned its supposed postwar economic recovery, attributed by many to the end of slavery and diversification of the Southern economy through industrialization. Woodward vehemently denied that there was an economic recovery. Instead, he painted a picture of a region mired in poverty and backwardness as appalling as that of pre-Petrine Russia. He denied that genuine industrialization came to the South or that it created a diversified economy. In his judgment the minimal industrialization that did occur in the South was almost always a result of Northern exploitation of the cheap labor pool in the South, eagerly welcomed by Southern business and political leaders, who were indifferent to the plight of their labor force, largely women and children. Northern investment did not result in a sophisticated, modern economy in the South, but in a subsistence, colonial one. Industrial development, manufacturing, railroads, and to a certain extent, even the distribution of food were controlled by outside capital.[46]

Under such dismal conditions, it was no surprise to find Southern farmers ready to enlist in the Populist movement. Woodward had already returned a favorable judgment on Southern Populism in *Tom Watson, Agrarian Rebel*. Contrary to his friend Hofstadter, who dismissed the Populists as bigoted and anti-intellectual, Woodward affirmed in *Origins* that Populists were not opportunists manufacturing grievances or clinging to precapitalist agrarian myths and that several Southern Populists tried to unite white and black farmers, at least for political and economic purposes.[47]

Woodward's interest in the Southern Populism brought him to race relations, and it was on this subject that he made his most original and timely contribution to Southern history. Concerned to understand the origins of segregation and bigotry, Woodward noted that prominent Southern white leaders had advocated the enfranchisement of blacks in the years following the war, but had quickly abandoned the idea. The concept of disfranchisement, articulated by Southern leaders in the 1880s and 1890s, was cloaked in the noblest of rhetoric. Defenders argued that depriving blacks of votes would eliminate fraudulent elections and that disfranchisement would remove the "Negro Question" from politics, enabling Southerners to concentrate on other issues.

Woodward further demonstrated that at the core of the debates on disfranchisement and race relations was a bitter struggle between white interest groups. The very laws that successfully disfranchised blacks also deprived poor whites, unable to meet property qualifications or pass literacy tests, of the vote as well. These poor whites were also those who had supported the Populist movement. Thus it was the struggle for white supremacy that united the "Solid South," not the other way around, and it was a class struggle in which blacks were virtually forgotten.[48]

Consideration of race relations allowed Woodward to combine two of his greatest and most recurring themes: that things have not always been the same in the South and that racism and segregation were not somehow inherently an element of the Southern personality. These themes were developed vigorously in Woodward's next book, *The Strange Career of Jim Crow*, published in 1955. The book was based on research done for *Origins* and originally developed as the Jefferson Lectures at the University of Virginia. Like Kenneth Stampp's *The Peculiar Institution*, *The Strange Career of Jim Crow* appeared against the tense and at the same time exhilarating background of the civil rights movement.[49]

Woodward amassed considerable evidence to demonstrate that whites and blacks had mingled freely before the Civil War and before 1890. Woodward was by no means arguing that the pre–Jim Crow South was a land of racial harmony, but simply that the elaborate structure of segregation, which even most Southerners believed was timeless, had not been implemented until some time after the end of Reconstruction. Woodward cited evidence of the peaceful mingling of whites and blacks before Reconstruction in saloons, restaurants, and trains. His work, while expressed in the most guarded terms, held out the promise that since racism and segregation had been created, they could be eradicated. Advancing this theme, *The Strange Career of Jim Crow* became in the words of Martin Luther King, "the Bible of the Civil Rights movement," and sold over half a million copies.[50]

In *The Strange Career of Jim Crow* Woodward was perhaps the first to argue and support with the weight of historical evidence the idea that race relations in the South and the United States were by no means rigid and immutable. Woodward in essence asserted that there was hope for the civil rights movement. In another sense Woodward told his Virginia audience that it could support civil rights and desegregation without violating their Southern principles. Tom Watson and Southern Populism demonstrated that there was a tradition of tolerance in the South reaching across racial lines that could be embraced. Conservative Southerners could also draw from a paternalistic tradition that directed them to care for the less fortunate.[51]

While Woodward was harsh on his native region, remorselessly demolishing the myth of the land of cavaliers and emphasizing in its place unseemly class struggles and racist demagoguery, he also leveled criticism at the North and resolutely defended Southerners from some of their critics. In his judgment the abdication of moral responsibility on the part of Northern leaders was crucial to the plight of Southern blacks, and he considered the Northern industrialists in the South as exploitive as any of the Robber Barons.

Woodward's work parallels in many respects that of Kenneth Stampp. Both remained true to the Beardian tradition that their friend Hofstadter and others had rejected by the 1950s. Both based their work on extensive archival research. Both wrote with controlled rage at racial injustice and intended that their work be a tool in overcoming that injustice. When David Potter wrote in 1969 that Woodward's greatest significance to historiography was that "he has made himself the foremost practitioner of a concept of history which holds that the experience of the past can find its highest relevance in the guidance which it offers in living with the problems of the present," he could have been writing about Stampp.[52] Both also shared their generation's sense of irony, that even the best-intentioned schemes for reform were likely to have completely different consequences from the ones their creators imagined.

In several regards Woodward also shares a more unexpected resemblance with Geoffrey Elton. Both were archival historians, who early in their careers advanced bold theses that redirected their fields of study. Both spent their careers primarily defending and refining those theses. Just as Geoffrey Elton spent the rest of his professional life defending his thesis of a Tudor revolution in government, Woodward spent much of the rest of his professional life defending his ideas, particularly those in *The Strange Career of Jim Crow*. And both defended their positions with the skill and tenacity of a mother bear defending her cubs from an intruder in the den.

By the 1960s critics had begun to chip away at the main thesis of *The Strange Career of Jim Crow*, that blacks and whites had lived together in general compatibility in the South before Reconstruction and that it was not until 1890s that the legal structure of segregation began to be imposed in earnest. Historians soon found plenty of evidence of segregation before the 1890s and extensive regional differences and believed they had uncovered the smoking gun necessary to indict Woodward. But they had not reckoned with their man. Woodward was not going to go gently into the night, and in response he noted that he had carefully qualified his more striking generalizations, both in the original text and in subsequent editions. For example, it became clear that Woodward's claims about the fluidity of race relations before the 1890s did not include churches, militias, companies, schools, state and private welfare institutions, and numerous other aspects of Southern life where segregation was fairly rigid. Writing in the 1950s, Woodward based his argument on issues that seemed important at that time, such as segregation in hotels, theaters, and restaurants and other places of public accommodation. While he was not wrong to base his argument on the evidence of public places, it did mean that his thesis was much narrower than originally conceived.[53]

In the face of criticism, Woodward remained generally unrepentant. Like Elton, he would admit to overstatement and occasional exaggeration, he would point to his careful qualifications, he was shrewd enough to find at least some things in the works of his critics that supported his ideas even if their overall findings did not, and he would conclude that with a few caveats his overall picture of the development of segregation in the South was still sustainable. With good reason, one of Woodward's critics expressed his frustration and admiration at "the Master's ability to absorb . . . knockout blows and even to incorporate adversaries' weapons into his own arsenal."[54]

In the larger scheme Woodward managed to both embrace and stand apart from the greatest historiographical trends of his time. At a time when several leading American historians, including his close friend Hofstadter, were developing grand syntheses of American history based on the idea of an emerging consensus and rejecting the Beardian emphasis on economic motivation, *Origins of the New South* was one of the last great books written in the Beardian tradition. It was clearly embedded in Woodward's Southern heritage and in the class struggles of the 1930s. At its core *Origins* embraced a Beardian view of human nature and historical methodology: find out who is in power and what they want; assume that the truth lies not on the surface reality of public records, but must be excavated from sketchy recollections of murky backroom deals, all based on economic interest, which can be uncovered only through the most painstaking archival analysis.[55] There were no heroes in Woodward's South. The only truly sympathetic characters in *Origins* were those too powerless to exploit anyone. The closest thing to a hero in Woodward's work is Tom Watson. But even with Watson, Woodward was compelled to record Watson's ugly transformation from the gallant champion of the underdog in the early 1890s to the viciously anti-Semitic, Catholic-hating racist of the twentieth century.[56]

Woodward was out of the mainstream of historiography in other ways. In contrast with Hofstadter who stressed the overall continuity of American history, Woodward emphasized the discontinuity of Southern history in particular. In a reconsideration of W.J. Cash's *The Mind of the South*, Woodward wrote, "The history of the South . . . has always seemed to me characterized by discontinuity, and I have suggested this as one trait that helps account for the distinctiveness and its history. . . . Southerners, unlike other Americans, repeatedly felt the solid ground of continuity give way under their feet."[57] At the time same time, in contrast of notions of the "Solid South" or the "New South," Woodward stressed the profound internal divisions in the South, between agrarian and industrial forces, class interests, and racial antagonisms. When the mood of consensus history crumbled in the 1960s as equally profound divisions threatened the foundations of American life, Woodward seemed vindicated.

In another sense, the history of the South provided Woodward with a vantage point from which American history could be studied. Seen from Washington, New York City, or other points north and east, there may be a certain continuity to American history. But seen from Savannah, Montgomery, or other points south, there was only discontinuity. Over and over in his work, Woodward stressed the differences in the history and development of the South in contrast with the overall flow of American history. The South, for example, arrived too late at the "Great American Barbecue" of the Gilded Age. Industrial development came later and only haphazardly to the South.

For all the theoretical advances that Woodward's history contained, it should be remembered that the great books that he produced in the decade after World War II were the products of extensive archival research. As in the case of Stampp and U.B. Phillips, Woodward's predecessors in Southern history had worked in archives, but Woodward took their use to a higher level. His appointment at Johns Hopkins allowed him the easy plunder of Washington's archives. During leaves of absence and summer terms he worked in all the important archives of the Southern states from Virginia to Texas. Two other summer terms teaching at Harvard and Chicago allowed the pillaging of New England and Middle Western repositories. After he had finished and began to sort through the massive file of notes he had taken, it seemed to him that he had acquired a huge sack full of jigsaw puzzles and thousands of pieces all jumbled together. It was not until yet another archival journey, this time among the papers of General Grenville Dodge at the Iowa State Historical Society in Des Moines and later at a library in Fremont, Ohio, that he began to piece together the sequence of events leading up to the Wormley House Conference and their significance.[58]

But Woodward's Southern vantage point did not exhaust potential points of view. When Stampp and Woodward wrote about the South, they studied it primarily from the perspective of Southern men, white and black. Women played only marginal roles in the stories they had to tell. In the 1960s Anne Firor Scott took one of the first steps toward redressing the balance and adopting a new vantage point. She had already studied the Progressive movement from a Southern point of view, and in the course of her research she noticed that she kept coming across "well-dressed, well-spoken Southern ladies taking a strong stand in social and political issues." Earlier work on Southern history did not prepare her to find these women. But there they were, speaking out and making a difference. She also discovered, while reading the records of congressional hearings, that Jane Addams was taken very seriously by members of Congress. And during the summer after her year of teaching at Haverford College, Scott began to study the Addams papers, conveniently housed at the Swarthmore College Library, just twenty miles away. Just then her husband took a new job in North Carolina, and with three young children and little money, the chances of a return to the Addams papers were slim. Granting agencies provided no help, but Scott did find a precarious part-time job in the history department at the University of North Carolina in Chapel Hill. A young colleague asked her to give a paper to a departmental seminar. Remembering the women in the Progressive movement and the women she encountered in the Addams papers, she decided to study Southern women through the Southern Historical Collection at Chapel Hill, at first thinking only about producing a respectable paper for the all-male and quite traditional history faculty.[59]

But the ultimate product of that research was *The Southern Lady*, published in 1970. *The Southern Lady* broke new ground in several ways. First, in the 1960s the study of Southern women was almost as romanceless as Woodward's study of the post-Reconstruction South. *The Southern Lady* demonstrated that Southern women, particularly those of the middle and upper classes, had a legitimate history and that their story raised the same challenging questions of interpretation that other subfields of history did.[60]

The second way in which *The Southern Lady* broke ground was in the field of women's history. Women had of course been studied and written about before the publication of *The Southern Lady*. An older generation of historians, such as Mary Beard, Julia Spruill, Elizabeth Anthony Dexter, and Mary Benson had published important works on women. But before the 1970s women's history was scarcely taught in the leading history departments, and it was regarded as secondary to more important history involving men. But in the 1960s attitudes towards women's history began to change. In 1970 Joan Kelly published "Did Women Have a Renaissance?" which argued that the standard historical periodizations usually pertained to men and had little relevance for women.[61]

Women's history developed most rapidly in the United States. By the 1960s the traditional emphasis on the study of male political elites was challenged by the rise of social history, which gave primacy to nonelite groups, including women. Women's history also merged with contemporary political struggles, such as the antiwar, civil rights, and feminist movements. At the same time a younger generation of women entered graduate school eager to study the history of women. In the absence of course offerings (Scott did not teach her first course in women's history at Duke until 1971) small groups formed to conduct their own reading and research. Thus inspired, women's history began to acquire more theoretical sophistication. In 1966 Barbara Welter examined the involvement of middle-class women in nineteenth-century reform movements and found a rigid separation between male and female spheres in reform efforts.[62]

Scott's *The Southern Lady* was a critical part of this transformation. The book began with her discovery of a paradox. The records of political reform movements revealed the presence of women or groups of women who had played significant roles well before women had secured the right to vote. As a Southern woman, Scott knew, or thought she knew, that a woman's place was not in the political arena. *The Southern Lady* therefore was an exploration of the difference between the image of Southern women and the reality of their behavior. Scott attempted to describe the culturally defined image of the Southern lady, the effect of this definition on women's behavior, and the struggle of women to free themselves from the cultural expectations imposed by this definition.

In the first part of *The Southern Lady* Scott examined images of women presented in literary journals, sermons, novels, and commencement addresses. Usually articulated by men, the ideals expressed in these writings usually challenged women to observe their proper and subordinate role in the family and society. Women were expected to please their husbands, attend to their physical needs, cook, clean, make clothes, raise children, manage their estates and businesses in their husband's absence, and cover up male indiscretions while having none of their own. "Be a lady and you will be loved and supported. If you defy the pattern and behave in ways considered unladylike, you will be unsexed, rejected, unloved, and you will probably starve," Scott summed up the message of Southern society to its women.[63]

While many accepted the ideal, others railed bitterly against it. Many Southern brides were teenagers suddenly expected to assume enormous domestic responsibilities of a large estate and to understand the skills involved with spinning, weaving, sewing, gardening, care of the sick, and food preparation. Many of these women had little training in these skills and found themselves unable to cope with the expectations imposed upon them, nor were they comfortable with their relationship with their slaves. "I cannot, nor will not spend my days following after and watching Negroes," wrote one irritated woman.[64] Most Southern women regarded female slaves as little more than prostitutes and lived in fear of contracting venereal disease.

The Civil War, according to Scott, passed through the South like a tidal wave, shattering the old institutions and assumptions of traditional society and helping forge new ones. One of the assumptions crushed by the war was the ideal of the perfect but subordinate lady. Scott had already demonstrated that the antebellum Southern lady was not just a plantation belle, but a real participant in Southern life. She now quoted with approval a contemporary's belief that in 1860 the South became a matriarchy. With many of the men gone to war, the women assumed even more responsibility. It fell to them to increase the food supply, to expand the production of cotton and wool, to keep the troops supplied, and even to resist the invasions of Northern armies. Generally discontented with their subordinate roles and eager to find meaning in their lives, Southern women for the most part responded heroically to the new demands imposed upon them.[65]

In the years after the war women were presented with more opportunity. Their numerical superiority over men meant that they could no longer count on making their place in society through marriage. Women were forced into the workplace. Factories needed cheap labor; businesses needed secretaries; schools needed teachers. These conditions combined to create what Scott called "the New Woman." The collapse of plantation culture, increased educational opportunities, and widening job prospects diminished the need to find a husband. Women also flocked to join voluntary organizations, including those working for temperance, labor reform, and racial cooperation. Voluntary organizations helped unite women and create a collective female consciousness. The right to vote added another dimension to women's lives and another option for women who wanted more than a purely domestic experience.[66]

Like Stampp's *The Peculiar Institution*, *The Southern Lady* was the product of extensive archival research in a variety of repositories, including the Library of Congress, Duke University, the University of North Carolina, Louisiana State University, Tulane University, Radcliffe College, the University of Georgia, the University of Michigan, and the University of Kentucky. Also like *The Peculiar Institution*, *The Southern Lady* was written in a tone of controlled passion. Scott clearly celebrated the liberation of women from the constricting prewar stereotypes imposed by Southern society, but there were also some irritations. She noted that the postwar entrance of women into the workplace was born only of necessity and economic expedience, not liberated attitudes. Only when factory owners needed cheap labor did it become acceptable for women to work in the mills. Only when businesses needed secretaries or when children needed teachers were the existing social barriers to women's work overcome.[67]

The Southern Lady had begun with the discovery of the paradox between ideal and reality, and in recent years *The Southern Lady* has been subjected to one of its own. In 1995 to mark the twenty-fifth anniversary of its publication and recognize its stature as a classic, the University Press of Virginia reissued it. But in 1996 Drew Gilpin Faust, a historian then at the University of Pennsylvania, published *Mothers of Invention*, which covered some of the same ground, but took a different point of view.[68]

When Scott treated the struggle of women to survive during the Civil War in *The Southern Lady*, she emphasized their resilience. When Faust examined their struggle in *Mothers of Invention* she was struck more by their petulance, racism, and elitism. Faust, for example, related tales of women energetically whipping their slaves and gloating at their profits from the "nigger trade." She also placed more emphasis on those women who felt overwhelmed by the war. Women who tried to be nurses, for example, were often repulsed by the indelicacies of the job and having to associate with the lower classes. Women who tried to assume their husbands' duties while the husband was off at war complained bitterly at their burden. Faust quoted Texan Lizzie Neblett, "I am so sick of trying to do a man's business when I am nothing but a poor contemptible piece of multiplying of human flesh tied to the house by a crying young one, looked upon as belonging to a race of inferior beings." In a particularly poignant passage Faust described Lizzie Neblett beating her ten-month old baby in frustration.[69] In the end Faust concluded that Southern women were largely whining elitists, disgusted by having to consort with the lower-class women with whom the war threw them and devoting themselves to trying to find new ways to maintain their social and racial dominance. Far from being incipient feminists, they willingly returned at the end of war to earlier patterns of submission and dependence and sought ways to bolster the shattered men who returned from the war.

In her defense Scott conceded that Faust had produced a remarkable book, but insisted that the new interpretation was mistaken. In Scott's view Faust placed too much emphasis on the women who left written records, who were usually upper class, highly educated, and were responsible for plantations with large numbers of slaves. These women were therefore more likely to find themselves helpless and resenting their contact with the lower classes. According to Scott, the women who came from families with just a few slaves were not as passive as the women examined by Faust.[70]

For many of the historians considered here, controversy was the engine of history, driving them toward new discoveries and a deeper understanding of the past. Geoffrey Elton and Lawrence Stone even appeared to thrive on it; others, such as Woodward or Stampp, if they did not thrive on it, did not shrink from it either. Woodward dedicated his *Thinking Back: The Perils of Writing History* to his critics, "without whom, life would have been simpler, but less interesting."[71]

For Richard Cobb, however, history should never be an intellectual debate. For him such debates were invariably sterile, allowing authors to cover up with rhetoric their lack of research and engagement. After World War II Cobb found himself working in the Bibliothèque Nationale with Albert Soboul on the Hébertistes. Cobb was immediately struck by a contrast in their working habits. Upon finding his subject, Soboul worked with single-minded determination, concentrating fully on Hébertism, and never following any other line of inquiry that would sidetrack him from his immediate purpose. Cobb, on the other hand, found himself continually diverted as the excitement of research and the discovery of new materials became ends in themselves. The chance discovery of a bulky dossier delighted him; it could contain love letters, intercepted correspondence from London, a merchant's account books, or an eyewitness account of the September massacres. All of it had to be investigated.[72]

The joy of discovery in the archives was not confined to the Bibliothèque Nationale. Cobb scoured provincial archives as well, visiting around forty. Because he liked working in them, he kept finding excuses to return. Most historians read documents to find what the authors of those documents say on the specific topics of interest to the historian at that moment. Cobb, on the other hand, when he stumbled onto the register of a municipality for 1794, wanted to know what happened in 1795 and 1796 and so on, how it all came out. More interested in individuals than in groups, when he came across people who seized his interest, he wanted to follow them through life, through marriage and family, triumph and tragedy, to the grave.[73]

Cobb's approach to history mirrored his approach to people in his own life. He had a passion for people and wished, if they caught his interest, to envelop them, to eat, drink, and work with them. Students or friends willing to accept his terms found a person willing to take them with total seriousness and to teach without their being aware they were being taught. Those unwilling to be enveloped or unwilling to indulge him found themselves overwhelmed.[74]

While he had a brief, youthful dalliance with Marxism, Cobb soon developed a contempt for the deep forces of history. Like Elton, he believed the historian should have no parti pris, no prior conceptualization of what he or she should find in the archives. In the same way Cobb believed that as an Englishman studying the French Revolution he had an advantage over the French historians studying the Revolution because he brought no ideological baggage to it. Distrusting the deep forces, Cobb preferred instead to study people and personal relationships and to judge individuals in their own terms and from what they say about themselves. "The servant girl who gets pregnant," he once said, "that's my history."

Not surprisingly, Cobb's work is filled with images. Two of the most powerful and recurring are that of a second identity and that of a man watching, *homo observicans*. Regarding the first, in his books Cobb conveys to the reader a sense of slipping into another world, like Alice sliding through the looking glass. His first attempt at autobiography was titled *A Second Identity*. In his best work he is able to take the reader into unexplored places, such as the Parisian underworld of the 1790s, as skillfully as Lawrence Stone took the reader into the world of English aristocracy.

The second image seems irrevocably connected to his work habits. Cobb began his work in the archives around ten o'clock in the morning and worked straight until closing time, refusing or forgetting lunch. He spent the rest of the evening eating dinner, reading *Le Monde*, drinking in cafés, wandering the streets, and watching people. In his history Cobb often appeared the same way, as a man watching. He was particularly fascinated by the individual, man or woman, alone in the city, eating alone, with no occupation, who receives no mail and has no friends.

Not surprisingly he chronicled in gruesome detail the squalid lives and lonely deaths of criminals, prostitutes, and others from the French revolutionary underworld of the 1790s.[75] The discovery in the Archives of the Seine, of a file, box D4 UI7, titled "Basse-Geôle de la Seine Procès Verbaux de Mort Violence (ans III-IX)," formed the basis for Cobb's *Death in Paris*, published in 1979. The *procès-verbaux* lists the particulars of 404 persons who met violent deaths through accidents, murder, and natural causes from April 1795 to September 1801. Unlike most historians, who introduce their work by explaining its significance, usually in the context of earlier work on the subject, Cobb provided no background, no justification for the study of Parisian death, no theoretical point of departure. He simply began by examining the deaths.

Suicides were numerous, especially among women, and suicide was Cobb's principal interest in *Death in Paris*. Drowning was the easiest and most common form of suicide since firearms were not readily available to ordinary citizens. April was the cruelest month and spring the cruelest season, with April–May and May–June having the highest numbers of suicides. Sundays, Mondays, and Tuesdays were the most frequent days of commission.[76]

But Cobb was seeking more than statistical veracity. His real interest in *Death in Paris* was to observe the lonely people of Paris and what happened to them. Two-thirds of the suicides were people who had always been single or had recently become so. The prevalence of Sunday suicides suggested to Cobb a connection between suicide and leisure. Cobb was relieved to find that in a supposedly brutal and callous society, authorities were prepared to spend at least a little time on the administrative formalities arising from the sudden deaths of nameless individuals and the last activities of people suddenly overtaken by death whether by suicide or while lying unattended in a squalid room. Every effort was made to identify the deceased and accord them some dignity in passing. In Cobb's phrase, "the silent dead . . . may tell us more about the living."[77]

Generalizing about any group of people, perhaps especially historians, is a bit difficult, but some generalizations are possible. For most of the historians of this generation, not just the archivalists, their great books emerged from a particularly intense "Storm and Stress" period, usually the decade after the end of World War II. Kenneth Stampp wrote *The Peculiar Institution* at the end of a lengthy period of hard work that reached its peak in the decade right after the end of the war. At the same time Vann Woodward was going through a similarly intense period of hard work. He began his work with his study of Tom Watson in the 1930s, but the research that made his reputation as a great historian, like Stampp's, was conducted right after the end of World War II. In England immediately after World War II Geoffrey Elton, Lawrence Stone, and J.H. Plumb threw themselves into exhaustive archival investigations. "I was young; I was energetic," Kenneth Stampp recalled of the period in his life during which *And The War Came* and *The Peculiar Institution* were written.[78] Due to her late start as a historian and family commitments, *The Southern Lady* occupied Anne Scott for most of the sixties rather than the postwar period.

In most cases, however, the level of work and intensity was not sustained. While Lawrence Stone and Richard Cobb continued to produce new books, usually archivally based, at a regular pace and to take on different subjects, the production of most of the others slowed after 1960, or like Elton and Woodward, they refashioned their ideas in light of criticism. And those who continued to publish did not continue the same level of serious work in archives. Kenneth Stampp followed *The Peculiar Institution* with a remarkable and shrewd synthesis of the Reconstruction published in 1965, but it contained little archival work. His most recent book, *America in 1857*, however, seems to mark a return to his old role as an archival historian. J.H. Plumb turned to the writing of popular history and became extremely wealthy from it.

The motivations behind their work were often political. The World War II generation of historians, especially the Americans, believed that history can be used to understand the present, and that the construction of a usable past was a decent and honorable task if the evidence warrants. Both Stampp and Woodward were involved in the civil rights movement, and their books were intended to contribute to it. The source of their work was in many ways the sense of social justice that both had acquired in the 1930s. Anne Scott was involved in several of the left-wing movements of the 1960s but especially the women's movement. There were of course other motivations. Career advancement, fame, and continuing brawls with old opponents all played their part. But in several cases the archivalists were as concerned to construct a usable past as the cultural critics.

The use of irony was one of the most recurring techniques in the works of these historians. Particularly the Americans believed that in the writing of history they were casting a cold realist's eye over the foibles of human nature by exposing the contradictions between lofty rhetoric and sordid reality, noble intentions and sleazy consequences, or between idealized images and the real world. Nineteenth-century America, with its confidence in progress, belief in manifest destiny, high-minded reform movements, and moralistic foreign policy pronouncements, was a particularly inviting target, and it is not surprising that the use of irony is most pronounced in the work of Stampp, Woodward, and Scott, historians of the nineteenth century.

Vann Woodward wrote an essay devoted to the ironies of Southern history, and in *Origins of the New South* he repeatedly exposed the pretension and hypocrisy particularly of Southern reformers and Northern politicians. In *And the War Came* Kenneth Stampp wrote that the "Yankees went to war animated by the ideals of the nineteenth century middle classes. . . . But what the Yankees achieved—for their generation at least—was a triumph not of middle class ideals but of middle class vices. The most striking products of their crusade were the shoddy aristocracy of the North and the ragged children of the South. Among the masses of Americans there were no victors, only the vanquished."[79] And Anne Scott framed *The Southern Lady* around the contradiction between the views of what women should be with the reality of what women actually were.

But the most important contribution of this group of historians remains their elevation of archival research to the height of the historian's craft. When Lawrence Stone arrived at Princeton in 1963, not one historian, faculty or graduate student, was engaged in archival research. Now virtually all of them are. Moreover, there is no evidence that Richard Hofstadter, usually regarded as the preeminent American historian of his generation, did much work with manuscripts. It would be very hard today to achieve such a level of eminence without having done some archival work.

While earlier historians utilized archives, this generation took their use to a much higher level and made work in them essential for those who wished to rise to the top of the profession. No one could hope to challenge the work of Elton, Stampp, Woodward, Scott, or any of the others without serious labor in the archives.

Chapter 12

SYNTHESIS, PRINTED SOURCES, AND OTHER KINDS OF HISTORY

In 1621 an African who came to be known as Anthony Johnson arrived in Jamestown, Virginia. At some point in the 1620s he was a free man. He owned land, sued white people in court, voted, purchased an African servant, and emerged as a respectable citizen. The case of Anthony Johnson, reported by Oscar and Mary Handlin in 1950, raised some interesting questions about the nature of race relations in colonial Virginia. One might have expected that Johnson, a black, would have been a slave. But there he was, in 1625, a free citizen enjoying the same freedoms as white settlers. To make matters more interesting, Anthony Johnson was not an isolated case. There were dozens of other free blacks in the Chesapeake region of early Virginia.[1]

As we have seen, the study of slavery and race relations was a recurring interest of the World War II generation of historians. In the 1950s, few subjects had more contemporary relevance. At about the same time as the Brown v. Board of Education decision was being rendered, Kenneth Stampp was brilliantly reevaluating the nature of the slave system as practiced in the antebellum South. The Handlins uncovered another critical issue. The case of Anthony Johnson raised the issue of the origins of slavery and of racial prejudice itself. Why wasn't Anthony Johnson a slave? How did he become free? And why was he able to enjoy the same freedoms as a white settler? The freedoms enjoyed by Anthony Johnson suggested that slavery and perhaps even racial prejudice did not exist immediately in Virginia, but developed later. If slavery and prejudice were behaviors and attitudes learned by Americans, they could be unlearned.[2]

Slavery and prejudice were different issues, but they were closely linked. Several scholars sought explanations for their origins. In 1959 Stanley Elkins proposed what came to known as the "Sambo thesis," by which he argued that Africans were regarded as inferior by whites because the slave system forced them to behave as if they were inferior. They were wrenched from their own cultures and cast into a new and bewildering environment, in which strange and ruthless people dominated their lives. For Elkins the only way to survive in such an environment was to be docile and passive, to avoid drawing attention to yourself. He cited the cases of Jews who survived the Nazi death camps as examples of how passivity was necessary to survive in similarly hostile environments. Elkins concluded, however, that by behaving passively Africans convinced their white masters that they were inferior and could be treated as inferiors.[3]

Elkins implied that racial problems could be solved to some degree by education and social reform. But another historian, Winthrop Jordan argued that prejudice was inherent in the white character. In a book called *White over Black* Jordan argued that racial prejudice was seared into the mental world of Elizabethan Englishmen long before they ever laid eyes on a black man. Examining Elizabethan literature, the Bible, and numerous contemporary pamphlets, Jordan found hundreds of examples to indicate that Elizabethan Englishmen believed that blacks were inferior, and that they were sons of Hamen, cursed with black skin. At the same time, the expression "black" denoted evil and treachery in Elizabethan England, notions that were transferred onto Africans. For Jordan this evidence suggested that Englishmen came to the New World already conditioned to hate Africans.[4]

Thus the nature of slavery and prejudice in early America raised a number of intriguing historical questions and was at the same time inextricably connected to contemporary events. Historians were writing on slavery as Governor Orval Faubus of Arkansas called out the Arkansas National Guard on the pretext of preserving order but in reality to deny black students entry to Little Rock Central High School, as blacks staged sit-ins at lunch counters and bus stations and other "white-only" facilities, as civil rights demonstrators were attacked, beaten, and murdered by militant segregationists, and as momentous civil rights legislation was being enacted by Congress.

Perhaps the most sophisticated approach to the questions raised by race relations in early America was presented by Edmund Morgan. In earlier books Morgan had ranged widely over many aspects of colonial America, focusing especially on the Puritans and the origins of the American Revolution. In the mid-sixties he took up the subject of servitude in early Virginia, producing several path-breaking articles and arguably his most far-ranging and greatest book, *American Slavery, American Freedom: The Ordeal of Colonial Virginia*, published in 1975.

All of Morgan's books were written in collaboration with Helen Morgan. Although she was only willing to have her contribution acknowledged in *The Stamp Act Crisis*, she was vitally involved with all her husband's work. She went to conferences and archives with him and was his most trusted editor. When they finished their research he would write a draft and give it to her. She would go over it carefully, raising questions about style and content. The much-admired style and coherence of his work owes much to her editorial skill.

Like many books, *American Slavery, American Freedom* started out as a book on something else. Morgan originally intended to write a history of attitudes toward work in America from colonization to the present, and had actually written several chapters of such a book. He had studied the attitudes about work English settlers brought to America along with views of the New World available to the English. Then he got to Virginia. There was plenty of material about what Virginians thought and did up to about 1625. After that there was an abrupt drop-off, particularly in the availability of private letters and memoirs. The materials that survive for colonial Virginia in the greatest profusion after 1625 are mainly county court records. As he worked his way through these records, Morgan realized that he was really working on Virginia. His study of attitudes toward work bore directly on the problems of the early settlement of the colony and his work in court records helped establish a demographic context for understanding that settlement.[5]

Two other facts about Virginia kept hitting Morgan in the face. The first was that Nathaniel Bacon, leader of Bacon's Rebellion and sometimes called the "torchbearer of freedom," was authorized to enslave any Indians he captured. The second was that Virginia recruited soldiers during the American Revolution by promising them not only land but slaves after the war.

Thus, *American Slavery, American Freedom* began with the exploration of a paradox that had always confounded the study of early America. The men who founded the United States repeatedly proclaimed their commitment to freedom and equality, but either held slaves or accepted the enslavement of blacks in principle. At the same time, in many cases their wealth and the freedoms they enjoyed depended upon slave labor. While Thomas Jefferson was defending his inalienable rights to life, liberty, and pursuit of happiness, he was personally depriving nearly two hundred men, women, and children of the same rights.[6]

Thus, perhaps the freest society of the eighteenth-century world was dependant upon slave labor. The key to understanding this paradox in Morgan's view, was early Virginia, where the system began and where Virginians owned more than 40 percent of all the slaves in the new nation. If it was possible to understand the meaning of the American paradox, the strange marriage of slavery and freedom, Virginia was the place to start.

For Morgan, the explanation of the American paradox rested primarily in the labor and settlement patterns of early Virginia. The early settlement of Virginia was undertaken by private investors, in this case, the Virginia Company of London, which, beginning in the early 1600s sent several ships of settlers and supplies to found a colony at Jamestown. These early attempts at settlement ended in tragedy. After one early attempt the captain of a ship sent by the company to resupply the initial settlers was shocked to discover that most of the original settlers had starved to death and many of those who were left were bowling. Yes, people on the verge of starvation were bowling. Other settlers resorted to the most desperate measures to avoid starvation. One man chopped up his wife, salted the pieces, and ate her. Others dug up graves and ate corpses.

How can we explain starving people not trying to grow the food or do the work that would sustain them? For Morgan the answer was fairly simple. The company's rules allowed people to eat whether they worked or not, and the company also found it difficult to attract settlers with the kinds of skills the colony needed. Most of the settlers tended to be either vagrants or gentlemen. Neither group possessed the work ethic or technical skills necessary to survive in the Darwinian laboratory of early America.[7]

In the next few years the company took steps to correct its early mistakes. Private property was introduced. All settlers were required to work, and the company offered inducements, called indentures, to improve the quality of the work force. Under this system, one served a period of indenture, usually five to seven years. At the end of the indenture, the settlers received land as well as the tools and supplies necessary to strike out on their own.

Still the colony struggled, unable to grow in terms of population without repeated resupply from England. Climate, disease, difficulty in cultivation, and conflicts with the indigenous population all took their toll. In about 1616, however, the colony received a stroke of luck. The Indians showed a settler named John Rolfe how to grow tobacco just when the tobacco market was about to expand. The colonists now had a cash crop, but a new set of problems came with it.

The first problem was that there was so much money in tobacco that the colonists grew it at the expense of attention to grain crops, causing the price of food to increase. Second, the profit in tobacco meant that the more workers a tobacco farmer had the more money he could make. It was at this point that Anthony Johnson and others like him appeared in Virginia.[8]

Why were they not enslaved? Why were they allowed to gain their freedom and pursue life, liberty, and happiness? Morgan offered several ingenious answers. To grasp them fully, it is necessary to understand the demography of early Virginia. The most important demographic fact was the exceptionally high mortality rate among the settlers. Disease, hardship, and Indian wars made life in early Virginia precarious. The colony was unable to sustain itself without a constant stream of settlers from England.

Armed with this information, Morgan tried to put himself in the place of the planter. Labor is scarce, but you need it desperately. You can invest in slaves or indentured servants. Slaves cost more, but you get them for life and they will produce more slaves so you might not have to buy more. Indentured servants are cheaper, but you only get them for a few years. Under normal circumstances, slaves would probably be the best long-term investment, but in early Virginia life is truly Hobbesian: nasty, brutish, and above all short. Thus, if you invest in indentured servants, not only will they cost you less to begin with, but life is so precarious you might never have to pay them off. If Morgan's logic is correct, it would explain why there were so many black indentured servants in early Virginia and why slavery came later.[9]

Morgan further suggested that as the population of Virginia grew and the number of blacks in Virginia grew, whites could no longer afford to be so generous. The land was plentiful in early Virginia, but profits from tobacco lured more settlers into the colony and the most desirable land was quickly taken. Slowly, the population of blacks and the amount of land held by them increased. By 1700 whites turned increasingly to the legal system to maintain their hold on society.[10]

American Slavery, American Freedom represented a significant departure from Morgan's previous work. As we have seen elsewhere in this book, many of the most distinguished members of his generational cohort relished ironic detachment in the writing of history. They delighted in exposing the sordid motives behind seemingly noble behavior and deflating the pretensions of groups like the Puritans and the Founding Fathers, and they worked from the assumption that the stated motivations of historical actors were rarely their actual motivations. It was the job of the historian to dig beneath the platitude to uncover the ugly reality. By contrast in his work before *American Slavery, American Freedom* Morgan took very seriously what his subjects had to say. While he had never accepted their pronouncements uncritically, his great achievement in writing about the Puritans was in demonstrating that they actually tried to accomplish what they said they wanted to accomplish. Morgan's stress on the importance of what historical actors said about themselves was, to be sure, more of a reaction against Charles Beard's emphasis on underlying economic motivations than against his own generation.

At the same time Morgan displayed considerable affinity with his Puritan subjects and a desire to understand them in their own context, not slam them for hypocrisy. Many historians and commentators have used the Puritans to get off some good lines at Puritan expense, such as Mencken's comment that Puritanism was the lurking fear that somewhere someone was having fun or Macaulay's complaint that Puritans hated bearbaiting not because it was painful to the bear but because it gave pleasure to the spectator. Morgan rescued the Puritans from these stereotypes and showed that Puritans were not the killjoys of popular legends, and he revealed their human side. They could be loving parents and spouses and were a much earthier lot than earlier commentators imagined. They laughed and had fun, and were by no means prudish about sex. Morgan also showed that the American colonists did have a coherent ideology in their protests against British policies in the 1760s by which they upheld their rights as Englishmen.[11]

But *American Slavery, American Freedom* departed abruptly from Morgan's earlier work and was the book which followed most closely the imperatives of his historical generation. It was a joyless tale of brutality, exploitation, and hypocrisy. The book began with the exposition of the irony of Jefferson as a lover of freedom and a slaveowner. And where Morgan had previously explained the Puritans and the American Revolution primarily in terms of ideology, the explanation he advanced about the nature of life in early Virginia emphasized demographic and economic conditions. In this sense, Morgan was probably the historian of this group least led by contemporary historical trends, events, or politics.

American Slavery, American Freedom was unusual for its utilization of a wide range of source materials. New Englanders and eighteenth-century colonists wrote a great deal about themselves and their goals. Hundreds of Puritan sermons have survived along with most of the writings of the founding fathers, almost all of it in print, so it was relatively easy for Morgan to read and absorb them. Seventeenth-century Virginians, however, especially those after 1625, said very little. So Morgan had to seek information about Virginia in other ways, and he spent more than ten years doing the research for *American Slavery, American Freedom.*

The book also represented another kind of history, one at which the World War II generation also excelled. While *American Slavery, American Freedom* utilized records in Virginia archives, it was also a work of synthesis, based on printed sources that could be found in any good university library and on the works of other historians. For works that examine a big subject, like the relationship between slavery and freedom and cover a wide geographical and chronological span, from sixteenth-century England to seventeenth-century Virginia, one must of necessity depend in some measure to the work of others. Understanding why English men and women were willing to risk their lives by coming to Virginia, Morgan needed to understand the social and economic conditions in England in the sixteenth century. He was fortunate that by the time he wrote *American Slavery, American Freedom,* important work had been done on these subjects by English social historians, such as Lawrence Stone, Joan Thirsk, and Peter Laslett. At the same time, important work had been done on other subjects of significance in early Virginia, such as the origins of slavery and Bacon's Rebellion. Thus, *American Slavery, American Freedom* continued in the archival tradition of earlier historians, but it was also a work based in part on the work of others, designed to tie together a number of big themes.

Other historians of the World War II generation tackled big subjects and large periods of time. These subjects and the length of the time period necessary to treat them properly made it difficult for the historian to examine all the available documents. This chapter considers those historians whose work is based primarily on the work of others, printed primary sources, or a combination of the two.

While slavery remained a riveting historical issue, emphasis on it obscured other parts of the black experience. Not all blacks were slaves, and they lived and worked in other parts of the country besides the South. One thing that was badly needed was an overview that would tell all parts of the story from the first appearance of blacks in the New World to the present day.

This synthesis was provided by John Hope Franklin in *From Slavery to Freedom*, though Franklin came to the subject with reluctance. As early as his graduate studies at Harvard, Franklin decided that he would be a historian without regard to race. Only in the later stages of graduate work did he "back into" his dissertation topic of free blacks in North Carolina. This dissertation, supervised by the pro-Southern Paul Buck, placed Franklin in the field of Southern history, and he turned energetically to his next project, which would become *The Militant South*. His work on the militant South was interrupted by a call from Roger Shugg, a history editor for Alfred A. Knopf. Shugg wanted to commission a survey text on black history. Arthur Schlesinger Sr. had recommended Franklin for the job. Not wishing to suspend his work on *The Militant South*, Franklin refused Shugg's offer. But Shugg, vitally committed to the project, made a special trip to North Carolina State College in Durham where Franklin was teaching to convince him. Impressed by Shugg's sense of purpose and the high standing of Knopf in the publishing world, Franklin finally agreed.[12]

Franklin also agreed to write a survey text because he was aware of the need for an overall synthesis of existing research on black history. *From Slavery to Freedom*, published in 1947, was then an attempt to see the big picture and was based primarily on the works of others. As Franklin wrote in the introduction, "I have undertaken to bring together the essential facts of the history of the American Negro from Africa to the present time." Franklin also devoted his attention to the experience of Negroes in the Caribbean, Latin America, and Canada, not just the American South, and tried to be attentive to regional variations. In all cases he sought to explore the "interaction between the Negro and his environment" with careful consideration of the outside forces that have affected his development.

After discussing ancient slavery, the African background, and the impact of the European conquest of the African coast, Franklin turned his attention to the problem of early Virginia. Anticipating Morgan, he contended that the choice of the seemingly inexhaustible supply of black slave labor had consequences. With the expanding black population, white Southerners came to have genuine reason to fear Negroes, and Southern colonies began enacting black codes designed to hold the black population in their proper and subordinate place.[13]

Franklin also considered slavery outside the South and paid particular attention to its practice in Pennsylvania. Slavery did exist there, although only a few slaveowners owned more than one or two slaves. But Pennsylvania was a state, like North Carolina, where religion was a force in shaping social conditions. Quakerism in Pennsylvania served as a humanitarian impulse to reduce the impact of slavery and to achieve a genuine accommodation between blacks and whites.[14]

Franklin also ruminated on the paradox between freedom and servitude in early America. For him, the period following the American Revolution promised great improvements in race relations. Not only was there considerable discussion of what constituted human rights, but the Northwest Ordinance of 1787 prohibited slavery north of the Ohio River, several states passed laws forbidding slavery, and such laws were even given serious consideration in several Southern states.

For a brief, shining moment, American race relations seemed poised to make a decisive turn. But for Franklin the post–Revolutionary War era was the great turning point in Negro history where history failed to turn. Several factors spoiled its promise. The manufacture of cheap cotton cloth by machine, the invention of the cotton gin to expedite production, and the extension of slavery into new territories destroyed the possibility of accommodation. The Industrial Revolution offered fabulous profits to those who cultivated and manufactured cotton, and the ideals of freedom bowed before the powerful forces of King Cotton. The Industrial Revolution and the cotton gin thus determined the course of the American future. Cotton unified the South by committing it to slavery and to defense of the slave system against any group or section that threatened it.[15]

Franklin then proceeded to describe slave life before the Civil War. Much of his description was utilized by Stampp in *The Peculiar Institution*, a title that Franklin had already used for his chapter on slave conditions in *From Slavery to Freedom*. Franklin also exposed the hypocrisies of Northerners, who were often as bigoted as Southerners and opposed even such things as the recruitment of black soldiers at the beginning of the Civil War.

The era of Reconstruction was a second turning point where black history failed to turn. The state constitutions drawn up during the Radical Reconstruction was the most progressive the South had ever known: no race or property qualifications for voting or officeholding. Under these enactments, Negroes won many elections. At one point they comprised a majority of the members of the South Carolina legislature, though they were never able to control it, nor did they ever claim political control of the South.[16]

What Negro success in politics triggered of course was a Southern reaction, taking the form of a guerilla war, designed to deprive the Negro of his political equality. That reaction, especially in the hands of such groups as the Ku Klux Klan, eventually took on the character of a jihad whereby the ends justified the means. It was clear by the end of the nineteenth century that while slavery was gone, Negroes were still in servitude, marginally if at all better off economically than they had been before.

The early twentieth century saw important improvements across the United States in education for Negroes and in the creation of new advocacy organizations, such as the NAACP and the Urban League. But prejudice and discrimination persisted. When the United States entered World War I, Negroes who were eager to serve their country found themselves barred altogether from serving in the Marines, consigned to menial positions in the navy, and subjected to much hostility from white soldiers and civilians in other branches of service. In Europe they discovered there was less prejudice against them and soon recognized that Woodrow Wilson's pledge to "make the world safe for democracy" did not include them.[17]

Negro veterans returned to a society that was hostile rather than grateful to them. In the first year after the war alone, more than seventy Negroes were lynched. And as Negroes moved into the fringes of white neighborhoods in Northern cities, they encountered increasing hostility, which led to an unprecedented outbreak of racial violence in 1919.

The next pivotal moment for Negroes occurred with the Great Depression and the New Deal. The decade of the 1930s was a turning point where history actually turned. The migration of Negroes to Northern industrial cities gave them some degree of political power, and Roosevelt shrewdly courted Negro votes. He established what was called the "Black Cabinet" of Negro advisors, who actually had input into policy matters, and many of Roosevelt's New Deal programs were designed to help the poor, white and black.[18]

Half a million Negroes saw military service during World War II, though few of them had any illusions that white society would recognize their contribution. Negroes contributed heavily to the war effort by working in defense industries. But as they moved to Northern industrial cities to work in defense plants, they found substandard housing, resentment from white workers, and political demagogues willing to use race-baiting as a path to power.

The fifties saw some significant changes in race relations, which Franklin discussed in later editions of *From Slavery to Freedom*. The roles of the military and the courts in these changes were critical. President Truman integrated the armed services and made all branches of the military open to qualified personnel. In the Korean War, General Matthew Ridgeway insisted upon the integration of Negroes into combat forces. The Supreme Court rendered favorable decisions, including the famous 1954 Brown v. Board of Education decision that overturned an earlier decision legalizing separate but equal facilities. By 1956 concluded Franklin, Southern whites despaired of maintaining segregation, and Negroes had become an integral part of Western culture.[19]

Even more than *American Slavery, American Freedom, From Slavery to Freedom* was a work of synthesis. While Franklin had done considerable archival research for other books, *From Slavery to Freedom* depended primarily on the works of others. In any event to have consulted all the primary sources for black history over as broad a period as that covered by *From Slavery to Freedom* would have been impossible. Franklin was forced to rely upon the work of others. His achievement lay in his ability to assimilate an enormous amount of material, tie it together, and create a coherent narrative.

At the same time his work embodies many of the same characteristics as the work of Morgan and the more archivally oriented historians, such as Stampp and Woodward. This generation relished the exposure of hypocrisy and paradox and explored thoroughly the role of the individual and groups trapped by social and economic forces beyond their control. In *From Slavery to Freedom* Franklin easily demonstrated that black history was more than slavery and more than the South, and that there was plenty of hypocrisy to go around from Jefferson to Woodrow Wilson. More painfully, at almost every nodal moment where blacks and whites appeared to be on the verge of accommodation, those moments were destroyed by outside economic and social forces.

A similar irony underpins Oscar Handlin's greatest book, *The Uprooted*. Americans in the 1950s who regarded slavery as a generally benign institution had similar ignorance about immigration, often congratulating themselves on the opportunities that America had provided for the huddled masses yearning to breathe free. America celebrated itself as a "melting pot" in which various ethnic groups had been welcomed and assimilated into American society.

Even though he was the child of immigrants, Oscar Handlin came to the subject of immigration by accident. He had gone to Harvard to study medieval history, but found it impossible. He sought Arthur M. Schlesinger Sr., who regarded himself as a social historian, as an advisor. When Handlin asked for suggestions for a dissertation topic, Schlesinger suggested a study of Boston's immigrants. Another student had tried it, but had just given up. "Why don't you do it?" Schlesinger asked.[20]

Thus, almost entirely by accident, Handlin found the topic that would lead to his greatest book. At the time, there was little to guide him. There were books on immigrants, but no systematic study. There was no urban or ethnic history. Social history was still in its infancy. There was no history "from the bottom up" or "history of mentalities" or demography, though Handlin pioneered the treatment of those subjects without using those exact names. The research that resulted in *The Uprooted* began with Handlin's dissertation on Boston's immigrants, published in 1941 as *Boston's Immigrants, 1790–1880: A Study in Acculturation.*

Working on Boston's immigrants required long hours of drudgery in

Boston's libraries, reading newspapers and pamphlets. Handlin quickly discovered that even by the 1840s Boston was still relatively undeveloped in industrial terms and had a relatively nomadic population. By 1850, for example, only half of the descendants of 1820s Bostonians still lived there. The demography of Boston changed with the great Irish Potato Famine of 1845. Starvation combined with other gross injustices in Irish society to drive several million Irish to flee to the United States.

The arrival of the Irish in Boston provided the cheap labor necessary for industrialization. But almost all who profited from industrialization were native Americans. The Irish, possessing few skills, took the menial jobs as laborers and domestic servants. Factory conditions were of course harsh and degrading, including fifteen hour workdays, no days off, under the lash of alien masters. The fortunes of the great Boston mill owners were made on the backs of Irish labor.

Boston was transformed by the immigrant population. The city was unprepared for their arrival, and there was insufficient housing available. Thus the Irish swarmed by the dozens, even hundreds, into dwellings originally intended for one family. Sanitation was virtually nonexistent. Filth, disease, crime, drunkenness, and prostitution proliferated. The Irish eventually established their own neighborhoods where they could be free from the attacks of the native population, often preferring to remain in them even after they could afford to move to better ones.[21]

Like Franklin, Handlin was more interested in understanding accommodation than in chronicling injustice. Like Africans in America, the Irish in Boston were strangers in a strange land, forced to adapt to new circumstances and customs. Almost every phase of their experience in America heightened the disparity between their heritage and that of their neighbors. And like the other historians of his generation, Handlin was repelled by the irony of a system that forced the Irish to work at slave labor for pitiful wages and live in squalor and then blamed them for being lazy and drunken.

But Handlin revealed that irony could cut both ways. The Irish, victims of racism, were themselves racist. Under the influence of the Catholic Church, which was reluctant to offend Southern Catholics, Irish leaders defended slavery and opposed the emancipation of blacks. During the election of 1860 Irish leaders opposed Lincoln and supported the Democrats. It was the mission of the church, not the government, to eradicate injustice. The Boston Irish followed the church's conservatism in other areas. Where most Americans approved of the European revolutions of 1848, the Boston Irish, following church decree, opposed them as the abomination of revolutionary change. Only when the Southern states seceded from the Union, did the Irish display any sympathy for the Northern cause. But the issue was unity, not injustice.[22]

The Catholic Church did help the Irish maintain their identity, and

Handlin was particularly sensitive to the ways in which an immigrant sense of community developed. Not only did many Irish cling to Catholicism as a means of retaining their sense of being Irish, but the church sponsored dances, religious processions, hospitals and schools, all of which were designed to promote a sense of Irish identity amidst the Brahmins.[23]

In the decade and a half following the Civil War, there was an appearance of stability and tranquility in Boston. The great migration appeared to be over; Boston industry thrived, and new fortunes were made rapidly. But appearances were deceptive. Conditions in factories and slums were still appalling; vicious anti-Irish prejudices pervaded. At the same time, traditional Boston society began to recoil at what their city had become. "Silas Lapham," wrote Handlin, "had become as repellent as Dennis or Bridget." In 1880 Boston was a city divided. A new tide of immigration would shortly expose the fissures and differences between the city's various competing groups. Handlin seemed to be saying that the relatively stable Boston before immigration was superior to the divided society that had emerged after the Civil War.[24]

Just as Franklin's work on North Carolina Negroes during the Reconstruction had served as a base for *From Slavery to Freedom*, *Boston's Immigrants, 1790–1880* was the foundation for *The Uprooted*. *Boston's Immigrants* was a study of a specific immigrant group based upon archival study; *The Uprooted* attempted to explore the immigrant experience on a grander scale and to place it in a larger historical perspective.

"Once I thought to write a history of the immigrants in American history. Then I discovered that the immigrants *were* American history."[25] With these words, now almost as famous as Stampp's declaration in *The Peculiar Institution* that Negroes were simply human beings in black skins, Handlin began an epic saga, almost biblical in its theme and rhythms. Handlin described the life of the European peasant communities from which most immigrants migrated, the perils of their exodus to America, and the appalling conditions they encountered in passage and upon their arrival. They were like the children of Israel, but there was no Moses to deliver them. As in *Boston's Immigrants*, Handlin was not primarily concerned to make his book a chronicle of injustice; he was most interested in explaining how the immigrants survived, how they retained their own cultures and adapted to new ones. As he had in *Boston's Immigrants*, he examined the importance of neighborhoods, the church, schools, theaters, newspapers, and magazines in helping immigrants retain their Old World identity, while at the same time adapting to their new surroundings.

Politics came to be the strongest force for immigrant accommodation. In the old world the state was basically external to the life of peasant. Government was clearly the tool of the upper classes. Its powers appeared to be most terrifying when it declared war, and the agents of the state appeared in villages and towns to take away young men to fight in wars in which they had no stake or understanding of the issues. In America there was a similar distrust of government and a recognition that, for example, when it came to immigrants, the regular police had minimal interest in the judicious enforcement of the law. But government in America held possibilities that did not exist in Europe. Immigrants eventually turned to informal ways of protection and enforcement. More important, several immigrant leaders were astute enough to see that in a democratic society the large immigrant population afforded the opportunity to taste political power that they had never known in Europe. Leaders who could deliver the vote could in return get improvements in housing, sanitation, jobs, and other things needed in immigrant neighborhoods. With the immigrant assumption of political power of course came corruption.[26]

Consideration of corruption led Handlin to another area of hallowed ground of his generation, the Progressive movement. The corruption spawned in the immigrant cities gave birth to the Progressive movement for reform. Reformers correctly blasted the corruption of big city political machines, which they connected to immigrants. Few of them, however, noted the degrading conditions that led to corrupt practices.

The Uprooted resembles in many ways *From Slavery to Freedom* and *The Peculiar Institution*. All three deal with a burning injustice in American society, with a tone of understated passion. But *The Uprooted* resembles most closely Franklin's book. Unlike *The Peculiar Institution*, neither *The Uprooted* nor *From Slavery to Freedom* advanced a provocative thesis; both books merely wished to assert the importance of a particular experience in American life. Few can read *The Uprooted* without absorbing a strong sense of what it would have been like to be an immigrant in nineteenth-century America. Also, like *From Slavery to Freedom, The Uprooted* was a work of synthesis rather than of original research. It was too much to expect Handlin to master all the archival materials pertaining to the immigrants. A book like *The Uprooted* was possible only if the author could draw on the work of many others.

The Uprooted was also distinctive for its unusual narrative techniques. Handlin decided the story he wanted to tell would not fit the forms of traditional historical narratives. Chronology was abandoned in favor of a thematic approach; footnotes were sacrificed to simplicity, and the text contained numerous italicized phrases lifted from documents. In the middle of a paragraph Handlin sometimes would interpose the words of an actual immigrant or Handlin's own rendering of them. These interjections occasionally gave the text a haunting, poetic quality, and an almost Joycean sense of narrative.

At the same time Handlin's work also resembled that of the French historian Fernand Braudel. Braudel was the product of the French *Annales* School of historians. He tried to write *total history*, and probably came reasonably close to it in his masterpiece, *The Mediterranean World in the Age of*

Philip II, published in 1949. To write the total history of the Mediterranean world, Braudel turned to the social sciences, particularly sociology and anthropology, for insight. As J.H. Hexter, Handlin's friend from the Harvard graduate school in the 1930s, once suggested, Handlin was the American historian of his generation most worthy of comparison with Braudel. In *The Uprooted*, along with his erudition and multitude of other interests, Handlin rivaled Braudel in the enormity of his vision. Concerned to draw on the insights of the social sciences long before it was fashionable, Handlin could also rival Braudel in the subtlety and scope of his work. *The Uprooted* not only was based on traditional historical sources, but also drew insights from folklore, the sociology of religion, novels, and newspapers.[27]

The initial reaction to *The Uprooted* was overwhelmingly favorable. The book captured the Pulitzer Prize for 1952. But it did receive some criticism. Some critics argued that Handlin romanticized preindustrial America while painting too dismal a picture of immigrant life. Others thought it generalized too broadly. Not all the immigrants, for example, left pastoral villages, nor did immigrants farther west experience the alienation that those on the east received. Other critics objected to the lack of documentation and the departure from traditional historical narrative.[28]

Despite these criticisms, *The Uprooted* is characteristic of much of the best work of the World War II generation. Like many of this generation's great books, *The Uprooted* was short, fluidly written, and therefore accessible to a nonacademic audience. More importantly, Handlin provided a serious treatment of immigration, like Franklin's or Stampp's serious treatment of blacks. At the time of its publication, ethnicity, like race, was not a term given a great deal of thought by most Americans, and when they did think about it, it was generally in optimistic terms. Even historians, especially those associated with the "Consensus School" generally thought that the United States had achieved a desirable unity. Handlin revealed the fragility of that unity.[29]

If the histories of blacks and immigrants remained subjects worthy of attention for the World War II generation of historians, so, too, did Hitler, the Nazis, and so-called German question. In 1946 Hugh Trevor-Roper published his analysis of Nazism, *The Last Days of Hitler*. In the early 1950s Carl Schorske took up the issue of the failure of German liberalism in *German Social Democracy*. Others of this generation such as Leonard Krieger, Peter Gay, and Alan Bullock also studied the Nazis, even though in several cases their training had been in other areas. In 1956 Gordon Craig considered the closely related subject of Prussian and, later, German militarism in *The Politics of the Prussian Army, 1640–1945*.

Between 1870 and 1939 Germany was responsible for starting two wars and played a significant, if not decisive part, in starting a third. Thus, the question of whether there was a peculiarly militant aspect to the German character was an intriguing subject. Long before Hitler, Sombart said of Prussia that "the state did not create the army. The army created the state." Of course the phrase "German militarism" covered a multitude of sins. In some instances it meant that German military officers were ruthless and arrogant. In other instances it meant that the German state was dominated by the needs of the military. Finally, it might mean that the German people were obedient and docile, subservient to authority.

Craig only really dealt with the second instance, the question of the extent to which the Prussian or German state was controlled by the needs of the military. *The Politics of the Prussian Army* considered the role of the Prussian and German Armies in the formulation of policy. Craig quickly demonstrated that the army was not always a force in Prussian society. During the age of religious wars, Prussian leaders depended, not always successfully, upon diplomacy to escape the horrors of religious war. It was not until Frederick William I (1713–40), who believed that the army was the key to power, that Prussia developed a substantial military force. Frederick William passed along his wisdom to his son Frederick the Great, who reformed and expanded the army. Despite Frederick's military success and reform, the army that emerged after his death embodied the worst excesses of Old Regime Europe. Position and promotion were based on patronage and pedigree. Soldiers of ability were passed over in favor of those with connection and money.[30]

The French Revolution made no impression on Prussia until Napoleon crushed the moribund Prussian army at Jena in 1806. The contrast between the French and Prussian armies was striking. The Prussian army was the province of old men and patronage. The average age of a Prussian general was sixty; and young officers of ability entertained little hope of advancement. By contrast the Napoleonic army was propelled by ambitious younger men who knew that by demonstrating ability and aptitude, they could be promoted. After Jena, Napoleon foolishly allowed the Prussians enough autonomy to reform their army along French lines. The leading reformers, Schnarnhorst and Gneisenau, wished to rid the high command of entrenched older officers and open the officer corps to men of talent, which meant that the bourgeoisie would be admitted to it. These reforms were greeted with squeals of horror by old-line officers who recognized them as an attack on their class and station. Three hundred Prussian officers resigned in protest, but the reformed army defeated Napoleon at Leipzig, Ligny, and Waterloo.[31]

As in the history of blacks in America, there were many points at which the history of Prussia might have turned in a liberal direction. The French Revolution was one such point. But outside of the army, there was little liberal reform in Prussia following the French Revolution. And once Napoleon had been defeated the army gradually returned to its old ways, and liberal reform made little progress elsewhere in Prussia. In 1848 demand for reform

again shook the Prussian monarchy to its foundations. Inspired by the eruption of insurrection across Europe, huge crowds in Berlin demonstrated on
behalf of liberal reform. When soldiers fired on them, angry mobs threatened to destroy the monarchy. With the city in complete chaos and his crown
hanging by a thread, Frederick William IV of Prussia ordered the troops out
of the city and promised a liberal government, elections, and universal suffrage. One of the goals of the liberal reformers was civilian control of the
army. But the promised liberal government, known as the Frankfurt Parliament, collapsed amidst bickering and self-interest. It was quickly dissolved
by Frederick William in April 1849, and the army appeared to have dodged
another bullet. In the 1860s, however, Prussian liberals made a last attempt
to secure civilian control over the military.[32]

In desperation army leaders turned to Otto von Bismarck to save them
from the liberals. Bismarck has been usually regarded as the epitome of Prussian militarism, but Craig easily refuted this charge. Bismarck did rescue the
army from the liberals in the 1860s and allowed it to maintain a large force.
On the other hand, Craig revealed the constant tension between Bismarck
and the army's high command. While Bismarck protected the army from
liberal reform, he also needed liberal support and had to allow constitutional
government to keep the liberals on his side. Army leaders constantly pes-
tered Bismarck to abolish constitutional government, but were firmly re-
buffed. The army also had little involvement with Bismarck's plans to unify
Germany. Craig showed that military leaders were shut out of important
decisions, such as the decision to invade Denmark in 1864. Even during later,
more crucial wars, such as those against Austria in 1866 and France in 1870,
Bismarck expected the generals to conduct the war; civilians made policy. It
was not until the reign of William II that the army eluded civilian control,
and that was more attributable to civilian lethargy than army initiative.

By World War I, however, the generals did achieve political as well as
military hegemony. But that control resulted from the cruel necessities of
war rather than design. By 1916, however, as casualties mounted, civilian
leaders began to explore the possibilities of a negotiated peace. They were
angrily denounced by the generals, who demanded total victory and still believed that it could be won. The generals were adamant against even the
suggestion of negotiated peace, a position that had consequences. The great
German offensive of 1918, for example, might have succeeded if the prospect of a negotiated peace had been floated informally before its beginning.
For the first few weeks of the offensive, the Germans enjoyed unprecedented
success. The British army crumbled at the onset of German attack, the Americans had yet to arrive, and the French were useless. If the British had known
that the Germans might accept a negotiated settlement, they would have
leapt for it, and on conditions favorable to Germany. The generals, even
though they were aware that their men were exhausted and overextended,

still refused to consider the possibility.[33] How different the course of the twentieth century might have been if World War I had ended with a negotiated peace in the spring of 1918. Arguably, the world might have been much better off if peace had been negotiated on terms favorable to Germany in the spring of 1918!

By 1930 the army was threatened by another liberal government. Again fearing the possibility of civilian control, the army acquiesced to Hitler's assumption of power. The generals were certain that Hitler could be managed, and, if not, he could be disposed of. Craig wrote, "of all the mistakes made by the political generals in the long history of the Prussian army, this was greatest, and for the nation the most tragic."[34] At first Hitler did not seek to dominate the army and often expressed his respect for it. For its part the army stood by while Hitler destroyed his political enemies. The turning point in the relationship between Hitler and the army came in 1936, when the generals opposed his reoccupation of the Rhineland. Hitler decided they were pessimists and made his plans without them. A key general was murdered and another was disgraced. In 1938 army leaders considered a strike against Hitler, but decided the German people were too much under his spell. After this failure of nerve, Hitler steamrolled over them. He informed the generals of his plans to attack Poland and negotiated the Russo-German Pact of 1939 without them. Swallowing their pride, the generals goose-stepped in cadence with Hitler to the bitter end.[35]

Craig painted an ambiguous picture of the relationship between the army and Prussian-German state. Neither Germany nor its people seemed to him particularly militaristic. During World War I, the military gained control of the state, but at other times, it could be controlled by an effective civilian leader. Most of the time the military stayed apart from domestic policies and was often inept when it did intervene.

Politics and the Prussian Army is, like the other works examined here, mainly a synthesis. Covering more than three hundred years of German history, Craig could not be expected to examine all the pertinent manuscripts. The discovery of material from the German military archives now in Washington allowed him to add some detail to the story. But he did not visit German archives, and most of the book is a skillful synthesis of printed sources and the works of other historians, such as that of Hans Gatzke for World War I.

To say that Craig's work is synthetic is not in any way to diminish it. Detailed manuscript investigations of key events are essential to historical knowledge, but the historians who are good at microscopic investigations are not always good at seeing the big picture. This is because archivalists and synthesizers generally have two different casts of mind. Archivalists tend to work microscopically; they take one historical issue, such as the role of Thomas Cromwell in English government in the 1530s, and examine as much detail, context, and connection as they can. They delight in the discovery of new manuscripts, and such discovery is often the key to their success. By contrast synthesizers tend to have what J.H. Hexter called the "Great Mother Earth" approach to history. They study large subjects, such as slavery and race relations, German militarism; and they wish to understand change and impact over centuries. They delight in intellectual epiphanies where connections between events suddenly become clear to them. The key to their research is often the appearance of a new monograph by someone else based upon archival research that can be incorporated into their synthesis. There is of course considerable overlap. Synthesizers need detailed monographs on which their works are constructed. Both kinds of history are necessary, and many of the historians considered here, such as Kenneth Stampp and Lawrence Stone, did both.

Like Gordon Craig, Barbara Tuchman was interested in the German question, though it was not central to her work. In her best book, *The Guns of August*, which was awarded the Pulitzer Prize in 1962, she examined the events leading up to World War I. There were significant differences between her approach and Craig's. Where Craig told the story from the German perspective over several centuries, Tuchman told the story of one month, August 1914, from the points of view of people in several different countries. Where Craig was most interested in the analysis and meaning of events, Tuchman was most interested in telling a story. Both, however, worked mostly from printed, primary sources and secondary authorities.

The story Tuchman wanted to tell concerned the opening days of World War I and the events leading up to them, a story that Winston Churchill called a "drama never surpassed." Leaders on all sides were too eager to fight. The British Prime Minister Asquith described Churchill's prowar attitude as "Winston with all his war paint on." War fever developed in part because the general staffs told the leaders the war would be over quickly, a belief that the leaders eagerly conveyed to the public. "You will be home before the leaves have fallen from the trees," the Kaiser told his troops as they marched off to war in the late summer of 1914.[36]

All sides had strategic misconceptions. The Germans, surrounded by France on one side and Russia on the other, elected to adhere to a strategy called the Schlieffen Plan, by which they hoped to avoid fighting a two-front war. The Schlieffen Plan was a nineteenth-century general's dream come true, a chance to imitate Hannibal's classic envelopment of the Roman armies at Cannae. Schlieffen called for the Germans to defeat the French as quickly as possible so they could then turn to the Russians. The plan, however, had a fatal flaw. It required the German army to sweep through Belgium, which would violate Belgian neutrality, thereby running the risk of bringing England into the war.

The Germans were not alone. The French, haunted by their humiliation by the Germans in 1870, still dreamed of reviving Napoleonic glories and continued to dress in the resplendent blue and red uniforms of 1830, while the British had already turned to khaki and the Germans to gray. For their part, the British tried to find the smallest number of men possible to send to France. "Britain's weapons were ready," Tuchman wrote, "but not her will." Hoping to improve the discipline of their troops, the Russians cut off the sale of vodka to the entire nation. But the sale of vodka was a state monopoly. By forbidding its sale, the Russians eliminated one-third of the country's revenue just as it was going to war.[37]

The conduct of the war brought as much folly as the planning. In the execution of the Schlieffen Plan, General von Kluck, the commander of the German right wing, was to sweep as far to the west as possible to prevent the German army from being outflanked. "Let the last man on the right brush the English Channel with his right sleeve," Schlieffen had admonished. Several weeks into the war, however, Von Kluck began to fear that his army was overextended, and he turned away from the Channel toward Paris. Disbelieving French generals watched as Von Kluck violated one of the most inviolable rules of warfare. "They offer us their flank," two of them shouted incredulously as they tracked the progress of Von Kluck's army.[38] Von Kluck's failure of nerve ruined any chance that the Schlieffen Plan had of succeeding. Instead, both sides dug in and fought a desperate battle along the Marne River. Almost before anyone realized it, new technologies, including machine guns, superior artillery, and air power, condemned Europe to a war of attrition in the trenches.

Tuchman's strength as a historian rested in her narrative skill. "Will the reader turn the page?" was her constant motto. Conrad Russell once remarked that studying history is like reading a murder mystery already knowing who the murderer is. As Tuchman tells the story, we know what will happen: that efforts to reach peace will fail, that the Germans will go forward with the flawed Schlieffen Plan, that the British will enter the war after the violation of Belgian neutrality, that the ponderous Russian armies will be defeated in separate battles by a much smaller German army, and that Von Kluck will make his fatal turn. Yet Tuchman's narrative skill keeps the reader feverishly turning page after page wondering how things will turn out.

The suspense is sustained in part because of Tuchman's eye for the telling details that make an event come alive in readers' minds or transport them to the scene. She told readers what was in the knapsack of a German soldier and the soldiers' horror of snipers. Many of her details have an ominous, foreboding quality, portents of the tragedy to come. She relates how on the night before the war began "rain was pouring in Berlin," how a rag doll was crushed by a German gun carriage as the German army barreled through Belgium, and how on the afternoon that the British army landed in France there was the sound of summer thunder in the air and how the sun set with a blood-red glow.[39]

The generals lent themselves to striking descriptions, and Tuchman also possessed a flair for style. "Of the two classes of Prussian officer, the bullnecked and the whipwaisted," she remarked, "Schlieffen belonged to the second." She likened the entry of German armies into Belgium to "a swinging scythe." Joffre, she said, "looked like Santa Claus and gave the impression of benevolence and naivete—two qualities not noticeably part of his character." Her description of Gallieni, the French general who saved France by convincing Joffre to attack Von Kluck's exposed flank, was particularly memorable: "He wore a pince-nez and a heavy gray moustache that was rather at odds with his elegant, autocratic figure. He carried himself like an officer on parade. Tall and spare, with a distant untouchable, faintly stern air, he resembled no other French officer of his time. Poincaré described the impression he made: 'straight, slender and upright with head erect and piercing eyes behind his glasses, he appeared to us as an imposing example of powerful humanity.'"[40]

Like other historians of her generation, Tuchman had a keen sense of irony. She noted that the German General Hindenburg was an undistinguished, retired general still wearing his old blue Prussian uniform when the war broke out, but his victories over the blundering Russians at Tannenburg and Mansurian Lakes transformed him into the most powerful man in Germany. Even more ironic, the Germans, having committed themselves to the Schlieffen Plan to avoid a two-front war, ended up fighting one. There was also irony in sentences like "the cavalry, once so strong in polished boots and bright uniforms, now stained and muddy, sway in their saddles, dazed with fatigue." Above all, *The Guns of August* ruminated on the supreme irony of World War I, that what was expected to be a quick, glorious war to create a better world turned out to be an illusion. "The mirage of a better world," Tuchman wrote, "glimmered beyond the shell-pitted wastes and leafless stumps that had once been green fields and waving poplars."[41]

Some might feel that Tuchman spent too much time with personal detail. Do we really need to know that the English Prime Minister Sir Henry Campbell-Bannerman loved France so much that he often took quick trips across the Channel just to have lunch? The anecdote is interesting, but Campbell-Bannerman concluded his time as prime minister in 1908 and did not figure significantly in the frantic diplomacy of the late summer of 1914. Do we really need to know that the Russian general Sukhomlinov was a scoundrel who framed the husband of a beautiful young woman so he could take her as his fourth wife? The anecdote certainly clarifies the nature of Sukhomlinov's character, but it occurred well before 1914 and Sukhomlinov plays little role in the rest of the story. One suspects that Tuchman sometimes just relishes a good yarn.

More seriously, Tuchman has sometimes been charged with reducing history to human folly and incompetence and the interplay of personality.

There is something to be said for this charge, particularly in the case of a historian who selected World War I as a subject. The obstinacy, inflexibility, and incompetence of the generals come through over and over again in *The Guns of August*, and Tuchman also wrote a later book, *The March of Folly*, in which she explored the various blunders of Greek leaders during the Trojan wars, medieval and Renaissance popes, British ministers before the American Revolution, and American policymakers before the Vietnam War.

But Tuchman's historical world is more complex; her characters are more like Shakespeare's, or perhaps Stampp's or Handlin's. They are ordinary people, both flawed and gifted, caught in the fury of events and forces beyond their control. Generals on all sides had their moments of stupidity and opacity, but that was not really Tuchman's theme. Her theme was that they were ordinary men condemned to blunders by their training, background, immediate political circumstances, and the old wounds and prejudices in the recent histories of their countries. If there was a way out, they could not have seen it; if they had seen a way out, they could not have taken it. *The Guns of August* was a Greek tragedy, lacking only a chorus, of all too human men chained by forces they could neither understand nor control. Again Tuchman relates an anecdote pregnant with symbolism. Just before the outbreak of war a confused moose wandered across the Russian frontier and unluckily emerged from the woods within the sight of the German army's hunting lodge at Romintern, where he was immediately shot by the Kaiser. The world in 1914 was as confused and unlucky as the moose.[42]

Carl Schorske began his scholarly career with a study of why German liberalism and social democracy had failed to resist Hitler. He is more famous for his later work, *Fin-de-Siècle Vienna*, a collection of essays, published between 1961 and 1979, which appeared in 1981 and for which he won a Pulitzer Prize. Interestingly, Schorske was not trained as a historian of either Vienna or the Hapsburg Empire. *Fin-de-Siècle Vienna* grew from his teaching. Taking up his first teaching post at Wesleyan University shortly after World War II, Schorske began to develop a course in European intellectual history. The course soon acquired the stamp of the American neo-Enlightenment tradition in which Schorske had been taught at Columbia. Its central theme was the history of rational thought and intellectual progress in the context of their relation to social and political change. This framework worked well enough for constructing a narrative of European thought until the late nineteenth century, but then floundered. As the twentieth century approached, rationalism and the historicist vision allied with it, crumbled before the onslaught of such post-Nietzschean categories as irrationalism, abstractionism, and subjectivity.[43]

Nietzsche was the last intellectual to fit reasonably into Schorske's rationalist framework. Nietzsche appeared as the principal herald of the modern condition and as a bridge between the rationalist world in which Schorske was raised and the post-Enlightenment world emerging in America after World War II, at once frightening and enticing in its possibilities. Nietzsche was comprehensible in the progressive framework in which Schorske intended to teach, but after him, wrote Schorske, "whirl was king, and I felt rudderless." The new categories were seemingly bereft of foundation or logic and were profoundly antihistorical. They represented in the words of the composer Arnold Schoenberg, "a death-dance of principles."[44] How does one teach the history of intellectual movements that lack principles and rational foundation?

Schorske's colleagues at Wesleyan and friends helped him cope with new intellectual currents. The postwar period was a time of turmoil for American intellectuals. As they confronted the collapse of the New Deal coalition in American politics, the coming of the Cold War, and the McCarthy nightmare, many of them abandoned the optimistic social and philosophic platforms of postwar liberalism. Realistic thinkers like Reinhold Niebuhr and Perry Miller, and existentialists like Kierkegaard and Sartre among intellectuals emerged as the cultural deities. Renewed interest in Freud indicated that the premises for understanding man in society had again shifted from social-historical to the psychological. Schorske recalls vividly a dinner party at his house in 1952 in which two of his friends, the Wesleyan classicist Norman O. Brown and the philosopher Herbert Marcuse, suddenly discovered they were both traveling along the same road from Marxism to Freudianism, from political to cultural radicalism.[45]

The various forces of post–World War II intellectual world converged to redefine Schorske's scholarly agenda. He resolved to explore the genesis of modern cultural consciousness with its explicit rejection of history. He also decided that only in a specific historical context could the totality of the experience be grasped. A city therefore presented the best opportunity for study. Schorske tried out several possibilities, such as Paris, London, Berlin, and Vienna, on his Wesleyan students. Vienna proved the most satisfactory. The city was a cultural center in art, architecture, music, and literature and possessed a well-defined intellectual elite.

Fin-de-Siècle Vienna consisted of seven essays, published between 1961 and 1979. Three of them appeared in the *American Historical Review*; one in the *Journal of Modern History*. The essays focus on figures who defined culture and politics in turn-of-the-century Vienna. Schorske shows how most of them retreated from politics and society and rejects history as the field from which meaning and direction can be ascertained. The four essays that appeared in major journals are the most famous.

In the first, "Politics and the Psyche in Fin-de-Siècle Vienna: Schnitzler and Hofmannsthal," Schorske tried to set the context for the entire book. In Austria, as in most European countries, the first half of the nineteenth century had been characterized by the struggle of liberal reform against a calcified aristocracy. By the 1860s the liberals had come to power and established a constitutional regime. But the triumph proved ephemeral. The liberals were forced to share constitutional power with the aristocracy and imperial bureaucracy. At the same time new social groups, such as the peasantry, urban workers, and Slavic peoples, emerged to demand political rights and challenge the liberal hegemony. In the end by 1900 the liberal reform had collapsed in the face of various mass and antiliberal movements.

In the essay on the playwright Arthur Schnitzler and the poet Hugo Hofmannsthal, Schorske explored the connection between psychological commitment and political engagement, a recurring theme in the book. Both faced the problem of the dissolution of the classical liberal view of human beings in the wreckage of Austrian politics. For Schnitzler, where the French Revolution had once been a defining political moment, it had by the 1890s lost its meaning. Schnitzler vividly exposed the pretensions of both liberal reformers and defenders of traditional society, but failed to provide an alternative. By contrast Hofmannsthal was eager to do more than knock down walls. While he shared many of Schnitzler's insights toward existing society, he was also able to envision an art that would offer creative potential beyond the liberal and aristocratic paradigms. Only in the irrational and instinctive, he suggested, could the aesthete find the appropriate course of action and artistic inspiration.[46]

A similar tension between old world and new informs the second essay, "Politics in a New Key: An Austrian Triptych," in which Schorske examined several "new keys" of Viennese political engagement as developed by Georg von Schonerer, Karl Lueger, and Theodor Herzl. Schonerer led German nationalism into a radical and violent anti-Semitism. Lueger appropriated the hate politics of Schonerer to become mayor of Vienna in 1897, an election ratified by the emperor. Herzl was the father of Zionism. Treating the three men, two anti-Semites and the father of Zionism, in the same "key" surprised many readers. But for Schorske they were pioneers of "post-rational politics." The key to their success was their ability to summon from the vasty deep of popular feeling a torrent of unconscious fears and violent passions. Each exhorted a mass of followers on a program of fear and emotion, barely nodding toward rational argument. In this context, Schorske quoted Hofmannsthal, "Politics is magic. He who knows how to summon the forces from the deep, him they will follow."[47]

As Sigmund Freud stood at the center of modernist thought, the centerpiece of *Fin-de-Siècle Vienna* was Schorske's essay on Freud. The essay is based on a close reading of a single text, Freud's *The Interpretation of Dreams.* This work, primarily psychological, also had subtle political undertones. Faced with a Viennese establishment that rejected his ideas, Freud retreated from formal politics, but reserved a role for guerrilla warfare. "If I can not shake the higher powers, I will stir up the depths," he wrote in the famous epigram to *The Interpretation of Dreams*. Schorske also links Freud's retreat from politics to a personal crisis resulting from the death of Freud's demanding father, who believed that Freud would never amount to anything. In *The Interpretation of Dreams* Freud offered the liberals an ahistorical explanation why reform has failed. People weren't rational. Understanding this made the liberal failure understandable, though it held little hope for the future. Freud was the classic instance of a Viennese intellectual who retreated from politics in favor of either the psychological or the artistic.[48]

In his essays Schorske usually worked by pairing thinkers or artists. Several instances of this practice can be seen in *Fin-de-Siècle Vienna*, first in the essay that contrasted the careers of urban planners Camillo Sitte and Otto Wagner and their conflicting approaches to *Ringstrasse*. Sitte framed his assessment of Viennese urban life on an appeal to the past, while Wagner advanced a modernist, functionalist architecture. In another essay Schorske studied the painting of Gustav Klimt in ways that bore comparison with Freud. If Freud urged a retreat from the historical to personal, the painter Gustav Klimt used his art to shift from "public ethos to private pathos." The final essay in *Fin-de-Siècle Vienna* examines music and art in a way similar to that of the previous essays. Oskar Kokoschka's expressionist portraits expressed psychological realism; Arnold Schoenberg created a new musical language.

There was no conclusion to *Fin-de-Siècle-Vienna*. The reader finished the book suspended almost in mid-journey. There was no trumpet sounding, no admonition to historians to undertake more interdisciplinary study, and no salutary reminder that history is a mansion with many rooms. Schorske was clearly more interested in the book's intellectual evolution than in its future. He took up the subject of its evolution twice, once in the introduction to *Fin-de-Siècle Vienna* and later in his "Life of Learning" lecture to the American Philosophical Society. In a way his intellectual progress was more important than having a conclusion to the book. In *Fin-de-Siècle Vienna* he chronicled the loss of faith and the psychological, Freudian turn taken by Viennese intellectuals and artists, just as his own intellectual circle in the 1950s, mirroring the country, was suffering its own loss of faith and making its turn to Freud. Vienna at the end of the nineteenth century, then, was almost a dress rehearsal for Schorske's own intellectual experience in the mid-twentieth.

Perhaps the greatest of the synthesizers was William McNeill, and his *The Rise of the West*, the greatest synthesis. *The Rise of the West* was conceived in the 1930s while McNeill was a graduate student, written in the 1950s, and published in 1963. It was also a global history from the beginning of recorded history to the present, a daunting subject, for which he was only partly prepared by his education. His basic undergraduate humanities course at the University of Chicago in the 1930s was almost entirely Western in its orientation, but it was chronologically broad, which would ultimately become quite useful. The course started with the Greeks and swept through the entire breadth of Western civilization. McNeill did study non-Western peasant cultures with the anthropologist Robert Redfield. Redfield wasn't interested in historical development at all, but he was interested in village life in different and remote parts of the world.

McNeill was more influenced by his own reading. While he was a graduate student at Cornell, he stumbled accidentally upon the first three volumes of Toynbee's *A Study of History* while casually perusing the stacks at the White Library. A few years before, he read the work of the other great megahistorian Oswald Spengler, but Spengler had left him cold. Toynbee was an epiphany. It was as if McNeill had encountered his double. With his interest in the rise and fall of civilizations and panoramic vision, Toynbee wrote the history McNeill dreamed one day of writing. "His thoughts were my thoughts, or so it seemed to me when I first read him in my twenties," McNeill later recalled.[49]

In 1947 McNeill was able to meet Toynbee and the two became friends.[50] They talked at length about history, hiked together, even getting lost at one point. In 1950 McNeill spent some time in London and met often with Toynbee to discuss the final volumes of *A Study of History*. While continuing to admire Toynbee's erudition and panoramic vision, McNeill was less enthralled than he had been as a graduate student, and often expressed his reservations about Toynbee's arguments. For the eighth volume, McNeill provided Toynbee with a careful, written criticism of specific problems in the text, and was surprised when Toynbee included a direct transcription of McNeill's remarks in a footnote without taking any account of them in the text.

Writing in the 1950's, McNeill was also influenced by the temper of own times. *The Rise of the West* was written while the West was still rising. The 1950s saw the United States reach the height of its industrial and economic power. *The Rise of the West* may be seen in some sense as the expression of the triumphant American imperialism of the time. It also underscored the need for Americans to be aware of their place in world history and to understand the importance of continuing contact and dialogue with other parts of the world if they wished to maintain that place.[51]

The ambition of *The Rise of the West* was breathtaking. Like Toynbee, McNeill wanted to write a history of the world and was interested in the comparative consideration of the rise and fall of civilizations. Toynbee's perspective was broad, identifying twenty-one developed civilizations and several "arrested civilizations," such as the Eskimos, the Spartans, and the Ottoman Empire. McNeill's was broader, embracing Chinese dynasties, the Mughal and Ottoman Empires, Mongolia, India, the central Asian steppes, North American indigenous cultures, and Japan, as well as the West.

While McNeill was primarily interested in the ability of cultures to absorb new ideas, *The Rise of the West* ranged widely over a multitude of subjects and disciplines. McNeill's exposure while at Cornell to the *histoire totale* of the French *Annalistes* was revealed in his emphasis on the vitality of agricultural innovation in early civilizations. He also discussed common patterns behind the expansion of government in early societies, such as the growth of bureaucracy, professional armies, legal systems, and tax collection. And he also gave serious consideration to the role of religion in creating communities.

The rise of the West remained his central theme, and McNeill found several reasons for Europe's emergence. The first was the deep-rooted tenacity and utter ruthlessness of the European soldiers and adventurers who arrived in Western Hemisphere and behaved as if they had been absolved from ordinary norms of morality. Europeans also possessed a superior maritime technology that enabled them to navigate the immense distances required to explore the world and to chart with reasonable accuracy their discoveries. Finally, the Europeans unwittingly introduced into the Western Hemisphere their most potent weapon, disease. At the time, Cortez assumed that his conquest of the enormous Aztec civilization with just a few hundred men was attributable to his own moral and cultural superiority. But it is now clear that the invisible killers of smallpox and influenza, for which the indigenous population had little resistance, did most of the damage. The swift and brutal conquest of the Western Hemisphere, along with the goods appropriated from the indigenous population, facilitated the development of a market economy. The final stages of the triumph of the West commenced with the emergence of the twin forces of democratic and industrial revolutions.[52]

The overall theme that emerged the most consistently in *The Rise of the West*, however, was the importance of intercultural contact as a motor of social change. Societies that remain closed to outside influence will settle into repetitive and ultimately destructive patterns of behavior in which change will be slow and probably inconsequential. The vitality of a civilization is sustained by its interaction with other cultures and its willingness to assimilate new ideas, technologies, and attitudes from outside civilizations.

Ironically, McNeill's work stood in stark contrast with that of his inspiration, Toynbee. McNeill saw the story from the point of view of the winners; Toynbee saw it from the point of view of the losers. According to Toynbee, studying the history of the Western world in recent times was like watching a train in reverse. In his view the West had been in decline since the Renaissance because of the unwarranted destruction of the medieval religious unity. The Reformation, the scientific revolution, and the Enlightenment, generally regarded as critical moments in the story of human emancipation from empty authority, were to Toynbee simply minor blips in the otherwise fatal path of European decay.[53]

It was this antiliberal, regressive aspect of Toynbee's history that provoked Trevor-Roper's bitter review of *A Study of History*. Trevor-Roper saw the history of the West not as decline, but as the slow, but ultimately successful, battle of individual freedom and initiative against institutional and religious tyranny; Erasmus, Bacon, Montaigne, and Voltaire were Trevor-Roper's heroes, proof that the human spirit was endlessly resilient, that progress and freedom will prevail, and that the iron laws of history could be circumvented.[54]

It was not then an accident that when Trevor-Roper published a front-page review of *The Rise of the West* in the *New York Times Book Review*, it was a rave, and it helped propel *The Rise of the West* at least briefly onto the best-seller lists. Trevor-Roper clearly recognized the massive learning that comprised *The Rise of the West*, but his admiration for the book was also attributable to the fact that McNeill's position was much closer to his than Toynbee's. The West was not in decline; it remained vital. The great achievements of Western culture were undeniable. Most importantly, as long as the West retained its ideal of dynamic interaction and challenge with other cultures, there was no reason to think it could not remain its preeminent position. In the face of the Communist challenge, expressed by cries of "we will bury you," McNeill's argument was reassuring to Trevor-Roper and no doubt to others.

The Rise of the West had little impact on the historical profession. McNeill even doubts whether members of his own department at Chicago took it seriously. The book was long, and the discipline of history had already acquired a high degree of specialization by which historians tended to concentrate on relatively narrow fields and periods. Ironically, the themes of *The Rise of the West* were reiterated from different angles in two other books, *Plagues and Peoples* (1976) and *The Pursuit of Power* (1982), which were well received by the profession.[55] The two books may be regarded as footnotes to *The Rise of the West*. In *Plagues and Peoples* McNeill considered disease an ally in conquest. The introduction, for example, of common Eurasian "childhood diseases" into relatively isolated regions of the Western Hemisphere had a devastating effect on the indigenous population and enabled Europeans to conquer it with relative ease. Thus, civilized, disease-experienced populations have a lethal advantage over isolated communities when the two encounter each other. In *The Pursuit of Power* McNeill argued that a well-armed and equipped invading force has the same lethal effect on an isolated society that disease does. A society that, usually by isolation, has failed to keep up with improvement and innovations in military technology will fall quickly to one that has.

In the 1980s the fate of civilizations again became a subject of public interest. In 1987 Paul Kennedy published *The Rise and Fall of Great Powers*, a book similar in intent to *The Rise of the West*. Like *The Rise of the West*, *The Rise and Fall of Great Powers* was history on a grand scale and an unexpected best-seller. Its popularity derived in part because *The Rise and Fall of Great Powers* resonated as thoroughly with the 1980s as *The Rise of the West* did with the 1960s, and because Kennedy had an even more provocative thesis to propose than McNeill did. Kennedy coined the phrase "imperial overstretch" to designate civilizations that had acquired, usually by conquest, more territory than they could administer effectively. It is easier in historical terms to conquer territory than it is to hold on to it. Holding onto the territory requires the conquering civilization to expend more money through the soldiers, bureaucrats, and tax collectors necessary to administer the conquered land. The insistence on retaining the territory or control of it ultimately diverts attention and resources away from domestic problems, weakening the conquering civilization to the point where it either declines economically or can be conquered by an outside force.

The popularity of Kennedy's book did not stem entirely from its historical outlook; Kennedy argued that the United States was one of those powers that was falling victim to "imperial overstretch." From the Vietnam War to the bombing of Libya, the United States appeared to have committed itself to military superiority and to using it to intervene in events around the world. To achieve that superiority, the United States had indulged in deficit spending on an extravagant scale, allowing numerous domestic ills to fester. The national debt mounted exponentially; the United States was rapidly becoming the world's greatest debtor nation; its infrastructure was crumbling; its educational system was so feeble that a national report argued that someone who had set out deliberately to undermine the country couldn't have done any better than its own educational system already had; the nation could no longer care for its poor or elderly, nor could it take care of the sick.

Kennedy's book had a Toynbeesque quality, though it was far more sophisticated. In the 1980s his view of decline seemed more compelling than McNeill's view of hope. By the beginning of the new century, however, the perspective changed. The United States remained full of problems, but the break-up of the Communist bloc and the Soviet Union and the Asian economic crisis vaulted the United States back to the top of the world. In the 1990s the American economy grew beyond anyone's wildest expectations; the debt was substantially reduced, and the sense of doom that prevailed in the 1980s vanished.

McNeill is perhaps the finest practitioner of historical synthesis. In a generation that savored the exploration of big themes, *The Rise of the West* tackled the biggest. Almost all of McNeill's work is based upon the reading of secondary works, and practically all of the research for *The Rise of the West* or *Plagues and Peoples* could have been done from any good research library.

Synthesis is not an exclusively American phenomenon. English historians used it to rise above the occasionally insular traditions of English historiography. In 1953 a book titled *The Making of the Middle Ages* was published by Hutchinson and Company, an established English academic publishing house. Its author was Richard Southern, at the time a rather obscure Oxford don with only a modest record of publication. Originally commissioned as a textbook, *The Making of the Middle Ages* was quickly recognized as much more, a seminal work, decisively altering the landscape of received opinion about medieval history, and its success catapulted Southern somewhat unwillingly into academic prominence. A recent observer has dubbed Southern "the once and future king" of medieval studies.[56] Still in print after nearly fifty years, *The Making* has gone through more than 30 editions and can still be regarded as one of a half-dozen or so of the best books ever written on the Middle Ages.

What accounts for its success? Part of the answer is quite conventional. The book attacked, with prodigious learning and subtlety, an important subject, the formation of western Europe as a coherent entity from the late tenth through the early thirteenth centuries. During this time leadership roles passed from Germanic rulers and nobles to men of Romance speech who made western Europe "the chief center of political experiment, economic expansion and intellectual discovery." Unlike many English medievalists, Southern had a pan-European vision, ranging widely across the river valleys of France and Germany, the mountains of Italy and the papacy, and to the eastern borders of European Christendom. *The Making* also delivered flashes of profound insight on unexpected topics. A brief discussion of the medieval conception of freedom described the paradox that the more freedom one had the more laws one had to obey. One might have expected it to be the other around. Southern also observed that the celebrated battle of Marathon in 490 B.C. in which the Athenians defeated the Persians receives considerable discussion in historical works. By contrast the medieval battle of Lech in 955 in which Otto the Great of Germany defeated the Magyars is barely noticed in historical annals. In Southern's eyes they should be regarded as equally important. Both were essential in determining and ensuring the territorial boundaries and stability of western Europe.

But a second part of the answer to the question of the appeal of *The Making* concerned its divergence from the main currents of medieval history as they existed in the early 1950s. Medieval historians at the time focused on several themes. The first centered on the assiduous examination of surviving court and administrative records for the major governments of Europe, primarily because these documents had survived in the greatest abundance. Medievalists have often been concerned to elucidate the medieval origins of modern constitutional government. For decades in the Round Room of the Public Record Office in London, one could watch the students of medieval English government poring over these records of early English government. Another subject of great attention is the study of the ideas of the great medieval thinkers. One attraction of this subject is that most of the materials involved in this study are in print and are easily accessible in most university libraries. And of course medievalists have flocked to the study of the church along with the study of church and state relations. By the 1950s there were also smaller groups studying economics, demography, and peasant life as well as those who studied popular religion and the operations of individual dioceses and parishes.

In *The Making of the Middle Ages* Southern eschewed almost all of these themes, and the book reflected his dissatisfaction with traditional emphases, especially those on constitutional and institutional history. Southern devoted much of his attention to such relatively subordinate figures as Peter of Blois, Gratian, and Peter Lombard. At the same time, there was no reference to Thomas Aquinas, the greatest intellectual figure of the Middle Ages, and only one to the Magna Carta, its great document. Such events as the Norman Conquest of England, the evolution of medieval law, and the agricultural and commercial revolutions, received little attention. There was little material included on demography. Nor did Southern display much interest in such prominent political figures as William of Normandy, Henry II of England, or Louis VIII of France, nor in Peter Abelard, second to Aquinas, as the greatest intellectual figure of the period.

Instead, *The Making* endeavored to recreate the mental world of a number of figures, mostly noble and clerical, and usually somewhat modest, of the High Middle Ages. While Southern acknowledged no special debt to them, his book echoed the approach of the great French historian Lucien Febvre and his pupils, who developed the subfield of the history of *mentalités*, the study of the world views and mind-sets of important individuals and groups. Southern's approach very much echoed theirs. For example, Southern devoted a great deal of space to Gregory VII, the powerful pope who tried the most vigorously to assert papal rights against imperial and secular authority. Most historians might have begun with a chronologically based narrative of Gregory's life and achievement. By contrast Southern assumed basic knowledge of Gregory's achievement, and instead related some anecdotes about him and identified some key phrases from his writings ("I have loved righteousness and hated inequality") to indicate the intensity of his personality. At the same time, while Southern was quite interested in the ideas of St. Anselm, Archbishop of Canterbury under Henry I, he was more interested in what they told us about Anselm than in trying to place them, as most historians would, into the context of other lines of medieval thought.

But *The Making* was an idiosyncratic book in many other ways, something rather odd for a historical classic. It assumed a great deal of background knowledge and there were few guideposts in the text to lead the uninitiated reader to the promised land. *The Making* began with of all things a discussion of western Christendom and its neighbors, especially Islam and the Byzantine Empire, a subject generally ignored by most other historians, who maintained a decidedly western focus in their writing.

Another idiosyncratic feature of the book was its presentation. While it was brief (about 250 pages) and engagingly written, locating a thesis statement in it was difficult. The book was more a series of interpretive essays than an integrated whole. While Southern offered an alternative to the political and constitutional emphases of decades of historical writing on the Middle Ages, there was no strident point of departure, no gauntlet thrown down to erring predecessors. If Southern intended a revolution, no more unassuming revolutionary can be imagined.

But the most idiosyncratic feature of the book was the way it abandoned conventional historical narrative. Most historians specify a theme that they wish to develop, cite a barrage of facts and supporting material, consider contradictory evidence and the ideas of other historians and conclude by explaining why their new perspective is infinitely better than the old one. In *The Making* Southern rarely adduced facts to support his generalizations and rarely explained how his ideas fitted into earlier explanatory frameworks. Instead, he often demonstrated his contentions with anecdotes, usually derived from vast reading of printed chronicles. Thus, a point about the importance of marriage in aristocratic life was supported by a lengthy discussion of the problems posed by the marriages of Henry I's bastard daughters. *The Making of the Middle Ages* unfolded by anecdotal illustrations of particular points, almost in the manner of impressionist painter. A point about church power was illustrated with a marvelous story about Pope Leo IX visiting the cathedral city of Rheims on October 1, 1049, the day of the feast of St. Remigius. A large collection of the higher clergy has been summoned to join him. At their convocation he made an unusual request. He asked each bishop and abbot to rise and declare whether they had paid any money to obtain their office. A tense drama ensued in which some clergy tearfully confessed and others engaged in all manner of evasion. The bishop of Langres fled during the night. The anecdote conveys better than any assertion could the personal power and majesty exercised by medieval popes.[57]

This symphony of seemingly disconnected anecdotes and analysis along with the use of relatively subordinate figures gave the books a vague and ethereal quality, which seemed almost deliberate. A discussion of the bonds of medieval society began with a discussion of several episodes in the life of the eleventh century German Agnes of Poitou, not someone that most historians would place in the center of high medieval politics. A chapter on the ordering of Christian life began with the suggestion that church life before the eleventh century could be best glimpsed in Catalonia and followed by a discussion of the importance of a Catalan noble named Wifred the Hairy and his descendants. Neither Catalonia nor Wifred had ever figured greatly if at all in earlier accounts.[58]

But this was so much the charm of *The Making*, to explore other roads, the blue highways and off-ramps of medieval history, to consider who and what had not been considered before, and to consider it in a collective, anecdotal style, derived from extensive reading of printed chronicles and works of other historians in several different languages. Southern's greatest gift seemed to be a sensitivity for the revealing episode, the telling anecdote. This sensitivity was derived in part from the nature of tutorial teaching at Oxford at that time. The superior Oxford tutor possessed the ability to take an otherwise banal and predictable theme, especially one that might appear on final examinations, and make it come alive in terms of an episode or documents. In a sense one was taught idiosyncratically by the idiosyncratic to be idiosyncratic.

Southern's history, like that of the others discussed in this chapter, was different from that of the archivalists and the cultural critics. Southern had studied manuscripts, especially on Anselm, but none of them made it into *The Making of the Middle Ages*. While Southern wished to rescue the Middle Ages from those who thought it was a time of barbarism, there was no cultural criticism in the book either. In *The Making* Southern worked primarily from available printed sources. Southern's pupil Ved Mehta remembers that as he arrived for his tutorial, Southern would almost always be lost in the reading of a medieval chronicle.[59] *The Making of the Middle Ages* was a work of synthesis, a work whereby the historian tried to take a big chunk of history and explain its overall significance.

The greatest of the English synthesizers, however, was Eric Hobsbawm, and his greatest synthesis was contained in his volumes on the nineteenth century, particularly *The Age of Revolution*. Hobsbawm's most recurring historical interest was in the emergence of capitalism. It was he who launched the "crisis of the seventeenth century" debate, later taken up by Trevor-Roper, as an elaboration of the Marxist transition from feudalism to capitalism.

Hobsbawm, like Southern, was repelled by the insular traditions of English historians and repeatedly urged his comrades in the Marxist Historians' Group to situate their understanding of capitalist development in England in the context of European capitalism. It is doubtful that any historian of his time, with the exception of Braudel, can claim Hobsbawm's geographical or chronological range. Hobsbawm has written on topics from England and Europe to the Mediterranean and Latin America. And while his primary focus has been the nineteenth century, he has also published books and articles on other topics from the seventeenth century to the twentieth.

Hobsbawm's enormous range may be attributed to the influence of Maurice Dobb, whose *Studies in the Development of Capitalism* (1946) admonished historians to study the historical development of capitalism in the broadest terms. Himself a master of synthesis, Dobb considered capitalist development in England from the Middle Ages to the Industrial Revolution. In several respects Dobb gave additional substance to ideas already proposed by Marx, such as the class nature of society and the sixteenth-century origin of capitalism. At other points, Dobb struck out on his own. For Dobb, there were two decisive moments in the development of English capitalism, the seventeenth-century revolutions and the Industrial Revolution. By reducing governmental regulation of trade and business, the English revolutions facilitated the dramatic increase in the accumulation of capital that provided the economic base necessary for the Industrial Revolution.[60]

In his article on the seventeenth century crisis Hobsbawm tried to follow Dobb's lead and to rise above the customary narrow boundaries of the English historiography. During the middle of the seventeenth century, as we have seen, monarchies in England, France, the Netherlands, Spain, Portugal, and elsewhere across Europe faced rebellion. Hobsbawm tried to link these rebellions to economic causes, such as business slump, demographic stagnation, agricultural failure, and plague. These economic problems were in turn related to structural weaknesses within the European economies, such as concentration on the marketing of luxury items, wasting money on dicey colonial ventures, and the immobilization of wealth in unproductive resources. In Hobsbawm's view the economic failure of the seventeenth-century economy represented a process of economic natural selection by which capitalism began to emerge. The economic crisis weeded out the more fragile and stagnant economies; the stronger and more adaptable ones, like the Netherlands and Britain, emerged triumphant and capitalist.[61]

Despite the economic advances of the Netherlands and Britain, capitalism remained fairly limited and unsophisticated. Its real emergence, according to Hobsbawm, came in the nineteenth century under the impact of two dynamic revolutions, the French Revolution of 1789 and the Industrial Revolution. In *The Age of Revolution* Hobsbawm considered the impact of these two revolutions in the transformation of the world, particularly their role in the triumph of capitalist industry. While the forces that created the triumph of capitalist industry were already at work before 1789, the greatest strides were taken during the time of what Hobsbawm called the "dual revolutions."[62]

Hobsbawm began by describing the rigid society of the eighteenth-century Old Regime, its overwhelmingly rural orientation, its dominance by parasitical landlords, and its closed system of patronage and advancement. Across Europe nobles used their wealth and the legal system to exclude their baser born rivals from government offices, church positions, and the legal and political systems.

Even before 1789, the system met with opposition. Its greatest opponents were found in the most progressive classes, including merchants, financiers, manufacturers, entrepreneurs, and other elements of the middle classes, although there was occasionally an enlightened nobleman crying for reform. The philosophy of the Enlightenment was the mantra of the opponents of the Old Regime. The great thinkers of the Enlightenment argued for freedom from arbitrary authority, the possibility of advancement in society according to ability, and the right to speak and write freely. It is not accidental that the two chief centers of this ideology were also those of the dual revolution, France and England.

For Hobsbawm, the French Revolution emancipated the middle class from the legal and political tyranny of the landed classes. The Revolution's greatest texts, Rousseau's *The Social Contract*, Sieyes' "What Is the Third Estate?" and "The Declaration of the Rights of Man and Citizen," reflected essentially middle-class interests. After they had seized power from the king, middle-class leaders established a system by which the middle classes could vote and hold office, and they replaced aristocratic privilege and mercantilism with free trade and the elimination of guilds. The prime beneficiaries of the new system were the businessmen, entrepreneurs, and lawyers who had been stifled by the Old Regime. The triumphant middle class, however, ignored the lower classes, denying them the right to vote and doing nothing to alleviate the suffering caused by bad harvests and high prices. Lower-class discontent was picked up by the Jacobins who installed manhood suffrage and price controls to reduce the cost of food and win support from the masses. To eliminate resistance to this radical drift in the Revolution, Robespierre had to implement the Terror. When the Terror exploded out of control, Robespierre's opponents had to eliminate him. By 1795 France faced political chaos. It had tried just about every possible form of government from monarchy, to middle-class constitutionalism, to democracy. None of it had worked, and from 1795 to 1797, French leaders were stymied. In the end Napoleon Bonaparte rescued France from the horns of political dilemma, using military force to seize and to implement many of the goals of the Revolution. Foremost among these goals was the principle of advancement according to ability.

The Industrial Revolution also facilitated the triumph of the middle class, this time in England. The introduction of cheap cotton cloth into the British economy at a time when population was growing rapidly created a demand for goods that the old system of artisanal production could not meet. In its place a series of inventors and investors created a machine technology that could deliver the goods and endless opportunities for those who were astute enough to anticipate consumer demand and the possibilities presented by the new technology. Whether one invested in cotton mills, coal and iron mines, turnpikes, or machine shops, it was now more possible than ever before to get rich through shrewdness and initiative. Mill owners also needed an educated class to manage their work force, to keep their account books, fill their orders, and oversee their operations, thus creating a new, white-collar middle class.

Hobsbawm also considered the impact of the dual revolution upon other aspects of society, such as religion and intellectual life. While Hobsbawm did not try to establish simple cause and effect relationships between social and cultural change, he did see important connections. The most important

tions. Schlesinger was an early member of Harvard's Society of Fellows. Geoffrey Elton arrived in England without knowing a word of English, but within a few weeks had earned a school certificate and within a few years earned a first-class university degree.

It also helps to have inspiring teachers and mentors. To an extent several, including Anne Scott, Schlesinger, McNeill, and Elton, were inspired by their academic fathers. But having good teachers also helped. The History and Literature program at Harvard provided superb teaching for Schlesinger, Edmund Morgan, and Daniel Boorstin. John Hope Franklin was drawn to history by the dynamism of Theodore S. Currier at Fisk College, and Currier even borrowed money to help Franklin go to Harvard. Anne Scott found Oscar Handlin an inspiration throughout her career. Carl Schorske never forgot the dedication of William Scott Ferguson as a teacher, nor did Lawrence Stone forget the stimulation provided by the teaching of John Prestwich.

It also helps to be self-motivated, since many succeeded despite desultory or mixed university experiences. For example, with the exception of those at Balliol College, most of the Oxford historians got very little from their undergraduate experience, and they represent for the most part the last generation of English historians to enter professional history without taking advanced degrees. A first-class undergraduate degree and a research fellowship were what Oxford required for its teaching fellows, and success at the research fellowship required an individual who could learn on his or her own. Trevor-Roper in particular had to learn without supervision and wrote his first book with scarcely any historical training. He was not alone. Geoffrey Elton received barely five minutes of supervision from J.E. Neale, his thesis advisor at the University of London. J.H. Plumb received a little more, two supervisions a term from G.M. Trevelyan, though he ended up with far greater respect and admiration for Trevelyan than Elton did for Neale.

In the United States, J.H. Hexter received little encouragement from his Harvard mentors. John Hope Franklin encountered anti-Semitism at Harvard. At Wisconsin Kenneth Stampp found that while William Best Hesseltine was a superb lecturer, he was a difficult and abrasive mentor. Fortunately, Stampp got along better with others on the Wisconsin faculty. William McNeill arrived at Cornell to find that Carl Becker was well past his prime.

It also helps to have mentoring beyond graduation. R.H. Tawney proved more valuable to Lawrence Stone than most of his Oxford tutors. J.C. Masterman was a poor tutor, but he materialized again and again to help advance Hugh Trevor-Roper's career. Sir Richard Southern was never taught by F.M. Powicke, but Powicke was essential to the development of his career. In some cases members of the group mentored each other. Richard Hofstadter and Kenneth Stampp had a happy convergence at the University of Maryland. They talked history by the hour while reading and criticizing each other's writing. Stampp has acknowledged that after he left Maryland, the contribution of Richard Current to his work became even more important.

The ghosts of several historians loom over the World War II generation. Foremost among these were the twin specters of Charles Beard and R.H. Tawney. Beard was the principal inspiration to the Americans. Stampp and Woodward in particular took their inspiration from Beard's economic interpretation of history and never rejected it. Richard Hofstadter rejected Beard, but his greatest books emerged as he developed the reasons behind that rejection. Beard's influence even reached across the Atlantic, as J.H. Plumb found himself influenced by Beard's work.

Tawney exerted a similar influence on the English. We have already seen his personal magnetism with Lawrence Stone. But far greater was his intellectual influence. Christopher Hill and Hugh Trevor-Roper, along with Stone, were drawn to Tawney's interpretation of the rise of the gentry, even though Trevor-Roper later demolished it. In the same way that Hofstadter was inspired by Beard, much of Trevor-Roper's best work came from his need to find alternative explanations to Tawney's class struggle. Tawney, too, cast a transatlantic spell. Edmund Morgan went to the London School of Economics in the thirties to hear Harold Laski. He discovered Tawney instead.

Lewis Namier was another powerful influence. Along with Beard he championed the use of manuscripts. But, like Beard and Tawney, he also advanced an explanation of historical truth and how it could be discovered. Most people, to Namier, had no principles; they operated primarily on self-interest, which could be uncovered by meticulous examination of the records of an individual's private affairs. Namier's appeal was primarily to the English or to Americans who worked on English history. Christopher Hill still remembers the excitement of the year in which a new book of Namier's appeared at the same time as a new volume of T.S. Eliot's poetry. J.H. Hexter wrote his first book under Namier's influence. And J.H. Plumb devoted his early career to refuting him.

While Beard, Tawney, and Namier were very different as historians, they had one common theme, a theme that is central to the work of the World War II generation. That theme was the notion of submerged reality, meaning that historical truth, like an iceberg, is never what it appears on the surface. For Beard behind the lofty rhetoric of the American founding fathers, the historian must seek an underlying economic motivation; for Tawney behind the platitudes about liberty delivered in the speeches of the members of seventeenth-century English Parliament, was a reality of class tension and convulsive social change. For Namier expressed principles were usually camouflage for self-interest.

The difference between the ideal and the real, surface appearance and underlying reality underscores most of the best work of this generation.

Among the Americans, whether it was Anne Scott's *The Southern Lady*, Stampp's *The Peculiar Institution*, Woodward's *Origins of the New South*, Handlin's *The Uprooted*, or most of Richard Hofstadter's best work, irony, the difference between the stated aims of policy makers or of society's ideals and the reality beneath them, was a theme to which they repeatedly returned. The English were less devoted than the Americans to ironic detachment, but it still played at least a part in some of their work. Christopher Hill often exposed the contradictions between revolutionary rhetoric proclaiming the will of the people and how often the same speakers ignored what the people wanted. Hugh Trevor-Roper, like Conrad in *Heart of Darkness*, was pleased to savor the irony in which the witch hunters who considered themselves enlightened and civilized were in reality committing crimes more sinister and frightening than any committed by the witches they hunted.

Among the Americans, the influence of Reinhold Niebuhr was important. Through World War I and the Great Depression, this generation had lost its faith in human nature and the inevitability of progress. Niebuhr sought a philosophy by which one could retain some hope in a world of unrelenting self-interest. Niebuhr contended that the primary source of evil in the world was not social or political institutions; evil emanated from the imperfections and fallibility of human beings. It was nevertheless the task of democracy to protect the weak from the predatory. Niebuhr thus upheld a philosophy that held no illusions about the ugliness of life and human nature but justified social and political commitment. Richard Hofstadter, Arthur Schlesinger Jr., and Vann Woodward were the historians most influenced by Niebuhr.

Other influences on the work of this generation of historians include Gibbon, Toynbee, Mencken, the *Annales* School of French historians, and sociologists such as R.K. Merton. One might have expected to find Marx on the list, but outside of Hill and Hobsbawm, only a few seem to have read him. Almost all of them gave some thought to Marxist ideas, and a few were in essence *marxisant*, but Marx was himself a turn-off. Several, including Stone and Hexter, tried to read Marx, but gave up the effort.

The path to the pinnacle of the profession was not always straight and unimpeded. Several struggled to make ends meet in the midst of the Depression. There was a great deal of anxiety about finding jobs. World War II interrupted their careers, and the university they entered as teachers was different from our own. In the decade after the war both English and American universities retained an amateur quality, and the best American universities and Oxbridge colleges were still the playgrounds of the privileged. At the same time many American universities that became high-powered were somewhat remote and provincial in the late 1940s. Berkeley had little distinction in the humanities when Kenneth Stampp began teaching there. The Yale history department was highly inbred. The University of Maryland, which would now be regarded by many as a highly desirable place to teach, was in the 1940s an academic backwater, with a heavy teaching load, a tyrannical president, and little institutional support for research.

But skilled in the exposition of historical irony, the World War II generation of historians experienced an irony of their own. They entered teaching during one of the most difficult times in history to begin an academic career, but they pursued their careers during one of the best. While they experienced considerable anxiety about finding jobs, most of them got good jobs fairly quickly. Moreover, for the both the Americans and the English, the university and the historical profession reached the height of their growth and power in the 1960s. Surging enrollments and economic growth allowed for enormous expansion of the university and history departments. The history department at Berkeley, for example, had fifteen regular faculty members in 1941, twenty-five in 1954, and sixty-five by 1970.

John Hope Franklin and the women faced obstacles the others barely had to think about. For Franklin, it was of course the continuing presence of racism that made his career and life difficult. Gertrude Himmelfarb and Anne Scott faced colleagues who occasionally didn't understand their commitment to their children or the different nature of their career paths. Barbara Tuchman did all her work outside the academy and was never really accepted by professional historians, though she probably wasn't particularly bothered by the fact.

The social and cultural changes of the 1960s provided the greatest intellectual challenge to this generation. By the 1960s most had reached the pinnacle of their careers and achievements. But the sixties came for many as a shock to their value systems. While most were liberal, with support for civil rights and sympathies for the antiwar movement, most were irritated by the use of the university as a political tool and the overwhelming hostility to the American system. Even their prize-winning and groundbreaking books came under fire. The warning shots were fired by several critics who found among other things that the history written by the World War II generation was not radical enough.

Now that there is some distance between the publication of their great books and the reaction against some of them, it may be possible fairly to assess their collective achievement. First, they are the generation that moved the most decisively from the narrative, storytelling traditions of Parkman and Trevelyan to the history of themes and problems, such as slavery, the rise of the gentry, the Tudor revolution in government, the Puritans, the rise of fascism, and the transition from feudalism to capitalism. Slavery and race relations naturally engaged the Americans more than the English. Study of the transition from feudalism to capitalism naturally engaged English historians more than Americans. Christopher Hill and Eric Hobsbawm took the lead in asserting its importance in English history while Hugh Trevor-Roper and an American, J.H. Hexter were suspicious of it as an explanatory force.

The World War II generation of historians did not invent new kinds of history, but they were responsible for the elevation of several previously existing types. Foremost among these was a dedication to manuscript research. Before the emergence of this generation, it was possible to write great books based on printed materials. After the publication of such works as *The Tudor Revolution in Government*, *The Peculiar Institution*, or *Origins of the New South*, it became much more difficult.

Other types of history of course continued to be practiced. The historians of the World War II generation were not afraid to take on big subjects, which were often too vast to be approached archivally. Particularly in the 1950s, history as cultural criticism flourished in the hands of Daniel Boorstin, David Potter, Richard Hofstadter, and Arthur Schlesinger Jr. And despite the archival revolution, it was still possible to write great books without manuscripts, as *The Rise of the West*, *From Slavery to Freedom*, *The Guns of August*, and *Fin-de-Siècle Vienna* among others can testify.

Whatever type of history one chose to write, it was almost always about change. "If history is not about change," declared Lawrence Stone with typical boldness, "it is nothing." The favored subjects of the World War II generation of historians were usually either about change, attempts to initiate change, or about things they wanted to change. A later generation of historians sometimes tended to write, especially in the case of Jonathan Clark and the school of English Civil War revisionists, about how little things changed even in revolutionary times. In the histories written by the most recent generation of historians, there were few decisive changes, no Tudor revolution in government, no rise of the gentry, no English Revolution, and no Industrial Revolution.

Both the English and the Americans saw history as a socially purposeful activity, but there was a difference. The Americans tended to see history as the construction of a usable past to assist understanding of contemporary social and political issues and advance social justice. Getting the story straight remained paramount, but once you got it right, you could pursue its contemporary social and political implications. Americans were particularly conscious of the need to study underprivileged groups. Franklin, Stampp, Woodward, and Morgan were all concerned to elucidate the nature of race relations. Woodward also described the plight of poor Southern whites. Oscar Handlin wanted the public to understand the difficulties faced by immigrant groups. Anne Scott believed her work on the Southern lady had a similar purpose in advancing understanding of gender relations. Several of the Americans, especially Daniel Boorstin, Richard Hofstadter, and Arthur Schlesinger Jr., used history as a vehicle to criticize contemporary society. Boorstin celebrated American pragmatism, Schlesinger pleaded for the maintenance of a vital center, and Hofstadter deplored the menace of the masses. Their tradition is today upheld by Gertrude Himmelfarb. Among the English, only

Eric Hobsbawm seems to have a similar view, but civil rights and immigration were not the problems in English society that they were in American.

The English were more interested in the rise and fall of classes. The reason for this difference seems relatively clear. For the most part, this generation of historians did its seminal work in the decade and a half after the end of World War II. During this time the United States reached the zenith of the American Century. The Depression and the Nazis were defeated; the economy boomed. For the Americans, it did seem to some of them that it was time for progress in social justice to match material and economic progress. Race relations and immigration were less compelling issues to the English in the 1950s, and English historians also wrote in the context of decline. While England had survived the Depression and World War II, it had surrendered economic superiority and leadership of the democratic world to the United States. As the English aristocracy and England itself declined in the face of forces that were essentially beyond their control, English historians sought to understand the response of earlier classes to the stresses of other immutable social and economic forces.

From the vantage point of retirement, the members of this generation look uneasily at what their profession has become. Among the Americans, most are dismayed at the fragmentation of the profession, which they attribute primarily to the seeming obsession with race, gender, and ethnicity. Arthur Schlesinger and Gertrude Himmelfarb wrote books to temper some of the most extreme aspects of the new history. For Edmund Morgan the new social history removes from consideration one of history's most critical questions, that of power relationships, since women and minorities were ordinarily not particularly powerful.

Both the English and the Americans share a dismay at the cult of professionalism that pervades recent historical writing, which, ironically, stems in large part from the elevation of archival research for which this generation was largely responsible. Several, such as Hugh Trevor-Roper, J.H. Plumb, and Eric Hobsbawm, long ago warned of the danger of losing the reading public by bombarding it with exhaustively detailed, highly specialized studies. Historians who dare to advance bold hypotheses often find themselves ripped apart by specialists and retreat into either timidity or massively detailed tomes. Historians, remarked Hugh Trevor-Roper, are killing history just as classicists long ago killed the classics.

There are at least some signs that the trend of specialization is being reversed. Works of broad scope and bold generalization that also appeal to the educated public have appeared in recent years from the hands of Steven Ambrose, John Keegan, Paul Kennedy, Edward Countryman, John Patrick Diggins, David Cannadine, and others. Their success suggests that there is again room in the mansion of history for specialist and popular history and that the two need not always be separated.

So there may be at least some hope. Particularly among the Americans, there survives in this generation, a cautious optimism, not only about history, but about the world. Oscar Handlin, the author of *Truth in History*, the most pessimistic jeremiad about the state of the profession in the late 1970s, was still able to write in the 1990s, "my philosophy, such as it is, develops out of the study of the human past which persuades me that, despite the susceptibility to error and despite the frequent risk of failure, man has the capacity to make order and find purposes in the world in which he lives when he uses the power of his reason to do so." In a similar vein, Arthur Schlesinger Jr. has remarked, "I am a short-term pessimist, but a long-term optimist. I think some future crisis will rally the country and bring out new leaders. These are the cycles of history."

While harboring no illusions about the crooked timber of humanity, these remarks echo the novelist William Faulkner in his Nobel Prize acceptance speech, delivered in 1950, as most of this generation entered the prime of their careers and as their generation faced the prospect of nuclear apocalypse. Faulkner asserted that postwar writers of fiction had forgotten the problems of the human heart in conflict with itself and must strive to relearn the old universal truths without which any story is ephemeral and doomed. For the World War II generation of historians the contemporary historian must abandon the narrow and antiquarian and return to subjects that will engage and educate the interested public. Perhaps, like Faulkner, they also believe that historians who follow this advice will demonstrate to that public that human beings will not only endure, they will prevail.

Appendix: Biographies and Selected Works

Daniel J. Boorstin

Born: Atlanta, Georgia, October 1, 1914
Education: A.B., Harvard University, 1934; B.A., Oxford University, 1936; B.C.L., Oxford, 1937; J.S.D., Yale University, 1940

Selected Books:

The Mysterious Science of the Law (1941)
The Lost World of Thomas Jefferson (1948)
The Genius of American Politics (1953)
The Americans: The Colonial Experience (1958)
The Americans: The National Experience (1965)
The Americans: The Democratic Experience.
The Creators (1992)

Richard Cobb

Born: May 20, 1917
Education: Shrewsbury School; B.A., Merton College, Oxford, 1938; research in Paris 1946–55

Selected Books:

L'Armée Révolutionnaire a Lyon (1952)
Les Armées Révolutionnaires (vol. 1, 1961), (vol. 2, 1963)
A Second Identity: Essays on France and French History (1969)
The Police and the People: French Popular Protest, 1789–1820 (1970)
Reactions to the French Revolution (1972)

GORDON CRAIG

Born: Glasgow, Scotland, November 26, 1913
Education: B.A., Princeton University, 1936; M.A., Princeton, 1939; Ph.D.,
Princeton, 1941; B.Litt. (Rhodes Scholar), Oxford University, 1938

Selected Books:

The Politics of the Prussian Army, 1640–1945 (1958)
From Bismarck to Adenauer: Aspects of German Statecraft (1958)
Germany, 1866–1945 (1978)
The Germans (1982)
Force and Statecraft: Diplomatic Problems in Our Time, with Alexander George
(1983)

GEOFFREY ELTON

Born: August 17, 1921
Education: Rydal School, 1939; University of London, B.A., 1943; D. Phil.,
University of London, 1949

Selected Books:

The Tudor Revolution in Government (1953)
England under the Tudors (1955)
Reformation Europe (1963)
The Practice of History (1967)
Policy and Police (1972)
Reform and Reformation: England, 1509–1558 (1977)
F.W. Maitland (1987)

JOHN HOPE FRANKLIN

Born: Rentiesville, Oklahoma, January 2, 1915
Education: A.B., Fisk University, 1935; A.M., Harvard University, 1936; Ph.D.,
Harvard, 1941

Selected Books:

Free Negro in North Carolina (1943)
From Slavery to Freedom (1947)
Militant South (1956)
Reconstruction after the Civil War (1961)
The Emancipation Proclamation (1963)
George Washington Williams: A Biography (1985)

OSCAR HANDLIN

Born: September 29, 1915
Education: B.A., Brooklyn College, 1934; Ph.D., Harvard University, 1939

Selected Books:

Boston's Immigrants (1941)
The Uprooted (1951)
Fire-Bell in the Night: The Crisis in Civil Rights (1964)
The American College and American Culture (1970)
Facing Life: Youth and the Family in American History (1971)
Truth in History (1979)

JACK HEXTER

Born: Memphis, Tennessee, May 25, 1910
Education: B.A., University of Cincinnati, 1931; M.A., Harvard University, 1933; Ph.D., Harvard, 1937.

Selected Books:

The Reign of King Pym (1941)
More's Utopia: The Biography of an Idea (1952)
Reappraisals in History (1961)
The Vision of Politics on the Eve of the Reformation (1973)
On Historians (1979)

JOHN EDWARD CHRISTOPHER HILL

Born: February 6, 1912
Education: St. Peter's School, York, and Balliol College, Oxford; Fellow of All Souls College, Oxford, 1934–38

Selected Books:

The English Revolution, 1640 (1940)
Economic Problems of the Church (1956)
Puritanism and Revolution (1958)
Society and Puritanism in Pre-Revolutionary England (1964)
The World Turned Upside Down (1972)
Liberty against the Law (1996)

GERTRUDE HIMMELFARB

Born: August 8, 1922
Education: B.A., Brooklyn College, 1942; M.A., University of Chicago, 1944;
Ph.D., Chicago, 1950

Selected Books:

Lord Action: A Study in Conscience and Politics (1952)
Darwin and the Darwinian Revolution (1959)
Victorian Minds (1968)
The Idea of Poverty: England in the Early Industrial Revolution (1984)
The New History and the Old (1987)
On Looking into the Abyss (1994)

ERIC HOBSBAWM

Born: June 9, 1917
Education: Cambridge University, B.A., 1938

Selected Books:

Primitive Rebels (1959)
The Age of Revolution (1962)
Captain Swing (1969)
The Age of Capital (1975)
The Age of Empire (1987)
The Age of Extremes: A History of the World, 1914–1991 (1996)

WILLIAM MCNEILL

Born: Octboer 31, 1917
Eduation: B.A., University of Chicago, 1938; M.A., University of Chicago, 1939;
Ph.D., Cornell University, 1947

Selected Books:

The Greek Dilemma: War and Aftermath (1947)
The Rise of the West: A History of the Human Community (1963)
Europe's Steppe Frontier, 1500-1800 (1964)
Venice: The Hinge of Europe, 1091 to 1797 (1974)
Plagues and Peoples (1976)
Pursuit of Power: Technology and Armed Force in Society Since A.D. 1000 (1982)
Arnold J. Toynbee: A Life (1989).
Keeping Together in Time: Dance and Drill in History (1995)

EDMUND S. MORGAN

Born: January 17, 1916
Education: A.B., Harvard University, 1937; Ph.D., Harvard, 1942

Selected Books:

Puritan Family: Religion and Domestic Relations in Seventeenth-Century New England (1944)
The Stamp Act Crisis: Prologue to Revolution, by Morgan with Helen M. Morgan (1953)
The Puritan Dilemma: The Story of John Winthrop (1958)
American Slavery, American Freedom: The Ordeal of Colonial Virginia (1975)
Inventing the People: The Rise of Popular Sovereignty in England and America (1988)

JOHN PLUMB

Born: August 20, 1911
Education: B.A., University College, 1933; Ph.D. Leicester; Christ College, Cambridge, 1937; Ehrman Research Fellow, King's College, Cambridge, 1939–46

Selected Books:

England in the Eighteenth Century (1950)
West African Explorers (1951)
Walpole (1956)
The First Four Georges (1956)
The Renaissance (1961)
The Death of the Past (1969)

DAVID M. POTTER

Born: Augusta, Georgia, December 6, 1910
Education: A.B., Emory University, 1932; M.A., Yale University, 1933; Ph.D., Yale, 1940

Selected Books:

Lincoln and His Party in the Secession Crisis (1942)
People of Plenty: Economic Abundance and the American Character (1954)
The South and the Sectional Conflict (1968)
The Impending Crisis, 1848–1861, completed and edited by Don Fehrenbacher (1976)

ARTHUR M. SCHLESINGER JR.

Born: October 15, 1917
Education: B.A., Harvard University, 1938; Henry Fellow, Cambridge University, 1939; Society of Fellows, Harvard, 1940–43.

Selected Books:

Orestes A. Brownson: A Pilgrim's Progress (1939)
The Age of Jackson (1946)
The Crisis of the Old Order, 1919–1933 (1957)
The Coming of the New Deal (1959)
The Politics of Upheaval (1960)
A Thousand Days: John F. Kennedy in the White House (1965)
The Disuniting of America (1993)

CARL SCHORSKE

Born: March 15, 1915
Education: A.B., Columbia University, 1936; M.A., Harvard University, 1937; Ph.D., Harvard, 1950

Selected Books:

The Problem of Germany (1947)
German Social Democracy (1955)
Fin-de-Siècle Vienna (1980)
Thinking with History (1998)

ANNE FIROR SCOTT

Born: April 24, 1921
Married: Andrew Mackay Scott, June 2, 1947
Education: A.B., University of Georgia, 1940; M.A., Northwestern University, 1944; Ph.D., Radcliffe College, 1958

Selected Books:

The Southern Lady (1970)
One-Half the People, with Andrew MacKay Scott (1974)
Making the Invisible Woman Visible (1984)

RICHARD SOUTHERN

Born: February 1912
Education: Royal Grammar School, Newcastle upon Tyne, and Balliol College, Oxford; Jr. Research Fellow, Exeter College, Oxford, 1933–37; studied at Paris, 1933–34, and Munich, 1935

Selected Books:

The Making of the Middle Ages (1953)
Western Views of Islam in the Middle Ages (1962)
St. Anselm and His Biographer (1963)
Western Society and the Church in the Middle Ages (1970)
Robert Grosseteste: The Growth of an English Mind in Medieval Europe (1986)
Scholastic Humanism and the Unification of Europe (1995)

KENNETH STAMPP

Born: July 12, 1912
Education: Milwaukee State Teachers' College; B.A., University of Wisconsin, Madison, 1935; Ph.D., Wisconsin, 1942.

Selected Books:

Indiana Politics during the Civil War (1949)
And the War Came: The North and the Secession Crisis, 1860–1861 (1950)
The Peculiar Institution: Slavery in the Ante-Bellum South (1956)
The Era of Reconstruction, 1865–1877 (1965)
The Imperilled Union: Essays on the Background of the Civil War (1980)
America in 1857: A Nation on the Brink (1990)

LAWRENCE STONE

Born: December 4, 1919
Education: B.A., M.A., Christ Church, Oxford, 1946.

Selected Books:

An Elizabethan: Sir Horatio Palavicino (1956)
The Crisis of the Aristocracy (1965)
The Causes of the English Revolution, 1529–1642 (1972)
The Family, Sex, and Marriage in England, 1500-1800 (1985)
The Past and the Present (1981)
The Road to Divorce: England, 1530–1987 (1990)
Uncertain Unions and Broken Lives: Marriage and Divorce in England (1995)

HUGH TREVOR-ROPER

Born: Glanton, Northumberland, January 15, 1914
Education: Charterhouse and Christ Church, Oxford; Research Fellow, Merton
College, Oxford 1937–39

Selected Books:

Archbishop Laud (1940)
The Last Days of Hitler (1947)
The Gentry, 1540–1640 (1954)
Historical Essays (1957)
Religion, the Reformation and Social Change (1967)
Renaissance Essays (1985)

BARBARA TUCHMAN

Born: January 30, 1912
Education: B.A., Radcliffe College, 1933

Selected Books:

Bible and Sword (1956)
The Zimmerman Telegram (1958)
The Guns of August (1962)
Stillwell and the American Experience in China (1971)
A Distant Mirror (1978)

C. VANN WOODWARD

Born: November 13, 1908
Education: B.Phil., Emory University, 1930; M.A., Columbia University, 1932;
Ph.D., University of North Carolina, 1937

Selected Books:

Tom Watson, Agrarian Rebel (1938)
Reunion and Reaction (1950)
Origins of the New South, 1877–1913 (1951)
The Strange Career of Jim Crow (1955)
The Burden of Southern History (1960)
Mary Chestnut's Civil War (1982)
Thinking Back: The Perils of Writing History (1986)

NOTES

1. BEGINNINGS

1. Lawrence Stone, "As Seen by Himself," in A.L. Beier, David Cannadine, and James Rosenheim, eds., *The First Modern Society: Essays in English History in Honour of Lawrence Stone* (Cambridge: Cambridge University Press, 1989), p. 576.

2. Stone, "As Seen by Himself," p. 577.

3. Ved Mehta, *Up at Oxford* (New York: Norton, 1993), p. 156.

4. Donald Pennington and Keith Thomas, eds., *Puritans and Revolutionaries: Essays in Seventeenth Century History in Honour of Christopher Hill* (Oxford: Oxford University Press, 1978), p. 4.

5. Hugh Lloyd-Jones, Valerie Pearl, and Blair Worden, eds., *History and Imagination: Essays in Honor of H.R. Trevor-Roper* (New York: Holmes and Meier, 1982), p. 357.

6. William Palmer, "Interview with Hugh Trevor-Roper," May 16, 1996. See also Hugh Trevor-Roper, "Interview with Blair Worden" (London, 1993).

7. Palmer, "Interview with Sir Richard Southern," May 17, 1995.

8. Richard Cobb, *Still Life: Sketches from a Tunbridge Wells Childhood* (London: Chatto and Windus, 1983); Cobb, *Something to Hold Onto* (London: John Murray, 1988); Cobb's early life is also discussed in his posthumous autobiography *The End of the Line* (London: John Murray, 1997).

9. Cobb, *A Classical Education* (London: Chatto and Windus, 1985).

10. Neil McKendrick, ed., *Historical Perspectives: Studies in English Thought and Society in Honour of J.H. Plumb* (London: Europa, 1974), pp. 4–5.

11. Pat Thane, "Interview with Eric Hobsbawm" (London: Institute of Historical Research, 1988).

12. My sources for Geoffrey Elton's childhood include Barret Beer, "Geoffrey Elton," in Walter Arnstein, ed., *Recent Historians of Great Britain: Essays on the Post-1945 Generation* (Ames: Iowa State University Press, 1990), pp. 13–35; DeLloyd Guth, ed., *Elton Remembrances* (Washington, D.C.: privately printed, 1995); and a letter from David L. Smith of Selwyn College, Cambridge, who was kind enough to share with me his notes of a meeting with Geoffrey

Elton in August 1994, about four months before his death, in which Elton discussed his childhood at length.

13. Information on Barbara Tuchman's childhood can be found in Barbara W. Tuchman, *Practicing History: Selected Essays by Barbara W. Tuchman* (New York: Alfred Knopf, 1981), p. 13; *Newsweek*, Mar. 12, 1984; *Times* (London), Feb. 8, 1989, pp. 16f.

14. Richard Bushman et al., *Uprooted Americans: Essays to Honor Oscar Handlin* (Boston: Little, Brown, 1979), pp. 4–5.

15. Carl Schorske, *A Life of Learning: The Charles Homer Haskins Lecture* (Washington, D.C.: American Council of Learned Societies, 1987), pp. 1–3.

16. Lynne Cheney, "A Conversation with Gertrude Himmelfarb," *Humanities* 12, no. 3 (May–June 1991): 8–9; Jacob Weisberg, "The Family Way," *New Yorker*, Oct. 21 and 28, 1996, p. 182.

17. Information about Richard Hofstadter's youth may be found in Daniel Joseph Singal, "Beyond Consensus: Richard Hofstadter and American Historiography," *American Historical Review* 89, no. 4 (Oct. 1984): 976–1004; Susan Stout Baker, *Radical Beginnings: Richard Hofstadter and the 1930s* (Westport, Conn.: Greenwood Press, 1985).

18. Baker, *Radical Beginnings*, p. 11.

19. Ibid., p. 14.

20. J.H. Hexter, "Call Me Ishmael; or, A Rose by Any Other Name," *American Scholar*, (Summer 1983), pp. 341–42.

21. Palmer, "Interview with J. H. Hexter," Dec. 19, 1995.

22. John Sproat, "Kenneth Stampp," in Clyde Wilson, ed., *Dictionary of Literary Biography* (Detroit: Gale Research, 1983), 17:401.

23. Palmer, "Interview with Gordon Craig," Jan. 4, 1996.

24. Information about William McNeill's childhood comes from interviews in the *Historian* 53, no. 1 (Autumn 1990): 2–4; and Palmer, "Interview with McNeill," Dec. 22, 1995.

25. David Courtwright, "Fifty Years of American Colonial History: An Interview with Edmund S. Morgan," *William and Mary Quarterly*, 3d ser., 44, no. 2 (Apr., 1987): 337–38.

26. Edwin Miles, "Arthur M. Schlesinger, Jr.," in Wilson, ed., *Dictionary of Literary Biography*, 17:384.

27. John Herbert Roper, "C. Vann Woodward's Early Career: The Historian As Dissident Youth," *Georgia Historical Quarterly* 64 (Spring 1980): 7–21; Elizabeth Muhlenfeld, "C. Vann Woodward," in Wilson, ed., *Dictionary of Literary Biography*, 17:465–82; C. Vann Woodward *Thinking Back: The Perils of Writing History* (Baton Rouge: Louisiana State University Press, 1986).

28. Roper, "C. Vann Woodward," pp. 8–9.

29. David Potter, *The South and Sectional Conflict* (Baton Rouge, 1968), p. v.

30. Information about Anne Firor Scott's life can be found in her essay "A Historian's Odyssey," in her collection *Making the Invisible Woman Visible* (Urbana and Chicago: University of Illinois Press, 1984).

31. Frank Annunziata, "Daniel Boorstin," in Wilson, ed., *Dictionary of American Literary Biography*, 17:79.

32. Daniel Boorstin, *The Daniel Boorstin Reader* (New York: Vintage, 1996), pp. 893, 898–99.

33. The information on John Hope Franklin's youth is taken from John Hope Franklin, *A Life of Learning: The Charles Homer Haskins Lecture* (New York, 1988), pp. 1–17; and *My Life and an Era: The Autobiography of Buck Colbert Franklin* (Baton Rouge: Louisiana State University Press, 1997).

2. HARVARD, THE 1930S, AND THE MAKING OF A HISTORICAL GENERATION

1. Some other historians of renown who studied at Harvard in the 1930s include John King Fairbank (b. 1907), Edwin Reischauer (b. 1910), Myron Gilmore (b. 1910), and H. Stuart Hughes (b. 1916). Harvard also produced stars in other disciplines in the 1930s, including a cluster of Supreme Court justices and Nobel prize winners, along with such other figures of distinction as John Fitzgerald Kennedy (b. 1917), David Riesman (b. 1909), Robert K. Merton (b. 1910), Robert Lowell (b. 1917), and Leonard Bernstein (b. 1918).

2. Hexter, "Call Me Ishmael," p. 342.

3. H. Stuart Hughes, *Gentleman Rebel: The Memoirs of H. Stuart Hughes* (New York: Ticknor and Fields, 1990). p. 109.

4. Edwin O. Reischauer, *My Life between Japan and America* (New York: Harper and Row, 1986), p. 40.

5. Bernard Bailyn et al., *Glimpses of the Harvard Past* (Cambridge: Harvard University Press, 1986), pp. 126–28; Henry F. May's memoir, *Coming to Terms: A Study in History and Memory* (Berkeley: University of California Press, 1987), also contains recollections about Harvard in the 1930s.

6. John King Fairbank, *Chinabound: A Fifty-Year Memoir* (New York: Harper and Row, 1982), pp. 144–45.

7. Ibid., pp. 143–44.

8. William Langer, *In and Out of the Ivory Tower* (New York: Watson Academic Publications, 1977), p. 165.

9. Richard M. Dorson, *The Birth of American Studies: Inaugural Address Delivered at the Opening of the American Studies Center, Warsaw University, Warsaw Poland, October 5, 1976* (Bloomington: Indiana University Press, 1981), pp. 5–7; Frederick C. Stern, *F.O. Matthiessen: Christian Socialist As Critic* (Chapel Hill: University of North Carolina Press, 1981), pp. 8–9.

10. Schorske, *A Life of Learning*, pp. 2–5.

11. Ibid., p. 7.

12. Ibid.

13. Ibid. For a discussion of the role played by objectivity issues in the development of this generation of historians, see Peter Novick, *That Noble Dream: The Objectivity Question and the American Historical Profession* (Cambridge: Cambridge University Press, 1987).

14. Richard Bushman, et al., eds., *Uprooted Americans*, p. 4.

15. Oscar Handlin, "A Career at Harvard," *American Scholar*, (Winter 1996), pp. 47–48.

16. Ibid., p. 49.

17. Bushman et al., eds., *Uprooted Americans*, p. 4.

18. Handlin, "A Career at Harvard," p. 49.

19. Bushman et al., eds., *Uprooted Americans*, pp. 4–5.

20. Arnold Shankman, "Oscar Handlin," in Wilson, ed., *Dictionary of Literary Biography*, 17:192.

21. Josef Konvitz, *What Americans Should Know: Western Civilization or World History: Proceedings of a Conference at Michigan State University* (Lansing: Board of Trustees, Michigan State University, 1985), pp. 180, 197 n. 2.

22. Palmer, "Interview with Hexter," Dec. 19, 1995.

23. Ibid.

24. Ibid.

25. Ibid.; Novick, *That Noble Dream*, p. 172.

26. Palmer, "Interview with Hexter," Dec. 19, 1995; J.H. Hexter, *The Reign of King Pym* (Cambridge, Mass., 1941).

27. Ibid.

28. John Hope Franklin, *A Life of Learning: The Charles Homer Haskins Lecture* (New York, 1988), pp. 5–6.

29. Ibid., p. 7.

30. Ibid.

31. Ibid., p. 8.

32. Ibid.

33. Ibid.

34. Ibid., p. 9.

35. Tuchman, *Practicing History*, p. 14.

36. Ibid.

37. Ibid., p. 15.

38. Ibid., pp. 15–16.

39. Ibid., p. 16.

40. *Newsweek*, Mar. 12, 1984, p. 82.

41. Courtwright, "Fifty Years of American Colonial History," p. 338.

42. Kenneth S. Lynn, "Perry Miller," *American Scholar* (Spring 1983), pp. 221–27.

43. Perry Miller, *Orthodoxy in Massachusetts* (Gloucester, Mass.: Peter Smith, 1933), leading to the more famous *The New England Mind: The Seventeenth Century* (New York: Macmillan, 1939).

44. For Matthiessen, see Kenneth S. Lynn, "F.O. Matthiessen," *American Scholar* (Winter 1976–77), pp. 86–93.

45. Courtwright, "Fifty Years of American History," p. 340.

46. Ibid., pp. 340–41.

47. For more about Tawney, see Ross Terrill, *R.H. Tawney and His Times: Socialism as Fellowship* (London: Deutsch, 1974).

48. Ibid., pp. 341–42.

49. Ibid., p. 342.

50. Ibid., p. 343.

51. Ibid., p. 344.

52. Palmer, "Interview with Arthur Schlesinger Jr.," July 2, 1996.

53. Ibid.

54. Miles, "Arthur M. Schlesinger, Jr.," p. 384.

55. Palmer, "Interview with Schlesinger," July 2, 1996.

56. *Orestes A. Brownson: A Pilgrim's Progress* (Boston, 1939), interview with Schlesinger, July 2, 1996; Miles, "Arthur M. Schlesinger, Jr.," in Wilson, ed. *Dictionary of Literary Biography*, p. 384.

57. All of the material presented here on Daniel Boorstin's career in the 1930s may be found in Annunziata, "Daniel J. Boorstin," pp. 79–85.

58. Roger Adelson, "Interview with Caroline Walker Bynum," *Historian* 59, no. 1 (Fall 1996): 7.

59. Richard Norton Smith, *The Harvard Century: The Making of a University to a Nation* (New York: Simon and Schuster, 1986), p. 120; Palmer, "Interview with Schlesinger," July 2, 1996.

60. Schlesinger has suggested that Marxism was practically a badge of honor among English historians in the 1930s, while Marxism at Harvard was something to be concealed. For a discussion of British Marxist historians, all of whom were university undergraduates in the 1930s, see Harvey J. Kaye, *The British Marxist Historians* (New York: St. Martin's Press, 1985). Hugh Trevor-Roper's first book, *Archbishop Laud* (London: MacMillan and Company, 1940), was written in a crude Marxist framework, which Trevor-Roper came to regret, but never tried to disguise. See Trevor-Roper's introduction to the third edition of *Archbishop Laud*, published in 1962.

3. OTHER AMERICAN COLLEGES AND UNIVERSITIES

1. Palmer, "Interview with Gordon Craig," Jan. 4, 1996.

2. Palmer, "Interview with William McNeill," Dec. 22, 1995; Roger Adelson, "Interview with William McNeill," *Historian* 52, no. 1 (Autumn 1990): 5–7.

3. "Interview with William McNeill," *Intinerario* 3, no. 1(1979): 19.

4. Ibid.

5. Ibid., p. 20.

6. Adelson, "Interview with William McNeill," *Historian*, p. 6.

7. This and several recollections of Becker that follow came from the late Carl G. Gustavson, emeritus professor of history at Ohio University and, like McNeill, a Becker student at Cornell in the late 1930s and early 1940s.

8. L. Perry Curtis, ed., *The Historian's Workshop: Original Essays by Sixteen Historians* (New York: Alfred Knopf, 1970), p. 170.

9. Adelson, "Interview with William McNeill," *Historian*, p. 5.

10. Ibid., p. 5.

11. Roger Adelson, "Interview with C. Vann Woodward," *The Historian* 54, no. 1 (Autumn 1991): 3.

12. Woodward, *Thinking Back*, pp. 21, 85.

13. Palmer, "Interview with C. Vann Woodward," Dec. 19, 1995.

14. Ibid.

15. Ibid.

16. Elizabeth Muhlenfeld, "C. Vann Woodward," in Wilson, ed., *Dictionary of Literary Biography*, 17:469.

17. Palmer, "Interview with Woodward," Dec. 19, 1995.

18. Woodward, *Thinking Back*, p. 18.

19. Ibid., pp. 18–19.

20. Adelson, "Interview with C. Vann Woodward," *Historian*, pp. 9–10.

21. Woodward, *Thinking Back*, pp. 21–22.

22. Ibid., p. 22.

23. *Historian*, p. 9.

24. Palmer, "Interview with Woodward," Dec. 19, 1995.

25. Mark T. Carleton, "David Potter," in Wilson, ed., *Dictionary of Literary Biography*, 17:366.

26. Anne Firor Scott, "A Historian's Odyssey," p. xiii.

27. Ibid., pp. xiii–xiv.

28. Palmer, "Interview with Kenneth Stampp," Dec. 17, 1995.

29. Ibid.; Sproat, "Kenneth M. Stampp," pp. 401–2.

30. Susan Stout Baker, *Radical Beginnings*, 42–43.

31. Daniel Joseph Singal, "Beyond Consensus: Richard Hofstadter and American Historiography," *American Historical Review* 89, no. 4 (Oct. 1984): 976–1004.

32. Baker, *Radical Beginnings*, p. 49.

33. Paula S. Fass, "Richard Hofstadter," in Wilson, ed., *Dictionary of Literary Biography*, 17:213.

34. Alfred Kazin, *New York Jew* (New York, 1978), p. 15.

35. Quoted in Eric Foner, introduction to Richard Hofstadter, *Social Darwinism in American Thought* (Boston, 1992), p. x.

36. Singal, "Beyond Consensus," p. 980.

37. Fass, "Richard Hofstadter," p. 220.

38. Singal, "Beyond Consensus," pp. 980–81.

39. Foner, introduction, p. x.

40. Singal, "Beyond Consensus," p. 981.

41. Foner, introduction, p. xi.

42. Ibid.

43. Ibid.

44. Ibid., p. xii.

45. Ibid., pp. 12–13.

46. Jacob Weisberg, "The Family Way," p. 182.

47. Lynne Cheney, "A Conversation with Historian Gertrude Himmelfarb," p. 9.

48. Ibid.

4. The English University Experience in the 1930s

1. Curtis, ed., *Historian's Workshop*, p. 250.

2. Ved Mehta, *Up at Oxford*, p. 431.

3. Reba Soffer, *Discipline and Power: The University, History, and the Making of an English Elite, 1870–1930* (Palo Alto: Stanford University Press, 1994).

4. J.C. Masterman, *On the Chariot Wheel: An Autobiography* (Oxford: Oxford University Press, 1975), p. 15. Curtis, ed., *Historian's Workshop*, p. 251.

5. Masterman, *On the Chariot Wheel*, p. 152.

6. Lloyd-Jones, Pearl, and Worden, eds., *History and Imagination*, p. 358. Palmer, "Interview with Hugh Trevor-Roper," May 16, 1996.

7. Palmer, "Interview with Trevor-Roper," May 16, 1996.

8. Ibid.

9. Lloyd-Jones, Pearl, and Worden, eds., *History and Imagination*, pp. 358–59.

10. Palmer, "Interview with Trevor-Roper," May 16, 1996.

11. Palmer, "Interview with Lawrence Stone," June 8, 1996.

12. Lawrence Stone, "As Seen by Himself," p. 578.

13. Lawrence Stone to the author, Dec. 28, 1995.

14. Palmer, "Interview with Stone," June 8, 1996.

15. Mehta, *Up at Oxford*, pp. 151–52.

16. Pennington and Thomas, eds., *Puritans and Revolutionaries*, p. 1.

17. Ibid., p. 2.

18. Kaye, *The British Marxist Historians*; Mehta, *Up at Oxford*, p. 156; Peter Brown to the author, Apr. 1, 1996.

19. Kaye, *British Marxist Historians*, p. 102.

20. Mehta, *Up at Oxford*, p. 157; Palmer, "Interview with Sir Richard Southern," May 17, 1996.

21. Mehta, *Up at Oxford*, p. 158; Christopher Hill to the author, Aug. 6, 1996; Pennington and Thomas, eds., *Puritans and Revolutionaries*, p. 3.

22. Alastair MacLachlan, *The Rise and Fall of Revolutionary England* (New York: St. Martin's Press, 1996), p. 47.

23. Mehta, *Up at Oxford*, pp. 157–58; MacLachlan, *Rise and Fall*, p. 58.

24. Courtwright, "Fifty Years of American Colonial History," p. 341.

25. Ved Mehta, *Fly and the Fly-Bottle: Encounters with British Intellectuals* (Boston: Little, Brown, 1962), pp. 163–67; Ross Terrill, *R.H. Tawney and His Times*.

26. Pennington and Thomas, eds., *Puritans and Revolutionaries*, pp. 3–4.

27. Palmer, "Interview with Southern," May 17, 1996.

28. Ibid.; Richard Southern, "Vivien Hunter Galbraith," *Proceedings of the British Academy*, 45 (1964): 397–425.

29. Palmer, "Interview with Southern," May 17, 1996.

30. Ibid.

31. Richard Cobb, *A Second Identity: Essays on France and French History* (Oxford: Oxford University Press, 1969), p. 2.

32. Ibid., pp. 3–6.

33. A.J.P. Taylor, *A Personal History* (New York: Atheneum, 1983), p. 141; *The Times* (London), Jan. 17, 1996.

34. Materials on J.H. Plumb's university experience were taken from Neil McKendrick, ed., *Historical Perspectives*, pp. 4–5; J.H. Plumb, *The Making of a*

Historian: The Collected Essays of J.H. Plumb (Athens: University of Georgia Press, 1989), pp. 3–9; Palmer, "Interview with J.H. Plumb," May 19, 1997.

35. Pat Thane, "Interview with Eric Hobsbawm" (London, 1988).

36. Material for Geoffrey Elton's undergraduate career is taken from DeLloyd Guth, ed., *Elton Remembrances;* and a letter to the author from David L. Smith of Selwyn College, Cambridge, describing a conversation he had with Elton in August 1994 about four months before Elton's death about this period.

5. V WAS FOR VICTORY

1. Palmer, "Interview with J.H. Hexter," Dec. 9, 1995.

2. Langer, *In and Out of the Ivory Tower,* pp. 180–81.

3. Palmer, "Interview with Stone," June 5, 1996.

4. Material on Stone's military exploits may be found in Stone, "As Seen by Himself," pp. 580–81.

5. Information about Geoffrey Elton's military service comes from DeLloyd Guth, ed., *Elton Remembrances;* and from a letter to the author from David L. Smith, who related a conversation he had with Elton shortly before his death about these matters.

6. Palmer, "Interview with Southern," May 17, 1996.

7. Palmer, "Interview with Simon Schama," Jan. 22, 1997.

8. Christopher Hill to the author, July 9, 1996.

9. Information on the war experiences of Cobb may be found in his *A Second Identity,* pp. 22–33.

10. Material on Hugh Trevor-Roper's military career may be found in the introduction to his *The Last Days of Hitler,* 6th ed. (Chicago, 1992), pp. 10–52. Beginning with the third edition, all subsequent editions contain this introduction. Details on his earlier career may be found in Lord Dacre of Glanton, "Sideways into the S.I.S.," in Hayden B. Peake and Samuel Halpern, eds., *In the Name of Intelligence: Essays in Honor of Werner Pforzheimer* (Washington, D.C.: NIBC Press, 1995). I am grateful to Lord Dacre for giving me a copy of this article.

11. Malcolm Muggeridge, *Like It Was: The Diaries of Malcolm Muggeridge* (New York: Morrow, 1982), p. 284.

12. Adelson, "Interview with William McNeill," pp. 1–16; and my interview with McNeill, Dec. 22, 1995.

13. Materials for Craig's service during World War II are derived from my interview with him, Jan. 4, 1996.

14. Langer, *In and Out of the Ivory Tower,* pp. 180–82.

15. Palmer, "Interview with Craig," Jan. 4, 1996.

16. H. Stuart Hughes, *Gentleman Rebel,* p. 137.

17. Schorske, *A Life of Learning,* p. 8.

18. Adelson, "Interview with C. Vann Woodward," p. 11.

19. Ibid.

20. Palmer, "Interview with Woodward," Dec. 19, 1995.

21. Palmer, "Interview with Schlesinger," July 2, 1996.

22. Miles, "Arthur M. Schlesinger, Jr.," p. 385; Palmer, "Interview with Schlesinger," July 2, 1996.

23. Courtwright, "Fifty Years of American History," pp. 344–45; Palmer, "Interview with Edmund Morgan," Dec. 18, 1995.

24. Materials on Barbara Tuchman's wartime activities can be found in the *Times* (London), Feb. 8, 1989, pp. 16f.; *New York Times*, Feb. 7, 1989, A1.

25. Scott, "A Historian's Odyssey," p. xiv.

26. Franklin, *Life of Learning*, pp. 9, 13–15.

27. Annunziata, "Daniel J. Boorstin," p. 80.

28. Oscar Handlin to the author, Jan. 20, 1997.

29. Novick, *That Noble Dream*, p. 247.

30. Palmer, "Interview with Stampp," Mar. 24, 1997; Novick, *That Noble Dream*, p. 248.

31. Sproat, "Kenneth M. Stampp," p. 402; interview with Stampp, Dec. 17, 1995; Baker, *Radical Beginnings*, p. 177.

32. Novick, *That Noble Dream*, pp. 321–22; Baker, *Radical Beginnings*, p. 180.

33. Baker, *Radical Beginnings*, p. 258.

34. Ibid., pp. 175–88.

35. Ibid., pp. 176–77.

36. Ibid., pp. 178–79, 182.

37. Kazin, *New York Jew*, p. 17.

38. Palmer, "Interview with Trevor-Roper," May 16, 1996.

39. Palmer, "Interview with Stone," Dec. 7, 1995.

40. Palmer, "Interview with McNeill," Dec. 21, 1995.

6. Building Careers in the Postwar World

1. Scott, "A Historian's Odyssey," p. xiv.

2. Palmer, "Interview with Stampp," Mar. 24, 1997.

3. Novick, *That Noble Dream*, pp. 315–18. Read is quoted on p. 318.

4. Ellen W. Schrecker, *No Ivory Tower: McCarthyism and the Universities* (Oxford: Oxford University Press, 1986); see also Michael Rogin, *The Intellectuals and McCarthy: The Radical Specter* (Cambridge: Harvard University Press, 1967).

5. For Tuchman, see *Newsweek*, Mar. 12, 1984; *Times* (London), Feb. 8, 1989, pp. 16f.; *New York Times*, Feb. 7, 1989, p. B7.

6. Palmer, "Interview with Craig," Jan. 4, 1996; Palmer, "Interview with Edmund Morgan," Dec. 18, 1995; Palmer, "Interview with Schlesinger," July 8, 1996; Palmer, "Interview with Hexter," Dec. 19, 1995.

7. Carleton, "David M. Potter," p. 366.

8. Shankman, "Oscar Handlin," pp. 193–95.

9. Handlin, "A Career at Harvard," p. 50.

10. The material on Franklin comes from his *A Life of Learning*, pp. 11–17.

11. Annunziata, "Daniel J. Boorstin," pp. 81–82.

12. Novick, *That Noble Dream*, pp. 325–28; Schrecker, *No Ivory Tower*, pp. 41–42, 44.

13. The material on Scott in this section comes from her "A Historian's Odysessy," pp. xv–xvii.

14. Palmer, "Interview with McNeill," Dec. 22, 1995; Adelson, "Interview with William McNeill," pp. 8–9.

15. The material in this section on Morgan may be found in Courtwright, "Fifty Years of American Colonial History"; Palmer, "Interview with Morgan, Dec. 16, 1995; William D. Liddle, "Edmund S. Morgan," in Wilson, ed., *Dictionary of American Literary Biography*, 17:287–89

16. The material on Schorske's early career may be found in his *A Life of Learning*, pp. 8–13.

17. Carl E. Schorske, *German Social Democracy* (New York, 1955).

18. Palmer, "Interview with Craig," Jan. 4, 1996; and Norman Cantor, *Inventing the Middle Ages* (New York: William Morrow, 1991), pp. 257–63.

19. Fass, "Richard Hofstadter," p. 217.

20. Richard Hofstadter and Walter Metzger, *The Development of Academic Freedom* (New York: Columbia University Press, 1955).

21. Palmer, "Interviews with Stampp," Dec. 17, 1995; Mar. 24, 1997.

22. Novick, *That Noble Dream*, p. 322.

23. The story of the Berkeley history department in the 1950s and 1960s is told in Gene A. Brucker, Henry F. May, and David A. Hollinger, *History at Berkeley: A Dialog in Three Parts* (Berkeley: University of California Press, 1998), esp. pp. 37–45.

24. Palmer, "Interview with Stampp," Mar. 24, 1997; and additional material from an interview of Stampp conducted by Ann Lage for the Bancroft Library in 1996. I am extremely grateful to John Sproat for sending me portions of his copy of the transcript.

25. Material on this stage of Woodward's career is taken from my interview with him, Dec. 19, 1995; Adelson, "Interview with C. Vann Woodward," pp. 11–13; and Muhlenfeld, "C. Vann Woodward," pp. 470–74.

26. Adelson, "Interview with C. Vann Woodward," p. 12. Palmer, "Interview with Woodward," Dec. 19, 1995.

27. Palmer, "Interview with Hexter," Dec. 19, 1995.

28. J. H. Hexter, *More's Utopia: The Biography of an Idea* (Princeton, 1952); the quotation in this paragraph is on p. viii.

29. Hexter, "Call Me Ishmael," p. 339.

30. The material on Schlesinger in the next few pages may be found in my interview with him, July 6, 1996, and Miles, "Arthur M. Schlesinger, Jr.," pp. 386–89.

31. Material on Elton may be found in Guth, *Elton Remembrances*; Robert Scribner, "Interview with Geoffrey Elton," (London, 1990); David Smith to the author, Jan. 9, 1995.

32. Plumb, *The Collected Essays of J.H. Plumb*, 2 vols. (Athens, Ga., 1991), 1: 3–4.

33. The material on Stone is derived from my interview with Stone, June 7, 1996; and Beier, Cannadine, and Rosenheim, *The First Modern Society*, pp. 581–85.

34. Palmer, "Interview with Trevor-Roper," May 15, 1996.

35. Palmer, "Interview with Southern," May 17, 1996.

36. John Morrill, Paul Slack, and Daniel Woolf, eds., *Public Duty and Private Conscience in Seventeenth Century England: Essays Presented to G.E. Aylmer* (Oxford: Oxford University Press, 1993), p. 2.

37. Pat Thane, "Interview with Eric Hobsbawm" (London, 1987).

38. Henry Abelove, et al., eds., *Visions of History* (New York: Pantheon, 1984), p. 34.

39. MacLachlan, *Rise and Fall*, pp. 79–121.

40. Christopher Hill to the author, July 9, 1996.

41. The early history of *Past and Present* may be found in Christopher Hill, "John Morris," *Past and Present* 75 (May 1977): 3–4; Christopher Hill, R.H. Hilton, and E.J. Hobsbawm, "Origins and Early Years," *Past and Present* 100 (Aug. 1983): 3–13.

42. Palmer, "Interview with Stone," June 7, 1996; Palmer, "Interview with Sir John Elliott," May 15, 1996.

43. Richard Cobb, *A Second Identity*, pp. 13–14, 36–46; *Times* (London), January 17, 1996.

44. Cobb, *A Second Identity*, p. 17.

7. At the Pinnacle (Mostly)

1. William E. Leuchtenburg, *A Troubled Feast: American Society since 1945* (Boston: Little, Brown, 1973), pp. 142–79, esp. p. 178.

2. Scott, "An Historian's Odyssey," pp. xx–xxiv.

3. *Times* (London), Feb. 8, 1989, p. 16f.; *New York Times*, Feb. 7, 1989, p. A1.

4. Hexter, "Call Me Ishmael," p. 340.

5. Liddle, "Edmund S. Morgan," pp. 290–94; Palmer, "Interview with Morgan," Dec. 17, 1995.

6. Muhlenfeld, "C. Vann Woodward," pp. 479–81; Palmer, "Interview with Woodward," Dec. 18, 1995.

7. J.H. Hexter, *On Historians* (Cambridge, 1979), p. 10; Palmer, "Interview with Hexter," Dec. 19, 1995.

8. For these episodes and additional references see Jon Wiener, "Radical Historians and the Crisis in American History, 1959–1980," *Journal of American History* 76, no. 2 (Sept. 1989): 399–434.

9. Beier, Cannadine, and Rosenheim, eds., *The First Modern Society*, pp. 21–30; Palmer, "Interview with Stone," June 5, 1996.

10. Beier, Cannadine, and Rosenheim, eds., *The First Modern Society*, pp. 26–30; Mark Silk, "The Hot History Department," *New York Times Magazine*, Apr. 19, 1987.

11. Beier, Cannadine, and Rosenheim, eds., *The First Modern Society*, pp. 28–29.

12. Silk, "The Hot History Department," p. 62; Norman Cantor, "The Real Crisis in the Humanities Today," *New Criterion*, June, 1985, pp. 1–11.

13. Stone, "As Seen by Himself," pp. 590–91.

14. Schorske, *A Life of Learning*, pp. 14–19.

15. For an account of life at Berkeley during this time, see W.J. Rorabaugh, *Berkeley at War: The 1960s* (Oxford: Oxford University Press, 1989).

16. Colin Campbell, "History and Ethics: A Dispute," *New York Times*, Dec. 23, 1984, pp. 1, 19; Karen J. Winkler, "Brouhaha over Historian's Use of Sources Renews Scholars' Interest in Ethics Codes," *Chronicle of High Education*, Feb. 6, 1985, pp. 1, 8–9.

17. Silk, "The Hot History Department,"p. 63; Jon Wiener, "Footnotes to History," *Nation*, Feb. 16, 1985, pp. 180–83.

18. Miles, "Arthur M. Schlesinger, Jr.," pp. 389–400.

19. For a sampling of the works involved, see William Appleman Williams, *The Tragedy of American Foreign Policy* (Cleveland: World Publishing Company, 1959); Robert J. Maddox, *The New Left and the Origins of the Cold War* (Princeton: Princeton University Press, 1973); John Lewis Gaddis, *The United States and the Origins of the Cold War* (New York: Columbia University Press, 1972); and Oscar Handlin, *Truth in History* (Cambridge: Harvard University Press, 1979), pp. 145–61; Novick, *That Noble Dream*, pp. 446–57; Schlesinger's position may be found in his "Origins of the Cold War," *Foreign Affairs* 46, no. 1 (Oct. 1967): 22–52.

20. Annunziata, "Daniel Boorstin," pp. 82–85.

21. Shankman, "Oscar Handlin," pp. 195–97.

22. Handlin, *Truth in History*, pp. 3–24.

23. Ibid., pp. 145–61.

24. Interview with Stampp, Mar. 24, 1997.

25. August Meier and Elliott Rudwick, *Black History and the Historical Profession, 1915–1980* (Urbana and Chicago: University of Illinois Press, 1986), pp. 246–47.

26. Adelson, "Interview with William H. McNeill," pp. 1–16; Palmer, "Interview with McNeill," Dec. 22, 1995.

27. Adam Sisman, *A.J.P. Taylor: A Biography* (London: Mandarin, 1994), p. 376.

28. Fass, "Richard Hofstadter," pp. 223–30.

29. Palmer, "Interview with Morgan," Dec. 15, 1995.

30. Carleton, "David Potter," pp. 369–73; Palmer, "Interview with Craig," Jan. 4, 1996.

31. Palmer, "Interview with Craig," Jan. 4, 1996.

32. Pennington and Thomas, eds., *Puritans and Revolutionaries*, pp. 19–21; Anthony Kenney, *A Life at Oxford* (London: John Murray, 1997), pp. 5–6, 50, 54–55, et seq.; Palmer, "Interview with Sir Keith Thomas," May 14, 1997.

33. Interview with Thomas, May 14, 1997; Palmer, "Interview with Maurice Keen," May 15, 1997.

34. Cantor, *Inventing the Middle Ages*, p. 350.

35. See Maurice Keen's appreciation of Cobb in the *Balliol College Annual Record* (1996), pp. 17–19.

36. Palmer, "Interview with Trevor-Roper," May 16, 1996.

37. Quoted in Barret L. Beer, "Geoffrey Elton: Tudor Champion," in Walter Arnstein, ed., *Recent Historians of Great Britain*, pp. 13–34.

38. Interview with Sir John Plumb, May 20, 1997; J.H. Plumb, *The American Experience: The Collected Essays of J. H. Plumb* (Athens, Ga., 1989).

39. J.H. Plumb, *The Death of the Past* (Boston, 1970).

40. Plumb, *Collected Essays of J.H. Plumb, 2:* 47–50.

41. "Interview with Eric Hobsbawm," in Abelove et al., eds., *Visions of History*, pp. 29–46; Kaye, *The British Marxist Historians*, pp. 131–66.

8. TEACHING

1. Franklin, *A Life of Learning*, p. 10.

2. Carl E. Schorske, *Fin-de-Siècle Vienna: Politics and Culture* (New York, 1981), pp. xviii–xxii.

3. Materials on Hexter as a teacher were taken from J.H. Hexter, "Introductory College Course in Non-American History: An Ethnocentric View," in Josef Konvitz, ed., *Americans* (Lansing, 1985), p. 182; and Palmer, "Interview with Hexter," Dec. 19, 1995.

4. Material for Handlin's teaching was derived from Bushman et al., eds., *Uprooted Americans*, p. xi; Handlin, "A Career at Harvard."

5. Palmer, "Interview with Anne Firor Scott," Feb. 2, 1999.

6. Palmer, "Interview with McNeill," Dec. 22, 1995.

7. In discussing the teaching of Daniel Boorstin, I have relied on my interviews with John Alexander on Feb. 2, 1999, and Richard Beeman on Feb. 11, 1999.

8. Material on Morgan as a teacher is derived from Courtwright, "Fifty Years of American Colonial History," 346–47; Palmer, "Interview with Morgan," Dec. 15, 1995.

9. Franklin, *Life in Learning*, p. 10.

10. Ibid., pp. 13–14. Richard Beeman, one of the students who made the trip, related the story to me in my interview with him, Feb. 11, 1999.

11. Material on Craig's teaching is taken from my interview with him, Jan. 4, 1996. Additional material may be found in Cantor, *Inventing the Middle Ages*, pp. 256, 261, and 402.

12. Palmer, "Interview with Schlesinger," July 6, 1996.

13. Materials on Schorske as a teacher come from his *Life of Learning*, and my interview with him, Jan. 28, 1999.

14. Palmer, "Interview with Stampp," Dec. 7, 1995.

15. Carl N. Degler, "David M. Potter," *American Historical Review* 76 (Oct. 1971): 1273–75; Don E. Fehrenbacher, Howard R. Lamar, and Otis Pease, "David Potter: A Memorial Resolution," *Journal of American History* 58 (Sept. 1971): 307–10; Palmer, "Interview with Craig," Jan. 4, 1996.

16. Foner, introduction, pp. xxvi–vii.

17. Palme, "Interview with Woodward," Dec. 19, 1995.

18. Curtis, ed., *The Historian's Workshop*, p. 148.

19. Palmer, "Interview with Hexter," Dec. 19, 1995.

20. Palmer, "Interview with Morgan," Dec. 15, 1995; Palmer, "Interview with Woodward," Dec. 18, 1995.

21. Palmer, "Interview with Craig," Jan. 4, 1996.

22. Novick, *That Noble Dream*, pp. 428–29.

23. Fass, "Richard Hofstadter," p. 224.

24. My view of Boorstin's teaching in the 1960s is based on my interviews with Alexander, Feb. 2, 1999, and Beeman, Feb. 11, 1999.

25. Material for Hill as a tutor is derived from interviews with Thomas, May 13, 1997, and Keen, May 14, 1997, and Hugh Stretton's recollection in Pennington and Thomas, eds., *Puritans and Revolutionaries*.

26. Pennington and Thomas, eds., *Puritans and Revolutionaries*, p. 11.

27. Ibid., p. 17.

28. Ved Mehta, *Up at Oxford*, pp. 140–44.

29. Ibid., pp. 152–55.

30. Ibid., p. 154.

31. Pennington and Thomas, eds., *Puritans and Revolutionaries*, p. 18; Rhys Isaac, *The Transformation of Virginia, 1740–1790* (Chapel Hill: University of North Carolina Press, 1982), p. 360.

32. Mehta, *Up at Oxford*, pp. 95–99.

33. Ibid., p. 99.

34. Cantor describes his experience with Southern in *Inventing the Middle Ages*, pp. 343–48.

35. Palmer, "Interview with Colin Lucas," May 17, 1997.

36. Palmer, "Interview with Trevor-Roper," May 15, 1996; Palmer, "Interview with Michael Howard," May 17, 1997.

37. For recollections about Stone as a teacher, see Beier, Cannadine, and Rosenheim, eds., *The First Modern Society*, pp. 3–20.

38. For recollections about Elton as a teacher, I have relied upon many of the accounts collected by Guth, in *Elton Remembrances*.

39. Materials on Plumb's teaching were taken from an interview with him, May 19, 1997; McKendrick, ed., *Historical Perspectives*, along with discussions with Simon Schama and Derek Hirst.

9. The Cultural Critics

1. A good, recent edition of Tocqueville's masterpiece may be found in *Democracy in America*, translated by George Lawrence and edited by J.P. Mayer and Max Lerner (New York: Harper and Row, 1966). The best recent examination is James T. Schleifer, *The Making of Tocqueville's "Democracy in America"* (Chapel Hill: University of North Carolina Press, 1980).

2. For some comments on Riesman and Tocqueville's use of history, see Carl N. Degler, "The Sociologist as Historian: Riesman's *The Lonely Crowd*," *American Quarterly* 15, no. 4 (Winter 1963): 483–97; and William Palmer, "David Riesman, Alexis de Tocqueville, and History: A Look at *The Lonely Crowd* after Forty Years," *Colby Quarterly* 27, no. 1 (Mar. 1990): 19–27.

3. Frederick Jackson Turner, *The Frontier in American History* (New York: Henry Holt, 1920). Turner's biographer, Ray A. Billington, has also written on the development of Turner's "frontier hypothesis," in his *The Genesis of the Frontier Thesis* (San Marino, Calif.: Huntington Library, 1971). For critical assessments, see Thomas Perkins Abernethy, *From Plantation to Frontier in Tennessee* (Chapel Hill: University of North Carolina Press, 1932), along with David Potter, *People of Plenty* (Chicago, 1954), and Richard Hofstadter, *The Progressive Historians: Turner, Beard, Parrington* (New York, 1968), the second of which is discussed later in this essay.

4. Mills and the authors of *The Lonely Crowd* were not the only authors to place postwar America under critical scrutiny. William Whyte's *The Organization Man* (New York: Simon and Schuster, 1957) was another sociological study; Lionel Trilling's *The Liberal Imagination* (New York: Viking Press, 1950) and R.W.B. Lewis's *The American Adam* (Chicago: University of Chicago Press, 1955) used literature as a point of departure; and Sloan Wilson's *The Man in the Gray Flannel Suit* (New York: Simon and Schuster, 1955) was a popular novel that explored middle-class anxieties.

5. David Riesman in collaboration with Reuel Denny and Nathan Glazer, *The Lonely Crowd: A Study of the Changing American Character* (New Haven: Yale University Press, 1950). Critiques of *The Lonely Crowd* can be found in S.M. Lipset and Leon Lowenthal, eds., *Culture and Social Character: The Work of David Riesman* (New York: Free Press of Glencoe, 1961).

6. C. Wright Mills, *White Collar* (New York: Oxford University Press, 1951); Mills, *The Power Elite* (New York: Oxford University Press, 1958).

7. Daniel J. Boorstin, *The Lost World of Thomas Jefferson* (Chicago, 1948; new edition with a new preface, 1993).

8. Boorstin, *The Genius of American Politics*, (Chicago: University of Chicago Press, 1953), esp. pp. 8–35, 81–98, 99–132.

9. For some critiques of Boorstin's work, see John Higham, "The Cult of the American Consensus: Homogenizing American History," *Commentary* 27 (Feb. 1959): 93–100; Higham, "Beyond Consensus: The Historian as Moral Critic," *American Historical Review* 67 (Apr. 1962): 609–25; and John P. Diggins, "The Perils of Naturalism: Some Reflections on Daniel J. Boorstin's Approach to American History," *American Quarterly* 23 (1971): 153–80.

10. Boorstin, *The Genius of American Politics*, pp. 14–15.

11. Annunziata, "Daniel J. Boorstin," p. 81.

12. Boorstin, *The Genius of American Politics*, p. 164; see also Boorstin's assertion (p. 26) that "much of the work of Turner and his followers is actually a theory to justify the absence of any American political theory."

13. See the interview with Boorstin in *Contemporary Authors: New Revision Series* (Detroit: Gale Publishing, 1990), 28:81.

14. Boorstin, *The Genius of American Politics*, pp. 6–7.

15. Potter, *People of Plenty*. His reputation as a Civil War scholar had been established by an earlier book, *Lincoln and His Party in the Secession Crisis* (New Haven, 1942).

16. Potter, *People of Plenty*, p. xxiv. Riesman and Potter spent time together at Yale during the academic year of 1948–49. Riesman was in the process of completing *The Lonely Crowd*, and Potter was working on the lectures that became *People of Plenty*. David Riesman, now nearly ninety, remembers discussing issues relating to the American character with Potter and being impressed with Potter's extraordinary ability, but does not recall the nature of his criticism of *People of Plenty*. Palmer, "Interview with David Riesman," Nov. 2, 1997.

17. Potter, *People of Plenty*, pp. 194–208.

18. Ibid., pp. 110–127.

19. Ibid., p. 122.

20. Ibid., pp. 142–65, esp. 158.

21. See Don Fehrenbacher, preface to David Potter, *Freedom and Its Limitations in American Life*, ed. Fehrenbacher (Stanford, 1976), pp. vii–ix, for the sad story of Potter's ordeal in trying to complete the Civil War book.

22. Potter, *Freedom and Its Limitations in American Life*, p. 61.

23. The basic sources on Hofstadter and his work include Fass, "Richard Hofstadter," pp. 211–230; Baker, *Radical Beginnings*; and Singal, "Beyond Consensus."

24. Novick, *That Noble Dream*, p. 323.

25. Kazin, *New York Jew*, p. 17.

26. Richard Hofstadter, *The American Political Tradition and the Men Who Made It* (New York, 1948), p. 34.

27. Ibid., p. 228; this passage is also cited in Singal, "Beyond Consensus," p. 984; I am indebted to Singal's argument and I have followed it in the next few paragraphs.

28. Hofstadter, *American Political Tradition*, pp. 190, 193, and 200.

29. Ibid., pp. 164–65.

30. Ibid., pp. v–xi.

31. Arthur M. Schlesinger Jr. was the first to recognize the essential difference between Hofstadter's consensus and Boorstin's. See his "Richard Hofstadter," in Marcus Cunliffe and Robin W. Winks, eds., *Pastmasters: Some Essays on American Historians* (New York: Harper and Row, 1969), pp. 278–315. Hofstadter was still alive at the time *Pastmasters* was published, and Schlesinger sent Hofstadter, as a courtesy, a draft of his essay. At the passage about deploring the consensus, Hofstadter wrote in the margin, "Thank you." See Foner, introduction, p. xxii.

32. David Hawke, "Interview: Richard Hofstadter," *History* 3 (1960): 141, cited in Foner, introduction, p. xi.

33. Singal, "Beyond Consensus," pp. 986–91, does an excellent job of exploring the history of this change in Hofstadter's outlook, and in particular the importance of Hofstadter's 1952 article, "Manifest Destiny and the Philippines," in Daniel Aron, ed., *America in Crisis* (New York: Knopf, 1952), where Hofstadter noted that the motivations surrounding the acquisition of the islands were not as clearly economic as the Progressive historians had suggested.

34. Karl Mannheim, *Ideology and Utopia: An Introduction to the Sociology of Knowledge*, trans. Louis Wirth and Edward Shils (1936; New York: Harcourt,

Brace, 1968). See the discussion of Hofstadter and Mannheim in Singal, "Beyond Consensus," p. 987.

35. Singal, "Beyond Consensus," pp. 986–89.

36. Ibid., pp. 986–87.

37. Schlesinger, "Richard Hofstadter," p. 278.

38. Foner, introduction, p. xxvi. Foner noted that, ironically, the faculty member replaced by Hofstadter was his father, Jack Foner. In a further twist, Eric Foner now holds the DeWitt Clinton Chair in history at Columbia, once held by Hofstadter.

39. Richard Hofstadter, *The Age of Reform: From Bryan to F.D.R.* (New York, 1955), pp. 23–59.

40. Ibid., pp. 35, 41, 71, 78, 176–89, 293.

41. Nor did he appear to notice that while in his work he continually flayed politicians for their lack of courage and conviction, he displayed minimal political courage himself. In 1944 two of Hofstadter's friends at Maryland, Kenneth Stampp and Frank Friedel, discovered that Carlton J.H. Hayes, whom they regarded as sympathetic to Franco, was a candidate for the presidency of the American Historical Association. Stampp and Friedel started a petitioning campaign to prevent Hayes's election. Hofstadter signed the petition but did little else and showed minimal interest in the campaign. Several of his friends attributed Hofstadter's lack of interest to his unwillingness to do anything that might damage his chances to secure a position at Columbia. In defense Hofstadter confessed that he was quite "conservative, timid, and acquiescent." Baker, *Radical Beginnings*, pp. 180–81. He was repelled by McCarthyism, but declined Merle Curti's invitation to sign a petition opposing the firing of Communist professors at the University of Washington. Foner, introduction, p. xxiii.

42. Schlesinger's father, Arthur Meier Schlesinger Sr., was a distinguished historian who taught at Ohio State, the University of Iowa, and Harvard, and was elected president of the American Historical Association in 1942. His influence on his son may be seen in several areas. First, both were sympathetic, though not slavish, to Progressive historiography. Second, two of the father's themes, the importance of the city in American history and the recurring cycles in American history, turn up in the work of the son. See especially Arthur M. Schlesinger, Sr., *The Colonial Merchants and the American Revolution, 1763–1776* (New York: Columbia University Press, 1918); Schlesinger, "Tides of American Politics," *Yale Review* 29 (Dec. 1939): 217–230; Schlesinger, "The City in American History," *Mississippi Valley Historical Review* 27, no. 1 (June, 1940): 43–66. For insights on the son, see John Patrick Diggins, ed., *The Liberal Persuasion: Arthur Schlesinger, Jr., and the Challenge of the American Past* (Princeton: Princeton University Press, 1997). See especially the essays by Diggins, William E. Leuchtenburg, John Morton Blum, and Robert Remini.

43. Arthur M. Schlesinger Jr., *The Age of Jackson* (Boston, 1945), pp. 43, 334–36.

44. Ibid., pp. 263, 307, 74–131.

45. Miles, "Arthur M. Schlesinger, Jr.," p. 387.

46. Arthur M. Schlesinger Jr., *The Vital Center: The Politics of Freedom* (Boston, 1949), p. vii; James Neuchterlein, "Arthur M. Schlesinger, Jr., and the Discontents of Post-War Liberalism," *Review of Politics* 39 (Jan. 1977): 3–40.

47. Reinhold Niebuhr, *The Nature and Destiny of Man*, 2 vols. (New York: Scribner's, 1941, 1943); Niebuhr, *The Children of Light and Children of Darkness* (New York: Scribner's, 1944).

48. Schlesinger, *The Age of Jackson*, p. 522.

49. See Schlesinger's volumes on the Age of Roosevelt: *The Crisis of the Old Order, 1919–1933* (Boston, 1957), *The Coming of the New Deal* (Boston, 1959), and *The Politics of Upheaval* (Boston, 1960).

50. For Boorstin's critics, see n. 9.

51. See especially Barton Bernstein, "The Conservative Achievements of Liberal Reform," in Bernstein, ed., *Towards a New Past: Dissenting Essays in American History* (New York: Pantheon, 1968); and Howard Zinn, ed., *New Deal Thought* (Indianapolis: Bobbs and Merrill, 1966).

52. See especially Stanley Elkins and Eric McKitrick, eds., *The Hofstadter Aegis: A Memorial* (New York: Knopf, 1974).

53. Hofstadter, *The Age of Reform*, p. 326; Schlesinger, *The Vital Center*, p.1.

54. Hofstadter, *American Political Tradition*, p. xi.

55. Schlesinger, *The Age of Jackson*, p. iv.

56. Richard Hofstadter, "The Great Depression and American History: A Personal Footnote," a typescript of a lecture, box 36, Richard Hofstadter Papers, Rare Book and Manuscript Library, Columbia University. Cited in Foner, introduction, p. xxii n. 26.

57. Potter, *People of Plenty*, pp. ix–x.

58. Theodore S. Hamerow, *Reflections on History and Historians* (Madison: University of Wisconsin Press, 1987), pp. 12, 3; quoted in William E. Leuchtenburg, "The Historian and the Public Realm," in Diggins, ed., *The Liberal Persuasion*, p. 22.

59. See the appreciation of Himmelfarb's work by Bernard Semmel in *Humanities* 12, no. 3 (May–June, 1991): 11–12, 34.

60. Gertrude Himmelfarb, *The New History and the Old: Critical Essays and Reappraisals* (Cambridge, Mass., 1987), pp. 5, 10, 13–14. Although it is not entirely clear from her text, I assume that Himmelfarb means to take issue with the historian's claim that the American Revolution is not terribly significant in terms of the ordinary ebb and flow of everyday existence and not with his claim that in his research he could not "get at" the Revolution. Clearly if the changes wrought by the Revolution, whatever these might be, were not in the sources, he cannot (and should not) be expected to include them.

61. Gertrude Himmelfarb, *The Demoralization of Society: From Victorian Virtues to Modern Values* (New York, 1994), pp. 3–5, 12–20, 139–42, 221–57; Weisberg, "The Family Way," p. 187.

62. Gertrude Himmelfarb, *On Looking into the Abyss: Untimely Thoughts on Culture and Society* (New York, 1994); Lionel Trilling, "On the Teaching of Mod-

ern Literature," in *Beyond Culture: Essays on Literature and Learning* (New York: Viking Press, 1965), p. 27. Trilling, *The Liberal Imagination*.

63. Culler and Fish are quoted in Himmelfarb, *On Looking into the Abyss*, pp. 7–8.

64. Himmelfarb, *On Looking into the Abyss*, pp. 134–35, 151–55; For the works criticized by Himmelfarb, see Joan Wallach Scott, *Gender and the Politics of History* (New York: Columbia University Press, 1988), p. 4; and Ellen Somekawa and Elizabeth A. Smith, "Theorizing the Writing of History; or, 'I Can't Think Why It Should Be So Dull, for a Great Deal of It Must Be Invention,'" *Journal of Social History* 22, no. 1 (Fall 1988): 154–60.

10. THE CONTROVERSIALISTS

1. I use the term "the English Revolution," rather than "the English Civil War," or "the Great Rebellion," only as a matter of convenience, not defiance. Like John Morrill, I am not sure what we are to call "the blasted thing" anymore. See Morrill, *The Nature of the English Revolution: Essays by John Morrill* (London: Longman, 1993), p. vii; Hugh Trevor-Roper expresses similar annoyance in "The Continuity of the English Revolution," in *From Counter Reformation to Glorious Revolution* (Chicago, 1992), pp. 214–15.

2. Samuel Rawson Gardiner, *History of England from the Accession of James I to the Outbreak of Civil War* (New York: AMS Press, 1965); Gardiner, *History of the Great Civil War* (New York: AMS Press, 1965). See also Roland G. Usher, *A Critical Study of the Historical Method of S.R. Gardiner* (St. Louis, Mo.: Washington University, 1915); and R.C. Richardson, *The Debate on the English Revolution* (New York: Methuen, 1977).

3. Tawney's articles are "Harrington's Interpretation of His Age," *Proceedings of the British Academy* 27 (1941): 201–23; and "The Rise of the Gentry, 1558–1640," *Economic History Review* 11 (1941): 1–38; see also Ross Terrill, *R.H. Tawney and His Times*.

4. J.H. Hexter, *Reappraisals in History: New Views on History and Society in Early Modern Europe*, 2d ed. (Chicago, 1979), p. 174 n. 14; Lawrence Stone, "As Seen by Himself," p. 582; H.R. Trevor-Roper, "The Gentry, 1540–1640," *Economic History Review*, Supplement 1, 1953, p. 1; and Palmer, "Interview with Trevor-Roper," May 16, 1996.

5. Lawrence Stone, "The Anatomy of the Elizabethan Aristocracy," *Economic History Review*, 18 (1948): 1–53. For a scrupulously fair account of the affair by a leading participant, see Lawrence Stone, *The Causes of the English Revolution, 1529–1642* (New York, 1972), pp. 26–43.

6. H.R. Trevor-Roper, "The Elizabethan Aristocracy: An Anatomy Anatomized," *Economic History Review*, 2d ser., 3 (1951): 279–98.

7. Lawrence Stone, "The Elizabethan Aristocracy: A Restatement," *Economic History Review* 2d ser., 4 (1952): 302–21, in this instance, see p. 313.

8. Trevor-Roper, "The Gentry, 1540–1640," pp. 1–55; Cooper is quoted by Hexter in *Reappraisals in History*, p. 123.

9. Trevor-Roper, "The Gentry, 1540–1640," p. 44.

10. Christopher Hill, "Recent Interpretations of the Civil War," in his *Puritanism and Revolution: Studies in Interpretation of the English Revolution of the Seventeenth Century* (London, 1958), pp. 3–31; Perez Zagorin, "The Social Interpretation of the English Revolution," *Journal of Economic History* 19 (1959): 376–401.

11. Hexter, "Storm over the Gentry," in his *Reappraisals in History*, pp. 117–62.

12. Stone, *The Causes of the English Revolution*, p. 29.

13. Lawrence Stone, *The Crisis of the Aristocracy, 1558–1642* (Oxford, 1965).

14. Stone, *Crisis of the Aristocracy*, pp. 65–128.

15. Ibid., p. 12.

16. For a subtle review sensitive to both the strengths and weaknesses of Stone's work, see Hexter, "Lawrence Stone and the English Aristocracy," in Hexter, *On Historians: Reappraisals of Some of the Makers of Modern History* (Cambridge, Mass., 1979), pp. 149–226.

17. H.R. Trevor-Roper, "The General Crisis of the Seventeenth Century," in his *The Crisis of the Seventeenth Century: Religion, the Reformation and Social Change* (New York, 1968), pp. 46–89; Perez Zagorin, *The Court and the Country* (New York: Athenaum, 1969).

18. Stone, *Causes of the English Revolution*, pp. 30–31.

19. Ibid., pp. 114–15.

20. In the introduction to *Causes of the English Revolution*, Stone relates the importance of his experience in the student unrest at Princeton in 1968 in formulating the ideas developed in *Causes*. He made the point that watching events unfold at Princeton, convinced him of the importance of the response of those in power to the crisis. Clearly those in power at Princeton made the right response; Charles and Laud did not.

21. Stone, *Causes of the English Revolution*, p. 135.

22. Geoffrey Elton, "Tudor Government: The Points of Contract," *Transactions of the Royal Historical Society*, 5th ser., 24 (1975): 195–211, and 25 (1976): 211–28; for Elton's review of *Causes of the English Revolution*, see *Historical Journal* 16 (1973): 205–8.

23. Several historians have cited the publication of *Causes of the English Revolution* as a critical point in the development of a revisionist perspective. See Glenn Burgess, "On Revisionism: An Analysis of Early Stuart Historiography in the 1970s and 1980s," *Historical Journal* 33, no. 3 (1990): 609–27; John Morrill, *The Nature of the English Revolution*, p. 276

24. The "Old Hat" terminology is Hexter's, but see its development by Jonathan Clark in *Revolution and Rebellion: State and Society in England in the Seventeenth and Eighteenth Centuries* (Cambridge: Cambridge University Press, 1986) along certain lines suggested here.

25. Trevor Aston, ed., *Crisis in Europe 1560–1660: Essays from "Past and Present"* (New York: Basic Books, 1965).

26. For criticism of Trevor-Roper's views on the witch hunts, see Joseph Klaits, *Servants of Satan: The Age of the Witch Hunts* (Bloomington: Indiana Uni-

versity Press, 1985), pp. 48–49; Keith Thomas, *Religion and the Decline of Magic* (New York: Scribner's, 1971). For a survey of recent views, with specific reference to Keith Thomas, see Jonathan Barry, Marianne Hester, and Gareth Roberts, *Witchcraft in Early Modern Europe* (Cambridge: Cambridge University Press, 1996), esp., pp. 2–10.

27. H.R. Trevor-Roper, "History: Professional and Lay," in Lloyd-Jones, Pearl, and Worden, eds., *History and Imagination*, p. 13. Hill quote from interview in Geoff Eley and William Hunt, eds. *Reviving the English Revolution* (London: Verso, 1988) p. 20.

28. Hugh Trevor-Roper, "Arnold Toynbee's Millennium," in *Men and Events* (New York, 1957), pp. 299–324.

29. In discussing the Regius Professor situation I have followed the account presented in Adam Sisman, *A.J.P. Taylor*, pp. 246–52. It should be recorded that while I believe the account is essentially sound, it also appears to be an account derived in large from Hugh Trevor-Roper.

30. Mehta, *Fly and the Fly-Bottle*, p. 167.

31. Ibid., p. 112.

32. A.J.P. Taylor, *Origins of the Second World War* (New York: Atheneum, 1961); Mehta, *Fly and Fly-Bottle*, pp. 112–22.

33. Mehta, *Fly and Fly-Bottle*, pp. 116–18.

34. A.L. Rowse speculates on Trevor-Roper's taste for controversy in *Historians I Have Known* (London: Duckworth, 1995), pp. 103–4.

35. Mehta, *Fly and the Fly-Bottle*, pp. 132–34.

36. Trevor-Roper, *The Crisis of the Seventeenth Century*, pp. 88–89.

37. For a summary of Hexter as historian, see William Palmer, "The Burden of Proof: J.H. Hexter and Christopher Hill," *Journal of British Studies* 20, no. 1 (Fall 1979): 122–29.

38. Hexter, *Reappraisals in History*, p. 196 n. 61; see also Hexter's essay on Carl Becker and historical relativism in *On Historians*, pp. 13–41.

39. J.H. Hexter, "Power Struggle, Parliament, and Liberty in Early Stuart England," *Journal of Modern History* 50 (Mar. 1978): 24. Here the original version is slightly different from the revised version that appeared in the second edition of *Reappraisals in History*.

40. Hexter, *Reappraisals in History*, pp. 215–16; see also, Hexter, "The Early Stuarts and Parliament: Old Hat and the *Nouvelle Vague*," *Parliamentary History* 1 (1982): 181–215.

41. Hexter, *Reappraisals in History*, pp. 217–18.

42. Christopher Hill, *The English Revolution of 1640* (London, 1940), p. 1.

43. Thomas is quoted in MacLachlan, *Rise and Fall*, p. 325.

44. Christopher Hill, *The Economic Problems of the Church: From Archbishop Whitgift to the Long Parliament* (Oxford, 1956). There is quite a bit of speculation about how Hill's resignation from the Communist Party in 1957 freed him from the shackles of doctrinaire Marxism and enabled him to develop a more flexible interpretation. Others attribute his increased flexibility of mind to the death of his stern Methodist father at about the same time. Hill himself has observed that

The Economic Problems of the Church was finished and submitted to the Clarendon Press in 1954, two years before the Hungarian Revolution. See his interview with Penelope Corfield under the auspices of the Institute for Historical Research (London, 1988). Also his pupils noted that his divorce in the early 1950s moved him back into residence at Balliol College and gave him more time to work.

45. Christopher Hill, *Society and Puritanism in Pre-Revolutionary England* (London, 1964); Corfield, "Interview with Christopher Hill." (London: Institute of Historical Research, 1988).

46. Christopher Hill, *The Century of Revolution, 1603–1714* (Edinburgh, 1961).

47. John Morrill develops this point in, "Christopher Hill's Revolution," in Morrill, *Nature of the English Revolution*, pp. 279–80.

48. Christopher Hill, *Intellectual Origins of the English Revolution* (Oxford, 1965); for Trevor-Roper's comments see *History and Theory* 5 (1966): 61–82.

49. Hexter, "The Historical Method of C. Hill," in his *On Historians*, pp. 227–51.

50. Christopher Hill, *Change and Continuity in Seventeenth Century England* (London, 1974), p. 94.

51. Hexter, *On Historians*, p. 251.

52. See David Underdown, "Puritanism, Revolution, and Christopher Hill," in Geoff Eley and William Hunt, eds., *Reviving the English Revolution: Reflections and Elaborations on the Work of Christopher Hill* (London: Verso, 1988), pp. 333–42, for the shrewdest analysis of Hill's work.

53. Christopher Hill, "Letter to the Editor," *Encounter* (July 1958), p. 76. There are several letters of interest on pp. 73–76.

54. Hexter, *Reappraisals in History*, p. vi.

55. Hill, *Change and Continuity*, pp. 217–18.

56. In two interviews with Hexter, conducted in December 1995, Hexter denied being influenced by either of the possible motivations described here.

57. Christopher Hill, *The World Turned Upside Down: Radical Ideas during the English Revolution* (New York, 1972), pp. 278–91.

58. Peter Lake, "Retrospective: Wentworth's Political World in Revisionist and Post-Revisionist Perspective," in J.F. Merritt, ed., *The Political World of Thomas Wentworth, Earl of Strafford, 1621–1641* (Cambridge: Cambridge University Press, 1996), p. 253.

11. THE ARCHIVAL REVOLUTION

1. *Letters and Papers, Foreign and Domestic, of the Reign of Henry VIII*, J.S. Brewer, et al., eds., 21 vols., and addenda (London, 1862–1932); A.F. Pollard, *Henry VIII* (London: Longman's, 1902); the personal details that follow may be found in the Robert Scribner, "Interview with Geoffrey Elton," (Institute of Historical Research, London, 1990).

2. G.R. Elton, *The Tudor Revolution in Government* (London, 1953).

3. Guth, ed., *Elton Remembrances*, p. 1.

4. G.R. Elton, *England under the Tudors* (London, 1955).

5. Penry Williams and G.L. Harriss, "A Revolution in Tudor History?" *Past and Present*, no. 25 (July 1963): 3–58; the best recent criticisms are found in John Guy, *Tudor England* (Oxford: Oxford University Press, 1988), pp. 154–77, and in the works of the contributors to "The Elton Legacy," in *Transactions of the Royal Historical Society*, 6th ser. (Cambridge, 1997), pp. 177–336.

6. G.R. Elton, *Policy and Police: The Enforcement of the Reformation in the Age of Thomas Cromwell* (Cambridge, 1972); Elton, *Reform and Renewal* (Cambridge, 1973).

7. G.R. Elton, *Reform and Reformation, England, 1509–1558* (Cambridge, Mass., 1977); David Starkey, "The King's Privy Chamber, 1485–1547," Ph.D. diss., Cambridge, 1973; Brendan Bradshaw takes up the issue of the evangelical Cromwell in "The Tudor Commonwealth: Reform and Revision," *Historical Journal* 22, no. 2 (1979): 402.

8. Elton, *Reform and Reformation*, p. v. In a new edition of *England under the Tudors*, Elton wrote that "the massive research and publication of the past generation, though of course they demand some alterations in the book, have not, to my mind, undermined its main theses [on the Tudor revolution in government] and have indeed confirmed some of its originally rash speculations" (p. v).

9. David Starkey, "Representation through Intimacy: A Study in the Symbolism of Monarchy and Court Office in Early Modern England," in I. Lewis, ed., *Symbols and Sentiments: Cross Cultural Studies in Symbolism* (London: Academic Press, 1977), pp. 187–224; Penry Williams, *The Tudor Regime* (Oxford, 1979); for Elton's review, see *Times Literary Supplement*, Feb. 15, 1980, p. 183; Christopher Coleman and David Starkey, eds., *Revolution Reassessed: Revisions in the History of Tudor Government and Administration* (Oxford: Oxford University Press, 1986), especially Starkey's contributions, pp. 13–27 and 29–58; for the Elton and Starkey acrimony, see Elton, "A New Age of Reform?" *Historical Journal* 30, no. 3 (1987): 709–16; and Starkey, "Tudor Government: the Facts?" *Historical Journal* 31, no. 4 (1988): 921–31.

10. Linda Colley, *Lewis Namier* (London: Weidenfeld and Nelson, 1989), pp. 25, 44–45.

11. Lawrence Stone, "The Political Programme of Thomas Cromwell," *Bulletin of the Institute of Historical Research* 24 (1951): 1–18; for Elton's irritation with theory, see particularly his "History according to St. Joan," *American Scholar* (Autumn 1985): 549–55.

12. Stone, *Crisis of the Aristocracy*.

13. Stone, "As Seen by Himself," p. 586.

14. Ibid., p. 587.

15. Ibid.

16. Ibid.

17. Ibid.

18. Stone, *Crisis of the Aristocracy*, pp. 199–270.

19. K.B. McFarlane, *The Nobility of Later Medieval England* (Oxford: Ox-

ford University Press, 1973); see also George Bernard, ed., *The Tudor Nobility* (Manchester: Manchester University Press, 1991). For a position close to Stone's, see the essays of McFarlane's student, Mervyn James, collected in *Society, Politics and Culture: Studies in Early Modern England* (Cambridge, 1986).

20. Plumb, *The Collected Essays of J.H. Plumb* (Athens, Ga., 1988) 1: 45–50.

21. J.H. Plumb, *Sir Robert Walpole: The Making of a Statesman* (London, 1956); Plumb, *Sir Robert Walpole: The King's Minister* (London, 1960).

22. McKendrick, ed., *Historical Perspectives*, p. 8.

23. J.H. Plumb, *The Growth of Political Stability in England, 1675–1725* (London, 1967); Plumb, *The Making of a Historian*, p. 97.

24. Plumb, *Growth of Stability*, pp. 161–88.

25. E.P. Thompson, *Whigs and Hunters: The Origins of the Black Act* (New York: Pantheon, 1975); the phrases are quoted from Lawrence Stone's review of *Whigs and Hunters*, in Stone, *The Past and the Present* (Boston, 1981), p. 195.

26. Jonathan Clark, "Eighteenth-Century Social History," *Historical Journal* 27 (1987): 773–88; Clark, *English Society, 1688–1832: Ideology, Social Structure and Political Practice during the Ancien Regime* (Cambridge: Cambridge University Press, 1985); Clark, *Revolution and Rebellion: State and Society in England in the Seventeenth and Eighteenth Centuries* (Cambridge, 1986).

27. Clark, *English Society, 1688–1832.*

28. Joanna Innes, "Jonathan Clark, Social History, and England's 'Ancien Regime,'" *Past and Present*, 115 (May, 1987), 165–200.

29. Ulrich B. Phillips, *American Negro Slavery* (New York: Peter Smith, 1918).

30. Herbert Aptheker, *American Negro Slave Revolts* (New York: Columbia University Press, 1943); Gunnar Myrdal, *An American Dilemma: The Negro Problem and Modern Democracy*, 2 vols. (New York: Harper and Brothers, 1944); Richard Hofstadter, "U.B. Phillips and the Plantation Legend," *Journal of Negro History* 39 (April, 1944): 109–24; John Hope Franklin, *From Slavery to Freedom* (New York, 1947).

31. Palmer, "Interview with Kenneth Stampp," Dec. 15, 1995; Kenneth M. Stampp, "The Historian and Southern Negro Slavery," *American Historical Review* 57, no. 3 (Apr. 1952): 613–24; Stampp, *The Peculiar Institution: Slavery in the Ante-Bellum South* (New York, 1956).

32. Stampp, *The Peculiar Institution*, p. 364.

33. Ibid., pp. 30, 174–77, 404.

34. Stampp is quoted in Novick, *That Noble Dream*, p. 349.

35. Stampp, *The Peculiar Institution*, p. vii.

36. August Meier and Elliott Rudwick, *Black History and the Historical Profession*, pp. 139, 140, 246. Hofstadter, on the other hand, after reading a draft of *The Peculiar Institution*, told Stampp that Stampp was "too gentle, too quiet, too objective, and there are many points at which I wish you were a little more indignant, or quarrelsome. . . . You are far more vulnerable to the charge of icy detachment than you are to that of special pleading." Hofstadter is quoted in Meier and Rudwick, *Black History and the Historical Profession*, p. 140n.

37. Palmer, "Interview with Kenneth Stampp"; Kenneth M. Stampp, *Interpreting History* (Salt Lake City: Department of History, University of Utah, 1983), pp. 11–12.

38. Eugene Genovese, *Roll, Jordan, Roll: The World the Slaves Made* (New York: Vintage, 1972); see also Paul Escott, *Slavery Remembered: A Record of Twentieth-Century Slave Narratives* (Chapel Hill: University of North Carolina Press, 1972), esp. pp. 18–35. Genovese's general views were also expressed in an early review of *The Peculiar Institution* written under the nom de plume of Vittorio Della Chiesa; see *Science and Society* 21, no. 3 (Summer 1957): 259–63.

39. Meier and Rudwick, *Black History and the Historical Profession*, p. 292.

40. C. Vann Woodward, *The Strange Career of Jim Crow* (New York, 1974), p. 65.

41. Woodward, *Thinking Back*, pp. 44–45.

42. C. Vann Woodward, *Reunion and Reaction: The Compromise of 1877 and the End of Reconstruction* (Boston, 1951), pp. 3–21; Woodward, *Thinking Back*, pp. 49–53.

43. For two important criticisms of *Reunion and Reaction*, see Michael Les Benedict, "Southern Democrats in the Crisis of 1876–1877: A Reconsideration of *Reunion and Reaction*," *Journal of Southern History* 46 (1980): 489–524; and Allan Peskin, "Was There a Compromise of 1877?" *Journal of American History* 60 (June 1973): 63–75.

44. Woodward, *Thinking Back*, p. 59.

45. C. Vann Woodward, *Origins of the New South, 1877–1913* (Baton Rouge, 1951), p. 20.

46. Ibid., pp. 107–41, esp. 111–20.

47. Ibid., pp. 245, 257.

48. Ibid., pp.333–37. *Origins* has come under criticism largely on two fronts. First, it has been criticized by those who believe that the old planting aristocracy survived in much better shape than Woodward thought. For two of these critics, see Dwight B. Billings Jr., *Planters and the Making of the New South* (Chapel Hill: University of North Carolina Press, 1979), and Jonathan Wiener, *Social Origins of the New South: Alabama, 1860–1885* (Baton Rouge: Louisiana State University Press, 1978). A second strain of criticism, closely related to the first, emphasizes, in contradiction to Woodward, the continuity of the southern experience. For two works along these lines, see George B. Tindall, *The Persistent Tradition in New South Politics* (Baton Rouge: Louisiana State University Press, 1975), and Carl N. Degler, *Place over Time: The Continuity of Southern Distinctiveness* (Baton Rouge: Louisiana State University Press, 1977).

49. Woodward, *Strange Death of Jim Crow*, p. 9.

50. Joel Williamson, *A Rage for Order: Black/White Relations in the American South since Emancipation* (New York: Oxford University Press, 1986), p. 261.

51. Ibid., p. 262.

52. David M. Potter, "C. Vann Woodward," in Winks and Cunliffe, eds., *Pastmasters*, p. 407

53. Howard Rabinowitz, *Race Relations in the Urban South: 1865–1890* (New York: Oxford University Press, 1978); Rabinowitz, "More Than the Woodward Thesis: Assessing *The Strange Career of Jim Crow*," *Journal of American History* 75, no. 3 (Dec. 1988): 842–56, to which Woodward replied on pp. 857–68.

54. Rabinowitz, "More Than the Woodward Thesis," p. 846.

55. Woodward, *Reunion and Reaction*, p. ix.

56. Sheldon Hackney, "*Origins of the New South* in Retrospect," *Journal of Southern History* 38 (May 1972): 191.

57. Michael O'Brien, "C. Vann Woodward and the Burden of Southern Liberalism," *American Historical Review* 78 (June 1973): 589–604; Woodward views on W.J. Cash are quoted on p. 596.

58. Woodward, *Reunion and Reaction*, pp. 72–74.

59. Scott, "A Historian's Odyssey," p. xix.

60. Anne Firor Scott, *The Southern Lady* (Chicago, 1970).

61. Joan Kelly, "Did Women Have a Renaissance?" in her *Women, History, and Theory: The Essays of Joan Kelly* (Chicago: University of Chicago Press, 1984), pp. 19–50.

62. Scott, "A Historian's Odyssey," pp. xxiii, xxiv; Barbara Welter, "The Cult of True Womanhood, 1800–1860," in her *Dimity Convictions* (Athens: Ohio University Press, 1976), pp. 21–41.

63. Scott, *The Southern Lady*, pp. 20–21.

64. Ibid., p. 47.

65. Ibid., pp. 100, 81.

66. Ibid., pp. 106–33.

67. Ibid., p. 129.

68. Drew Gilpin Faust, *Mothers of Invention: Women of the Slaveholding South in the American Civil War* (Chapel Hill: University of North Carolina Press, 1996).

69. Ibid., pp. 64, 132.

70. See Scott's review of *Mothers of Invention* in the *Journal of Southern History* 62, no. 2 (May 1996): 382–85.

71. Woodward, *Thinking Back*, p. v.

72. Cobb, *A Second Identity*, pp. 15–16.

73. Ibid., p. 16.

74. I am grateful to Colin Lucas for these and other insights on Cobb's character and work.

75. Cobb, *A Second Identity*, p. 44; see Richard Cobb, *The Police and the People: French Popular Protest, 1789–1820* (Oxford, 1970), and Cobb, *Death in Paris, 1795–1801* (Oxford, 1978).

76. Cobb, *Death in Paris*, pp. 6, 8.

77. Ibid., pp. 9, 10, 27, 28, 33, 48.

78. Palmer, "Interview with Kenneth Stampp," Mar. 17, 1997.

79. C. Vann Woodward, *The Burden of Southern History* (Baton Rouge: Louisiana State University Press, 1968). Stampp is quoted on p. 207.

12. Synthesis, Printed Sources, and Other Kinds of History

1. T.H. Breen and Stephen Innes, *"Myne Owne Ground": Race and Freedom on Virginia's Eastern Shore, 1640–1676* (New York and Oxford: Oxford University Press, 1980), pp. 7–18.

2. Oscar Handlin and Mary Handlin, "Origins of the Southern Labor System," *William and Mary Quarterly*, 3d ser., 7 (1950): 199–222; for another point of view, see Carl N. Degler, "Slavery and the Genesis of American Race Prejudice," *Comparative Studies in Society and History 2*, no. 1 (Oct. 1959): 49–66.

3. Stanley M. Elkins, *Slavery: A Problem in American Institutional and Intellectual Life* (Chicago: University of Chicago Press, 1959).

4. Winthrop D. Jordan, *White over Black: American Attitudes Toward the Negro, 1550–1812* (Chapel Hill: University of North Carolina Press, 1968).

5. For a good discussion of the genesis of *American Slavery, American Freedom*, see Courtwright, "Fifty Years of American History," pp. 356–59.

6. Edmund S. Morgan, *American Slavery, American Freedom: The Ordeal of Colonial Virginia* (New York, 1975), p. 4.

7. Ibid., pp. 84–85, 86–90.

8. Ibid., pp. 107–9.

9. Ibid., pp. 175–77.

10. Ibid., pp. 296–99, 327–28.

11. See particularly such Morgan works as *The Puritan Family: Religion and Domestic Relations in Seventeenth Century Massachusetts* (Boston, 1944), *The Puritan Dilemma: The Story of John Winthrop* (New York, 1958), and *The Stamp Act Crisis: Prologue to Revolution* (New York, 1953).

12. Meier and Rudwick, *Black History and the Historical Profession*, pp. 117–18.

13. Franklin, *From Slavery to Freedom*, pp. 71–79.

14. Ibid., p. 98.

15. Ibid., pp. 154, 166.

16. Ibid., pp. 312–13.

17. Ibid., p. 467.

18. Ibid., p. 519.

19. Ibid., p. 604.

20. Oscar Handlin, *Boston's Immigrants, 1790–1880: A Study in Acculturation* (Cambridge: Belknap Press of Harvard University, 1941), revised and enlarged edition, with a new preface by the author, 1991), p. xi.

21. Ibid., pp. 110–14.

22. Ibid., p. 133.

23. Ibid., pp. 151–77.

24. Ibid., p. 228.

25. Oscar Handlin, *The Uprooted* (Boston: Little, Brown and Company, 1951), 2d ed. (Boston, 1973), p. 3.

26. Ibid., pp. 180–202.

27. Hexter, *On Historians*, pp. 83–84.

28. For a summary of criticisms, see Maldwyn A. Jones, "Oscar Handlin," in Cunliffe and Winks, eds., *Pastmasters*, pp. 256–58, 264–67; Shankman, "Oscar Handlin," p. 193.

29. It is also worth noting that Handlin gave considerable attention to racial injustice, first in the article cited at the beginning of this chapter and in later works such as *Fire-bell in the Night: The Crisis in Civil Rights* (Boston, 1964).

30. Gordon A. Craig, *The Politics of the Prussian Army, 1640–1945* (Oxford, 1956), pp. 20–21.

31. Ibid., pp. 43.

32. Ibid., p. 82.

33. Ibid., pp. 299–300.

34. Ibid., p. 467.

35. Ibid., pp. 46., 493, 502–3.

36. Barbara Tuchman, *The Guns of August* (New York, 1962), pp. 119, 150.

37. Ibid., pp. 37, 113, 266.

38. Ibid., p. 412.

39. Ibid., pp. 66, 126, 172, 202; Tuchman, *Practicing History*, pp. 18, 43.

40. *Guns of August*, pp. 17, 38, 341, 348.

41. Ibid., pp. 308, 344, 439.

42. Ibid., p. 66.

43. Schorske, *German Social Democracy*; Schorske, *Fin-de-Siècle Vienna*. Throughout the discussion of Schorske, I am indebted to Michael S. Roth's perceptive article, "Performing History: Modernist Contextualism in Carl Schorske's *Fin-de-Siècle Vienna*," *American Historical Review* 99, no. 3 (June 1994): 729–45.

44. Schorske, *Fin-de-Siècle Vienna*, p. xix; Schorske, *A Life of Learning*, p. 10.

45. Schorske, *Fin-de-Siècle Vienna*, pp. xxiii-iv; Schorske, *A Life of Learning*, p. 12; Palmer, "Interview with Schorske," Jan. 27, 1999.

46. Schorske, *Fin-de-Siècle Vienna*, p. 22.

47. Ibid., p. 134.

48. Ibid., p. 203.

49. "Interview with William McNeill," *Historian* 53, no. 1 (Autumn 1990): 6.

50. For this paragraph and an interesting approach to McNeill and world history in general, see Paul Costello, *World Historians and Their Goals: Twentieth Century Answers to Modernism* (Dekalb: Northern Illinois University Press, 1993), pp. 183–212, esp. p. 190.

51. William H. McNeill, *The Rise of the West: A History of the Human Community* (Chicago, 1963), p. xvi.

52. Ibid., pp. 569–72.

53. At the request of Toynbee's last surviving child, McNeill also wrote Toynbee's biography, published as *Arnold J. Toynbee: A Life* (Oxford, 1989).

54. Hugh Trevor-Roper, *Men and Events* (New York, 1957), pp. 299–324.

55. William H. McNeill, *Plagues and Peoples* (Garden City, 1976); McNeill, *The Pursuit of Power* (Chicago, 1982). One can also glimpse the recurring themes of *The Rise of the West* in other of McNeill's works, such as *Europe's Steppe Frontier, 1500–1800* (Chicago, 1964) and *Venice: The Hinge of Europe, 1081–1793* (Chicago, 1974).

56. Cantor, *Inventing the Middle Ages*, p. 337.

57. R.W. Southern, *The Making of the Middle Ages* (New Haven and London, 1972), pp. 79–80, 126–27.

58. Ibid., pp. 76–78, 118–19.

59. Ved Mehta, *Up at Oxford*, p. 98.

60. Maurice Dobb, *Studies in the Development of Capitalism* (London: Routledge and Kegan Paul, 1946).

61. Eric J. Hobsbawm, "The Crisis of the 17th Century: I," *Past and Present* 5 (May, 1954): 33–53, and Hobsbawm, "The Crisis of the 17th Century: II," *Past and Present* 6 (Nov. 1954): 44–65, subsequently revised and reprinted in Aston, ed., *Crisis in Europe*, pp. 5–58.

62. Eric Hobsbawm, *The Age of Revolution, 1789–1848* (London, 1962).

63. Alfred Cobban, "The Myth of the French Revolution," reprinted in his collected essays, *Aspects of the French Revolution* (London: Norton, 1968). Summaries of recent French Revolution historiography may be found in Francois Furet, *Interpreting the French Revolution* (Cambridge: Cambridge University Press, 1978); T.C.W. Blanning, ed., *The Rise and Fall of the French Revolution* (Chicago: University of Chicago Press, 1996); and Gary Kates, ed., *The French Revolution: Recent Debates and New Controversies* (London and New York: Routledge, 1998).

64. A.E. Musson, *The Growth of British Industry* (London: Holmes and Meier, 1978); Donald McCloskey, "The Industrial Revolution, 1780–1860: A Survey," in R. Floud and D. McCloskey, eds., *The Economic History of Britain since 1700*, 2 vols. (Cambridge: Cambridge University Press, 1981); Arno Mayer, *The Persistence of the Old Regime* (New York: Pantheon, 1981); Lawrence Stone and Jeanne C. Fawtier Stone, *An Open Elite? England 1540–1880* (Oxford, 1986).

65. E.J. Hobsbawm, *Primitive Rebels: Studies in Archaic Forms of Social Movement in the 19th and 20th Centuries* (Manchester, 1959); Hobsbawm, *Labouring Men* (London, 1964).

BIBLIOGRAPHY

♏

BOOKS

Abelove, Henry, et al., eds. *Visions of History*. New York: Pantheon, 1984.

Abernethy, Thomas Perkins. *From Plantation to Frontier in Tennessee*. Chapel Hill: University of North Carolina Press, 1932.

Aptheker, Herbert. *American Negro Slave Revolts*. New York: Columbia University Press, 1943.

Arnstein, Walter, ed. *Recent Historians of Great Britain: Essays on the Post-1945 Generation*. Ames: Iowa State University Press, 1990.

Aston, Trevor. *Crisis in Europe, 1560–1660*. New York: Basic Books, 1965.

Bailyn, Bernard, ed. *Glimpses of the Harvard Past*. Cambridge: Harvard University Press, 1986.

Baker, Susan Stout. *Radical Beginnings: Richard Hofstadter and the 1930s*. Westport, Conn.: Greenwood Press, 1985.

Barry, Jonathan, Marianne Hexter, and Gareth Roberts, eds. *Witchcraft in Early Modern Europe*. Cambridge: Cambridge University Press, 1996.

Beier, A.L., David Cannadine, and James Rosenheim, eds. *The First Modern Society: Essays in Honour of Lawrence Stone*. Cambridge: Cambridge University Press, 1989.

Bernard, George, ed. *The Tudor Nobility*. Manchester: Manchester University Press, 1991.

Bernstein, Barton, ed. *Towards a New Past: Dissenting Essays in American History*. New York: Pantheon, 1967.

Blanning, T.C.W., ed. *The Rise and Fall of the French Revolution*. Chicago: University of Chicago Press, 1996.

Billings, Dwight. *Planters and the Making of the New South*. Chapel Hill: University of North Carolina Press, 1979.

Billington, Ray A. *The Genesis of the Frontier Thesis*. San Marino, Calif.: Huntington Library, 1971.

Boorstin, Daniel, *The Daniel Boorstin Reader*. New York: Vintage, 1996.

Breen, T.H., and Stephen Innes. *"Myne Owne Ground": Race and Freedom on Virginia's Eastern Shore, 1640–1676*. New York and Oxford: Oxford University Press, 1980.

Brewer, J.S., et al., eds. *Letters and Papers, Foreign and Domestic, of the Reign of Henry VIII.* 21 vols. and addenda. London, 1862–1932.

Brucker, Gene A., Henry F. May, and David Hollinger. *History at Berkeley: A Dialogue in Three Parts.* Berkeley: University of California Press, 1998.

Bushman, Richard, et al., eds. *Uprooted Americans: Essays to Honor Oscar Handlin.* Boston: Little, Brown, 1979.

Cantor, Norman. *Inventing the Middle Ages: The Lives, Works, and Ideas of the Great Medievalists of the Twentieth Century.* New York: William Morrow, 1991.

Clark, Jonathan. *English Society, 1688–1832: Ideology, Social Structure and Political Practice during the Ancien Regime.* Cambridge: Cambridge University Press, 1986.

———. *Revolution and Rebellion: State and Society in England in the Seventeenth Century and Eighteenth Centuries.* Cambridge: Cambridge University Press, 1986.

Cobb, Richard. *A Classical Education.* London: Chatto and Windus, 1985.

———. *The End of the Line.* London: John Murray, 1997.

———. *A Second Identity: Essays on France and French History.* Oxford: Oxford University Press, 1969.

———. *Something to Hold Onto.* London: John Murray, 1988.

———. *Still Life: Sketches from a Tunbridge Wells Childhood.* London: Chatto and Windus, 1983.

Cobban, Alfred. *Aspects of the French Revolution.* New York: Norton, 1968.

Coleman, Christopher, and David Starkey, eds. *Revolution Reassessed: Revisions in the History of Tudor Government and Administration.* Oxford: Oxford University Press, 1986.

Colley, Linda. *Lewis Namier.* London: Weidenfeld and Nelson, 1989.

Costello, Paul. *World Historians and Their Goals: Twentieth Century Answers to Modernism.* Dekalb: Northern Illinois University Press, 1993.

Cunliffe, Marcus, and Robin W. Winks, eds. *Pastmasters: Some Essays on American Historians.* New York: Harper and Row, 1969.

Curtis, L. Perry. *The Historian's Workshop: Original Essays by Sixteen Historians.* New York: Alfred Knopf, 1970.

Degler, Carl N. *Place over Time: The Continuity of Southern Distinctiveness.* Baton Rouge: Louisiana State University Press, 1977.

Diggins, John Patrick, ed. *The Liberal Persuasion: Arthur Schlesinger, Jr., and the Challenge of the American Past.* Princeton: Princeton University Press, 1997.

Dobb, Maurice. *Studies in the Development of Capitalism.* London: Routledge and Kegan Paul, 1946.

Dorson, Richard. *The Birth of American Studies: Inaugural Address Delivered at the Opening of the American Studies Center, Warsaw University, Warsaw Poland, October 5, 1976.* Bloomington: Indiana University Press, 1981.

Eley, Geoffrey, and William Hunt, eds. *Reviving the English Revolution: Reflections and Elaborations on the Work of Christopher Hill.* London: Verso, 1988.

Elkins, Stanley. *Slavery: A Problem in American Institutional and Intellectual Life.* Chicago: University of Chicago Press, 1959.

Elkins, Stanley, and Eric McKitrick, eds. *The Hofstadter Aegis: A Memorial.* New York: Knopf, 1974.

Escott, Paul. *Slavery Remembered: A Record of Twentieth Century Slave Narratives.* Chapel Hill: University of North Carolina Press, 1972.

Fairbank, John King. *Chinabound: A Fifty-Year Memoir.* New York: Harper and Row, 1982.

Faust, Drew Gilpin. *Mothers of Invention: Women of the Slaveholding South in the American Civil War.* Chapel Hill: University of North Carolina Press, 1996.

Floud, R., and D. McCloskey, eds. *The Economic History of Britain since 1700.* 2 vols. Cambridge: Cambridge University Press, 1981.

Franklin, John Hope. *A Life of Learning: The Charles Homer Haskins Lecture.* New York: American Council of Learned Societies, 1988.

———, ed. *My Life and an Era: The Autobiography of Buck Colbert Franklin.* Baton Rouge: Louisiana State University Press, 1997.

Furet, Francois. *Interpreting the French Revolution.* Cambridge: Cambridge University Press, 1978.

Gaddis, John Lewis. *The United States and the Origins of the Cold War.* New York: Columbia University Press, 1972.

Gardiner, Samuel Rawson. *History of England from the Accession of James I to the Outbreak of Civil War.* New York: AMS Press, 1965.

———. *History of the Great Civil War.* New York: AMS Press, 1965.

Genovese, Eugene. *Roll, Jordan, Roll: The World the Slaves Made.* New York: Vintage, 1972.

Guth, DeLloyd, ed. *Elton Remembrances.* Washington, D.C.: privately printed, 1995.

Guy, John. *Tudor England.* Oxford: Oxford University Press, 1988.

Hamerow, Theodore S. *Reflections on History and Historians.* Madison: University of Wisconsin Press, 1987.

Handlin, Oscar. *Truth in History.* Cambridge: Harvard University Press, 1979.

Hofstadter, Richard, and Walter Metzger. *The Development of Academic Freedom.* New York: Columbia University Press, 1955.

Hughes, H. Stuart. *Gentleman Rebel: The Memoirs of H. Stuart Hughes.* New York: Ticknor and Fields, 1990.

Issac, Rhys. *The Transformation of Virginia, 1740–1790.* Chapel Hill: University of North Carolina Press, 1982.

James, Mervyn. *Society, Politics, and Culture: Studies in Early Modern England.* Cambridge: Cambridge University Press, 1986.

Jordan, Winthrop D. *White over Black: American Attitudes toward the Negro, 1550–1812.* Chapel Hill: University of North Carolina Press, 1968.

Kates, Gary, ed. *The French Revolution: Recent Debates and New Controversies.* London and New York: Routledge, 1998.

Kaye, Harvey J. *The British Marxist Historians.* New York: St. Martin's Press, 1985.

Kazin, Alfred. *New York Jew.* New York: Alfred Knopf [distributed by Random House], 1978.

Keeney, Anthony. *A Life in Oxford.* London: John Murray, 1997.

Kelly, Joan. *Women, History, and Theory: The Essays of Joan Kelly.* Chicago: University of Chicago Press, 1984.

Klaits, Joseph. *Servants of Satan: The Age of the Witch Hunts.* Bloomington: Indiana University Press, 1985.

Konvitz, Josef. *What Americans Should Know: Western Civilization or World History: Proceedings of a Conference at Michigan State University.* Lansing: Board of Trustees, Michigan State University, 1985.

Langer, William. *In and Out of the Ivory Tower.* New York: Watson Academic Publications, 1977.

Leuchtenburg, William. *A Troubled Feast: American Society since 1945.* Boston: Little, Brown, 1973.

Ioan Lewis, ed. *Symbols and Sentiments: Cross Cultural Studies in Symbolism.* London: Academic Press, 1977.

Lewis, R.W.B.. *The American Adam.* Chicago: University of Chicago Press, 1955.

Lipset, S.M., and Leo Lowenthal, eds. *Culture and Social Character: The Work of David Riesman.* New York: Free Press of Glencoe, 1961.

Lloyd-Jones, Hugh, Valerie Pearl, and Blair Worden, eds., *History and Imagination: Essays in Honor of Hugh Trevor-Roper.* New York: Holmes and Meier, 1982.

Mannheim, Karl. *Ideology and Utopia: An Introduction to the Sociology of Knowledge.* Trans. Louis Wirth and Edward Shils. New York: Harcourt, Brace, 1936.

Masterman, J.C. *On the Chariot Wheel: An Autobiography.* Oxford: Oxford University Press, 1975.

May, Henry F. *Coming to Terms: A Study in History and Memory.* Berkeley: University of California Press, 1987.

Mayer, Arno. *The Persistence of the Old Regime.* New York: Pantheon, 1981.

MacLachlan, Alastair. *The Rise and Fall of Revolutionary England: An Essay on the Fabrication of Seventeenth Century History.* New York: St. Martin's Press, 1996.

Maddox, Robert J. *The New Left and the Origins of the Cold War.* Princeton: Princeton University Press, 1973.

McFarlane, K.B. *The Nobility of Later Medieval England.* Oxford: Oxford University Press, 1973.

McKendrick, Neil, ed. *Historical Perspectives: Studies in English Thought and Society in Honour of J.H. Plumb.* London: Europa, 1974.

Mehta, Ved. *Fly and the Fly-Bottle: Encounters with British Intellectuals.* Boston: Little, Brown, 1962.

———. *Up at Oxford.* New York: Norton, 1993.

Meier, August, and Elliott Rudwick. *Black History and the Historical Profession, 1915–1980.* Urbana and Chicago: University of Illinois Press, 1986.

Merritt, J.F., ed. *The Political World of Thomas Wentworth, Earl of Strafford, 1621–1641.* Cambridge: Cambridge University Press, 1996.

Miller, Perry. *The New England Mind: The Seventeenth Century.* New York: Macmillan, 1939.

———. *Orthodoxy in Massachusetts*. Gloucester, Mass.: Peter Smith, 1933.

Mills, C. Wright. *The Power Elite*. New York: Oxford University Press, 1958.

———. *White Collar*. New York: Oxford University Press, 1951.

Morrill, John. *The Nature of the English Revolution: Essays by John Morrill*. London and New York: Longman, 1993.

Morrill, John, Paul Slack, and Daniel Woolf, eds. *Public Duty and Private Conscience in Seventeenth Century England: Essays Presented to G. E. Aylmer*. Oxford: Oxford University Press, 1993.

Muggeridge, Malcolm. *Like It Was: The Diaries of Malcolm Muggeridge*. New York: Morrow, 1982.

Musson, A.E. *The Growth of British Industry*. London: Holmes and Meier, 1978.

Myrdal, Gunnar. *An American Dilemma: The Negro Problem and Modern Democracy*. 2 vols. New York: Harper and Brothers, 1944.

Niebuhr, Reinhold. *The Children of Light and Children of Darkness*. New York: Scribner's, 1944.

———. *The Nature and Destiny of Man*. 2 vols. New York: Scribner's, 1941 and 1943.

Novick, Peter. *That Noble Dream: The Objectivity Question and the American Historical Profession*. Cambridge: Cambridge University Press, 1987.

Peake, Hayden B., and Samuel Halpern, eds. *In the Name of Intelligence: Essays in Honor of Werner Pforzheimer*. Washington, D.C.: NIBC Press, 1995.

Pennington, Donald, and Keith Thomas, eds. *Puritans and Revolutionaries: Essays in Seventeenth Century History in Honour of Christopher Hill*. Oxford: Oxford University Press, 1978.

Phillips, U.B. *American Negro Slavery*. New York: Peter Smith, 1918.

Plumb, J.H. *The Making of a Historian: The Collected Essays of J.H. Plumb*. 2 vols. Athens: University of Georgia Press, 1989.

Pollard, A.F. *Henry VIII*. London: Longman's, 1902.

Rabinowitz, Howard. *Race Relations in the Urban South: 1865–1890*. New York: Oxford University Press, 1978.

Reischauer, Edwin O. *My Life between Japan and America*. New York: Harper and Row, 1986.

Richardson, R.C. *The Debate on the English Revolution*. New York: Methuen, 1977.

Riesman, David, in collaboration with Reuel Denny and Nathan Glazer. *The Lonely Crowd*. New Haven: Yale University Press, 1950.

Rogin, Michael. *The Intellectuals and McCarthy*. Cambridge: Harvard University Press, 1967.

Rorabaugh, W.J. *Berkeley at War: The 1960s*. Oxford: Oxford University Press, 1989.

Rowse, A.L. *Historians I Have Known*. London: Duckworth, 1992.

Schleifer, James. *The Making of Tocqueville's "Democracy in America."* Chapel Hill: University of North Carolina Press, 1980.

Schlesinger, Arthur M. Sr. *The Colonial Merchants and the American Revolution, 1763–1776*. New York: Columbia University Press, 1918.

Schorske, Carl. *A Life in Learning: The Charles Homer Haskins Lecture*. Washington: American Council of Learned Societies, 1987.

Schrecker, Ellen W. *No Ivory Tower: McCarthyism and the Universities.* Oxford: Oxford University Press, 1986.

Scott, Anne Firor. *Making the Invisible Woman Visible.* Urbana and Chicago: University of Illinois Press, 1984.

Scott, Joan Wallach. *Gender and the Politics of History.* New York: Columbia University Press, 1988.

Sisman, Adam. *A.J.P. Taylor: A Biography.* London: Mandarin, 1994.

Smith, Richard Norton. *The Harvard Century: The Making of a University to a Nation.* New York: Simon and Schuster, 1986.

Soffer, Reba. *Discipline and Power: The University, History, and the Making of an English Elite, 1870–1930.* Palo Alto: Stanford University Press, 1994.

Starkey, David. "The King's Privy Chamber, 1485–1547." Ph.D. diss., Cambridge University, 1973.

Stern, Frederick C. *F.O. Matthiessen: Christian Socialist As Critic.* Chapel Hill: University of North Carolina Press, 1981.

Taylor, A.J.P. *Origins of the Second World War.* New York: Atheneum, 1961.

———. *A Personal History.* New York: Atheneum, 1983.

Terrill, Ross. *R.H. Tawney and His Times: Socialism as Fellowship.* London: Deutsch, 1974.

Thomas, Keith. *Religion and the Decline of Magic.* New York: Scribner's, 1971.

Thompson, E.P. *Whigs and Hunters: The Origins of the Black Act.* New York: Pantheon, 1975.

Tindall, George B. *The Persistent Tradition in New South Politics.* Baton Rouge: Louisiana State University Press, 1975.

Tocqueville, Alexis. *Democracy in America.* Trans. George Lawrence, ed. J.P. Mayer and Max Lerner. New York: Harper and Row, 1966.

Trilling, Lionel. *Beyond Culture: Essays on Literature and Learning.* New York: Viking Press, 1965.

———. *The Liberal Imagination.* New York: Viking Press, 1950.

Tuchman, Barbara. *Practicing History: Selected Essays by Barbara Tuchman.* New York: Alfred Knopf, 1981.

Turner, Frederick Turner. *The Frontier in American History.* New York: Henry Holt, 1920.

Usher, Roland G. *A Critical Study of the Historical Method of S.R. Gardiner.* St. Louis, Mo.: Washington University, 1915.

Welter, Barbara. *Dimity Convictions.* Athens: Ohio University Press, 1976.

Whyte, William. *The Organization Man.* New York: Simon and Schuster, 1957.

Wiener, Jonathan. *Social Origins of the New South: Alabama, 1860–1885.* Baton Rouge: Louisiana State University Press, 1978.

Williams, Penry. *The Tudor Regime.* Oxford: Oxford University Press, 1979.

Williamson, Joel. *A Rage for Order: Black/White Relations in the American South since Emancipation.* New York: Oxford University Press, 1986.

Williams, William Appleman. *The Tragedy of American Diplomacy.* Cleveland: World Publishing, 1959.

Wilson, Clyde, ed. *Twentieth-Century American Historians.* Vol. 17 of *The Dictionary of Literary Biography.* Detroit: Gale Research, 1985.

Wilson, Sloan. *The Man in the Grey Flannel Suit.* New York: Simon and Schuster, 1955.

Woodward, C. Vann. *Thinking Back: The Perils of Writing History.* Baton Rouge: Louisiana State University Press, 1986.

Zagorin, Perez. *The Court and the Country: The Beginning of the English Revolution.* New York: Athenaeum, 1969.

Zinn, Howard, ed. *New Deal Thought.* Indianapolis: Bobbs and Merrill, 1966.

ARTICLES

Adelson, Roger. "Interview with Caroline Walker Bynum." *Historian* 59 (1996): 1–17.

———. "Interview with C. Vann Woodward." *Historian* 54 (1991): 1–18.

———. "Interview with William McNeill." *Historian* 52 (1990): 1–16.

Benedict, Michael Les. "Southern Democrats in the Crisis of 1876–1877: A Reconsideration of *Reunion and Reaction.*" *Journal of American History* 60 (1980): 489–524.

Bradshaw, Brendan. "The Tudor Commonwealth: Reform and Revision." *Historical Journal* 22 (1979): 459–76.

Burgess, Glen. "On Revisionism: An Analysis of Early Stuart Historiography in the 1970s and 1980s." *Historical Journal* 33 (1990): 609–27.

Campbell, Colin. "History and Ethics: A Dispute." *New York Times,* Dec. 23, 1984.

Cantor, Norman. "The Real Crisis in the Humanities Today." *New Criterion,* June 1985, pp. 1–11.

Cheney, Lynn. "A Conversation with Gertrude Himmelfarb." *Humanities* 12 (1991): 4–9.

Clark, Jonathan. "Eighteenth Century Social History." *Historical Journal* 27 (1987): 773–88.

Courtwright, David. "Fifty Years of American Colonial History: An Interview with Edmund S. Morgan." *William and Mary Quarterly,* 3d ser., 44 (1987): 336–69.

Davies, C.S.L., et al. "The Elton Legacy." *Transactions of the Royal Historical Society,* 6th ser. 7 (1997): 177–336.

Degler, Carl N. "David M. Potter." *American Historical Review* 76 (1971): 1273–75.

———. "Slavery and the Genesis of American Race Prejudice." *Comparative Studies in Society and History* 2 (1959): 49–66.

———. "The Sociologist as Historian: Riesman's *The Lonely Crowd.*" *American Quarterly* 15 (1963): 483–97.

Della Chiesa, Vittorio. "Review of *The Peculiar Institution.*" *Science and Society* 21 (1957): 259–63.

Diggins, John P. "The Perils of Naturalism: Some Reflections on Daniel J. Boorstin's Approach to American History." *American Quarterly* 23 (1971): 153–80.

Elton, Geoffrey. "History According to St. Joan." *American Scholar* 54 (1985): 549–55.

————. "A New Age of Reform?" *Historical Journal* 30 (1987): 709–16.

————. "Tudor Government: Points of Contact." *Transactions of the Royal Historical Society*, 5th ser., 24 (1975): 211–18.

Fehrenbacher, Don E., Howard R. Lamar, and Otis Pease. "David Potter: A Memorial Resolution." *Journal of American History* 58 (1971): 307–10.

Hackney, Sheldon. "*Origins of the New South* in Retrospect." *Journal of Southern History* 38 (1972): 191–216.

Handlin, Oscar M.. "A Career at Harvard." *American Scholar* (Winter 1996): 47–58.

Handlin, Oscar, and Mary Handlin. "Origins of the Southern Labor System." *William and Mary Quarterly*, 3d ser., 7 (1950): 199–222.

Hexter, J.H. "Call Me Ishmael; or, a Rose by Any Other Name." *American Scholar* (Summer 1983): 199–222.

Higham, John. "Beyond Consensus: The Historian as Moral Critic." *American Historical Review* 67 (1962): 609–25.

————. "The Cult of Consensus: Homogenizing American History." *Commentary* 27 (1959): 93–100.

Hill, Christopher. "John Morris." *Past and Present* 75 (1977): 3–4.

Hill, Christopher, R.H. Hilton, and E.J. Hobsbawm. "Origins and Early Years." *Past and Present* 100 (1983): 3–13.

Hobsbawm, Eric. "The Crisis of the 17th Century: I." *Past and Present* 5 (1954): 33–53.

————. "Crisis of the Seventeenth Century: II." *Past and Present* 6 (1954): 5–58.

Hofstadter, Richard. "Manifest Destiny and the Philippines." In *America in Crisis*, edited by Daniel Aron, 173–200. New York: Knopf, 1952.

Innes, Joanna. "Jonathan Clark, Social History, and England's 'Ancien Regime.'" *Past and Present* 115 (1987): 165–200.

Keen, Maurice. "Richard Cobb." *Balliol College Record* (1996): 17–19.

Lynn, Kenneth. "F.O. Matthiessen." *American Scholar* (Winter 1976–67): 86–93.

————. "Perry Miller." *American Scholar* (Spring 1983): 221–27.

O'Brien, Michael. "C. Vann Woodward and the Burden of Southern Liberalism." *American Historical Review* 78 (1973): 589–604.

Palmer, William. "The Burden of Proof: J.H. Hexter and Christopher Hill." *Journal of British Studies* 20 (1979): 122–29.

————. "David Riesman, Alexis de Tocqueville, and History: A Look at *The Lonely Crowd* after Forty Years." *Colby Quarterly* 27 (1990): 19–27.

————. "Sir Richard Southern Looks Back: Portrait of the Medievalist as a Young Man." *Virginia Quarterly Review.* 74 (Winter, 1998): 18–31.

Peskin, Allan. "Was There a Compromise of 1877?" *Journal of American History* 60 (1973): 63–75.

Rabinowitz, Howard. "More Than the Woodward Thesis: Assessing *The Strange Career of Jim Crow*." *Journal of American History* 75 (1988): 842–56.

Roper, John Herbert. "C. Vann Woodward's Early Career: The Historian as Dissident Youth." *Georgia Historical Quarterly* 64 (1980): 7–21.

Ross, Jean. "Interview with Daniel Boorstin." In *Contemporary Authors, New Revision Series*, 80–84. Detroit: Gail Research, 1990.

Roth, Michael. "Performing History: Modernist Contextualism in Carl Schorske's *Fin-de-Siècle Vienna*." *American Historical Review* 99 (1994): 729–45.

Schlesinger, Arthur M., Jr. "Origins of the Cold War." *Foreign Affairs* 46 (1967): 22–52.

Schlesinger, Arthur M., Sr. "The City in American History." *Mississippi Valley Historical Review* 27 (1940): 43–66.

———. "The Tides of American Politics." *Yale Review* 29 (1939): 217–30

Semmel, Bernard. "In Celebration." *Humanities* 12 (1991): 11–12, 34.

Silk, Mark. "The Hot History Department." *New York Times Magazine*, 19 Apr. 1987.

Singal, Daniel Joseph. "Beyond Consensus: Richard Hofstadter and American Historiography." *American Historical Review* 89 (1984): 976–1004.

Somekawa, Ellen, and Elizabeth A. Smith. "Theorizing the Writing of History; or, 'I Can't Think Why It Should Be So Dull, for a Great Deal of It Must Be Invention.'" *Journal of Social History* 22 (1988): 154–69.

Starkey, David. "Tudor Government: The Facts?" *Historical Journal* 31 (1988): 921–31.

Stone, Lawrence. "The Anatomy of the Elizabethan Aristocracy." *Economic History Review* 18 (1948): 1–53.

———. "The Elizabethan Aristocracy: A Restatement." *Economic History Review*, 2d ser., 4 (1952): 302–21.

———. "The Political Programme of Thomas Cromwell." *Bulletin of the Institute of Historical Research* 24 (1951): 1–18.

Tawney, R.H. "Harrington's Interpretation of His Age." *Proceedings of the British Academy* 27 (1941): 201–23.

Trevor-Roper, Hugh. "The Elizabethan Aristocracy: An Anatomy Anatomized." *Economic History Review* 18 (1951): 279–98.

———. "The Rise of the Gentry." *Economic History Review* 11 (1941): 1–38.

Weisberg, Jacob. "The Family Way." *New Yorker*, Oct. 21 and 28, 1996.

Wiener, Jon. "Radical Historians and the Crisis in American History, 1959–1980." *Journal of American History* 76 (1989): 399–434.

Williams, Penry, and G.L. Harriss. "A Revolution in Tudor History?" *Past and Present* (July 1963): 3–58.

Winkler, Karen J. "Brouhaha over Historian's Use of Sources Renews Scholars' Interest in Ethics Codes." *Chronicle of Higher Education*, Feb. 6, 1985.

Zagorin, Perez. "The Social Interpretation of the English Revolution." *Journal of Economic History* 19 (1959): 376– 401.

INTERVIEWS

Several kinds of interviews were used in this book: interviews that I did myself, videotape interviews conducted by the Institute of Historical Research in London, and printed interviews in journals. The printed interviews are listed in the article section of the bibliography. The interviews that I did are listed below and cited in the notes with "Palmer," followed by the name of the subject and the date; the interviews done by the Institute for Historical Research are listed below and cited in the text with the name of the interviewer listed first, followed by the subject.

INTERVIEWS BY WILLIAM PALMER

John Alexander, February 2, 1999
Richard Beeman, February 11, 1999
Gordon Craig, January 4, 1996
Sir John Elliott, May 15, 1996
J.H. Hexter, December 19, 1995
Sir Michael Howard, May 17, 1997
Maurice Keen, May 15, 1997
Colin Lucas, May 17, 1997
William McNeill, December 22, 1995
Edmund Morgan, December 18, 1995
J.H. Plumb, May 19, 1997
David Riesman, November 2, 1997
Arthur M. Schlesinger Jr., July 2, 1996
Carl Schorske, January 28, 1999
Anne Scott, February 2, 1999
Simon Schama, January 22, 1997
Sir Richard Souther, May 16, 1996
Kenneth Stampp, December 17, 1995; March 24, 1997
Lawrence Stone, June 5 and June 8, 1996
Keith Thomas, May 14, 1997
Hugh Trevor-Roper (Lord Dacre of Glanton), May 16, 1997
C. Vann Woodward, December 19, 1995

INTERVIEWS BY THE INSTITUTE OF HISTORICAL RESEARCH, LONDON

Corfield, Penelope. "Interview with Christopher Hill." London: Institute of Historical Research, 1988.
Scribner, Robert. "Interview with Geoffrey Elton." London: Institute of Historical Research, 1990.
Thane, Pat. "Interview with Eric Hobsbawm." London: Institute of Historical Research, 1988.
Worden, Blair. "Interview with Hugh Trevor-Roper." London: Institute of Historical Research, 1993.
Wrightson, Keith. "Interview with Lawrence Stone." London: Institute of Historical Research, 1988.

ACKNOWLEDGMENTS

A great many people helped with the writing of this book. I am particularly grateful to the historians for their time and effort on my behalf. Hugh Trevor-Roper, Sir Richard Southern, and Jack Plumb allowed me to interview them in person, while I interviewed Edmund Morgan, Vann Woodward, Jack Hexter, Lawrence Stone, Arthur Schlesinger Jr., Carl Schorske, William McNeill, and Gordon Craig over the telephone, sometimes more than once. Oscar Handlin, Gertrude Himmelfarb, and Anne Scott referred me to material in print.

Writing this book also gave me a great excuse to talk to a lot of other interesting and distinguished people I wanted to talk to anyway. I would like to thank John Alexander, Richard Beeman, Peter Brown, Carl Degler, Sir John Elliott, Eric Foner, Steven Gunn, John Guy, Christopher Haigh, Derek Hirst, Dale Hoak, Sir Michael Howard, Charles Joyner, Mark Kishlansky, Maurice Keen, Leon Litwack, Colin Lucas, Ved Mehta, John Morrill, Michael Perman, David Riesman, Simon Schama, David Smith, John Sproat, Sir Keith Thomas, Penry Williams, and Blair Worden for sharing with me their opinions and recollections of the historians under consideration. The book is immeasurably better because of the interest they took in it.

I am also grateful to Jack Hexter, Christopher Hill, Edmund Morgan, John Morrill, Arthur Schlesinger Jr., David Smith, Hugh Trevor-Roper, Penry Williams, Lawrence Stone, and Blair Worden, along with my Marshall colleagues Bob Sawrey and David Duke for reading parts of the book and offering useful suggestions, although they are in no way responsible for any of the errors or misjudgments that may appear in the text. Having one's drafts scrutinized by such superb stylists as Arthur Schlesinger Jr., Jack Hexter, and Hugh Trevor-Roper was daunting, but I'm glad I did it. Several of my students provide testimony that teachers can learn from their pupils. Megan Flynn, Jeff Lavender, and Elizabeth Grujovski helped with the research, and Alison Gerlach performed exemplary duty in helping me say what I wanted to say as concisely as possible, although I persist in the belief that sentences, though not too many, can start with "but" and "and." I am also grateful to the West Virginia Humanities Council for a research grant that enabled me to travel to Great Britain in the summer of 1996.

In the end my greatest debt is to Gretchen and our sons Aaron and Clark for being there to come home to. I am proud to be her husband and their father. I'm especially glad I was able to send the first draft of the manuscript off to a publisher just before the start of youth baseball in Huntington. There are a lot of little boys with dreams who need to be coached, hours of bp to be pitched, numerous grounders to be hit, many hot dogs to be eaten, and dozens of games to be played and watched, and I'm going to be there to do it all. I can hardly wait.

INDEX

✻